THE FAILURE OF THE NORTHERN IRELAND PEACE PROCESS

THE FAILURE
OF THE
NORTHERN IRELAND
PEACE PROCESS

G. K. PEATLING

University of Guelph

IRISH ACADEMIC PRESS
DUBLIN • PORTLAND, OR

First published in 2004 by
IRISH ACADEMIC PRESS
44 Northumberland Road, Dublin 4, Ireland

and in the United States of America by
IRISH ACADEMIC PRESS
c/o ISBS, Suite 300
920 NE 58th Avenue
Portland, Oregon 97213-3786

Website: www.iap.ie

© G.K. Peatling 2004

British Library Cataloguing in Publication Data

An entry is available on application

ISBN 0-7165-2808-8 (cloth)
ISBN 0-7165-3336-7 (paper)

Library of Congress Cataloging-in-Publication Data

An entry is available on application

Contents

Illustrations

Glossary

AIA:	Anglo-Irish Agreement, signed by the British and Irish governments in 1985
ANC:	African National Congress, the party that has governed South Africa, under Presidents Nelson Mandela and Thabo Mbeki, since apartheid ended in 1994, and that has been closely associated, at different times or possibly even the same time, with the PIRA and the British Labour Party
anti-agreement unionism:	of or pertaining to unionists opposed to the peace process under the GFA, who are also known as 'rejectionist' unionists. Strictly speaking, a distinction should be made between those who opposed the agreement at its signing and those who have subsequently become opposed to the peace process, although it remains to be seen whether that istinction will have any political significance. Anti-agreement unionism includes the DUP and a sizeable minority within the UUP.
APNI:	Alliance Party of Northern Ireland, which is broadly unionist by tradition and inclination, and regards itself as the largest non-sectarian party in the province
BBC:	British Broadcasting Corporation, the publicly owned provider of a number of television and radio stations, and ancillary activities, in the United Kingdom (and, through the BBC World Service and other subsidiaries, around the world)
BIC:	British–Irish Council, the body created under the GFA to institutionalise meetings of representatives from the governments of the United Kingdom and

	the Irish Republic, the devolved governments of Scotland, Wales and Northern Ireland, and the governments of the British Crown territories of the Channel Islands and the Isle of Man; sometimes called the 'Council of the Isles'
Britain:	alternative name for the state known as the United Kingdom of Great Britain and Northern Ireland; not to be confused either with 'Great Britain', which is the name of an island, or with 'the British Isles', thestandard geographical term for the group of islands of which Great Britain and Ireland are the two largest
CLMC:	Combined Loyalist Military Command, a body set up in 1991 that has occasionally spoken for all loyalist paramilitary groups, such as when announcing ceasefires
conservatism:	the view that the preservation of established political, social and religious institutions is the highest political end
Conservatism:	of or pertaining to the British Conservative Party
ContinuityIRA	Continuity Irish Republican Army, sometimes referred to as the CIRA, an organisation that broke away from the PIRA around the time of its ceasefire in 1994 and has remained active in pposition to the GFA
dissident republicanism:	of or pertaining to those republicans who oppose the GFA, as represented by paramilitary organisations such as the Continuity IRA, the Real IRA and the INLA, and by political bodies such as the 32-County Sovereignty Movement; defined in contrast to the 'mainstream republicanism' associated with the Provisionals
DUP:	Democratic Unionist Party, founded in 1971 by Ian Paisley and often seen as 'hardline', especially in its opposition to the GFA
GFA:	Good Friday Agreement, signed in 1998 by representatives of the British and Irish governments, and of most political parties in

Northern Ireland: the defining achievement of the Northern Ireland peace process

Great Britain: the larger island to the east of Ireland, comprising England, Wales and Scotland, and linked constitutionally with Northern Ireland in the United Kingdom of Great Britain and Northern Ireland. ('Britain'serves as an informal term for the United Kingdom as a whole, not for Great Britain alone.)

IICD: Independent International Commission on Decommissioning, the body, headed by the Canadian General John de Chastelain, set up under the GFA to facilitate the decommissioning of paramilitaries' weapons, the idea being that dealing with an 'international' and 'independent' body would seem less like surrender for certain paramilitary groups than handing weapons in directly to governments. The most significant role of the IICD to date has been the involvement of its representatives in, or their presence at, acts of decommissioning by the LVF and, more significantly, the PIRA.

INLA: Irish National Liberation Army, a republican paramilitary organisation that broke away from the Official IRA in 1975 and now opposes the GFA, but is currently officially regarded as being on ceasefire

IRA: Irish Republican Army, a paramilitary organisation with origins in the struggle for Irish independence from the United Kingdom after the end of the First World War. Groups claiming the name have still been active after the original IRA declared a ceasefire following the Anglo-Irish Treaty of 1921. Late in 1969 the then IRA split into the Official IRA and the Provisional IRA, the latter becoming of greater significance: 'IRA' soon came to be commonly used to refer to the PIRA alone. This usage has been avoided in these pages, not least because it suggests that the PIRA has stronger genealogical links than it actually has to the original struggle for independence that resulted in the creation of the 26-county state in the South of Ireland.

Ireland: the whole island, traditionally divided into thirty-two counties, and split in 1921 between Northern Ireland (six counties) and the remainder, now the Irish Republic. Use of the term 'Ireland' as a synonym for the Republic has been avoided here, although inhabitants of the Republic very largely identify with an imagined Ireland and 'Ireland' is the official name of the 26-county state in English.

labour: of or pertaining to predominantly working-class and left-leaning political movements and organisations such as trade unions

Labour: of or pertaining to the British Labour Party

liberalism: the political doctrine that emphasises the importance of individual liberty

Liberalism: of or pertaining to the former British Liberal Party and its successor organisation (following a merger with the Social Democratic Party), the Liberal Democrats

loyalism: this term is sometimes used to denote those within Northern Ireland who, from a broadly unionist perspective, identify primarily with what they call 'Ulster' (the six-county province of Northern Ireland) rather than primarily with the United Kingdom; according to this usage 'loyalism' can include the DUP and even sections of the UUP and other unionists. Here, however, 'loyalism' is used specifically to refer to formations and individuals pertaining to loyalist paramilitary organisations, such as the UDA (or UFF), the UVF, the LVF or the RHD, and associated political parties, such as the PUP and (formerly) the UDP, in order to help in distinguishing between those who are closely linked to paramilitary activity (loyalists) and those who are not (unionists), a distinction that parallels the deployment of the terms 'republican' and 'nationalist'.

LVF: Loyalist Volunteer Force, a paramilitary organisation that never formally supported the GFA, but called a ceasefire soon after it was signed, possibly in an attempt to have prisoners who belonged to it released under the terms of the agreement. It has since ended its ceasefire.

mainstream
republicanism:see 'Provisionals'
MLA: Member of the Legislative Assembly of Northern
              Ireland established under the GFA
MP: Member of Parliament, an elected member of the
              House of Commons, the lower house of the British
              Parliament (not used of members of the upper house,
              the House of Lords)
nationalism: in Irish contexts, of or pertaining to political
              movements and their affiliates, or assumed affiliates,
              avowing the objective of an independent and united
              Ireland, whether as an aspiration or at any other
              level, and whether by peaceful means, by the use of
              force, or by a combination of both approaches. In the
              late nineteenth and early twentieth centuries the main
              legally functioning and politically influential body
              advocating this objective was the Nationalist Party,
              also referred to as the Irish Parliamentary Party, led
              by Charles Stewart Parnell and, later, John Redmond.
              In Northern Ireland from 1922 to 1970 the objective
              was upheld by the Nationalist Party in the province's
              Parliament and elsewhere, as well as by illegal
              republican groups. Since its foundation, in 1970, the
              SDLP has usually attracted most of those in Northern
              Ireland who pursue the same aspiration, while
              emphasising peaceful and constitutional means
              towards it: hence the distinction often made between
              'nationalists', meaning members of the SDLP or other
              non-violent advocates of a united Ireland, and
              'republicans'. However, 'nationalism' is still often
              used to cover not only the 'nationalists' in this
              narrower sense, but also the republicans and the
              linked 'nationalist community'. In the context of
              Ireland as a whole the term can be used to include the
              main parties in the Republic, although sometimes
              such usage is intended to exclude northern
              republicans and thus approximates to the parties that
              participated in the New Ireland Forum in 1984.
              Where such usage does include republicanism

qualified terms, such as 'pan-nationalism' or 'the nationalist family', are sometimes adopted to emphasise that fact. More generally, nationalism refers to the view that the preservation or attainment of the political sovereignty and/or cultural integrity of a certain nation is the highest political aim; this involves an act of imaginative construction as to the nature of that nation and is to be distinguished from a less specific pursuit of the interests of the inhabitants of a given territory or sovereign political unit (described elsewhere as 'territorialised patriotism').

neoliberalism: of or pertaining to the project of removing impediments to international and national trade, involving indifference to, if not enthusiasm about, the implicit extension of the power of wealthy multinational corporations

NI: Northern Ireland

NILP: Northern Ireland Labour Party, a political party active in the province in the years after partition, often forming the second largest parliamentary group after the UUP and long associated with, although organisationally separate from, the British Labour Party. Ultimately it accepted partition and received much of its support from members of the Protestant working class. It ceased to be a significant force after the onset of the Troubles and was finally dissolved in 1987.

NIWC: Northern Ireland Women's Coalition, a political party that emerged in 1996, with the particular purpose of representing women's interests in Northern Ireland, and has since become supportive of the GFA and the peace process

NSMC: North–South Ministerial Council, an institution created under the GFA, consisting of representatives from the Northern Ireland Executive and the government of the Irish Republic, that comprises the most significant 'Irish dimension' of the GFA

OIRA: Official Irish Republican Army, the name used to denote the rump of the IRA that did not join the

PIRA after the IRA split late in 1969, in the main over the rump's interest in ending the IRA's policy of political abstention.   Links have been suggested between the 'Officials', as the OIRA and the former Official Sinn Féin were jointly known, and what still survives as one of the smaller political parties in Northern Ireland, the Workers' Party.

PIRA: Provisional Irish Republican Army, a republican paramilitary organisation that emerged late in 1969 from a split in the IRA, at the time in opposition to a proposal that republicans end their policy of electoral abstention. The PIRA also retreated from the Marxist rhetoric that had previously been predominant within the IRA. The PIRA has links to PSF. Over the past three decades it has often been referred to simply as 'the IRA'.

PR: proportional representation

Provisionals: members of PSF/PIRA, also referred to, in these pages and elsewhere, as mainstream republicans

PSF: Provisional Sinn Féin, the main republican political party in Northern Ireland, currently led by Gerry Adams. PSF has its origins in the split in the IRA in 1969–70 and has links to the PIRA. It is often referred to simply as Sinn Féin and, indeed, has dropped the word 'Provisional' from its official title, but the word has been retained here to distinguish it from earlier groups called Sinn Féin.

PSNI: Police Service of Northern Ireland, the new police force created under the GFA and as a result of the recommendations of the subsequent Patten Commission, replacing the RUC

PUP: Progressive Unionist Party, a loyalist political party, founded in 1979, that has links to the UVF

Real IRA: a republican paramilitary group that emerged in 1997 in opposition to the PIRA's ceasefire and has since opposed the GFA, regarding it as a betrayal of republican ideals. It rose to global prominence in August 1998, when it carried out the bombing of Omagh, shortly after which it declared a short-lived ceasefire. It is alleged that it has links to a political group, the 32-County Sovereignty Movement, although both the Movement and the Real IRA deny this.

republicanism:of or pertaining to republican paramilitary organisations such as the PIRA, the Continuity IRA, the Real IRA and the INLA, and associated political parties such as PSF; not to be confused either with 'republicanism' in the more general sense of opposition to monarchy and fidelity to equal rights, or with the 'Republicanism' associated with the US Republican Party

RHD: Red Hand Defenders, a loyalist paramilitary organisation that first appeared shortly before the GFA, which it opposed. More recently the name has been used as a cover name for terrorist activities by both the LVF and the UDA.

RUC: Royal Ulster Constabulary, the police force created in Northern Ireland after partition, whose membership swiftly became overwhelmingly Protestant as the proportion of Catholic members fell to a single-figure percentage. Several hundred RUC officers lost their lives during the Troubles, many of them targeted by republicans. Reform of the RUC was promised under the GFA. Unionists pressed strongly for the new force to retain the title RUC, but ultimately it was renamed the PSNI.

SAS: Special Air Service, a special operations unit of the British Army

SDLP: Social and Democratic Labour Party, founded in 1970 by elements from the old Nationalist Party and those involved in civil rights agitation; led by John Hume from 1979 until recently; the largest nationalist party in Northern Ireland for most of its existence

Sinn Féin: a political party in Ireland, founded in 1905 by Arthur Griffith and consisting of more 'advanced' nationalists than those in the Irish Nationalist Party. Sinn Féin was confirmed as the most popular political party in Ireland in the general election of 1918 and its leaders negotiated the independence of the 26-county Irish Free State with the British government in 1921. More recently the name has often been used to refer to PSF.

Taoiseach: the office of Prime Minister of the Irish Republic and its incumbent

TD: Teachta Dála, elected member of the Dáil, the lower house of the Irish Parliament

UDA: Ulster Defence Association, a loyalist paramilitary organisation founded in 1971, which sometimes also uses the name Ulster Freedom Fighters (UFF)

UDP: Ulster Democratic Party, a loyalist political party that emerged in the 1980s and was linked to the UDA. After the UDA's ceasefire was ruled to have ended in 2001 the UDP collapsed. Since then the body calling itself the Ulster Political Research Group has acted as a political link to the UDA.

UDR: Ulster Defence Regiment, a regiment of the British Army, created in 1970 and recruited in Northern Ireland, with the purpose of serving the functions of the former Ulster Special Constabulary (the 'B-Specials'). The UDR was merged with the Royal Irish Rangers in 1992.

UK: United Kingdom of Great Britain and Northern Ireland ('Britain' for short)

UKUP: United Kingdom Unionist Party, a unionist party that emerged in the mid-1990s, following its leader Robert McCartney's secession from the UUP. It has since opposed the GFA and has since been reduced itself by secessions

Ulster: an ancient province of Ireland comprising the six counties of modern Northern Ireland along with Counties Monaghan, Cavan and Donegal, which are in the Irish Republic. Many inhabitants of Northern Ireland, and some academic and media commentators, refer to the six counties alone as 'Ulster', while some institutions, such as the RUC, the UDA, the UDP, the UDR and the UUP, have used, or still use, the name, even though they lacked, or lack, any presence in

Counties Monaghan, Cavan and Donegal (with the exception, due to the vagaries of transmission, of the commercial broadcaster Ulster Television).

unionism: of or pertaining to political movements and their affiliates, or assumed affiliates, avowing the objective of maintaining the constitutional position of Northern Ireland as part of the United Kingdom (although some unionists have occasionally entertained the notion of an independent Northern Ireland). In Northern Ireland unionism equates to the UUP and the DUP; smaller unionist parties, such as the UKUP; the loyalist parties; and the linked 'unionist community'. The term 'Ulster Unionist' is avoided here, since it is unclear whether it refers to all unionists in Northern Ireland, or only to members of the UUP, and in any case involves a non-standard definition of 'Ulster'. In Great Britain the Conservative Party has also been known as the Conservative and Unionist Party in England and Wales, and as the Unionist Party in Scotland, and was long linked with unionists in Northern Ireland. The other main British parties, the Labour Party and the Liberals/Liberal Democrats, have also generally been committed to maintaining the union ever since Northern Ireland was created (although some members of both these parties, and, briefly and ambivalently, the leadership of the Labour Party in the 1980s, have espoused the ideal of a united Ireland).

United Kingdom (UK):   a state comprising Great Britain (England, Wales and Scotland) and Northern Ireland, also commonly known as 'Britain'

UUC: Ulster Unionist Council, the governing body of the UUP

UUP: Ulster Unionist Party, the oldest and for long the most popular unionist party in Northern Ireland. The majority in the UUP supported the GFA, but there is a significant and possibly growing minority within its ranks opposed to peace process, a minority that has included, among others, the MPs David Burnside and, until December 2003, Jeffrey Donaldson.

UVF: Ulster Volunteer Force, a loyalist paramilitary organisation formed in 1966, although its name has a very old ancestry in unionist/loyalist history. The UVF is still officially on ceasefire and is linked to the PUP.

Acknowledgements

I would like to thank the Daily Express newspaper London, for permission to reproduce Fig. 1, and Martyn Turner for permission to reproduce Fig. 2, and to acknowledge the Nationl Archives, and the Deputy Keeper of the Records, Public Record Office of Northern Ireland, for permission to reproduce quotations from unpublished manuscripts. Fig. 3 is produced by permission of Telegraph Group Limited and is © Telegraph Group Limited (2001). Fig. 4 is copyright Pressdram Limited 1998, reproduced by permission. I would like to thank the Democratic Unionist Party for permission to reproduce the cover illustration.

This book is dedicated to the courage and perseverance of the people of Northern Ireland.

Introduction

If the thought were not invidious and macabre, it would be tempting to suggest that, given the dimensions of the political problem, Northern Ireland has, over the past thirty years, already received more than proportionate attention. Northern Ireland, with fewer than two million inhabitants, is demographically smaller than many cities. For all the pain, death and destruction caused by the conflict, devastating to its victims and their families, friends and associates, it is still of a low enough intensity to make a minimal impact on the daily lives of many of the province's inhabitants. Yet the quantity of scholarly work, as well as less scholarly or more media-friendly output, engendered by the Northern Ireland conflict is already daunting enough. The evidence over the past thirty years that this literary prognostication has advanced a 'solution' to the Northern Ireland 'problem' is so unconvincing that any decent human being undertaking further study must feel moments of futility analogous to Thomas Hardy's sense of being addressed by the Moon in 1917:

> I've been scanning pond and hole
> And waterway hereabout
> For the body of one with a sunken soul
> Who has put his life-light out.
>
> Did you hear his frenzied tattle?
> It was sorrow for his son
> Who is slain in brutish battle,
> Though he has injured none.
>
> And now I am curious to look

> Into the blinkered mind
> Of one who wants to write a book
> In a world of such a kind.[1]

Such doubts are particularly potent for those who feel impelled to advance a thesis such as the present book's, which is intended to challenge the basis of the faith of many in the imminence of a 'solution' to the Northern Ireland conflict. Such a hypothesis could surely seem to be inspired by a voyeuristic fascination with the pain of others, or, still worse, the desire to advance an academic or commercial reputation from that pain, a motivation identified piercingly by Theo Hoppen in his description of elements of the 'peace studies' industry in Northern Ireland as academic crows feeding off the carrion of conflict.[2]

The opposite, however, is true of this study, which is intended as a departure from the 'invented tradition' of such academic and journalistic work. It is not, contrary to appearances, a book about the 'Northern Ireland problem' or 'conflict in Northern Ireland'. Indeed, the basis of the prevailing view that it is necessary to keep faith and persist with the peace process comprises assumptions that are paradoxically pessimistic about the nature of Northern Ireland. The essence of this view, and the consonant euphoria that greeted the defining achievement of the peace process, Belfast or Good Friday Agreement (GFA) itself, are epitomised in one reported comment of a White House aide on hearing of the agreement: 'Hell just froze over. There's going to be peace in Ireland.'[3] Similarly, Philip James Currie, reflecting on the Canadian General John de Chastelain's role in the peace process, suggested that it demonstrated that, while Canada has moved on, 'Ireland [*sic*]' was still fighting 'yesterday's battles'.[4] The idea that the Northern Ireland peace process has failed appears, when presented to those adopting these perspectives, to be a doctrine of doom, because it presages the return of the province (indeed, of 'Ireland') to a Hell of fossilised ethnic dispute, which is assumed to have been the condition of Northern Ireland before the agreement. That assumed condition is further ably summarised in a critical analysis by Joseph Ruane and Jennifer Todd:

> the people of Northern Ireland are out of step with contemporary cultural trends . . . Each community, it is

claimed, is trapped in its ancestral myths, extreme in its nationalism, archaic in its religious beliefs, tribal in its loyalties, intransigent in its political attitudes and prone to violence. Some identify a deeper cultural problem: a degeneration of Christian or moral standards; a narrow essentialist concept of identity and an inability to cope with cultural difference.[5]

Such assumptions implicitly invoke facile images of the nature of Northern Ireland prior to the GFA, patronising conceptions of the people of Northern Ireland and an inflated view of the peace process as commonly defined by the GFA. Northern Ireland was not a Hell of fossilised conflict before the agreement. The position was fluid and a good deal more complicated: social attitude surveys in Northern Ireland have not depicted a society that was, or that its people thought was, unchanging. Further, the people of Northern Ireland do not have an atavistic predisposition to murder each other, from which fate they have been rescued only by the miraculous attributes of the GFA and of a handful of political leaders. Both the nature of that accord and the abilities of many of the leaders concerned are too limited to have achieved such a feat. The implication of assumptions underlying valorisations of the GFA, and with it the peace process, is that Northern Ireland should be conceptualised and studied as a 'place apart', generating a distinct violent culture. There is mileage in such an approach, as scores of academic and other commentators have shown, but such media and academic pathology also distorts the reality of life in Northern Ireland, even before the current peace process, which to a considerable extent was, and is, ordinary and uneventful, as its inhabitants were, and are, largely decent and law-abiding. It is an approach that Ruane and Todd reject for another significant reason. They argue that:

> the conflict is generated by a structural bind within Northern Ireland which is reproduced and stabilised outside its boundaries, by the internal structures and mutual relations of the two sovereign states [the United Kingdom and the Irish Republic] . . . If the Northern Ireland conflict is to be resolved, it has to be addressed at the wider level of the structures of the two states and the relationship between them.[6]

In other words, to focus on conflict specifically *in Northern Ireland* is unhelpful and a source of distortion. Ian MacBride and Graham Walker in part agree with Ruane and Todd, although their considerations lead them to focus on only one of the 'two sovereign states': in their view the 'Northern Ireland problem' pertains to 'the hap-hazard and in some ways artificial development of the UK. It is about the multi-definitional character of "Britishness", the United Kingdom.' The 'common English perception of what Britishness should mean' has thus become artificially prevalent, and excludes the claim of unionists in Northern Ireland to a 'Britishness'.[7]

There is indeed a pressing need for British academics and commentators to understand how Northern Ireland's conflicts and politics relate to, and interact with, British culture and history. However, this study differs from the work of the scholars cited above in suggesting that conflict in Northern Ireland pertains to structural binds, not only in the United Kingdom, or in the United Kingdom and the Irish Republic, but to all or many modern societies, and that the conflict should be studied accordingly. One wonders even in Canada whether the debates surrounding Québecois separatism quite deserve a positive, modern designation. Indeed, it can be contended that the current (or, as will be maintained, recent) peace process, or, more particularly, the political dynamics that have accompanied it, have actually tended to consolidate the separation and exoticisation of Northern Ireland from surrounding societies, in a development that is cognate to the failure of the process. To acknowledge failure in the Northern Ireland peace process is thus by no means itself a justification for despair, but it does instead comprise a call for renewed (or, so far as some peripheral actors to the conflict are concerned, initial) effort to improve the quality of life of the people of Northern Ireland.

Some political actors, largely in Northern Ireland itself, declared themselves opposed to the GFA at the outset. Other commentators, in Northern Ireland and elsewhere, have suggested that the peace process has since taken an erroneous course. Still others would suggest that particular policies pursued by some or any of its leading actors (particularly the alleged entrenchment of communalism) were and are misguided, and require correction. Yet practically no one, and certainly no academic commentator, has to date fully explored the hypothesis that the GFA and peace process have failed, in the sense of having served useful purposes once, but now having come to a terminal halt. Mick Fealty, Trevor Ringland and David Steven outline the three possible futures for the peace processes: progress, stalemate or disaster.[8] Failure, which, it is contended in this book, has now arisen, corresponds not to disaster, but to a continued and protracted stalemate beyond serious hopes of revival. The suspension of the Northern Ireland Assembly at the time of writing is a symptom of that failure, but it does not define it: even a new agreement between the parties and the Assembly's resumption would not, without other events that now appear unlikely, signify the transcending of the fundamental long-term weaknesses in the process, since there would be still harder obstacles to surmount on the road to stability (see Chapter 2).

WHY SPEAK OF FAILURE?

Commentators and journalists are generally averse to speaking of 'failure' in connection with the Northern Ireland peace process. There is a desire to prolong political dialogue between parties in Northern Ireland for as long as possible, lest there be a reversion to conflict. This has both interested and disinterested bases. At the time of another phase of political dialogue in Ireland, the ill-fated Irish Convention of 1917–18, one British commentator, F.E. Smith (later Lord Birkenhead), stated: 'Let them keep on talking. If they don't agree it's the fault of Irishmen and not of the English, for there is not an Englishman on the Convention. It's an Irish problem and not an English problem.'[9] There is today undoubtedly at some level a hope that internal political dialogue can continue so that 'England', the 'United Kingdom' or the wider world will be left alone and not bothered again with these apparently petty disputes. In some cases, as in F.E. Smith's, there may also ultimately be a hope that, if dialogue does break down, the Irish will still stew in their own juice. In any case, there are important if unconscious political implications to this attitude: 'it's an Irish problem' presupposes that the solution too must be Irish.

Hopes that the peace process will continue also have much better motives. Commentators have a sense that they should avoid exacerbating difficulties by using a performative language of crisis and that they should encourage continued support for political engagement among the constituencies in Northern Ireland to which its political parties are ultimately responsible. Commentators, in short, recognise the importance of encouraging pacific attitudes on the ground by 'talking up' the peace process, much as governments have long known the value of engendering commercial confidence by 'talking up' the economy. When presented in able formulations, this case can appear compelling. Two of the best recent books on Northern Ireland that adopt this perspective (or indeed, any perspective) are Jeremy Smith's *Making the Peace in Ireland* and Paul Arthur's *Special Relationships*. Smith argues that 'even the most limited and pessimistic interpretation' would accept the view of the experienced and informed journalist David McKittrick that 'it has (now) become safe to join the optimists'.[10] Arthur, while suggesting that 'it is much too early to be definitive about the degree to which we have put our ancient quarrel behind us', describes his own book as 'guardedly optimistic in that it assumes that we have reached the beginning of the end'.[11]

Smith's suggestion that 'a flawed peace is surely better than no peace'[12] appears on humanitarian grounds to be beyond question. The bare statistics of rates of death from the conflict in Northern Ireland since the paramilitary ceasefires of 1994 provide, as the British journalist Jonathan Freedland suggested in 2001, a further strong argument:

> Whatever else happens, peace processes have to keep on. For all its flaws, the Northern Ireland effort can claim to have saved nearly 600 lives: until the IRA cessation in 1994, approximately 100 people were killed in each of the 30 years of the Troubles. With more than 100 dead since 1994, that leaves close to 600 saved in seven years.[13]

To question the beneficence of the linked political process appears perverse: all commentators have a human and ethical responsibility, if not a legal obligation, to avoid language that may inflame old hatreds. The sense of responsibility is well-expressed by Mike Morrissey and Marie Smyth:

> The data we collect has been used by one or other parties to the Northern Ireland conflict to 'prove' their cause. Researching and publishing such data in the midst of a continuing conflict brings with it responsibilities. Once [it has been] published, the authors lose control over how the work is used or interpreted. Our work might be used in ways that will contribute to the entrenchment of positions, and thence to more bloodshed and loss of life. There is no possible evasion of this responsibility.[14]

Since evasion is impossible, there appears little political space in which to speak of the failure of the Northern Ireland peace process, and still less of an audience for what might appear to be doom-saying. While a small number of depraved or grossly misguided individuals in Northern Ireland itself doubtless continue to see a recrudescence of conflict on a large scale as likely to advance congenial political goals, it is surely fair to suggest that even most critics of the peace process would not want to see conflict on such a scale in the province and elsewhere, and thus, in a sense, would like to be proved wrong. Few would share Conor Cruise O'Brien's thoughts on the peace process: 'I'm glad to see this bloody thing crash.'[15]

Commentators' duty to accentuate the positive in the peace process in Northern Ireland is further emphasised where it is suggested that the process has inspired analogous confidence in efforts at conflict resolution around the world. The decision of the Basque separatist organisation Euskadi Ta Azkatasuna (ETA) to call a ceasefire in 1998 in the light of the Provisional IRA's ceasefire is a prominent example.[16] The GFA 'was hailed as an example of how even the most intractable conflicts can be made more malleable given a fair wind. . .'[17] In the predominantly liberal academy, to be seen to pronounce the intractability of conflict all over the world would be to acquire an unenviable reputation.

Yet there are six pressing reasons for questioning the desirability of reiterating optimistic discourses about peace in Northern Ireland. First, it may not be readily apparent that such discourses are at least cognate, in a number of contexts, to party-political perspectives. The reputations of certain parties, or certain individual politicians, in Great Britain and Ireland have a lot invested in the talking up of the peace process.

This was most evident in the general election of spring 2002 in the Irish Republic, in which the supposed success of the peace process featured alongside the performance of the 'Celtic Tiger' economy as a major selling point of the sitting Fianna Fáil-led coalition government, which duly recorded a crushing victory at the polls. Hagiographic accounts of the Taoiseach (Prime Minister) Bertie Ahern paint him as a peacemaker,[18] a trait found similarly in literature glorifying the role in the peace process of nationalists and republicans, especially John Hume and Gerry Adams,[19] and, to an extent, of the Clinton administration and Irish America.[20]

In the British context, similarly, it is suggestive that optimistic commentators on the process, such as Smith and Peter Taylor, cite the rise of 'New Labour' to government as a positive influence on Northern Ireland.[21] A further development of this argument suggests (albeit contentiously) that the previous Conservative governments of 1979–97 made a mess of running Northern Ireland.[22] The assertion that there is no alternative to the peace process – or, in Peter Mandelson's words from October 1999, that 'there is no Plan B'[23] – is very much the language of New Labour. The British Prime Minister Tony Blair, in particular, relies heavily on events in Northern Ireland to underpin his kudos as a peacemaker. In a phone-in on the BBC World Service on 4 December 2002 Blair told a questioner that he regarded the GFA and the peace process as the achievement in office of which he was proudest. Most suggestively, Blair made this claim at a time when the Northern Ireland Assembly was suspended and political dialogue between parties in Northern Ireland had almost completely ground to a halt.[24]

It should also be noted in passing, however, that one could argue that the British Conservative Party's formal renunciation of bipartisanship with Labour over Northern Ireland policy in December 2001 could be read as suggesting that it is not only New Labour that plays politics in Britain with Northern Ireland. This writer's view, however (for what it is worth), is that the renunciation of bipartisanship was not necessarily inappropriate. The allegation of playing politics with Northern Ireland could perhaps more fairly be levelled at the procedure adopted by the then Conservative leader, William Hague, in September 1999, when he claimed to be maintaining bipartisanship even after having accused Blair of betraying the people of Northern Ireland.

Academic and journalistic accounts affirmative of the peace process themselves may be derivative of its personnel. Arthur, for example, was himself involved in 'track two' diplomacy in earlier stages of the process,[25] while Jeremy Smith's *Making the Peace in Ireland* is in key places, and even in its title, derivative of George Mitchell's account of his own role in the negotiations, *Making Peace.*[26] Jonathan Freedland's sympathy for Provisional Sinn Féin (PSF)[27] should cast something of a pall over his depiction of the peace process solely in terms of saved lives, since it obscures the agency of those who would have taken those lives. Three thousand, six hundred people did not die just because of the lack of a set of political conditions, but because of grave moral and political errors on the part of those, the Provisional IRA (PIRA) principal among them, who were involved in killing. To obscure this agency is to trivialise the emotive questions of, for instance, forgiveness, remorse and reconciliation raised by the release on licence of paramilitary prisoners,[28] and to occlude the need for concrete gestures of contrition, without which the political process can appear to be a series of submissions to threat and unilateral political gain to the 'men of violence': hence, in part, the strength of anti-agreement unionist opinion. Among the major actors in the peace process it is perhaps only David Trimble who surrounds himself and is surrounded in a lower-key language about the blessings of the peace process, Trimble's speech on accepting the Nobel Peace Prize of 1998 being of course a crucial example.[29]

Second, one may argue that there is some sleight of hand at work in any optimism about the 'peace process' that moves from suggesting that some recent developments in Northern Ireland have been beneficial to justifying a wide and disparate array of political actions. It may be the case that to desire 'peace', in the sense of continued diminutions in the numbers of casualties in Northern Ireland, is the only sensible and humane alternative, but defences of the 'peace processes' go beyond this. An argument that there is no alternative to a particular policy may be appropriate to some contexts, but if it is used to justify, or curtail discussion of, a large body of measures, so that a 'process' becomes a great irreversible abstraction, it can carry profoundly undemocratic implications. This is most evident in the demonisation of critics of the British government's policy in Northern Ireland, whom Blair occasionally depicts as desiring a return to violence in Northern Ireland,[30] as when he reviled 'the malignant whisperings of those opposed to the process, always pointing out its faults, never aiding its strengths … At every step, those working for peace, trying to make the agreement function, were being undermined, often from within their own community.'[31] Yet surely it must be conceded that some objections to particular aspects of the peace process, such, for instance, as the release of paramilitary prisoners, even if mistaken, are understandable. More contentiously, it can be argued that particular details of governments' policies in Northern Ireland since the agreement was signed are hard to defend at all. A still more important cognate point should be noted in Arthur's comment on the access to Downing Street permitted to PSF's leaders Gerry Adams and Martin McGuinness in the autumn of 1997 that the 'politics of inclusion were back in vogue'.[32] Arthur omits to note that the admission of PSF to this status within high political councils also produced the (arguably self-imposed) exile from all-party talks on Northern Ireland of segments of unionist opinion, namely Ian Paisley's Democratic Unionist Party (DUP) and the United Kingdom Unionist Party (UKUP), which in combination had almost as much electoral support in Northern Ireland as PSF at the time, and now have more. Arthur's description of this 'peace process' as the 'politics of inclusion' is statistically inaccurate, because overt criticism of associated policies is heavily concentrated within Northern Ireland itself within one community, the unionists. To affirm the 'peace process' in a way that dismisses such critics as obscurantist or pernicious thus implicitly involves a highly contentious and teleological approach to Northern Ireland politics, with dramatic, and arguably explosive, implications for the future. Failure to represent at least the existence, even if not the rationale, of such a body of opinion, by leaving significant numbers of people voiceless and frustrated, could be at least as much a source of violence as pessimism.

    While the actual arguments advanced in the late Edward Saïd's book on the Israeli–Palestinian peace process can be criticised, Saïd at least identified not only the possibility that a 'peace process' orchestrated over the heads of those most affected by a conflict can contain an effective bias against one party, but also that an associated public discourse of 'peace' can furnish outsiders with a deluded sense of the beneficence of policies and developments.[33] In relation to Northern Ireland too, optimistic academic and journalistic discourses about the 'peace process' can, third, be criticised for entrenching uncritical definitions of the term 'peace'.[34] Only certain aspects of life in Northern Ireland have been improved by the 'peace process' and only certain categories of violence have abated. Indeed, it seems likely that some types of violence *within* each of the two communities in Northern Ireland, as opposed to violence *between* them, have actually increased during the peace process, particularly in the form of what are euphemistically described as paramilitary 'punishment beatings'. Paramilitary involvement in protection rackets and smuggling, tension surrounding parades and marches, and increasingly segregated residence patterns in parts of Northern Ireland can also be cited as limits to peace. The effect of the peace process in diminishing instances of conflict-related death may also be exaggerated. Talk of more than 100 people being killed in every year from 1969 to 1994 is something of a distortion, since the average is inflated by including the worst years of the conflict, which were the early 1970s: in fact, death rates had diminished long before the paramilitary ceasefires of 1994. It is true, of course, that these nonetheless brought an improvement, but it has been a more marginal improvement than is sometimes suggested, and one that – at least for those coming from certain perspectives – has to be weighed against political change that is hard to bear.

Fourth, indeed, when the types of violence that have actually decreased are considered, it becomes apparent that in a sense commentators, particularly from certain locations, actually have an ethical responsibility *not* to overstate the extent of peace in Northern Ireland. One intelligent commentator on Northern Ireland from continental Europe, Richard Deutsch, accuses the media of hypocrisy in its attitude towards the peace process: 'the British and Irish media hailed the Peace Process, [and] praised the GFA[,] and now they bitterly criticise its implementation'.[35] It will be emphasised in this book that hypocritical attitudes in the media, especially in Britain, have indeed had a negative influence on the context of Britain's relations with Northern Ireland over the past thirty years, but the hypocrisy in question is not accurately identified by Deutsch. It is true that elements of the British media have loudly condemned the execution of certain measures anticipated in the GFA, such as the release of paramilitary prisoners on licence, but even right-wing British newspapers are distinctly selective in such criticisms. The right-wing *Daily Telegraph*, for instance, has, it is true, taken an ambivalent attitude to the GFA since its signature,[36] but it has argued that it supports the implementation of the GFA itself and criticises only what it regards as the unbalanced application of aspects of its content.[37] Even the right-wing *Daily Mail* has had a good word in passing for Tony Blair's 'courage' in Northern Ireland.[38] Further, in one important respect it can be argued that the British press has definitely not overstated problems with the peace process, in that, since the PIRA called its second ceasefire in July 1997, violence in Northern Ireland – with the exception of certain set-piece occasions – has been relatively *under*-represented in Great Britain. (As is argued elsewhere in this book, the reporting of the series of annual stand-offs over the Portadown Orange lodge's desire to parade its established route down a nationalist section of the Garvaghy Road has itself some performative political implications.) This under-representation is the product of a consistent tendency in British reporting of the conflict to give discriminating levels of representation and rhetoric to certain categories of violence. In general, the deaths of people from Great Britain as a result of the conflict have been guaranteed a higher level of profile and condemnation, especially in British newspapers, since it is tacitly believed that so to feed an assumed addiction to a contrived sense of national injustice is a way to gain access to the lucrative British market for 'news'. The shrillest press complaints about the release of paramilitary prisoners rather demonstrate this, in so far as they tend to arise from the release of the killers of British individuals, such as service personnel in Northern Ireland. Yet this is one of the categories of violence that the peace process has definitely diminished: whatever else a PIRA ceasefire entails – and its definition appears somewhat flexible – it is clearly deemed incompatible by the PIRA itself with bombing campaigns in Great Britain and attacks on British service personnel. In this sense there is *already* an exaggerated perception in certain locations of the diminution of violence and, by extension, of the success of the peace process. Academics, journalists and newspaper-readers, particularly if they are based in Great Britain, are among those who have profited most from the peace process in terms of a greater proportionate diminution of any risk of falling a victim to violence associated with the conflict. It is arguable, therefore, that those of us with substantive connections to Great Britain – particularly if we are academics rather than journalists and thus not so prone to pander to the basest nationalistic instincts assumed of their readers – actually have a responsibility to represent the experience of those bystanders still at a greater risk of encountering the continued violence associated with the conflict, even if this entails the risk of feeling the chill embrace of apparent pessimism and accusations of stirring up trouble.

A fifth point pertains to another problematic dimension of common ideas of 'peace', across a temporal rather than a spatial frame. Unless one adopts an extreme pacifist position, it must be accepted that there are circumstances in which 'peace' – even in a fully literal sense that does not apply to the present in Northern Ireland – can simply be bought at too high a price. An example would be a case where a more powerful foreign state invades a nation: if the invaded people were to offer no resistance, peace would in a sense prevail, but under circumstances that would ordinarily be deemed intolerable. The more hysterical unionist suggestion that the GFA actually comprises such a foreign takeover of Northern Ireland can be dismissed. The agreement certainly has, however, for instance, underpinned an 'Irish' dimension to the government of Northern Ireland. Further, from a unionist perspective, there are observable dynamics in the republican movement, demonstrated by its fractious nature and its perceived reluctance about weapons decommissioning, that suggest a possibility of scenarios in the none too distant future that pose serious questions about the present prosecution of the 'peace process' and certainly casts doubt on the optimistic view that the limited measures of republican decommissioning to date show that the 'war is over'.[39]

In the relevant nightmare scenario for unionists, the mainstream republican movement will continue to press for acts of completion by the British government and the unionists in areas of the agreement, such as policing reform and demilitarisation, that represent a further diminution of British or unionist ability to control executive power and authority in the province, delaying further acts

The Failure of the Northern Ireland Peace Process

of PIRA decommissioning for as long as possible by way of bargaining chip or threat.[40] Such concessions to republicans and nationalists having been delivered, whether it would ultimately prove possible to press the PIRA for full acts of decommissioning, or even to disband itself, might then be revealed as of less significance than is imagined, for these would not affect the magnitude of a growing dissident republican threat. The membership and military hardware of groups such as the 'Real' IRA might be enhanced at this juncture by the active co-operation of sections of the Provisionals' leadership. Precedents for such a development exist, for instance in the defection of the Provisionals' Quartermaster to the Real IRA around the time of the GFA.[41] Even if PSF's leadership, especially Adams and McGuinness, co-operate sincerely with other pro-agreement parties at this point, this need not prevent a large secession of the Provisionals' rank-and-file from a recently self-abnegated movement to an increasingly militarily potent dissident faction. Indeed, by this point the acts of demilitarisation imposed upon the PSF/PIRA would have weakened any possibility of its neutralising the dissident movement. The upshot of such a scenario would thus be a renewed conflict with 'the IRA' in a new form, weaker than earlier incarnations only in some respects, but facing a unionist side in an infinitely weaker position. On constitutional matters, the new status quo that unionists would be defending would embody all the concessions on sovereignty and power-sharing that they have made with such great misgivings, and in terms of military strength the forces protecting unionist communities would be handicapped in numbers and cohesion. Perhaps thirty years after this new conflict was joined the Real IRA too would call a ceasefire and its political wing would enter negotiations. What a British government would then press unionists to concede can only be imagined. The possibility even then of a splinter fragment of the Real IRA renewing the conflict, if it was dissatisfied with this new set of concessions, could not be dismissed.

For a number of reasons, however, this scenario is not likely. For one thing, questionable assumptions are made in it about the evolving attitudes of the Irish and British governments to dissident republicanism. The Real IRA would surely be unlikely ever to receive the level of latitude granted to the PIRA by Jack Lynch's government in the Irish Republic in the 1970s.[42] Nevertheless, as is argued in this book, the potency of dissident republicanism – especially if it is enhanced by factors within the control of unionists and loyalists themselves – can be underestimated. The fears of anti-agreement unionists on this score are worthy of consideration, if only as a demonstration of why, from certain political perspectives, it is entirely legitimate to question the beneficence of the Northern Ireland peace process, and why it is not sufficient passively to accept the prevalent assumption of outsiders that to continue to co-operate with that process is the only logical and moral course of action. Academics have a duty to recognise the existence of such fears, even if they do not agree with them.

There is a sixth and final reason why optimistic journalistic and academic assumptions about the Northern Ireland peace process must be criticised. Whatever duty commentators have to avoid inflaming volatile situations, academics also have an important ethical responsibility to address unwelcome realities, not least because to deny such realities may be to contribute to the creation of further problems in the future. There have always, of course, been commentators and actors who have claimed that the peace process was fundamentally flawed. For some, especially on the unionist side, the GFA was a waste of time, a betrayal by the British government, or worse still. This is not the definition of failure here advanced. However, the GFA, or the process by which it was obtained, can still be criticised. Jeremy Smith, Paul Arthur and many lesser commentators are correct that there are aspects of political and social change in Northern Ireland over the past five years or so that it would be chary to bemoan. Yet *additional* progress along existing lines is unlikely and failure, in this specific sense, was almost necessarily 'hard-coded' into aspects of the process at its outset. The agreement is in some respects a chronically vague document, which represents a far smaller level of accord between key parties than casual commentators chose to represent. This is most evident in the clauses on decommissioning, the ambiguity of which even able commentators refuse to address (see Chapter 3). Indeed, so open to differing interpretation is the agreement that it created sources of disagreement as it resolved others.

Beyond the agreement itself, the peace process represents a set of assumptions and a certain trajectory in Northern Ireland politics the limited utility of which it is tempting to compare to a computer and its hard drive. While the hard drive is in use, an able operator can turn it to excellent purposes. In another sense, however, the operator can be the victim of such success by becoming dependent on the use of the drive. The life of even the best hard drive is finite: even if terminal failure does not occur, the appearance of new analogous possible products on the market will make its continued use less attractive. It is at this point that the real difficulties arise. If the old computer has been of long utility, the operator may have developed an irrational affection for it or an inertia that is inimical to the disruptions inherent in moving to a new system. Even if the necessity is appreciated, considerable dexterity is required in transferring the accumulated data, skill and experience from the old drive to use on a new system. This book maintains that as the November 2003 election results suggested, the painful transition to a new set of assumptions about and in Northern Ireland has become necessary, sooner rather than later, and marks a modest attempt to apply accumulated recent experience to the new environment.

SYMPTOMS AND FALSIFICATION OF FAILURE

One further disincentive to talking about failure in the Northern Ireland peace process is its appearance of possessing a charmed life. Time after time it appears to have overcome apparently terminal difficulties through new initiatives, especially from governments or republicans, and/or through the affirmation of a viable if tenuous basis for and by pro-agreement unionism, by the narrowest of margins.[43] As Marianne Elliott reminds us, in mid-1993 very few in Northern Ireland thought that the talks process would succeed.[44] Mallie and McKittrick wrote early in 1997, at a time of no great promise, that the peace process 'at many points looked dead in the water, yet time after time was revived against all the odds. The hope will obviously be that it can happen [again].'[45]

This optimistic approach appears vindicated in comparison, for instance, to Kevin Myers' suggestion, at a similar time, that the peace process was finished.[46] In retrospect Myers had to eat his words, which, to his credit (and unlike many), he did publicly.[47] To speak of failure is thus, like Myers, to invite the confounding of one's predictions, and to risk an appearance that certainly would not impress in academic circles. Yet academics too can sit on the fence too much. To cite Karl Popper, an unfortunately unfashionable influence in academia these days, human understanding is best advanced by risky predictions or improbable projections, based on powerful theories, which can be subjected to refutation and which survive this testing.[48] If such theories are falsified, individual reputations may be shattered, but commentators should not be too sensitive about such self-inflicted injuries: at least the reasons for such mistakes can be deduced and the corpus of human knowledge can thus be advanced. Myers' prediction is still helpful in that it is useful to consider why he was mistaken. As is argued in this book, his error arose not because he was simply too pessimistic, but because his understanding of republicanism was awry (see Chapter 3).

The symptoms of failure in the Northern Ireland peace process are twofold: the chronic lack of workable confidence in the peace process in the unionist community; and the multi-dimensional lack of room for manoeuvre of key parties to the agreement. Unionist support for the agreement has barely stood at a majority ever since the referendum of May 1998 and, according to some recent estimates, only about a third of unionists support the agreement.[49] Local, Northern Ireland, Westminster and European elections in the North since the referendum have largely confirmed this impression. David Trimble's nominally pro-agreement Ulster Unionist Party (UUP) until recently retained a narrow lead over the DUP and there may even have been, as has been argued,[50] some moderating of the DUP's position. The smaller unionist and loyalist parties are, however, increasingly disaffected with the peace process, with the sole exception of the Alliance Party of Northern Ireland (in so far as it may still be regarded as a unionist party). Surely it is most significant that important sections of the UUP were opposed to the agreement from its outset, or since became disaffected. Trimble's ability to obtain ratification by narrow majorities of his party's highest decision-making body, the Ulster Unionist Council, both indicates the problems of unionist confidence in the peace process and actually lead to an exacerbation of them. Trimble's apparent capacity to prevail narrowly against his unionist critics itself has encouraged a cavalier attitude among some to this problem: if the peace process has survived to date with a marginal level of support among unionists, why can it not go on doing so? This misplaced sense of confidence, at several conjunctures in the process to date, may have encouraged governments' decisions to implement policies – such as aspects of policing reform, prisoner releases, or the latitude given to the PIRA over decommissioning – that it has been hard for many unionists to accept.[51] This has thus stored up even greater trouble in the medium term, by giving moderates within the unionist movement less and less credibility or breathing space with consequences seen in November 2003 elections. In this way, denial of serious problems in the peace process may have intersected with a merely marginal level of unionist support to bring about failure: if diagnosis of failure may seem premature, denial of failure can exacerbate the problems.

In some cases, the popularity of the anti-agreement unionist position and the cognate problems in the peace process have been denied. An article in a republican journal argues: 'In the wake of every crisis, politicians of all persuasions now repeat the mantra about needing to "save the peace process" and "protect the Good Friday Agreement" – showing that they have nothing else to argue or fight for.'[52] Many observers, however, are quite aware of the lack of unionist support for the process, but have rarelyt accepted, for one of two reasons, that the process has failed. First, some republicans and even some nationalists appear to take the attitude that lack of unionist support should not matter and, indeed, it is often implied, would not have mattered if pro-agreement forces had a stronger leader than Trimble, whose demise is not infrequently openly anticipated and even desired.[53] This evinces a touchingly naïve view of the state of universal happiness that would have ensued if the UUP had any other leader besides Trimble. Trimble's admiring biographer may not be entirely correct to depict Trimble as expendable to neither unionism nor the peace process,[54] but it is surely fair to suggest that any other leader of moderate unionism would have faced equivalent difficulties in obtaining the support of the UUP in the circumstances. A second and more interesting upbeat response to the problem of lack of unionist support for the process emanates from commentators who are broadly pro-agreement and sympathetic to unionism, and who see the problems of the peace process to date as largely arising from wanton appeasement of republicans. In this view, lack of unionist support for the agreement certainly is a serious problem: a pro-agreement majority within unionism at the Assembly elections in 2003 was unsurprisingly not obtained, and even pro-agreement unionists are not likely to accept Gerry Adams as Northern Ireland's Deputy First Minister even though PSF emerged from the poll as the largest nationalist party.[55] On these assumptions, the lack of unionist support for the process could still be (or could have been) alleviated by the requisite measures of decommissioning from the PIRA, which are in any case overdue,[56] and could be delivered if courage from the Provisional leadership, and appropriate firmness from the British and Irish governments, were applied. According to this interpretation, Trimble's hands would then be strengthened against anti-agreement unionist critics and the pro-agreement vote would recover (or would have recovered). This, however, is where the second symptom of failure – the multi-dimensional lack of room for manoeuvre of several parties to the agreement – becomes important. Put simply, it is not just pro-agreement unionists who need more breathing space: it is possible for other key players also to look at the behaviour and treatment of opposite forces, hemmed in by the restraints of their own location, and see abundant reasons to give no ground.

It is argued in this book that violence by loyalists has probably been repeatedly underreported throughout the conflict by the mainstream media, especially in Britain (see Chapter 3). This has probably still been the case during the more recent peace process. There is also an analytical neglect, at the political and academic levels, of the question of loyalist decommissioning. As David Trimble puts it, 'the Republican movement's obstinacy to disarmament will not be tolerated', when the evidence suggests that reluctance to decommission is actually greater among loyalists.[57] The assumption that loyalism is reactive to republicanism, and thus that loyalists will react to completed PIRA decommissioning or disbandment in kind, has been widely endorsed by politicians, journalists and even informed scholars, such as Steve Bruce.[58] Cautioning in 1995 that it is 'foolish to predict the future in Northern Ireland', Bruce proves that prediction is in this context also necessary and difficult by anticipating that only a resumption of PIRA violence, 'no constitutional crisis', will bring an end to loyalist ceasefires.[59] This

thesis, and the shared assumptions that underlie the entire peace
process, stand up poorly to the evidence. Special pleading cannot
explain the behaviour of those loyalist groups, such as the Red Hand
Defenders, that never recognised the constitutional developments
embodied in the GFA,[60] nor the two loyalist organisations on
ceasefire around the time of the GFA, the Loyalist Volunteer Force
(LVF) and the highly significant Ulster Defence Association (UDA),
which subsequently overtly resumed paramilitary activities. The
loyalist position on decommissioning should also not be represented
as solely reactive to republicans' positions. Although the UDA,
following an internal feud, restored its ceasefire in February 2003
(albeit the British government has been reluctant to recognise this),
the linked Ulster Democratic Party (UDP), which committed itself, in
a vague sense, to working for UDA decommissioning by signing the
GFA, cannot deliver on this, since it disintegrated in November 2001
following the collapse of the UDA's ceasefire. The Ulster Political
Research Group has since stepped into the political vacuum resulting
from the UDP's collapse, but has not obviously advanced any
immediate intention on behalf of loyalists to decommission. The
Progressive Unionist Party (PUP) is still in close relations with the
other main loyalist paramilitary group, the Ulster Volunteer Force
(UVF), which has remained formally on ceasefire, but the same
factors that have placed the other loyalists under such great strain
also affect the PUP. Namely, it feels unable to press the UVF towards
full decommissioning, since even the limited measures of republican
decommissioning to date have, to loyalist minds, been purchased at
such a high price in concessions from the British government as to
undermine the integrity of the process.

Loyalist reluctance to advance the peace process thus also has a
rationale. Nevertheless, this reluctance means that analysts need to
be wary of underestimating the separate dimension to the peace
process that comprises the threat posed by loyalist violence to
Catholics and nationalists. It cannot be assumed that all or most
loyalists would decommission even if the PIRA were to complete its
decommissioning.

Many analysts appear to assume that dissident republican
groups, such as the so-called Real IRA and the political group that
appears to be linked to it, the 32-County Sovereignty Movement,
could not posture plausibly as defenders of Catholic communities in

the North, even in a situation where the Provisionals were almost completely unarmed, thus abrogating this function that they themselves assumed a generation ago. Dissident republicans appear on such assumptions to have been utterly delegitimised by the Omagh atrocity and mainstream republicans, on this analysis, are seen as having repeatedly 'talked up the danger of a split'.[61] Yet this may itself evince too cavalier an attitude to the internal dynamics of republicanism (see Chapter 3). Caution is certainly needed in underestimating how extreme the circumstances would appear to exposed Catholics and nationalists in such a scenario, and it can be argued that increasing identification with dissident republicanism would be found in such locations. Indeed, there is some evidence in terms of grass-roots republican disaffection with the process that in some parts of the North this has already occurred, although on a very small scale. After all, around the early 1970s not a few analysts – even if well-informed, but disposed to precipitate moral judgements about the iniquities of 'terrorism' – mistakenly took the view that Provisional activities such as 'Bloody Friday' had effectively terminally deprived the Provisionals of any position where they could convincingly posture as protectors of Catholic communities.[62] Admittedly, a parallel between the dissidents and the IRA campaigns of 1939–41 and 1956–62, which failed to accrue much popular support, may be more accurate than a parallel with the PIRA's activities in the 1970s: the issue depends on the context. In a context where the PIRA did disarm, there is a potential source of significant political gain for the dissidents republicanism in whatever form may then appear most plausible.

Thus, mainstream republican reluctance about decommissioning may be regarded as comprehensible, rather than as sheer bloody-mindedness, in terms of controlling the dissident republican threat. This would imply that the concessions towards non-violence required from mainstream republicans, which pro-agreement unionists need in order at least to recoup their electoral position within the unionist community, will prove harder to obtain than many assume. If conceding the potency of dissident republicanism helps to explain (if not justify) the delicacy of mainstream republicans' position, this potency would also lead one to regard the unionist nightmare scenario outlined above as not beyond the realms of possibility and thus helps one to understand the mindset of anti-agreement unionists. Interpreting developments within the republican movement on the most charitable basis for mainstream republicans thus, paradoxically, shows us that anti-agreement unionism, contrary to republican insistence and (frequently) wider understandings, is not simply compounded of supremacism and intransigence but has an evidential basis.

Each party to the agreement, as well as many outside, feels under sufficient pressure that they require a polar opposite to take the very next initiative in the peace process in order to let them off the hook, yet each seems trapped by a combination of foes and erstwhile friends. Without the freedom to move there is no process, and a new approach appears to be required. It is hard to see how that new impetus would arise without major changes in attitudes. A scenario in which the PIRA might be encouraged to disarm entirely by the offer of a role in a new coalition government in the Irish Republic would provide an impetus, but the Provisionals sharing in power in Dublin would also surely exacerbate long-held unionist suspicions of a pan-nationalist or pan-republican conspiracy against them. Certainty is, of course, almost impossible in predictions of this kind, and there are possible developments that could give a new impetus to the peace process along the current lines. The most likely such impetus would appear to be errors by extremist or anti-agreement parties. These have occurred before: indeed, one might suggest that the decision of the DUP and the UKUP to leave the talks in July 1997 constituted such a 'helpful error'. It was an error in so far as it deprived these parties of input into the negotiations, and it was helpful to the peace process in so far as it helped to frame and define the combination of parties that signed the GFA. The possibility of such errors, in another form, bailing out the peace process cannot be denied, although it is necessarily hard to estimate their likelihood. The possibility does, however, help us to specify the falsification and refutability of the argument here advanced. If workable expressions of majority pro-agreement opinion reappear within unionism, without the impetus of diametrically new attitudes and approaches to Northern Ireland and without such errors, this would comprise the falsification of the theory advanced in these pages. If such errors intervene, with or without a new 'deal', the theory would merely have been, to adopt a phrase of which the PIRA are fond, 'overtaken by events'.[63]

ALTERNATIVES TO THE PEACE PROCESS?

The failure of the Northern Ireland peace process has long been predicted by anti-agreement parties and commentators. For some it was only ever likely to survive as long as the Sunningdale arrangements did;[64] for others it was depraved, misguided and utterly without benefit from the outset. This is not the view advanced in these pages. Ultimately Peter Mandelson was right when he suggested in February 2000 that there was a greater political will behind the peace process than there had been behind Sunningdale and that thus, even if one accepts the idea of irreversible failure now, it has survived for longer.[65]

It is also some tribute to the peace process that positing alternatives is difficult. Even so, it is helpful to reconsider the concepts of 'peace' and 'solution', and to problematise their simplistic usage. No society is completely peaceful, and Northern Ireland in fact has had until recently a history of absence of certain categories of (non-political) violence. Further, 'peace' in the specific sense meant in 'the peace process' entails the delivery of short-term reductions in *certain categories* of violence by certain actors, usually necessitating either dramatic concessions towards, or coercion of, those actors, neither of which would in fact produce 'peace' in the long term. The ambiguities are indicated in the fact that the peace process has always co-existed with a certain level of violence in Northern Ireland. This suggests that the discourse of 'solution' should be avoided in connection with the Northern Ireland conflict, since it is suggestive of only one section of a spectrum of imaginable desirable political and social developments, and can therefore distract attention from achieving other desirable objectives, some of which may be more easily within reach. Similarly, it is more accurate to conceive, not of a single peace process with no viable alternative, but of possible alternative *negotiation processes*, meaning the array of possible different dialogues that could conceivably be structured between different sets of political actors. This means that, even if it is accepted that the current peace process has failed, an alternative array of conceivable negotiation processes remains available and that it may even be possible to implement a different such process that is ultimately more productive. To illustrate alternatives – paths not taken in a conflict situation – can liberate awareness of the array of human possibilities and thus challenge assumptions about the inevitability of violence. It is the doctrine that there is no alternative to current policies that instead conduces to despair.

In this connection the role played by the British and Irish governments' decisions on what preconditions to impose upon PSF/PIRA's readmission to talks in July 1997 appears crucial. Recovering the possibilities at that point in time demonstrates two important aspects of the process. First, developments from that point forward, including the GFA, have to only a limited extent actually represented significant progress in Northern Ireland, as opposed to the repeated suspension from consideration of the objects of the most serious controversy. Second, if the peace process thus is to be considered as a certain amount of progress along one thread of one of many conceivable negotiation processes, the summer of 1997 becomes a point when at least one alternative track was clearly not taken. The anti-agreement unionist position, representing the clearest alternative negotiation process, remains derivative, in its personnel and its proposals, of this moment. Such unionists(who are growing in popularity and subtlety) propose the renegotiation of the agreement on a basis that would almost certainly exclude reblicans, unless totally unarmed. These proposals are discussed in Chapter 4 of this book and, ultimately, are not considered realistic.

Because of these difficulties, an alternative negotiation process is not here proposed. Recognising the failure of the peace process is not the same as suggesting that a 'bloodbath' (or a 'Hell') in Northern Ireland is imminent or should be precipitated, or that the PIRA's ceasefire is over or should be regarded as such: it means that further progress along the lines so far pursued is not foreseeable. What can be comprehended here is the nature of the difficulties, and what is proposed are certain attitudinal shifts, in Northern Ireland and elsewhere, that could form a modest contribution to relieving the difficulties. It is useful to have an alternative policy such as anti-agreement unionists propose in view, in order to understand these difficulties. These do not have roots solely in Northern Ireland, but arise also because of the lack of political legitimacy that certain groups within Northern Irish society, especially the unionists, possess within the wider world and in Great Britain. Political legitimacy is, however, constructed by politicians and other commentators, and conditioned by a wider political context. The future of Northern Ireland will thus not just be created within the province in isolation, but via a range of wider cultural and political formations, which pertain as much to the problems of British, Irish and other societies as to Northern Ireland itself. Political and academic attitudes, within and outside Northern Ireland, to terrorism, ethnicity and nationality, postmodernism, capitalism and disadvantage, multiculturalism, immigration and asylum all currently delimit political possibilities in Northern Ireland. This book analyses these broader dynamics, which are currently fundamentally transforming all western and non-western societies; explains how they affect Northern Ireland; and attempts to suggest some related steps that might, if external conditions allowed, enhance the prospects of greater stability in the province. A broad perspective on politics and culture, inside and outside Northern Ireland, and the use of a full range of sources, popular and elite, written, audio and visual, is needed in an attempt to penetrate these wider dimensions of the Northern Ireland conflict.

WHAT THIS BOOK COMPRISES

This book thus comprises an introduction to the Northern Ireland problem for the general reader; an interpretative contribution to political debate on the future of the peace process; and some consideration of issues of far wider and greater academic and political significance.

There is certainly no shortage of surveys of the recent history of Northern Ireland. Nevertheless, to attempt the specific and new tasks here intended, it is necessary to begin with a summary of the key phases in Northern Ireland's history (Chapter 2), in order to isolate further the key influences on the current impasse. The more analytical third chapter identifies, from a range of suspects, the key causes of failure in the Northern Ireland peace process; it then delimits the operation of these causes and the relations between them. Chapter 4 considers ultimate reasons why alternative negotiation processes prior to the GFA were (and are) not implemented and demonstrates that the relevant reasons are far from relating solely to the dynamics of Northern Irish society. The fifth and final chapter demonstrates that the failure of the Northern Ireland peace process, while it is certainly a great misfortune, is no cause for an immobilising capitulation to fate. A short postscript then brings the narrative of events from Chapter 2 as up-to-date as is possible.

To offer a solution is beyond the ambitions of this study, and may even, as is suggested above, not be desirable. Yet there is much that can be done and it is argued here that many who believe themselves to have neither responsibility for, nor organic relation to, the core issues can take small steps, and adopt new attitudes and new approaches that might, taken together, contribute to the recovery of political potentialities and an improvement in the lives of inhabitants of Northern Ireland.

Northern Ireland and the
Peace Process

This chapter is intended to summarise the course of main events in the Northern Ireland conflict and peace process. However, it is not possible to approach this subject without surveying the modern history of Northern Ireland in the broadest sense, taking as the point of departure the beginnings of Northern Ireland's cultural and, ultimately, political separation from the rest of Ireland. Particular attention is paid within this chapter to the Northern Ireland conflict since the 1960s and, within this, the most detailed attention is given to the peace process from 1985. This is intended to provide the crucial context for the later analysis of the failure of the peace process.

THE FOUNDING OF NORTHERN IRELAND

Ireland was largely treated as a single administrative unit by its English and British rulers from Elizabethan times, a fact confirmed by the Act of Union 1800, which incorporated the island within the new United Kingdom of Great Britain and Ireland. However, important differences between the North, especially the Northeast, of Ireland and the rest of the island have a long genealogy.[1] Differences in politics, economics, religion and society undoubtedly became of greater significance as a consequence of a number of processes during the nineteenth century, including a decline in the proportion of the population of the nine counties of Ulster that was Catholic, and a Protestant revival in that province in the 1850s; the growth of industry in the province and of closer economic links to

Great Britain;[2] the effect of the Famine of the 1840s on material circumstances and popular beliefs across Ireland;[3] and the decline of Liberalism and the hegemony of Conservatism among unionists from the later nineteenth century.[4] In the late nineteenth century the growing movement for independence or home rule in Ireland was strongest outside Ulster. Nevertheless, while Ulster was referred to in the late nineteenth-century debates on the government of Ireland occasioned by the Liberal Prime Minister William Gladstone's two Home Rule Bills, it was largely assumed by both opponents and proponents of home rule at this time that Ulster was not to be a separate facet of the issue.[5] The partition of Ireland was rarely proposed in the nineteenth century, for several reasons, some of which retain a relevance to the issue. Partition had no precedent (especially not in Irish history); it would entail the difficult task of drawing a boundary between two parts of one island; and it would leave minorities at the mercy of majorities on both sides of any border. In any case, throughout the nineteenth century unionism was strong enough in every part of the British Isles to defeat proposals for home rule or independence in Ireland. As a result, any proposals for partition remained largely theoretical.

The partition of Ireland was certainly not inevitable before the unionist position was weakened by another Liberal government's reduction of the powers of the House of Lords in 1911. Under the Parliament Act of that year, the Lords found their right to veto home rule replaced by the power merely to delay the measure for two years. This removed a critical obstacle to home rule, while the reliance of the Liberals on Irish nationalists for a parliamentary majority made it certain that a third Home Rule Bill would be introduced. This Bill was presented to the House of Commons in April 1912. Details of proposals for separate self-government in Ireland, including the relationship of largely unionist areas of Ulster to the proposed institutions, took on a more immediate importance. Ulster unionists organised separately to resist the Bill, notably signing the Ulster Covenant of September 1912.[6] Unionists in Britain offered their Ulster brethren moral and practical support, but for many British unionists 'Ulster' still remained a way of defeating home rule outright.[7] The Irish nationalists, meanwhile, largely advised their Liberal allies to ignore the unionist mobilisation in Ulster, fearing that an attempt to repress it would create unionist martyrs. As the Lords' two-year veto slowly expired, although the British Liberal government belatedly started to address the importance of the Ulster dimension to home rule, it became clear that the issue had reached a point beyond the control of the leaders of all the relevant political parties.[8] An effort to resolve the controversy, at a conference at Buckingham Palace in July 1914, failed to defuse the threat of violence in the North of Ireland if home rule were put into effect, to the evident dismay of King George V among others.[9]

In the event, the start of the First World War largely delayed the outbreak of violence in Ireland, but did not prevent it. The famous Easter Rising of April 1916, while orchestrated by a small group of separatists and by no means initially popular in nationalist Ireland, eventually struck a chord with a population alienated by the heavy-handed repressive measures of the British authorities, suspicious on account of the long delay in granting home rule and aggrieved on a score of other aspects of British policy before and during the war. A number of subsequent efforts to effect a compromise that would bring home rule into immediate operation, largely motivated by the evident rise of the Sinn Féin movement in Ireland at the expense of more moderate nationalists, were unsuccessful, as Ulster once again proved a sticking point in negotiations. Although the British empire was to emerge victorious from the war, for many observers events during it had demonstrated the limits of Irish nationalists' willingness to adapt themselves to British and imperial interests, as well as the stubborn opposition of Ulster unionists to a united home-rule Ireland. Further evidence of the extent of divisions within Ireland was provided by the results of the general election of 1918 – when Sinn Féin candidates replaced members of the nationalist Irish Parliamentary Party in most Irish seats, but unionist candidates were successful in much of Ulster – and then by the opening of the Anglo-Irish War, fought between the Irish Republican Army (IRA) and British forces from 1919.[10]

Partition was not imposed on Ireland, but rather stumbled upon by a British political class inclined for ideological and practical reasons to alternative forms of settlement.[11] The Government of Ireland Act 1920 reflected conflicting tendencies within British policy-making. On the one hand, the Act created Northern Ireland, consisting of six of the nine counties of Ulster, with a parliament and government subordinate to the sovereignty of the United Kingdom, and separated from the rest of Ireland. This reflected the concerns of those in Britain, such as Andrew Bonar Law and Arthur Balfour, that as much as possible of the unionist sections of Ulster be protected from the nationalist majority in the whole of Ireland. On the other hand, the Act created a Council of Ireland, on which representatives from northern and southern Ireland were to meet to discuss items of common concern. The possibility was envisaged, by at least some at the time, that this body would acquire growing powers and importance, possibly even furnishing the basis of a large degree of political unification between the two parts of Ireland.

In the event those sections of the Bill applying to southern Ireland were obviated by the Anglo-Irish Treaty of December 1921, negotiated and signed by representatives of the British government and of the government formed in Dublin by Sinn Féin, which granted dominion status to a 26-county Irish Free State. This treaty appalled many unionists, both because a British government had negotiated with and empowered men whom they regarded as 'murderers', and because clause twelve of the treaty seemed to pose a threat to the territory of Northern Ireland, by promising the creation of a boundary commission to review the frontier between the two new entities. However, the treaty also divided Sinn Féin, since many of its most prominent leading members were especially unhappy with the limits placed on the independence conceded to the Free State, and a bitter civil war was fought between 'treatyites' and 'anti-treatyites' in the South in 1922–23.[12] In the longer term, however, the treaty served to consolidate partition and the northern 'province' (as it came to be called). The Free State's leaders had formed audacious expectations of how the Boundary Commission could advance the unification of Ireland and the prospect of boundary revision placed the leaders of the new Northern province in a difficult dilemma.[13] The commission was eventually established by the short-lived British Labour government in 1924, but that government shortly collapsed in an unrelated political crisis and was replaced by a Conservative ministry. Perhaps influenced by this political context, the commission proposed such limited transfers of territory that the Free State government chose to accept a package of financial concessions instead.[14] The Council of Ireland proposed in 1920 never formally sat,[15] although similar concepts have continued

FIGURE 1
Cartoon by Cummings, *Daily Express*, 12 August 1970

"How marvellous it would be if they DID knock each other insensible!"

to influence later attempts at an Irish settlement. Although Northern Ireland contained from the outset a sizeable and often disaffected Catholic minority, unionist hegemony within the new province was to prove secure for almost fifty years. Until the reintroduction of direct rule, in 1972, the Protestant-dominated Ulster Unionist Party (UUP) was never out of government in Northern Ireland.

The nature of the new province in the period from 1921 to the 1960s has retrospectively been criticised from a number of political perspectives. Among some unionists and some on the British right, there is regret that Northern Ireland was not fully integrated within the United Kingdom: the experiment of devolution in Northern Ireland is said by such commentators to have been the source of the forces that were to shake the links between Northern Ireland and Great Britain. However, in view of the sustained interest of British policy-makers in obtaining a settlement with the leaders of nationalist Ireland, the alternative possibility must be conceded: that, if devolution had not been put into effect in the North, a British government would have eventually instead promoted the unification of Ireland as a way of putting the troublesome province at arm's length. It is noteworthy that, at Great Britain's moment of most acute difficulty, during the Second World War, British policy-makers suggested the unification of Ireland, in an unsuccessful attempt to lure the South into the conflict on the Allied side.[16]

A more serious point pertains to the extent to which the integration of Northern Ireland within the imagined British nation could be and was achieved. Northern political leaders, such as Lords Craigavon (James Craig) and Brookeborough (Basil Brooke), were not as naïve about public relations issues as it is sometimes assumed unionists have been, and made efforts to 'market' Northern Ireland and project a positive 'British' image of the new province, although some visible differences could never be surmounted.[17] Attempts were also made to alleviate what unionists regarded as misunderstandings of Northern Ireland in Britain and elsewhere, on points such as the relations between Britain and Northern Ireland.[18] An at times bizarre battle was joined between governmental and non-governmental representatives concerned with the semantics of the two Irish political entities. Officially, following its progress towards becoming a republic under its Constitution of 1937, the southern state, overtly aspiring to govern the whole of the island, styled itself 'Ireland'. Strenuous efforts could be made by its officials to avoid reference to Northern Ireland altogether and, where these did not suffice, some preferred the somewhat dismissive term 'the six counties'.[19] Unionist leaders, meanwhile, pressed for the southern state to be described with a more specific label: in the 1960s it was noted that 'the Cabinet Office have had to take up this question of correcting nomenclature on many occasions in the last few years, since the Irish Republic takes every opportunity to have their territory described as "Ireland"'.[20] Unionists also pressed not just for the existence of Northern Ireland to be recognised, but for it to be named with a term consonant with its assumed dignity and Britishness: 'Ulster' and even 'Northwest Britain' were both officially considered for this purpose. References to 'the United Kingdom' within Great Britain that seemed to neglect the existence of the part of the state that lay across the Irish Sea were also a sore point in Northern Ireland, especially when they figured in one of the Queen's Christmas messages.[21] However, unionists obtained some satisfaction from the British state following its formal recognition of the South's standing as a republic, when the United Kingdom Parliament enacted its clearest legislative guarantee of the status of Northern Ireland within the union, as part of the Ireland Act 1949.

Controversy – and violence – have raged more directly in connection with the nature of government and society within Northern Ireland itself. Northern Ireland in this period of rule from Stormont[22] has been depicted as a province under the sectarian, even 'fascist', control of an 'apartheid', 'police' or 'one-party' regime dominated by the reactionary influence of the Orange Order.[23] Northern Ireland had a bloody initiation: both minority and majority suffered casualties, harassment and expulsions in a largely forgotten arena of the Irish War of Independence and the Civil War, especially in 1920–22, in which northern Catholics came off worst.[24] Subsequently, throughout the province's history, few Catholics felt entirely at ease in it, while few unionists felt able to extend much trust towards the minority.[25] The suspiciousness of many unionists towards the Catholics was perhaps accentuated by the arrival of numbers of Protestants from the South – fleeing what they regarded as an unsympathetic regime and, in some cases, actual violence – some of whom, such as members of Andrew Philip Magill's family, went to work for the Stormont regime.[26] The Catholic minority, it has been suggested, was held in a subservient economic position and excluded from political and social power and influence by the numerically dominant unionists, protest being stifled by a sequence of emergency legislation and a sectarian system of policing, especially the notorious Ulster Special Constabulary or 'B-Specials'.[27]

Academic assessments and interpretations of the extent of discrimination in Stormont-ruled Northern Ireland, in areas such as enfranchisement, public-sector employment or the allocation of housing, vary greatly and are often impassioned.[28] The most thought-provoking work on the period before the 1960s suggests a programmatic, if limited, use of discrimination to maintain the political hegemony of the UUP within the Protestant community, fear being inspired as much by the challenges to this hegemony posed by labour and socialist movements within that community as by Irish nationalism itself.[29] At the outset, under the terms of the Government of Ireland Act 1920, elections to local government bodies and to the Northern Ireland Parliament were conducted under proportional representation (PR), but this system was abolished as soon as divisions within unionism seemed to pose a threat to the previously assured majorities of the ruling party. While the British government protested, when PR was abolished in local government in 1922, its protest was ineffectual: a degree of complacency and negligence, which often surprises retrospective observers, had quickly entered into dealings between the United Kingdom government, in particular the Home Office, and the Northern Ireland government. Thus, in 1928, as the abolition of PR for elections to the Northern Ireland Parliament was being mooted, William Joynson-Hicks, then Home Secretary in the Conservative government in London, responded to a petition from members of the Northern Ireland Labour Party against the proposed change by informing Lord Craigavon, the Unionist Prime Minister of Northern Ireland, in a strikingly deferential tone: 'I don't know whether you would care at any time to discuss the matter with me; of course I am always at your disposal. But beyond that I "know my place", and don't propose to interfere.'[30]

While it would be inaccurate to describe Stormont-ruled Northern Ireland as a 'one-party state', the continued domination of the UUP meant that relations between the government and the party were intimate. Even peaceful political movements opposed to partition were greeted with suspicion and harassment.[31] The archives of the province reveal that legislation on matters such as electoral boundaries was considered with a close eye on the political fortunes of the party. Famous instances of gerrymandering resulted: for example, after a redistribution of the ward boundaries in Londonderry/Derry in 1936, local government in that city, which contained (as it still does) a majority of Catholics, was controlled by unionists for the remainder of the period.[32] For those involved in such proceedings, however, they simply seemed necessary to the stability and good government of the province. Many unionists felt that nationalists, or even all Catholics, simply could not be trusted with political or social power. Some believed that the government of Northern Ireland indeed was far too indulgent in this respect. Two correspondents complained to Craig in 1923 at having to deal with the mixed Royal Ulster Constabulary (RUC) rather than the sectarian 'B-Specials': 'Surely the Northern Government have learnt from past experience that all the Roman Catholics in the Police Force cannot be trusted.'[33]

By the 1960s proposed reforms to the electoral system in Northern Ireland seemed innocuous and just, but the extent of resistance to such reforms from unionists in areas such as Londonderry/Derry cannot be understood unless it is realised that such measures were perceived as handing unionists over to the mercies of politically empowered sworn enemies. Bitterness was particularly aroused whenever it was perceived that bargains were being done with these enemies to entrench the position of unionists in more secure local majorities. During electoral reorganisation in 1929, R. Dawson Bates, Northern Ireland Minister for Home Affairs, was told that Tyrone unionists felt 'much what the Monaghan Protestants felt when left out of Northern Ireland'.[34] Even in the Stormont years of practically unchallenged unionist hegemony, unionist leaders were occasionally deluged with similar missives from grassroots supporters, complaining that too much sympathy was being shown by the government to Catholics, and not enough protection being offered to the loyal men and women of 'Ulster' (meaning, for such people, the six-county province of Northern Ireland created in 1921, not the ancient nine-county province of Ulster). One Orangeman complained in 1949 of 'the flying of the tricolour, which the police seem to protect better than they do the Union Jack'.[35] Revealingly, in a number of cases the province's government was moved to circumspection in according privileges to its supporters, not by any calculation as to what was right for Northern Ireland, but by a sense of what they could get away with. When discussing schemes for redistribution in local government with Londonderry/Derry unionists in 1936, a civil servant emphasised the importance of not making the gerrymander obvious: this 'would obviously very much ease the Minister's position if he were attacked on the matter in the [Northern Ireland] House [of Commons]'. He was told, however, 'that whatever was done the Nationalists in Derry would be dissatisfied and it was therefore perfectly idle to do anything to attempt to satisfy them, and we might as well "go the whole hog"'.[36]

Two partial defences of the unionist rulers of Northern Ireland during this Stormont period can be offered. Unionists have suggested that Catholics in Northern Ireland did not do enough to help themselves out of a lowly economic and social status, which was largely the product of Catholic underachievement. More reasonably, it is true that the full integration of Catholics within Northern Ireland at this time would have proved desperately difficult, even given the fairest of political and social systems. Nationalists within the six counties unwisely greeted the creation of Northern Ireland by boycotting its Parliament, a practice they subsequently repeated in relation to many of its political institutions and initiatives. This left unionists in unchallenged control in a key formative period, depriving nationalists' retrospective criticisms of the province of much of their moral force.[37]

Second, a lack of accommodation with the South and, possibly, the entrenching of unionist hegemony in the North may be explained in part by the actions of the South's political classes. The leaders of the new southern state can be judged too harshly, especially when the political pressures to which they were subject,[38] and their measures to suppress periodic IRA activity, are considered (even though the latter hardly satisfied unionists).[39] Nonetheless, the South's formal neutrality during the Second World War, while mediated by less public measures,[40] the close relationship between the state and the Catholic Church, the proportionate decline of the Protestant population, and the rhetorical claim to the whole of the island in the Constitution of 1937 all created distaste among the majority in the North,[41] although there remained a level of practical North–South co-operation between some agencies.[42] It is possible to suggest that in some respects the two Irish political entities, both of them sectarian, conservative, illiberal and insular, had much in common for at least their first forty years.[43]

POLITICS FOR NON-LEARNERS, 1963–74

By 1963 Northern Ireland had a deceptive air of stability. The attempt of the IRA, in its border campaign of 1956–62, to appeal to northern Catholics was an acknowledged failure. The fruits of the United Kingdom's post-war welfare reforms, as well as other influences, ensured that many Catholics in Northern Ireland were probably better disposed to the province they inhabited than ever before. The appointment in 1963 of a new UUP government under the moderate Terence O'Neill seemed to herald further reforms and also a more practical relationship with the southern state: O'Neill's relations with the Republic's Taoiseach (Prime Minister), Sean

Lemass, attained an unprecedented level of cordiality.[44] Yet, in spite of all this promise, by the early 1970s Northern Ireland was reputed throughout the world as the place mired in the ugliest ethnic conflict in western Europe.

Academic and other commentators, and those involved, have naturally struggled to explain this development. The 'default mode' of political discussion of these origins has been as partisan and zero-sum as the conflict itself: the outbreak of violence is explained either through the injustices inflicted on the minority by Northern Ireland governments and the supremacist nature of unionism;[45] or as the consequence of the 'grievance culture' nurtured in the North by Irish Catholicism, the reactionary nature of Irish nationalism or the machinations of republicans.[46] While academic perspectives are largely more nuanced,[47] even some important recent academic analysts of this question continue to parallel one or other of these positions.[48] These two perspectives on the North's political crisis are derivative of, or parallel, a common highly politicised debate about the nature of revolution, derivative respectively of what one might call the Marxian perspective, which sees revolution as the product of social, political and economic oppressions;[49] and the Burkean theory, which links it to revolutionaries' ambitions and misguided ideologies.[50]

Both of these positions are ultimately inadequate to explain revolutionary crises in most cases, including the North's, since they highlight, at most, some necessary rather than sufficient causal conditions. Contingencies in the onset of revolution that should particularly be highlighted are the role of a political order's loss of legitimacy; the failure of authorities to take steps that might head off the crisis; and the obstacles to such policies. Despite pressure from the British government and other sources, the authorities in Northern Ireland felt they *had* to stall or obstruct reforms.[51] This was due, among other factors, to the geography of Northern Ireland and to fears of division within unionism itself.[52] The worst cases of perceived abuse in Northern Ireland, such as the local government of Londonderry/Derry, which exposed the province's ruling institutions to the greatest external criticism and aroused the greatest internal opposition, could not be targeted by specific reforms without particularly exposing grassroots unionists in such areas to the threat of nationalist rule and thus the risk of raising potent grassroots unionist movements opposed to the official leadership. Even apparently unrelated considerations, such as the United Kingdom's possible entry into the European Economic Community, aroused political anxieties about 'a considerable increase in the flow of labour into Northern Ireland, with serious implications in such places as Londonderry'.[53] If a smaller, more homogeneous Northern Ireland had been created in the 1920s it might not have faced such problems, but such an assertion depends upon the benefit of hindsight and many debatable assumptions. Unionist authorities, already limited in their capacity to face down the civil rights agitation that began in the 1960s by their dependence on British authorities, were thus hampered until a fatally late stage in their ability to apply such reforms, both by the fissiparous nature of unionism and by the variegated nature of local circumstances in Northern Ireland.

O'Neill's efforts, therefore, while arguably well-intended, raised expectations that could not be met and provoked fears that could not be allayed. From the mid-1960s a number of civil rights groups were formed in Northern Ireland and elsewhere to highlight abuses in the province, and to attempt to ensure that reforming energies were concentrated. Some of these movements were overtly inspired by the moral example of the civil rights movement led by Martin Luther King in the United States, although this influence can be exaggerated.[54] The most important such group was the Northern Ireland Civil Rights Association, established in 1967.[55]

There have been two significant angles of criticism of this civil rights movement. The first suggests that its complaints about the Stormont regime were impractical and pedantic. Instancing the higher levels of social security available at the time in the United Kingdom compared to those in the Irish Republic, it has been suggested that whatever the level of discrimination in Northern Ireland in terms of employment, the unemployed in Northern Ireland were financially better off than unskilled workers in the Republic. This, however, is no defence of the lack of *political power* accorded to Catholics in Northern Ireland at the time; and it implies that unemployment benefit was in some way something that Catholics did not really deserve and for which they should have been grateful. A second and more serious criticism, articulated by a number of unionists at the time, was that the civil rights movement was a cloak for a republican conspiracy designed to bring down Northern Ireland. For some unionists this thought indeed marred (and still mars) not only nationalist complaints about discrimination, but also the entire nationalist agenda.[56] It is true that there was some level of republican involvement, and a larger amount of naïvety about how the agitation could cohere to sectarian objectives, particularly in the People's Democracy organisation, which emerged late in 1968.[57] However, the support for reform of groups such as the Northern Ireland Labour Party suggests the commitment of at least some to improving rather than bringing down the political institutions of the province,[58] and it is at least arguable that, if the subsequent set of political confrontations had not been triggered, the civil rights movement could have proved the agent of greater Catholic adaptation to the status quo in Northern Ireland.[59]

Events were swiftly to disempower moderates on both sides. Political attention was focused by a confrontation between civil rights marchers and the RUC in Londonderry/Derry on 5 October 1968, for the march and the injuries sustained by many of the marchers, such as the prominent nationalist politician Gerry Fitt, were widely reported in the international media. Although O'Neill applauded the RUC's action, he told the Northern Ireland government that it now had no alternative but to implement reforms:

> Northern Ireland's standing and reputation had been most seriously damaged . . . He must remind his colleagues of Northern Ireland's utter financial dependence; in these circumstances a directive from Downing Street could have grave repercussions. He was aware that in some quarters there had been idle talk of a Northern Ireland 'U.D.I.' [unilateral declaration of independence, as by the white minority in Rhodesia (now Zimbabwe) in 1965]. Any such talk must be dismissed as wholly irresponsible, bearing in mind not only Northern Ireland's financial and economic dependence but also its lack of any defence forces under its control.[60]

Further obstacles to pressure for reform were to emerge from outside the institutions of the province. Unionist opponents of reform believed that the civil rights movement posed a serious threat to the stability of the province, and to Protestant liberties and livelihoods in Northern Ireland. These groups, among whom the Reverend Ian Paisley was emerging as a political force, picketed civil rights activities and organised counter-demonstrations. A paramilitary group claiming the title of the Ulster Volunteer Force (UVF), a name with genealogical links to a past of unionist counter-mobilisation, was also reviving. To a large extent it can be argued that the first blows in the Northern Ireland conflict were struck by such groups: the UVF was involved in a bombing campaign in 1969 with the aim of bringing O'Neill down.

Late in 1968 O'Neill appeared to have restored order by bringing forward a package of limited reforms and dismissing his colleague William Craig, the province's firebrand Minister for Home Affairs, from his government. The ensuing events remain highly contentious. Some reformers, notably in People's Democracy, were not satisfied by O'Neill's proposals, which fell short, for instance, of providing for one person, one vote in local government. Such reformers did not accept the need for a moratorium on the practice of political marches, which O'Neill had proposed to try to calm tensions. A provocative march began on 1 January 1969 and produced a famous confrontation, in which loyalist counter-demonstrators attacked civil rights protestors at Burntollet Bridge, while the RUC appeared to stand side.[61] Each side could blame the other. The equilibrium disturbed, O'Neill resorted to calling elections to the Northern Ireland Parliament, but the desired vote of confidence for the restoration of order was not forthcoming. Unionists could claim that precipitous action by civil rights activists had destabilised the province and that the germ of a more equitable political order – including the much sought after one person, one vote in local government – had been conceded before O'Neill's resignation (which followed the elections).[62] Nationalists could claim that this was offered only after violence and threats had exhorted it, and could also draw attention to the UVF's bombings during the elections, which were blamed at the time on the IRA.[63] Either way, O'Neill acknowledged his defeat by resigning.[64]

Within a few months O'Neill himself was upbeat, believing that without his provocative presence the cause of reform was advancing. His doubts, however, proved more accurate.[65] Some of the annual marches of the loyalist institutions have a long history as potential political flashpoints, although very many have gone off peacefully for decades and even continue to do so. In the summer of 1969 they were the trigger for an intensification of the level of violence in Londonderry/Derry to which it proved beyond the resources of the government of Northern Ireland to bring a semblance of control. With limited military resources and with stern determination being displayed by Catholic protestors in the Bogside area of Londonderry/Derry, James Chichester-Clark, O'Neill's successor as Prime Minister, felt that he had to ask London for assistance.

While the deployment of troops in the summer of 1969 is often taken as the starting date of the 'Troubles', neither the nature of the subsequent political controversy nor the character of the long and bloody accompaniment was clear, or seemed inevitable, at the time. The attitudes of the various protagonists were in flux. The British government continued officially to propound the doctrine that the disturbance comprised an internal issue that raised no question pertaining to the sovereignty of Northern Ireland and rebuffed the concerns expressed by the government of the Irish Republic.[66] Internally, however, several British officials thought about Ireland in a very different way, inclining to see unification as a desirable consummation and another inevitable aspect of Britain's contemporary decolonisation, while recognising certain obstacles. As one put it, what was required was 'seduction, not rape'. Dublin would have to make itself more attractive to the northern unionists, and even then there would be difficulties: 'it is least certain of all that the Republic would be wise to contemplate incorporating within its borders a Protestant minority of such Bible-thumping bloody-mindedness as is to be found in Belfast'.[67] On the other hand, a Foreign Office memorandum of 1970 was to suggest that Britain could not be neutral on the question of unity: 'The moderate Unionists represent the only real hope.'[68] British policy towards the province was to remain highly ambiguous.

While the assumption behind much later media depiction of, and policy towards, the conflict has been that 'the IRA' is the source of the problem, the Provisional IRA did not exist as such as the troops were deployed in 1969. Disturbances initially occurred largely between loyalists and civil rights supporters, and, to an extent, between sections of the Protestant and Catholic communities. Far from being an obvious source of violence, in the summer of 1969 the IRA was being excoriated in some quarters for not making its presence felt. The conflict itself triggered the rethinking that led to yet another split in both the IRA and the political party linked to it, Sinn Féin. One set of republican factions – the Official IRA and Official Sinn Féin, as they became known – eventually ceased to be significant either as a paramilitary force or as a political movement.[69] Late in 1969 and early in 1970, however, the other factions in both organisations emerged as the Provisional IRA (PIRA), under Seán MacStiofáin as 'Chief of Staff', and Provisional Sinn Féin (PSF),[70] under its first President, Ruairi Ó Brádaigh. The new organisations represented a retreat from the brief flirtation with Marxist ideology inspired by the 'Official' leader Cathal Goulding and a return to older nationalist objectives. It was not until 1971 that the Provisionals began to treat the British Army as a legitimate target and killed British soldiers for the first time. Efforts were made by the PIRA to build up a reputation and a following by posturing as defenders of Catholic communities from loyalist activity and, not for the last time, the sometimes heavy-handed attentions of the authorities.[71] Yet these developments were by no means guaranteed to obtain even the limited level of support that they ever achieved from a sizeable minority of Catholics. The creation in August 1970 of a more moderate new political party, the Social Democratic and Labour Party (SDLP), was indicative of the more general response among Catholics and nationalists to the political crisis. The party was at first led by Gerry Fitt, and featured Paddy Devlin, a young John Hume and others who had become involved in the civil rights protests.[72]

Different emphases were evident at different times in the approach taken by the government of the Republic, as was the case with the British government. A threat of intervention from the South had been one factor leading Chichester-Clark to request British troops. In 1970 two ministers in the Republic's government, Neil Blaney and Charles Haughey, were tried for attempting to supply the northern republicans with guns, but were acquitted, Haughey, suggestively, because he was deemed to have acted with state sanction.[73] However, no government of the Republic could give more than limited latitude to an insurgent republican movement that ultimately denied the legitimacy of the 26-county Republic itself. In the early 1970s British officials and, especially, Northern

Ireland unionists felt and occasionally expressed irritation, particularly with the Fianna Fáil Taoiseach Jack Lynch, over the Republic's perceived failure to do more about the use of operations bases in the South by the republican factions. There was also occasionally awareness that Irish political leaders, of whatever party, were obliged for domestic political reasons to take a protective interest in the Catholic population of the North. Indeed, given the territorial claim in the Republic's Constitution of 1937, Irish governments were under something of an obligation to appear to work and hope for a united Ireland. In any case, the Republic's authorities did have some success against republicans in the South.

The more spectacular developments in Northern Ireland doubtless created a good deal of bewilderment among the population at large in Britain as in the Republic. In so far as British public opinion had responded articulately to the emergence of conflict in Northern Ireland, there was a predominant sense that hard-pressed British troops had been drawn into the thankless task of trying to preserve order between two uncivilised 'Irish' factions, or even into protecting the minority Catholic community.[74] Some famous political cartoons that appeared in the British press at this time evince particularly clearly the wish that the two groups of inhabitants of the island of Ireland could just be left to fight the issue out among themselves, preferably tearing each other to pieces in the process.[75] Only the most partisan commentators would now adopt such an uncritical view of the British Army's role in Northern Ireland,[76] but at the time many were shocked and horrified that the very armed forces supposedly protecting the Catholics of Northern Ireland should be coming under vicious attack from the PIRA, a force that undoubtedly obtained a level of support from sections of that same Catholic community. Army representatives were largely unable to understand the grievances to which its attentions to Catholic areas of the province, avowedly in pursuit of terrorists, gave rise, while trying to make clear to Catholics that 'they were lucky to have the British Army as no other Army would have behaved so well as the British had done'.[77] Such suppositions were disseminated in Britain by mass media that, while not as uncritical and one-dimensional as is sometimes suggested,[78] were generally sympathetic to British aims in Ireland and subject to a low level of political influence.[79]

The Conservative government of the United Kingdom, elected in June 1970 and headed by Edward Heath, responded to this situation at several levels. A secret channel of communication was opened with the PIRA, most notably during a brief Provisional truce in 1972, but such discussions proved forlorn. Continued attacks on British troops and, later, a particularly devastating series of bomb explosions in Belfast that left nine dead on 21 July 1972 ('Bloody Friday') confirmed the impression that the Provisionals were beyond political redemption. Efforts to contain the security threat, notwithstanding successes such as Operation Motorman against republican 'no go' areas in the North in summer 1972[80] also proved problematic. The adoption of internment without trial in August 1971 appeared overtly to target Irish Catholics and nationalists, and heightened the siege mentality of that community. The justification of the first internment 'swoop' of 9 August 1971 provided by the then British Home Secretary, Reginald Maudling, reads with hindsight as disastrously complacent: it was 'imperative', Maudling explained, in combating 'a vicious and ruthless enemy', 'to obtain all available intelligence in order to save the lives of civilians and members of the security forces; and it is therefore essential to interrogate suspects who are believed to have important information'.[81] Logically, and in practice, the use of interrogation in pursuit of 'all available' intelligence could be used to justify the detention of large numbers of Catholics who often proved to be unconnected to the PIRA, and, since only republicans and not loyalists were being conceived of as 'a vicious and ruthless enemy', this proved an effective way of spreading hostility to British rule far more widely throughout the Catholic community. Internment was indirectly to provide a still more potent and infamous source of recruitment to the PIRA in Londonderry/Derry in January 1972: it was at an anti-internment rally that British troops apparently opened fire on unarmed protestors, in the incident known as 'Bloody Sunday'.

The bloodiest phase of the Troubles had begun. The retaliatory burning down of the British Embassy in Dublin by an enraged crowd further soured British–Irish relations. In the aftermath of 'Bloody Sunday' the British cabinet noted 'some political solution of the conflict would need to be in prospect' in order to assuage public opinion in Britain, Ireland and elsewhere: 'In order to promote a political settlement it might be necessary to take major political risks, which might involve a substantial modification of earlier policies and even the possibility of considerable bloodshed.'[82] The destructive bombing campaign waged by the PIRA brought that possibility much nearer. The British were beginning to doubt that the PIRA could be militarily defeated[83] and proposed a reform package, but it was immediately scuttled by the unanimous refusal of the Unionist government of the province to countenance the transfer of responsibility for law and order in Northern Ireland from Stormont to Westminster.[84] In March 1972 the British felt they had no choice other than to suspend the institutions of the Stormont regime and resume direct rule of the province after fifty years. It is worth noting, however, notwithstanding subsequent complaints in Britain of unfair publicity for its policies in Northern Ireland, that British officials believed that foreign press reaction to 'Bloody Sunday' was, in the main, fair; found 'no cause for complaint' about coverage in the United States around the same time; and also found little to complain of in the attitude of the Papacy.[85]

As violence in Northern Ireland became harder to control, the British searched more widely among the available political alternatives. The repartition of Ireland, including transfers of populations, and even progress towards a united Ireland were considered by the British government and British diplomats, and on the opposition Labour Party benches, around this point.[86] Dialogue between the more mainstream parties proved more productive than communications with the Provisionals. Following a conference of moderate unionist parties at Darlington in September 1972 and the subsequent launch of the British government's relatively well-received consultation document (or 'Green Paper'), *The Future of Northern Ireland*,[87] representatives of the UUP led by Brian Faulkner, and of the non-sectarian but unionist Alliance Party of Northern Ireland (APNI), encouraged by William Whitelaw, the UK's Secretary of State for Northern Ireland, were tentatively able to advance towards agreement with the SDLP, which had emerged as the voice of mainstream nationalism. The proposals advanced in 1973, and enlarged with the then Irish Taoiseach Liam Cosgrave in the Sunningdale Agreement of December 1973, in different respects both anticipated the later Good Friday Agreement (GFA) – hence the famous but misleading description of the GFA, by Seamus

Mallon of the SDLP, as 'Sunningdale for slow learners' – and also harked back to the proposals of the 1920s. Devolution in Northern Ireland was to be resumed on the basis of cross-community power-sharing in government, while the discussion of issues common to the two parts of Ireland would be pursued on an 'all-Ireland' basis in a Council of Ireland consisting of a consultative assembly and a council of ministers. The consensus reached in 1973 came under pressure from many sides from the moment it was achieved. The Sunningdale Agreement suggested that the consent of the majority in Northern Ireland was a precondition for a united Ireland, the first time such a proposition had been formally accepted by a government of the Republic. This met with a legal challenge in the South from opponents of the Agreement, on the grounds that it was contrary to the opening articles of the Republic's Constitution, which laid a claim to govern the whole of the island of Ireland. Similar difficulties were to dog later developments in British–Irish relations, such as the Anglo-Irish Agreement of 1985.[88] The Republic's constitutional claim to the North seemed like an arrogant imposition to unionists, but political progress towards its removal would be slow. Meanwhile, the first elections to the new devolved Assembly in Northern Ireland, held prior to the reaching of agreement, had confirmed the eclipse of the once-proud Northern Ireland Labour Party.[89]

The Achilles' heel of the Sunningdale settlement proved to be the growing tide of unionist unease at developments ever since the civil rights protests. In the elections to the Assembly supporters of power-sharing and the Sunningdale settlement formed only a minority of the unionists elected. Key voices of disaffection with the allegedly supine nature of 'official' unionism included Ian Paisley's Democratic Unionist Party, formed in 1971, and the Vanguard movement created by William Craig, who had at first remained active within the UUP after O'Neill dismissed him from office (see above), but emerged in 1973 as the leader of this separate party. These rifts within unionism continue to have serious consequences. The resumption of direct rule had proved terminal to the more intimate dimensions of the relationship between 'official' unionism and British Conservatives. A key perceived guarantee of the unionist position had been the adoption by the British government of the principle that any change in the constitutional position of

Northern Ireland should require the consent not of the people of Northern Ireland but of its *Parliament*.[90] Since Stormont, even after O'Neill's reforms, had underrepresented the minority, not least owing to republican abstention, this seemed to make the British connection much safer. The suspension of Stormont in March 1972 had swept this safety net away and unionist support for a settlement engineered by a British Conservative administration could thereafter certainly not be assumed.[91] Loyalist paramilitaries were an increasingly important force, with the Ulster Defence Association (UDA), another body emerging to rival the UVF in 1971, posturing, as its name implies, as the defender of the Protestant community, much as the Provisionals did across the sectarian divide.[92] In July 1972 Whitelaw was moved to recommend to the British cabinet that the security forces be told to be prepared in the last resort to open fire in certain circumstances on unarmed members of the UDA, although Prime Minister Heath demurred at this.[93] The calling of a referendum in March 1973, permitting a reaffirmation of the majority unionist view in the North favouring partition, and security successes such as Operation Motorman,had done only a little to ease unionist and loyalist discontent. By 1974 some elements of the UDA were sufficiently disaffected with British policy to consider whether their main political objective should be, not the preservation of the union, but the creation of an independent Northern Ireland (or 'Ulster'), although this has never been the view of the majority of unionists.[94] Such tendencies within the broad unionist community helped to focus what is often referred to as the Protestant backlash against the Sunningdale Agreement.[95]

Early in 1974 dissenters within the UUP unseated Faulkner as its leader, although he remained Chief Executive of the new power-sharing government of Northern Ireland. A general election called in February in the United Kingdom facilitated another concentrated expression of unionist discontent: unionists opposed to Sunningdale received only just over 50 per cent of the votes cast in the North, but won eleven of the twelve (then) Northern Ireland seats in the British House of Commons. The general election also replaced Heath's government in London with a Labour government under Harold Wilson. In May 1974 a general strike was declared by a body calling itself the Ulster Workers Council.[96] Such a method of protesting at aspects of British policy had been tried in 1972 and would be used again in 1977, both times with limited success, but in May 1974 it struck a chord among the wider unionist community. Around the same time loyalists detonated a series of bombs in Dublin and Monaghan in the Irish Republic, killing thirty-three people and providing the Troubles with their bloodiest single day. The impasse created between the loyalists and the British government ended only with Faulkner's resignation as Chief Executive and the consequent collapse of the Northern Ireland government. The first attempt at power-sharing in Northern Ireland had failed, at the hands of representatives of a movement styling itself 'loyal' yet bitterly denounced by the Prime Minister of the state to which it avowed loyalty as 'people who spend their lives sponging on Westminster and British democracy, and then systematically assault democratic methods'.[97]

A LONG WAR, 1974–85

Some still argue that the British Labour government should have faced down the loyalist revolt of May 1974, while others argue that it was hampered in this by a fifth column within its own intelligence services, which had its own agenda antagonistic to government policy.[98] For the rest of that government's life its policies belied, in Paul Arthur's view, the reputation of the British Labour Party as anti-partitionist.[99] While the late 1970s were not without their political initiatives, the emphasis from Britain was rather on exerting some control over the republican movement, epitomised by the contentious Prevention of Terrorism Act 1974.[100] While hints about the withdrawal of British troops from the province tempted the PIRA into calling a truce in 1975, it seems in retrospect that the British continued to toy with this suggestion only to place the Provisionals at risk of terminal fissure and decline. Officially the PIRA's truce continued into 1976, but in fact the movement lost discipline before this and drifted under provocation into an exchange with loyalists of vicious sectarian killings. A British policy of criminalisation to an extent deprived the Provisionals of the opportunity of engaging the British Army as the enemy, challenging the PIRA's preferred propaganda image as an anti-British or 'anti-colonial' force. Collusion between the security forces and loyalists is also alleged to have occurred from this period, the imprisonment of one such linkman, Brian Nelson, until his death in 2003, providing at least one piece of corroboration.[101] Also in 2003, to the embarrassment of both the British government and republicans, there were revelations concerning the high-level infiltration by the British of the Provisional organisation through a double agent, 'Stakeknife', the protection of whose identity apparently implicated the authorities in acquiescing in the sectarian killing of at least one unconnected Catholic.

Further pressure was placed on republicans in the mid-1970s by the attitude of the Irish Republic itself. As Minister of Posts and Telegraphs in a Fine Gael–Labour coalition government, Conor Cruise O'Brien, who had emerged as a vociferous critic of republicanism, enacted a broadcasting ban on representatives of both of the Provisional organisations.[102] While the PIRA undoubtedly still found moral and material support from some sections in the Republic, all this was a far cry from the gun-running trials of 1970. These years did not, even so, see nothing but gains for anti-republican strategies. The PIRA protected itself against erosion by organising in a more impermeable structure[103] and learned from these years a greater suspicion of British policy, and of the kind of political change that might expose it to splits. The glacial development of political thought and strategy in the republican movement, for instance in the aftermath of the Downing Street Declaration of 1993, while it infuriated political opponents, is surely directly connected to these experiences.

The period was also punctuated by PIRA 'spectaculars', notably the infamous pub bombings in Birmingham in central England on 21 November 1974 (which became the occasion for one of the English legal system's most embarrassing mistakes, the ultimately quashed convictions of the 'Birmingham Six'); the assassination in Sligo in 1979 of Earl Mountbatten of Burma, a close relative of both the Queen and her husband; and, on the same day, the killing of eighteen British soldiers at Warrenpoint. Such events consolidated an unfortunate strategy in British media reporting of Northern Ireland (not imposed by British governments) which tended to concentrate almost exclusively on the deaths of people from Great Britain at the hands of republicans. This proved productive of distortions in British public opinion and, ultimately, British policy, on the issue, as Irish governments, Irish nationalists or even 'the Irish' were treated by newspapers as complicit in the murder of innocent 'British people' by 'the IRA'.[104] Although the stark statistics of the conflict do reveal that republicans have been responsible for the greater part of the fatalities during the Troubles, one would certainly have gleaned from sections of the British press the impression that the proportion was greater than the actual 58–59 per cent. As Phillip Elliott observed, a surface reading of the British media in the 1970s would have suggested that *only* the PIRA were responsible for killings during the conflict.[105] Further, given that it was the loyalists who tended to adopt the more nakedly sectarian strategy in these years, arguably, if the term 'innocent' has any

FIGURE 2
Cartoon by Martyn Turner, 1998

meaning in this context, it was innocent Catholics in Northern Ireland who, almost unnoted in the British media, bore much of the brunt of the conflict.[106]

To make this point is not to fall into the error of accepting republicans' own lame retrospective apologetics for their 'long war' strategy. While the Provisionals proved able to accrue political gains on the back of posturing as a group seeming to protect Catholics, in many instances their reckless activities helped to expose ordinary Catholics to loyalist retaliation and other violence. The convicted PIRA bomber Patrick Magee has justified the PIRA's strategy as ultimately advancing a peace process in the long term, by showing the British that a solely military solution was impossible and by propounding a 'republican analysis'.[107] If this may be felt to be a colossal euphemism, Magee's argument that the PIRA never targeted civilians, bomb explosions that took civilian life being due to logistic or technical errors,[108] may be frankly felt to be dishonest in some quarters. Even assuming Magee's honesty, the placing of explosives in the proximity of civilians demonstrated a reckless attitude to human life and helped to exacerbate a conflict in which many of the victims would be ordinary Catholics or the ordinary Protestants whom, in theory, Provisionals claimed as fellow citizens of the true Irish Republic. In any case, if the Provisional military strategy is to be defended as encouraging the British away from seeking a solely military solution, it should be acknowledged that military victory was also the Provisional objective at times: 1972, after all, was their trumpeted 'year of victory'. Thus, according to Magee's logic, and notwithstanding his assertions to the contrary, the British military campaigns against the PIRA, including such morally dubious operations as the killing of PIRA 'volunteers' at Loughgall in 1987 and on Gibraltar in 1988, and even the security forces' collusion with the loyalists, were entirely justified contributions to the peace process.[109]

In the short term, however, a less successful dimension of the British government's attempt to criminalise republicans was provided by the attempt to remove 'special category status' from republican prisoners, since it provided republicans with an opportunity to invoke a favourite strategy, the hunger strike, thereby presenting their movement with more martyrs. Whatever the rights and wrongs of this issue (and the continued representation of Bobby Sands, the first hunger striker to die as a hero disturbs many), the election of the Conservative Party under Margaret Thatcher to government in Britain in 1979 provided the Provisionals in this context with the kind of stubborn adversary who constituted a propaganda gift. John Hume had recently become leader of the SDLP and turned its policy in a nationalist direction, which meant that it had difficulty in doing other than follow the lead of the Provisionals on the hunger strikes. An untimely by-election, in which the SDLP, under duress, declined to offer a rival candidate, provided a means of electing Sands to the UK Parliament in his dying days, and demonstrated that the PIRA's political wing,

Provisional Sinn Féin, was capable of finding a popular constituency in Northern Ireland. After the issue of prisoners' status had been more quietly resolved, this was confirmed in the British general election of 1983 by the election of Gerry Adams of PSF as member of Parliament (MP) for West Belfast, although he declined to take his seat at Westminster, following the long-established republican policy of abstention from British institutions.[110]

Further political prestige may have been handed to republicanism through the 1980s by (depending on one's view) the iniquities of British security policy or the unwarranted interference of bodies such as Amnesty International and the European Commission on Human Rights, both of which condemned aspects of British policy.[111] PSF/PIRA meanwhile retained the ability to kill while winning votes: notable bomb outrages in Hyde Park in London in the summer of 1982 and at the Harrods department store in London in December 1983, and Magee's attempt to assassinate the Prime Minister and her cabinet at the Grand Hotel in Brighton in October 1984, confirmed most British newspapers' view as to the utter depravity of Irish republicanism.

Beyond the rhetoric, however, a number of significant political initiatives were attempted in the 1980s. Given that the New Ireland Forum of 1984 was organised among the SDLP and parties from the Irish Republic, it may have seemed a foregone conclusion that it would reassert a preference, within the 'nationalist family', for a united Ireland, but it did represent a stage of considering variant models within John Hume's SDLP, which was at the time under considerable electoral pressure from PSF.[112] The British Conservatives had promoted the policy of integrating Northern Ireland within the United Kingdom at the general election in 1979. After their victory, and the assassination shortly beforehand of the party's staunchly pro-unionist Northern Ireland spokesman Airey Neave[113], the party withdrew from these policies, which were strongly favoured anyway by only a few ideologues in its ranks.[114] The early years of Thatcher's government instead featured attempts to make progress towards devolution, which failed to obtain nationalist co-operation, and an attempt to pursue more collaborative relations with the Irish government. Pressure on Britain from its ally the United States,[115] and a period of government in the Irish Republic by a moderate coalition dominated by Fine Gael and led by Garret

FitzGerald, improved the prospects of a formal Anglo-Irish accord. The Anglo-Irish Agreement (AIA), signed by the two governments late in 1985, represented a significant breakthrough, in spite of the inauspicious events that followed it. The British acknowledged an 'Irish dimension' to the government of Northern Ireland, through the creation of an Anglo-Irish Intergovernmental Conference, while for its part the Irish government acquiesced in the reiterated formula that any prospect of a united Ireland would be dependent upon its acceptance by the majority in the province, and also promised co-operation with British security policies against the republican paramilitaries.[116]

RETHINKING AND REALIGNMENT, 1985–93

The negotiation of this agreement by a Prime Minister who still continued to boast so sonorously of her commitment to the union of Great Britain and Northern Ireland[117] was a major shock to unionists, and the UUP, led by James Molyneaux, acted with Paisley's Democratic Unionists in a concerted protest. Northern Ireland's unionist MPs resigned their seats in unison in order to facilitate the expression of discontent, Northern Ireland's opinion on the Agreement not otherwise having been sought. Although more than 80 per cent of those who voted in the ensuing by-elections, most of them unionist, rejected candidates supporting the AIA, this proved a fruitless exercise, in so far as the sovereign governments of the United Kingdom and the Irish Republic could ride roughshod over such expressions of provincial dissatisfaction. Seeking an independent Northern Ireland was again considered in these years by some unionists, including David Trimble, but remained at most a second-best option.[118] Part of the intention on the British side in signing the AIA may have been to press unionists to come to an arrangement in Northern Ireland with nationalists, which could form the basis of devolution in the province. Indeed, Article 2 of the AIA implied that devolution would substantially reduce the Irish government's new consultative role in the province, which would have been an attraction for unionists. Although no such arrangement proved possible, unionists did reluctantly begin to rethink their political position. One representation of this reassessment was the development of parties attached to the loyalist paramilitaries, among whom a somewhat surprisingly creative trend of thought has since been in evidence.[119]

This would by no means be the last shock for unionists to absorb, however. During the 1980s, if it had not been apparent earlier, more parties to the conflict began to accept that a purely military solution was improbable, although in 1989, for example, Peter Brooke, then Secretary of State for Northern Ireland, still found it useful to deny such a conviction under unionist interrogation.[120] It was not only pieties on the unionist side that were being challenged in the late 1980s. The British famously expressed dissatisfaction with the degree of co-operation on the question of anti-republican security that they received from the South after the signing of the AIA,[121] not least after the return of the British bugbear Charles Haughey to the post of Taoiseach. From a nationalist perspective, British criticisms of problems in extraditing terrorist suspects from the Republic had something of a hypocritical appearance, given that the English legal system (the separate Scottish legal system not being involved) was moving at glacial speed towards reversing a number of unsound convictions on terrorist offences, notably of the Birmingham Six, the Guildford Four and the Maguire Seven.[122] Nonetheless, the AIA suggested that both literal interpretation of the opening articles of the Constitution of the Irish Republic, and the republican teleology that depicted Britain as the only obstacle to a united Ireland, were no longer viable. A southern government had again formally accepted that northern opinion would have to be persuaded before Ireland could be united.

The ending of the Cold War was another influence affecting the perspectives of several actors in Northern Ireland. According to Adrian Guelke, an attendant diminution of anti-colonialist rhetoric in international politics led unionists to take a more positive attitude to international interest and dimensions to the Northern Ireland conflict.[123] Such attitudinal change was, however, largely limited to moderate unionism: other unionists continued to respond with irritation to rhetorical and other interventions into Northern Ireland politics from continental Europe and the United States, especially during the presidency of Bill Clinton. Connections can also be posited between the ending of the Cold War and Brooke's declaration in 1990 that Britain had no 'selfish strategic or economic interest' in Northern Ireland. Whether this constituted a material shift in the British government's mindset is another question: after all, British governments were hardly insistently avowing a strategic and selfish purpose in Northern Ireland even before the fall of the Berlin Wall[124] and, since the strategic danger to the United Kingdom posed by the Soviet Union was surely rhetorically exaggerated by the British Conservative government in the late 1980s, for the purpose of seizing electoral advantage from the then-unilateralist Labour opposition, it is easy in turn to exaggerate the effect that strategic considerations had ever had on British policy in the North during the Cold War.

Nevertheless, the ending of the Cold War and the signing of the AIA did facilitate a sense within PSF/PIRA that British strategic interests in Northern Ireland, contrary to earlier assumptions,[125] were indeed negligible. The new global environment also may have further problematised the PIRA's residual and always minor links with Marxist thinking, and threatened previous sources of weaponry, which, in addition to American sympathisers, had most notably included Colonel Gadafy's regime in Libya. As commentators now realise, considerable debate then took place, in private, within republicanism, but it was by no means always a productive debate. The issue of electoral participation in the Republic, involving an implicit recognition of the hated 26-county state, illustrated the fissiparous tendencies in republicanism by producing the first major split in the Provisional movement.[126] In addition, the Provisionals hardly appeared to many British commentators to be demonstrating a beneficent face in these years. In particular, the bombing of a Remembrance Day service at Enniskillen in November 1987, in which eleven people died, inspired some of the rare expressions of broad support for a British presence in Northern Ireland from the British public in these years.[127] Blanket condemnation was also elicited by the bombing of the British Army's barracks in Deal in Kent in September 1989 and by the assassination of the pro-unionist Conservative MP Ian Gow on 30 July 1990.

At the same time, sections of the British media also criticised weaknesses of British government policy in Northern Ireland, such as the handling of an inquiry by John Stalker, then Deputy Chief

Constable of Manchester, into the alleged adoption of a 'shoot to kill' policy by the security services in Northern Ireland,[128] and an attempt by the government to ban Thames Television's documentary *Death on the Rock*, an investigation of the killing of three unarmed PIRA operatives on Gibraltar on 16 March 1988. Yet for other sections of the media such reactions only demonstrated how global opinion, including 'we British', were far too hard on 'ourselves'. Many British newspapers were uncertain how to react to the bizarre actions of one loyalist, Michael Stone, who murdered mourners at the funeral at Milltown Cemetery in Belfast of the PIRA members killed on Gibraltar, but explored in detail the certainly barbaric lynching of two British soldiers in civilian clothes at the further funeral a few days later.[129] Another major influence on the British media's representation of the conflict was the imposition in October 1988 of a ban on broadcasting direct statements by members of certain organisations, including PSF and the UDA.[130] This ban was actually less stringent than analogous measures still effective from O'Brien's days in the Irish Republic, leaving television companies, for instance, free to broadcast the words of representatives of such organisations if they were spoken by an actor. Opinion remains divided as to whether or not the ban had an adverse effect on the fortunes of the organisations affected, even some opponents of PSF, for instance, feeling that it protected the party from the possibility of having the threadbare nature of its arguments exposed in broadcast debate.

Where the pronouncements of Gerry Adams, PSF's most prominent leading figure, did reach an audience at this time, analysis of his discourse suggests that, notwithstanding a characteristic reluctance publicly to criticise any Provisional action, he was issuing signals that some forms of PIRA violence were counterproductive.[131] Striking evidence of these counterproductive effects was provided in the limitations of electoral support for republicanism in the North and, especially, in the South. In military terms too there were setbacks for the Provisionals in the late 1980s, including a number at the hands of the British special operations unit the Special Air Service (SAS), notably at Loughgall in May 1987 and on Gibraltar the following year, the two events leaving a total of eleven active PIRA 'volunteers' dead.

Meanwhile, Father Alex Reid, one of the few actors in the events of March 1988 in Northern Ireland to emerge with credit, helped to facilitate clandestine contact between John Hume and Gerry Adams. Initially their dialogue was unproductive, since PIRA outrages made it harder on Hume's side,[132] and a round of talks between unionists and mainstream nationalists in 1991–92, facilitated by Brooke and his successor as Secretary of State, Patrick Mayhew, as well as by brief loyalist ceasefires, seemed a more likely opening. Although such talks made little tangible progress,[133] the flexibility of some unionists, the effectiveness of loyalist attacks and the increasing difficulties of mainstream republicanism – Gerry Adams lost his parliamentary seat in the general election of 1992 – may have facilitated a desire among Provisionals to acquire a foothold in mainstream politics, and the dialogue between Hume and Adams was resumed.

The early 1990s also brought new prime ministers to both Britain and the Irish Republic, respectively the Conservative John Major and Albert Reynolds of Fianna Fáil. Whereas relations between Haughey and Thatcher had been somewhat fraught, Reynolds' interaction with Major was more cordial. By 1992, when loyalists were actually starting to kill at a quicker rate than republicans were, the British government also showed an awareness of this factor in the situation and banned the UDA. Into 1993 a secret channel of communication between the British government and the PIRA was exploited, but a series of developments rendered these contacts difficult. In March that year a PIRA bomb exploded, killing two children, in Warrington in northwest England. In October Adams served as a pallbearer in the funeral cortege of Thomas Begley, a PIRA member recently killed in the act of laying a bomb on the Shankill Road in Belfast that killed nine other people: memorably, this led the British tabloid the *Sun* (owned by Rupert Murdoch) to suggest that 'Gerry' and 'Adams' were 'the two most disgusting words' in the English language.[134] In Major's view, however, while Adams' action, which may have been an attempt to keep republican hardliners on board, was deplorable, by prompting a reaction against the Provisionals in the Irish Republic it actually facilitated progress in talks with Reynolds.[135] John Major's upbeat speech at the Guildhall in London on 15 November indicated a commitment to dialogue that the embarrassment of being forced to admit to recent contact with the Provisionals did not derail. An agreement between the British and Irish governments was finalised, and issued as the Downing Street Declaration (also known as the Joint Declaration for Peace) in December 1993. The British government recognised the imperative of an 'Irish dimension' to the government of Northern Ireland, and declared its lack of 'selfish strategic or economic interest' in Northern Ireland (the phrase first used by Brooke three years before), while the Republic's government again recognised the need for the 'freely given consent of a majority of the people of Northern Ireland' before a united Ireland could become a possibility.[136] It remained to be seen if the content of the declaration could draw the Provisionals into mainstream politics.

CEASEFIRES AND PROXIMITY, 1994–97

For unionists this was an increasingly difficult position. Contrary to Margaret Thatcher's famous comparison restated in a book published at this time, one wondered if a British government would ever declare that Britain had no strategic interests in holding the borough of Finchley.[137] The fast-diminishing size of the Conservatives' working majority in the British House of Commons, which had been reduced but not eradicated in Major's unexpected general election victory in 1992 gave the Conservatives some reason to be concerned about unionist disaffection, even apart from any ideological considerations. Yet a dialogue of sorts with republicanism was also pursued. PSF's request for clarification of the declaration, ultimately met by the British government on 19 May 1994, bought those within the republican movement who were keenest on a political process only a limited amount of time. The Provisionals were under pressure, in the form of both carrot and stick, from the Irish government and others to show a commitment to peace. The carrot was most evident in the highly contentious decision of the Clinton administration in the United States to grant Gerry Adams a short-term US visa, the stick in suggestions that the Irish and British governments might combine to hound the PIRA into submission. A brief PIRA ceasefire at Easter 1994 initially seemed only an intermission, especially when a PSF Ard Fheis (conference) in Letterkenny in the summer of that year apparently rejected the declaration.[138] However, the mood was rapidly reversed by the PIRA's announcing of a ceasefire beginning on 1 September.

The two-edged nature of the British media's reductive focus on the PIRA's violence was quickly revealed by the enthusiastic response to the ceasefire in most newspapers: because, in the lazy view of most British observers, 'the IRA' were the problem, a PIRA ceasefire seemed to them to mean virtually the end of the conflict. Dissentient notes were sounded only by commentators such as Conor Cruise O'Brien, who was particularly exercised by the renewed access to broadcasting networks recently secured for PSF,[139] and Ian Paisley, whom John Major threw out of Downing Street after a fraught meeting in early September 1994.[140]

The prevailing British assumption that the activities of the loyalist paramilitaries were merely a response to those of the PIRA at least created an expectation that the loyalists would also respond with a ceasefire. The Combined Loyalist Military Command (CLMC) played its part, in both senses, declaring a cessation from 13 October 1994, the permanence of which, it declared, would 'be completely dependent upon the continued cessation of all nationalist/ republican violence, [for] the sole responsibility for a return to war lies with them'.[141] Some journalists' criticisms of the loyalist response at this time seem disproportionate.[142] For keen observers, however, the ambiguities of the PIRA's ceasefire, which was eventually to prove disruptive to the 'peace process', were quickly evident. The PIRA's 'complete cessation of military operations'[143] never meant a 'continued cessation of all nationalist/republican violence', for it did not entail an end to the PIRA's recruiting, drilling, targeting, involvement in organised crime or administering of punishment beatings. In calling a ceasefire the PIRA's commanders also did not speak for rogue units within their own organisation, such as those who apparently shot a postal worker dead during a robbery on 10 November 1994, or for the smaller republican INLA, or, more ominously, for a significant splinter group, the Continuity IRA, which seceded from the PIRA at the time, determined, as its name implied, to continue the 'armed struggle'. The collapse of the government in the Irish Republic and the formation of a new coalition led by John Bruton of Fine Gael caused some anxieties lest Reynolds be proved critical to the peace process, but there were few grounds for this fear. Even organs of publishing groups that would quickly emerge as the most sceptical about this phase of the peace process were, at the end of 1994, happy to inflate the prevailing mood of already exaggerated optimism by talking of the 'best chance of peace in Ireland for 300 years'.[144]

In February 1995 the British and Irish governments published the 'green tinted' *Frameworks for the Future* (known as the Framework Documents).[145] The three-stranded model for the future government of Northern Ireland that they proposed largely remained intact in the eventual GFA three years later, as well as summarising elements that had been on the negotiating table for some time previously, although the documents contained a more substantial 'Irish dimension' than would appear in the GFA. In a proposed cross-border institution that would exercise executive power over matters such as tourism and transport, it is not too far-fetched to see another revival of the Council of Ireland idea, adapted from its origins in 1920 and its relaunch in 1973.

It can be suggested that the more audacious implications of these proposals destabilised aspects of Northern Ireland politics by exacerbating unionist anxieties, although Major claimed that their presentation in pro-unionist newspapers unnecessarily fanned the flames.[146] These fears found several significant expressions. First, there was parliamentary denunciation of the Framework Documents even by relatively moderate unionists, such as Ken Maginnis.[147] Second, there was growing disenchantment with the process of certain British newspapers, especially the *Times* and the *Sunday Times*). Pro-unionist writers on the *Sunday Times*, for instance, responded hyperbolically to President Clinton's further extension of a visa to Gerry Adams in March 1995 by declaring the end of the Anglo-American 'special relationship'.[148] Third, and more tellingly, there was the commitment felt by many unionists in the emerging dispute pertaining to the Portadown Orange Lodge's annual parade along a contentious portion of the Garvaghy Road, symbolised in 1995 by the personal involvement of two prominent unionists, Ian Paisley and David Trimble of the UUP. In subsequent years this Drumcree dispute aroused intense emotions, as well as some wry humour, under the gaze of the bewildered global media.[149] Also in the summer of 1995, the UUP suffered the embarrassment of a by-election defeat in North Down by Robert McCartney, the leader of the new United Kingdom Unionist Party (UKUP):[150] Molyneaux's position as leader of the UUP became untenable. In September David Trimble, having a reputation, recently reinforced at Drumcree, as a hardliner, was elected leader in succession to him. Such expressions of unionist fears pressed the British government, with its tenuous parliamentary majority, to focus on aspects of its peace process policies that were more congenial to unionists. These included insisting that the PIRA decommission some weapons before PSF could participate in talks; pressing the PIRA to desist from punishment beatings; and suggesting elections to a 'Northern Ireland Forum' before all-party talks could take place. None of these may in themselves have caused the breakdown of the PIRA ceasefire: Major may be correct to suggest that internal strains within republicanism were the principal cause.[151] Nevertheless, Major's emphasis particularly on the mention of elections in the report on the peace process furnished by the former US Senator George Mitchell late in 1995 at least provided the PIRA with circumstances in which disengagement from its ceasefire earned it denunciations only in the expected quarters.[152]

Subsequent speculation centred on whether Adams and Martin McGuinness, PSF's other most prominent leading member, had known that the explosion that marked the end of the ceasefire, at Canary Wharf in London on 9 February 1996, was due to take place: how close, in other words, did the relationship between the PSF leaders and PIRA hardliners remain? Both Adams and McGuinness, predictably, denied advance knowledge of the event,[153] but this claim may at best represent only a confusing metonym for the disagreements within republicanism, which Provisionals remained reluctant to acknowledge in public.[154] In fact, no sooner had the PIRA's first ceasefire ended than there were rumours of a second ceasefire. In the spring of 1996 Major tried to create space for this development by suggesting that having the PIRA's decommissioning run concurrently with any talks, rather than take place before they started, would suffice to permit PSF's involvement in them.[155] Although a rapid attempt to back-pedal on this assurance, to avoid alienating pro-unionist backbench Conservatives, may have mixed the message,[156] PSF's improved showing in the elections to the Northern Ireland Forum of May 1996 could have suggested to some republicans that gains were available to a political strategy. However, the detonation of a huge bomb in the centre of

Manchester early in June, responsibility for which was belatedly admitted by the PIRA, and other PIRA activities in Great Britain and Ireland over the next year, suggested that a renewal of the ceasefire was unlikely without a major shift in attitudes among either British ministers or the Provisionals. Otherwise, however, the intensity of the PIRA's terrorist operations was relatively low, at least initially within Northern Ireland itself, and most loyalists, fortunately, failed to keep their word, in that they were not prompted by undoubted evidence of 'nationalist/republican violence' as ostentatiously to resume their own paramilitary operations. The loyalists had their reward in the participation of their parties, the Ulster Democratic Party (UDP) and the Progressive Unionist Party (PUP), in the post-Forum 'Stormont' talks and in the Forum itself, from both of which PSF was excluded. The talks, chaired by Mitchell, initially made sparse progress[157] and were to continue into the following year.

Restraint was also shown by the British and Irish authorities in not reinstating their former broadcasting bans on PSF/PIRA representatives. The governments' restraint caused some consternation among unionists and on the British right, both in politics and in the media. The *Times* had anticipated the collapse of the PIRA's ceasefire and endorsed the UKUP at the Forum elections, seeing it as a less sectarian option than the other unionist parties.[158] The *Times* also condemned Dublin and London for giving too much latitude to PSF.[159] In this the *Times* at least reflected a growing Conservative backbench revolt against the government on Northern Ireland. Any goodwill that unionists or the British government might have claimed in the eyes of global opinion was, however, severely reduced by the management of a second impasse over the annual Drumcree parade in July 1996. On this occasion the controversial section of the parade's established route was initially prohibited by the authorities, but violent loyalist protest led to a reversal of this decision, the march taking the route in the teeth of orchestrated resistance by nearby nationalist residents led by the republican activist Brendan MacCionnaith. The authorities had changed their initial decision due to the fear that greater violence would otherwise ensue. The intransigence of the Orange Order and, by extension, the perceived intransigence of the UUP's closely implicated new leader David Trimble, was as widely criticised as the alleged incompetence of the government and the security forces, although even John Bruton, who was otherwise deemed too tolerant of unionism by many in the South, publicly criticised the authorities' decision. Members of PSF/PIRA were presented with another opportunity to pose as protectors of an allegedly besieged Catholic community.[160] The Drumcree controversy also led the SDLP to boycott the Northern Ireland Forum for a while, which, with PSF already absent and the unionist parties arguing among themselves, further detracted from its usefulness.

As republicanism's vocal critics in the media predicted, neither the PIRA's disruption of the general election campaign in Great Britain in 1997, nor its other recent activities – the Provisionals killed their last British serviceman in Northern Ireland in February 1997 – lost PSF support in the republican heartlands.[161] Indeed, for the first time the Provisionals' political wing secured the return of two MPs, Adams and McGuinness, although their effort to gain access to the Palace of Westminster was given short shrift by the Speaker of the House of Commons, Betty Boothroyd, on the grounds that they could not enter as long as they refused to swear allegiance to the Queen. The election also significantly returned a huge majority for the self-styled 'New' Labour Party, led by the telegenic Tony Blair, and presently a general election in the Irish Republic returned a new coalition government, headed by Bertie Ahern of Fianna Fáil, as well as giving PSF one member of the Dáil, the lower house of the Republic's Parliament (or TD, from the abbreviation in Irish). Blair and his party made some efforts at this time to assuage unionist and 'middle England' anxieties at the appearance in government of a party that had been out of government for eighteen years and had, until relatively recently, flirted with the idea of 'unity by consent' in Ireland. First, during the PIRA's pre-election 'mainland' campaign, Labour had dropped its long-standing commitment to scrap the Prevention of Terrorism Act. Second, Blair's first major speech on Northern Ireland, on 16 May, contained the declaration that 'none of us in this hall today, even the youngest, is likely to see Northern Ireland as anything but a part of the United Kingdom'. Blair declared to PSF at the same time that 'the settlement train is leaving. I want you to be on that train. But it is leaving anyway, and I will not allow it to wait for you.'[162] This latter suggestion was, however, belied by communications with the Provisionals, which, it has since been argued, shifted the goalposts on decommissioning very much in their favour.[163] Early in July Labour's new Secretary of State for Northern Ireland, Dr Marjorie (better-known as 'Mo') Mowlam, anguished nationalists and republicans by permitting the Portadown Orange Lodge its annual parade down the Garvaghy Road,[164] but the resulting danger of meltdown into serious disorder throughout the province was prevented by the more realistic attitude taken by the Orange Order for the remainder of the marching season.[165]

Satisfied by the new British government's suggestions that it would accept PSF's participation in talks before the PIRA began decommissioning, the PIRA then announced a second ceasefire. Two unionist parties, the DUP and the UKUP, left the talks in protest, and the attitude of the UUP's spokesperson Ken Maginnis, as expressed in a memorable debate with Martin McGuinness on the television programme *Newsnight* (BBC 2) in August 1997, suggested that Maginnis' party would also enter talks with PSF only with great reluctance. PSF formally accepted the 'Mitchell principles' of non-violence (derived from Mitchell's report of November 1995) in early September, but unionist doubts must have been increased by suggestions from the PIRA at this time that it would never decommission its weapons. PSF's suggestion in response that it was 'not the IRA' probably convinced few critics, although suggestions of a split within PSF in the autumn did indicate some differences of view among the Provisionals. By then both the UUP and the British government had effectively crossed the Rubicon, as 'Stormont' talks, including PSF, resumed in the autumn.

The next source of disturbance to the peace process was provided by a neglected actor, the republican INLA. This group, which had never joined the PIRA on ceasefire, assassinated the loyalist leader Billy Wright in the Maze Prison in December 1997.[166] Mo Mowlam's decision to head to the Maze for a conference with prominent loyalist prisoners may have seemed bizarre, but may also have prevented a collapse of the loyalist ceasefires.[167] Thus, as 1998 opened, negotiations could proceed involving three unionist parties (the UUP, the UDP and the PUP), two nationalist or republican parties (the SDLP and PSF), the

APNI, and the Northern Ireland Women's Coalition (NIWC), a configuration of parties that many observers would have long deemed impossible.

A GOOD FRIDAY?

Unionists had reasons to be satisfied with the document, the 'Heads of Agreement', produced by the British and Irish governments in January 1998, which seemed to mark a withdrawal from the proposal for a powerful North–South body contained in the Framework Documents. The talks process, however, was jeopardised in the opening months of 1998 by evidence of major breaches of their ceasefires by both the UDA (acting under the cover name of the 'Ulster Freedom Fighters') and the PIRA. The British and Irish governments adopted the flexible if illogical procedure of expelling the linked parties, the UDP and, later, PSF from the talks for only brief 'decontamination' periods. More intense negotiations, chaired by Mitchell, opened in April 1998. An approach nearer to that of the Framework Documents seemed to be signified by a subsequent discussion document produced by the governments and introduced to the parties under Mitchell's auspices. Under pressure from unionists, all-Ireland institutions were reduced to less heroic dimensions. This aim was achieved at the price of concessions to republicans on other issues, with the SDLP already assured of its aim of a power-sharing government in the province. Flexibility was shown as the deadline initially imposed by Mitchell for negotiations to end, 9 April, was breached. On the following day last-minute doubts were aired as unionists struggled to swallow the clauses of the agreement pertaining to the release of prisoners, although most of Trimble's delegation were reassured, for the moment, by a letter from Tony Blair. The attainment of agreement was announced on Good Friday, 10 April 1998, and was greeted euphorically by the international media.[168] Even cartoonists usually noted for their wry cynicism about the conflict seemed shortly to enjoy the breakthrough.[169]

Detailed readings of aspects of the GFA are considered elsewhere in this book (see Chapter 3). In its immediate aftermath, with the agreement due to be put to referendums north and south of the Irish border, broad interpretations of its political significance were of obvious importance. For some, from disparate political perspectives, the GFA simply did mean, and has meant, sooner or later, a united Ireland. In Richard Deutsch's phrase, and in the view of right-wing British critics of the GFA, this was its 'ultimate and clear aim'.[170] Indeed, at this time PSF's representatives were making still more audacious predictions as to the proximity of a united Ireland. Unionist and British nationalist pessimists could also cite the anticipations of this result of an Irish Taoiseach firmly schooled in Fianna Fáil's traditions.[171] Such interpretations of the GFA seem to rest on two obviously flawed assumptions: that all Catholics in Northern Ireland (if not everywhere) support a united Ireland;[172] and that a proportionate demographic shift in Northern Ireland in favour of Catholics will rapidly take place. In fact, when it is considered that by no means all Catholic voters in the North support a united Ireland, and that the results of the census in Northern Ireland in 2001 (announced in December 2002) revealed significantly smaller increases in the percentage of Northern Ireland's inhabitants who are Catholic than many had anticipated, a united Ireland seems far from inevitable, especially within an immediate timescale. The right-wing journalist Peter Hitchens' suggestion that the conditional nature of the union recognised in the GFA marks a significant departure in British policy[173] is also historically challenged, since Northern Ireland's status in the United Kingdom has been declared dependent on the consent of the province, in whatever form, for almost as long as Northern Ireland has existed. The Parliament of Northern Ireland had to vote the six counties out of the Anglo-Irish Treaty in 1922 and consent was made a condition in the Ireland Act 1949, although this was met with bitter protests by nationalists at the time. The terms of consent had been shifted from 'parliament' to 'people' by the time of the border poll of 1973, long before 'New' Labour was dreamed of.

In this light, and given that the vast majority of opposition to the GFA has been unionist, it is tempting to follow Paul Bew and suggest that 'the unionists have won – they just don't know it'.[174] Bew, and other academic and journalistic commentators close to Trimble, are surely correct to point to the partitionist core of the agreement.[175] The pro-agreement unionist Antony Alcock agrees, suggesting that the main material point in the GFA was the promise that the articles of the Irish Constitution that claimed Northern Ireland as part of the Republic's territory would be amended.[176] From very different perspectives, the judgement that the GFA means victory for unionists is also endorsed by the former republican volunteer Anthony McIntyre[177] and by dissident republicans. To treat the GFA as a sign of a unionist victory is, however, to ignore the air of respectability, in the eyes of global and, especially, Irish opinion that PSF has acquired, a respectability most obviously indicated by the growth in the party's support both north and south of the border. The holding of offices in the Northern Ireland Executive by PSF leaders and the release of PIRA prisoners have, in combination with continued republican paramilitary activity and delays in PIRA decommissioning, become central to a key floating minority of unionists' fragile confidence in the peace process because this conjuncture of political issues suggests, when seen from the unionist perspective, that the Provisionals' new aura of respectability is utterly incongruous and that the linked political gains are entirely undeserved. The continued further ominous threat of republican violence, albeit posed in the different form of the new 'dissident' paramilitary group calling itself the 'Real' IRA (to which a political group called the 32-County Sovereignty Movement is understood to be linked), adds considerable and understandable impetus to the distaste felt by many unionists for the post-GFA order (see Chapter 1).

Opposition to the GFA in the subsequent referendum in the Republic was negligible, but in the concurrent referendum in Northern Ireland it had three key focuses: the Orange Order, Paisley's Democratic Unionists, and the further dissident secession from the Provisionals.[178] Unionist disaffection with the GFA became the key issue in the referendum and was focused by the lauding of Provisional prisoners, released soon after the signing of the agreement, by their fellow republicans. (A corresponding gesture was made to the loyalists at the same time.) The former republican Sean O'Callaghan surely errs, however, in representing this as a gratuitous undermining of moderate opinion by the British government, since it should be recalled that PSF had not formally declared its adherence to the GFA before this point.[179] The release of prisoners, and the associated dimensions of bereavement, forgiveness, trauma and remorse, remain among the thorniest and most poorly addressed issues in the peace process. In the event, majority unionist support for the GFA was achieved only by a narrow margin, and even then after a significant declaration by Blair in Belfast on 14 May 1998, in which he appeared to reinforce the message of his letter to Trimble the previous month and promise unionists that he would enforce preconditions on PSF's entry into the new Northern Ireland Executive, going beyond the stipulations of the GFA itself.[180] While prolonging the process in the short term, garbled versions of these words would be repeatedly used against Blair by his political opponents, exacerbate unionist disillusionment with the peace process and, perhaps, also diminish republican trust in the Prime Minister.

FROM THE FIRST SUSPENSION CRISIS TO THE SECOND, MAY 1998 TO MAY 2000

The level of unionist disaffection was confirmed almost immediately in the first elections to the new Northern Ireland Assembly. Trimble's UUP became the largest party in the new Assembly, but its support dipped to an all-time low. Further, when it is considered that a considerable segment even of Trimble's party itself had by this time publicly declared itself opposed to the GFA (a segment most obviously represented by Jeffrey Donaldson), it can be questioned whether a viable and active level of support for the peace process has ever existed within the unionist community. The Assembly soon opened its deliberations in a shadow format, but the formation of an executive (government) in Northern Ireland was to await progress on the contentious question of decommissioning.

A more obvious challenge to the new constellation in Northern Ireland politics was offered by the annual impasse at Drumcree. On this occasion the authorities took the decision not to allow the parade to pass down the contested Upper Garvaghy Road. This decision, unlike in 1996, was maintained, at the price of a huge and costly security operation, featuring the erection of huge barricades to keep the Orangemen and protesters from the contested territory, and an ill-tempered loyalist protest that reached an ugly finale in the murder of three Catholic brothers aged between eight and eleven, Jason, Mark and Richard Quinn, at Ballymoney in County Antrim on 12 July 1998, one of the most blatantly sectarian events of a conflict that was supposedly drawing to its conclusion. Any lingering optimism that Northern Ireland had stepped, with a few signatures on a single document, into a millennium of sweetness and light was finally shattered a month later by the worst single atrocity in the history of the Troubles: the detonation of a huge bomb planted by the Real IRA in the centre of Omagh on 15 August 1998, killing twenty-nine people, including one woman who was pregnant with twins. Even the dissident republicans were unable to withstand the flood of international condemnation and presently declared a ceasefire, although this lasted only a short while. In the circumstances the fact that PSF, while condemning the Omagh outrage, has offered little or no encouragement to the police investigation of the crime is surely indicative of mainstream republicans' continued fear of further splits within their fissiparous movement. The reluctance evinced by Adams about decommissioning, even at this stage, should surely also be related to the same dynamic.

Two other crucial developments in 1998, intended by outsiders as gestures of reconciliation, were to emerge as points of contention. Late in that year John Hume and David Trimble were jointly awarded the Nobel Prize for Peace. In some quarters this award is regarded as a curse or a waste of time (a previous award in connection with the conflict, to the 'Peace People' back in 1976, was not a good omen). There were also those who complained about the non-inclusion of Gerry Adams among the laureates. Perhaps a more concerning feature is the continued depiction of either Hume or Trimble as unworthy of the award by partisan affiliates of the other, a tendency by no means isolated to the Northern Ireland parties.[181] Of longer-term significance was the opening, even before the signing of the GFA, of a new public inquiry into the events of Bloody Sunday, under the chairmanship of Lord Saville. This denoted an acceptance of nationalist and republican complaints about the inadequacies of the earlier Widgery inquiry. The existence of the Saville inquiry, which is still sitting at the time of writing, doubtless nurtures a sense among many unionists, and among some in Great Britain, that disproportionate attention is paid to nationalists' supposed grievances, especially in the media of film and television,[182] including a number of 'docudramas' about Bloody Sunday prepared for the occasion of its thirtieth anniversary. The Saville inquiry did, however, elicit an admission from Martin McGuinness that he had had a senior role in the Londonderry/Derry PIRA in 1972, the sort of admission that PSF's leaders had long avoided.[183]

By the early months of 1999 considerable levels of disquiet were evident in Northern Ireland, and in Great Britain, on a number of issues. While the ceasefires of the PIRA and of most loyalist groups were still intact on the official minimalist definition, the groups' involvements in maimings, mutilations and other illegal activities appeared to be continuing. Meanwhile, no paramilitary group had decommissioned any weapons, with the exception of a gesture by the small loyalist splinter group the Loyalist Volunteer Force in December 1998 (the LVF in any case was presently to begin acting as if no longer on ceasefire). In this context the British government in particular came in for increasing criticism for releasing paramilitary prisoners 'on licence' (a form of parole) under the GFA: both pro-agreement unionists and nationalists were given pause by the release, respectively, of republican and loyalist paramilitaries, while newspaper headlines in Great Britain had predictably been seized by the release of the killers of British Army personnel and by released PIRA members such as Patrick Magee, the would-be assassin of the Conservative cabinet at Brighton in 1984. In 2000 Magee gave an interview in which he declared himself committed to the peace process. The interview still distressed many British Conservatives, however, since Magee sought to justify his involvement in the Brighton bombing on the grounds that it exerted pressure on the British government to negotiate with the Provisionals.[184] Another source of alarm for unionists was the prospect that a commission, then in progress under the chairmanship of Chris Patten, would recommend a radical scheme of police reform.

Meanwhile, the murder of a Catholic lawyer, Rosemary Nelson, in March 1999, responsibility for which was claimed by the Red Hand Defenders, demonstrated the continued potency of loyalist paramilitaries. Like the earlier murder of another Catholic lawyer, Pat Finucane, in 1989, this killing has since frequently featured in allegations of collusion between the security forces in Northern Ireland and the loyalists. In April 2003 an inquiry headed by Sir

John Stevens, now Commissioner of the Metropolitan Police Service in London, concluded that collusion between the security forces and loyalist groups had at least hampered the investigation of Finucane's murder. Critics of the Provisionals continue to suggest that Finucane was not merely a lawyer but was active in PIRA circles, although this is strongly denied by Finucane's widow and family.[185]

Alarmingly different levels of expectation among the pro-agreement parties continued to be in evidence in 1999 about the precedence of the creation of the Executive, with PSF members, and the decommissioning of paramilitary weapons, which, in this context, was almost always treated as reducible to PIRA decommissioning. The Hillsborough Declaration, issued on 1 April 1999, was swiftly denounced by PSF, even though it symbolised a greatly qualified level of accord between the relevant parties in its central recognition of a 'difference of view about [the] timing and the sequence' of implementation.[186] Unionist disquiet was represented in the elections to the European Parliament in June. Northern Ireland elects three members to the European Parliament, for which purpose the province functions as a single constituency under PR, the first three candidates in the poll being returned. Ian Paisley topped the poll once again in 1999, while the proportion of votes going to the UUP's candidate, Jim Nicholson, exhibited a sharp fall. (However, this may have been exacerbated by the nature of the electoral system and the weakness of the candidate, who barely managed to beat PSF's candidate for the third place.)[187]

The British government exhibited some audacity in this context in placing pressure on pro-agreement unionists to enter the Northern Ireland Executive with PSF members, although it is surely unfair to associate this procedure solely with the vanity of a Prime Minister whose stature on the world stage had been inflated by the concurrent conflict with Serbia.[188] The deadline set by Blair for the establishment of the Executive, 30 June, passed without a break in the deadlock. In July Ahern and Blair agreed to reinvoke the services of George Mitchell to undertake a detailed review of the peace process at the end of the summer. In the intervening period grave questions were posed in some quarters over the continuation of the process, with allegations of the PIRA's involvement in attempted gun-running from Florida and in the murders of a Belfast taxi-driver, Charles Bennett, and a PIRA informer, Eamon Collins.

The British government's judgement that the PIRA's ceasefire was still intact was sharply criticised in Great Britain and elsewhere.[189]

The political atmosphere appeared to improve following the appointment in October 1999 of Blair's close political ally Peter Mandelson as Secretary of State for Northern Ireland. The replacement of Mowlam by Mandelson was reassuring to those unionists who had increasingly regarded the former as naïvely pro-nationalist. Adams appeared to greet the arrival in office of the new Secretary of State with soothing suggestions that 'republicans need to address the concerns of unionists'.[190] By the end of Mitchell's review, in November 1999, the PIRA indicated its willingness to appoint a representative to liaise with General John de Chastelain of the Independent International Commission on Decommissioning (IICD). PSF's hope that this would be enough to facilitate the activation of the Northern Ireland Executive was to be fulfilled, but only for a short period. Motivated in part by knowledge of the extent of unionist distrust of the Provisionals, and perhaps also by disaffection with the radical reform of policing in Northern Ireland proposed in the recently published Patten report, David Trimble lodged a post-dated letter of resignation as First Minister of Northern Ireland for February 2000, to be activated if no start had been made on PIRA decommissioning by that date. Even with this caveat, which was condemned by republicans and some nationalists as an unwarranted ultimatum, the Ulster Unionist Council (UUC), the highest decision-making body of the UUP, supported entry into the power-sharing Executive only by 58 per cent to 42 per cent, hardly a resounding majority. Possibly a more positive achievement for unionists at the end of 1999 was the formal recasting, at last, of the opening clauses of the Irish Republic's Constitution, giving the claim to the whole territory of the island of Ireland a less threatening, more 'aspirational' air by explicitly 'recognising that a united Ireland shall be brought about only by peaceful means with the consent of the majority of the people, democratically expressed, in both jurisdictions in the island'.

In December 1999 devolved government returned to Northern Ireland when David Trimble was confirmed as First Minister and Seamus Mallon of the SDLP became Deputy First Minister. While hollow laughter in several quarters greeted both Martin McGuinness' appointment as Minister of Education for Northern

Ireland and the rapidity with which the Assembly's members (known as MLAs) voted increases to their salaries, the second suspension of the Northern Ireland Assembly and Executive, less than three months later, evoked a measure of despair. Amid a confused set of communications early in February 2000, it transpired that the PIRA had not done clearly enough, within the deadline suggested by Trimble, to satisfy Mandelson. Republican and nationalist sympathisers claimed, somewhat grandiosely, that this suspension violated the GFA and thus international law,[191] and Mandelson earned a level of hostility from republicans and some nationalists that he was never to escape. A few days later the PIRA broke off contact with the IICD and the difficulties of the process were made more apparent by the effects on the standing of David Trimble within his party. At the UUP's annual general meeting in March 2000 Trimble's leadership of the party was challenged by the experienced politician the Reverend Martin Smyth, who secured 43 per cent of the votes cast. The party also voted to remain outside devolved government unless the province's police force retained the name 'Royal Ulster Constabulary'.[192]

On 6 May 2000 the PIRA issued a statement indicating its willingness to begin a process that would put its arms 'completely and verifiably' beyond use. This process would comprise the inspection of select PIRA weapons dumps by two IICD arms inspectors, Cyril Ramaphosa, formerly a leading figure in the African National Congress (ANC) in South Africa, and Martti Ahtisaari, a former President of Finland. Given the close links between the ANC and the PIRA, Ramaphosa was certainly a not injudicious choice.[193] Mandelson and Trimble both declared their opinion that this would be sufficient to justify the reactivation of devolved government, and Trimble was able to carry his party with him, if by a still smaller margin than before. On this occasion significant influences on the narrowly affirmative response of the UUC included the unanticipated support of one of its most influential members, John Taylor and, more controversially, the opinion of the former republican Sean O'Callaghan that the PIRA's latest gesture indicated that the Provisionals' 'war' was over.[194] After a stuttering two years following the signature of the agreement, on 30 May 2000 devolution in Northern Ireland was back in operation.

DECOMMISSIONING, POLICING AND DISAFFECTION, JUNE 2000 TO DECEMBER 2001

In June 2000 it was announced that the promised inspection of the PIRA's weapons dumps had occurred. There were also measures of demilitarisation[195] by the British authorities, including the closure of five military installations in the spring and, in July, the completion of the release on licence of prisoners attached to paramilitary groups on ceasefire within the two-year timescale implied in the GFA. Mandelson was then, and has subsequently been, criticised for taking this latter step, since another two-year timescale set out in the GFA, on paramilitary decommissioning, had clearly not been kept to. In fact, attempts to establish explicit and close links between these two sections of the GFA are flawed, and, in any case, the mention of a procedure to 'review' paramilitary ceasefires under the GFA in connection with the release of prisoners allows a Secretary of State to revoke at least an individual prisoner's licensed release. This has been applied in a few cases to date, most notably that of the prominent loyalist Johnny 'Mad Dog' Adair. (Adair has been taken back into custody twice since his initial release, in August 2000 and January 2003, on both occasions in connection with activities pertaining to internecine feuding between loyalists.) Nevertheless, Mandelson's speedy fulfilment of British obligations under this section of the GFA demonstrated at least a surprising measure of goodwill towards the paramilitaries, and it was not only the most suspicious minds in the unionist camp who saw in this conjuncture a deal between the British government and the PIRA to encourage the latter to move towards decommissioning, even though loyalist prisoners, notably Michael Stone, were also released on licence at this time, in considerable numbers. (Like other prisoners previously released under the terms of the GFA, Stone declared his commitment to peace in Northern Ireland; he has since worked there for a time as a freelance artist.) The marching season and especially the annual stand-off at Drumcree arrived in time to focus unionist discontents, when Mandelson adopted the line of his predecessor in refusing the Portadown Orange Lodge permission to march down the Upper Garvaghy Road. Anti-agreement unionism may, however, have briefly been weakened by the evidently counterproductive nature of the province-wide protest at Mandelson's decision; by a feud between groups of loyalist paramilitaries over the summer, which left outsiders shaking their heads in bemusement; and perhaps also by the hypocrisy of the anti-agreement DUP in accepting ministerial offices in the revived Executive, the party's clear desire for the higher profile that came with involvement being modulated only by its ministers' gesture of periodically resigning the offices in order to be replaced by party colleagues.

Discontents in the latter half of 2000 were not limited to the unionist community. The nationalist SDLP, the Catholic Church and PSF all voiced opposition to the government's proposals for police reform, which fell short of a literal interpretation of the radical measures advanced by Chris Patten's commission. Mandelson's judgement also seemed to be exercised against nationalists and republicans in determining the issue of the flying of the Union flag on public buildings, the requisite level of cross-community agreement in the power-sharing institutions not having been achieved. Dissent of sorts was also registered by the Real IRA's activities in London in the summer of 2000, especially its attempts to disrupt celebrations of the Queen Mother's hundredth birthday and to mortar-bomb the headquarters of the British intelligence service, MI6.

Many commentators interpreted the outcome of the South Antrim by-election of September 2000 as a further setback for the peace process: the UUP's candidate, David Burnside, was defeated by Willie McCrea of the anti-agreement DUP. With another meeting of the UUC approaching in October, Jeffrey Donaldson, a prominent opponent of the GFA within the ranks of the UUP, made clear his intention to put forward a motion calling on Trimble to resign from the Northern Ireland Executive unless there was actual decommissioning of PIRA weapons. Publicly PSF was dismissive of calls from unionists and British government sources for the PIRA to proceed with decommissioning, claiming that it was not a significant factor in the peace process, since the guns of the PIRA were 'silent'. This was not an entirely convincing argument, since actions such as the murder of Edmund McCoy in May 2000 by 'Direct Action Against Drugs', which has been used as a cover name by the PIRA, demonstrated that the PIRA's guns were not entirely silent. PSF also accused Trimble of weakness in the face of his critics inside the UUP and the British of an unprincipled attempt to preserve Trimble's leadership rather than stick to the letter of the GFA. However, the fact that the Provisionals consented to a further inspection of their weapons dumps in advance of the UUC's meeting, facilitating an expression of the inspectors' view that the weapons contained therein were 'secure', surely suggests that the lack of concern that some commentators discern among mainstream republicans for the plight of pro-agreement unionists[196] is more apparent than real. In the event Trimble secured the endorsement of his party on this occasion only by offering to impose sanctions against PSF until the PIRA's decommissioning was effected. His declared intention to bar PSF's representatives from meetings of the North–South Ministerial Council (NSMC), the symbolic if weak representation under the GFA of the united Ireland to which republicans aspire, was well-selected to inspire republican displeasure. This sanction was effective pending an extended attempt by PSF to challenge Trimble's move through the courts.

It was with some relief that early in the new year republicans and some nationalists observed the news break of a scandal, not relating to Northern Ireland affairs, that led to the resignation of Peter Mandelson as Secretary of State. The reported initial reactions of McGuinness to his replacement, John Reid, a Scot from a Catholic background, were no more favourable than republicans had generally been to Mandelson. Criticism of the textured nature of the paramilitary ceasefires continued, and allegations also surfaced suggesting that the relationship between the Provisional IRA and the dissident Real IRA was cosier than might have been expected. Such suggestions were particularly sensitive, since it was still the case at that point that no one had been imprisoned on any charges relating to the Omagh crime. Freed of the responsibilities of government, Mandelson began politely intimating a personal view that more should be done in certain quarters to secure convictions.[197]

In advance of a new general election for the British Parliament and in the continued absence of decommissioning on any significant level by any paramilitary groups, Trimble imposed another deadline, declaring his intention to resign as First Minister on 1 July 2001 unless the PIRA commenced decommissioning. In spite of this show of resolve, which earned him a predictable condemnation from Provisionals, and a further inspection of PIRA weapons dumps, the general election, which made virtually no impression on the Blair government's huge parliamentary majority, yielded a disastrous result for pro-agreement unionists. Not only did the anti-agreement DUP advance its parliamentary representation to five of the eighteen Northern Ireland seats in the British House of Commons, but most of the six UUP representatives returned were or became opposed to the peace process, and it is possible that Trimble himself was returned to Parliament for his constituency of Upper Bann only because of the decision of the moderate APNI not to put forward a rival candidate and to advise its supporters in the constituency to vote for Trimble.

The other major development in the election occurred within the nationalist community. John Reid's expressed belief, or aspiration, that the continued practice of punishment beatings by the PIRA would delegitimise republicanism and result in a reduced vote for PSF was very wide of the mark, demonstrating again that one cannot just hope that a moderate majority in Northern Ireland will appear out of nowhere. In the event PSF made major progress, increasing its proportion of the overall number of votes cast, which for the first time exceeded that of the SDLP, and returning two further MPs, Pat Doherty and Michelle Gildernew, making four in all, although not without unionists advancing allegations of electoral malpractice in relation to both seats.[198] The British government responded coolly to these allegations, although the later implementation of new electoral registration procedures in Northern Ireland certainly seems to have been read in some circles as a measure particularly targeting republicans.

As no decommissioning by the PIRA had occurred by 1 July, Trimble's resignation came into effect. This created a six-week breathing space in which the Assembly could elect a First Minister and a Deputy First Minister, although in the event Secretary of State Reid twice adopted the device, at the end of each of two such six-week periods, of giving the parties more time to come to agreement by suspending the institutions of devolved government for twenty-four hours. After a meeting of pro-agreement politicians with representatives of the British and Irish governments at Weston Park in Staffordshire, new proposals were issued by the governments that included extended policing reforms, largely designed to sugar the pill of decommissioning for the Provisionals.[199] While these prompted the SDLP and the Catholic Church, but not PSF, to accept the revised reforms, the proposals included the abolition of the name 'Royal Ulster Constabulary'. If Trimble was to return to devolved government, he would have to go back on the proposition agreed by his party in March 2000 that the retention of that name was a condition of such participation. Trimble's position was thus further undermined, which may have been a reason why he felt unable to accept an imprecise offer by the Provisional IRA, issued on 9 August but subsequently withdrawn, to undertake decommissioning. The level of crisis in the peace process was further illustrated over the summer and autumn by the explosion of a Real IRA bomb in Ealing in London; by the arrest in Colombia of three alleged PIRA operatives who had established contact with a left-wing guerrilla movement in that country; and by the Secretary of State's ruling that the participation by the UDA and the LVF in violence in Northern Ireland constituted the ending of both their ceasefires. Given that a number of prisoners, especially from the UDA, had previously been released, the punitive sanctions open to a Secretary of State were nonetheless limited. Northern Ireland grabbed global headlines again for the wrong reasons early in September, when groups of loyalists began to picket the route taken by schoolgirls and their parents to Holy Cross Girls' Primary School, a Catholic institution in the Ardoyne district of North Belfast. The loyalists adopted this injudicious procedure in an attempt to protest at what they, and their supporters, claimed was the sorry plight of Protestants in North Belfast, who were said to be under siege from republican attacks: whatever the full facts behind this dimension of the event, they were less easy to catch on television cameras and therefore, it could be argued, escaped global attention. Later in the autumn a quieter settlement was reached, which included an increased presence of security forces in the areas that concerned the loyalists.

Holy Cross had in the meantime been quickly relegated down the order of news bulletins on and after 11 September 2001. The subsequent shift in global opinion against any group connected with terrorism, combined with the Provisionals' connection to events in Colombia (which was initially denied but later admitted), led to a weakening of the Provisionals' stance. Late in October it was announced that General de Chastelain had been present at an event where a significant quantity of the PIRA's arms had been put beyond use. Trimble could then claim that it was only when republicans were put upon the rack that they recognised their obligations under the GFA. In part because this act of decommissioning remained opaque – de Chastelain suggested that to make too many details public might jeopardise further decommissioning – Trimble was not guaranteed unionist support when he declared the action significant enough to justify his return to the Northern Ireland Executive alongside two of PSF's leading members, McGuinness and Bairbre de Brun (Minister of Health).

At this point the procedures for electing the First Minister and the Deputy First Minister under the GFA took on an unforeseen importance. To reconstitute the Executive it was necessary, among other conditions, for an Assembly vote to take place in which the appointment of Trimble as First Minister and of the SDLP's new leader Mark Durkan as Deputy First Minister received majority support from both unionist and nationalist MLAs voting separately. As the elections to the Assembly in 1998 had returned only a small excess of pro-agreement unionists over anti-agreement unionists, and as in the intervening period the UUP MLA Peter Weir had defected to an anti-agreement position, there were clearly possible difficulties in the way of the reconstitution of the Executive. In order to traverse this obstacle one of the NIWC MLAs, Jane Morrice, redesignated herself as a 'unionist' (having been an 'other') for this particular vote. At the same time, to preserve the NIWC's non-sectarian position, Monica McWilliams, a fellow MLA, reclassified herself as a 'nationalist'. However, this move was thwarted because of the unexpected conversion of a further UUP MLA, Pauline Armitage, to opposition to the peace process, and the initial Asssembly debates failed to obtain a majority among unionist MLAs for the appointment of Trimble and Durkan. 'Unionist' endorsement of their appointment was achieved only after consultation between the Secretary of State John Reid and the leader of the non-sectarian APNI, David Ford, after which the APNI MLAs also redesignated themselves 'unionist' (from 'other'). A second vote was attempted on 5–6 November. This procedure was possibly facilitated further by the fact that Lord Alderdice, also a member of the APNI, was the Presiding Officer of the Assembly.

The requisite 'unionist' majority was achieved by this contrived procedure, but not until after the passage of a formal deadline of six weeks from the Secretary of State's last suspension of the Assembly (itself a contrived procedure effected to buy the PIRA more time to deliver decommissioning), meaning that technically there was now a requirement for elections. The justifications articulated by Reid and his supporters – variously, that circumstances called for flexibility, or that a consultation period was implicit in the terms of the GFA – failed to disguise the fact that new Assembly elections were being avoided in order to stifle what seemed likely to be an overwhelming expression of unionist discontent with the peace process. The anti-agreement DUP protested, although there was in truth also something slightly ridiculous about an anti-agreement movement appealing to the terms of the agreement. Anti-agreement discontent was also expressed during the Assembly debates,[200] in an unseemly scuffle afterwards and in responses to a poll held by the *Belfast Telegraph*, which suggested that 52 per cent of the Protestants it surveyed simply did not believe General de Chastelain's report that significant decommissioning by the PIRA had taken place.[201]

The substance of the ground being conceded by mainstream republicans was keenly expressed in their condemnation by dissident republicans, such as Bobby Sands' sister Bernadette Sands-McKevitt, and by the Real IRA's planting of a car bomb in Birmingham. Yet the impression that any ground was being conceded by republicans was again almost negated, so far as many unionists were concerned, by complementary changes in the British government's policy. In addition to the earlier concessions on police reform, the government responded to the PIRA's first act of decommissioning with further measures of demilitarisation. More evidence of a surreptitious deal was provided late in 2001 when the British government introduced legislation into Parliament to permit access to facilities at Westminster for the PSF MPs, even without the MPs in question taking their seats in the House of Commons or swearing allegiance to the Crown. This was bitterly condemned in the right-wing British press and by individuals more attached than 'New' Labour was said to be to notions of the sanctity of British parliamentary institutions, a feeling that encompassed unionists, the Conservative opposition and some of Labour's own backbenchers. The Conservatives ostentatiously renounced the previous convention of bipartisanship on Northern Ireland policy between the two major British political parties.[202] While the government defended the measure as advancing the peace process and the integration of the republicans within constitutional politics, any consolation for unionists was perhaps more likely to be obtained from the further consequent condemnation of mainstream republicanism by its dissident critics. It is noticeable, however, that 'New' Labour was not alone in its view that the 'house-training' (in David Trimble's memorable phrase[203]) required of mainstream republicans was best done after having first admitted them to the house. Early in 2002 Alex Maskey became PSF's first Lord Mayor of Belfast, a position into which the support of the non-sectarian APNI was crucial in placing him.

CRISIS AND RECKONING, 2002–03

The year 2002 opened with the DUP promising to lodge a legal challenge to the procedures adopted by Reid in the autumn of 2001, which had prevented the holding of new Assembly elections. In March the PIRA's involvement was alleged in a break-in at a security centre in Castlereagh. It was announced in April that the PIRA had co-operated with General de Chastelain in another act of decommissioning. The fact that, around the same time, British government sources were airing the idea of offering an amnesty to members of the PIRA who were on the run could be used by the government's critics to distract attention from this second instalment of decommissioning;[204] it also provided a further suggestion for the suspicious that the PIRA was conducting decommissioning only as part of some sort of informal arrangement, involving reciprocal concessions. In any case, David Ervine, the leader of the PUP, felt able to use a political context apparently favourable to republicanism as an excuse not to recommend any decommissioning by the UVF, the loyalist paramilitary group to which he had once belonged and which was still associated with his party. The other main loyalist group, the UDA, was not then considered to be on ceasefire at all, so that the decommissioning of its weapons also seemed unlikely. Both of these facts, combined with the continued presence of dissident republicans, must have left the Provisionals unwilling to offer further decommissioning.

A further complication was provided by the revelation in April 2002 of evidence about the PIRA's intelligence-gathering activities, which included gathering detailed information about leading British Conservative politicians and other perceived opponents of republicanism. Many felt that the collation of such materials by a body at least formerly implicated in the work of political assassination could only have one meaning. Allegations in relation to the Provisionals' links with guerrilla groups in Colombia also embarrassed the movement and Adams found it convenient to absent himself from US Congressional hearings on the subject. PSF alleged, as over the Castlereagh break-in, that it was the victim of a smear campaign inspired by elements of the British establishment opposed to the peace process,[205] although others were surprised rather by the latitude allowed the Provisionals by the British government. Notwithstanding these allegations of impropriety, in the Irish general election of the spring of 2002, which confirmed Ahern's continuance as Taoiseach, PSF expanded its support base in the South. Even so it was not offered a place in the governing coalition, which some observers had thought a possibility. Later in the year PSF proved to be insufficiently powerful in the South to inspire a further rejection of the Treaty of Nice, which was concerned with the operations of the European Union, in the Republic's second referendum on the subject.

In July the PIRA issued an apology for past activities that had involved the killing of civilians. This fell short of an explicit declaration from the Provisionals that the 'war' was over, which unionists and some British politicians have sought since at least the first of the PIRA's ceasefires, and others were quick to note the lack of an apology for any actions that had involved death or injury to members of the British Army or the security services in Northern Ireland,[206] a fact that surely demonstrates the continued existence of clear water between republicans and the nationalist humanism of, for example, John Hume.[207] The apology also failed to head off (if this was the intention) the placing of more political pressure on the PIRA, in the form of an iteration in July 2002 by the British government of a definition of the activities that it regarded as inconsistent with a paramilitary ceasefire.[208] That this was hardly welcomed by PSF surely presaged the ensuing difficulties. Rioting in parts of the province throughout the summer indicated a level of popular disengagement from the peace process, even PSF apparently having failed to fulfil the demands of sections of its core constituency.

In September 2002 David Trimble faced yet another difficult challenge within the UUP and felt that the only way to hold his party together was to issue an ultimatum: unless there was an indication of full renunciation of violence by the PIRA by 18 January 2003, he and his UUP colleagues would resign from the power-sharing Executive. Trimble's use of a deadline was condemned by his opponents, not for the first time, as an unwarranted imposition,[209] but Trimble could certainly argue that such a strategy had proved effective in the past in evoking a response from the Provisionals. Nevertheless, it did not seem likely that republicans would be quite so obliging this time.

A more pressing problem was already emerging behind the scenes. According to John Reid, even before the government had given the impression of firming up its attitude to paramilitary violence in July, British security forces had obtained evidence of intelligence-gathering on a wider scale by the Provisionals. Those arrested in connection with this alleged intelligence-gathering included a senior PSF official based at Stormont, Denis Donaldson. The impression that PSF had been using its position within the institutions of devolved government, conceded so reluctantly by its opponents, to furnish itself and (it was widely assumed) the PIRA with sensitive information about those very opponents, completed the generation of an all-round sense of crisis in the peace process. On 14 October the Northern Ireland Assembly and Executive were suspended for the fourth time. Trimble expressed dissatisfaction that the innocent had thus been punished along with the guilty (meaning PSF), suggesting that he would have preferred the continuation of devolution with the removal of PSF's members from the Executive. According to a revelation from Mark Durkan, this was an option that Blair considered and it was perhaps thwarted only by the resistance of Durkan's own SDLP.

A major speech by Blair on 17 October 2002 indicated his perhaps belated concern for the plight of pro-agreement unionists, renewing the call for republicans and loyalists to eschew violence in a purer sense: 'we cannot carry on with the IRA half in, half out of this process. Not just because it isn't right any more. It won't work any more.' Blair remained, by his own admission, 'optimistic', but his interpretation of developments was marked by a considerable tension: 'People say [that] unionists now reject the agreement', he observed. 'I don't think that's true. It's not that they don't support the concept of it. They don't believe [that] it is being implemented properly whilst paramilitary activity remains.'[210] Here lies part of the difficulty: if all the parties that signed the GFA had accepted the same interpretation at the outset as to what the proper implementation of its provisions meant, perhaps it would never have been possible to get all the parties to sign it. The PIRA's public response to Blair's speech was lukewarm and leaks from Irish government sources suggested that the organisation was continuing with forms of paramilitary activity, such as targeting and training.

A British cabinet reshuffle that led to the appointment of a new Secretary of State, Paul Murphy, in the autumn of 2002 was not associated with the injection of new life into proceedings, in the way that Mandelson's appointment had been three years earlier, although this was no reflection of the quality of the appointment, for Murphy's experience was a good deal more relevant to the province than Reid's or Mandelson's. Trimble, meanwhile, capped his demands with a request for the full disbandment of the PIRA, claiming that this was the only way to restore the trust that mainstream republicans had forfeited. By the end of the year he was clearly encountering political difficulties in engaging in dialogue with PSF at all. By the time that his initial deadline of 18 January 2003 passed without significant progress, both the PIRA and the UVF had withdrawn from contacts with General de Chastelain and the other members of the IICD.

The latter part of 2002 and the start of 2003 were times when nationalists and republicans could perhaps legitimately suggest that, while republican paramilitary activity received (as it usually has) the larger proportion of media attention, loyalist paramilitary activity was the more potent. This included both internal feuding among loyalists and aggression against predominantly Catholic areas, such as in Larne and in Short Strand in Belfast.[211] Early in 2003 a feud between sections of the UDA came to a head. After Johnny Adair's licence was revoked yet again and he was taken back into custody, his supporters in the so-called 'C' company of the UDA were effectively forced out of the province. This not only effected at least a truce in the UDA feud, but facilitated the announcement in February 2003, on behalf of the organisation, of a twelve-month resumption of its ceasefire, although the British government has been reluctant to recognise it.

Progress towards decommissioning by the UDA still appeared unlikely, but this was still a more positive contribution to the context of ongoing discussions designed to break the deadlock, and reactivate the Executive and the Assembly. Once again a deadline appeared to be focusing minds. In this case there was a clear desire on the part of several affected parties to have the institutions operating again in advance of new Assembly elections, which were due in May 2003. As the timetable appeared to dictate that pro-agreement parties would have to come to some form of arrangement early in March, analysts were floating – often with surprising optimism – the prospect of a new 'Shrove (or Pancake) Tuesday Agreement'. The crux of the issue was, once again, framing a formula acceptable to both mainstream republicans and pro-agreement unionists: the prospect of the PIRA's disbandment had receded, but it seemed possible that more measures of republican decommissioning to satisfy the UUP leadership could be offered, if they could be met by concessions to republicans by the British government in areas such as policing and demilitarisation. Mainstream republicans' wish to avoid further disruption to the institutions of the GFA and unionists' wish for the availability of just such sanctions proved the sticking points. Early in March a four-week delay in the Assembly elections, until the end of May, was announced, in order to facilitate further discussions.

The start of US and British military action in Iraq in the intervening period was a major distraction from the local problems of Northern Ireland, especially from the British perspective, but it also offered some potentially helpful dynamics. Nationalist and republican parties in the North opposed the British government's support for US policy (as well as the more muted support offered by the Irish government), while unionist parties were supportive. Even Ian Paisley found a rare good word for Tony Blair at this time, although he qualified it with the suggestion that the Prime Minister should declare war on IRA as well as Iraqi 'terrorism'.[212] This set the

Provisionals at odds with elements of their lucrative support base in the United States, and suggested that a context of US events and influences – as after 11 September 2001 – might press the Provisionals into reconsidering their position and giving ground. A brief visit to Northern Ireland by President George W. Bush in April 2003 both further suggested this possibility and demonstrated the goodwill that Blair had purchased in the White House by his support of Bush's policy on Iraq.

In mid-spring, with the adjusted timetable of Assembly elections again imposing another deadline, the British and Irish governments became involved in intense attempts to break the deadlock. However, an exasperating quarrel broke out between the British government and PSF regarding the extent of the commitments that the Provisionals were prepared to make to a complete ending of paramilitary activities. The British government judged the Provisionals' statement on this score not rigorous enough, or at least not enough to be likely to satisfy Trimble and the UUP. In spite of repeated suggestions from the Irish government to the effect that agreement was nearly within reach, it proved elusive. The British government further delayed the Assembly elections until November, since it was not judged desirable to hold them during the marching season. This decision was welcome to the UUP, although disliked by both the Irish government and the Provisionals, and the latter, not for the first time, withdrew proposals for decommissioning that it had made in the course of negotiations. PSF's disappointment can have been only partly mollified by the decision of the British and Irish governments, even in spite of the lack of agreement, to publish their Joint Declaration.[213] This advanced the possibility of accelerated demilitarisation in Northern Ireland and inducements to PSF to take up membership of the new policing authority, from which it was still abstaining. The document, and parallel British and Irish government proposals, exerted more strain on pro-agreement unionists within the UUP.

In June 2003 Trimble faced yet another challenge within his party from his old rival Jeffrey Donaldson. The Joint Declaration framed the issue for Donaldson's attack on the peace process and Trimble's leadership, but other contemporary events could also have been used to illustrate its failing, including the continued evidence of anti-agreement paramilitary activity. At least one killing, in May 2003, was linked to the loyalists, and dissident republicans were still capable of endangering life in the province. In the vote held by the UUC on 16 June 2003, Donaldson's call for the outright rejection of the Joint Declaration was narrowly defeated. Trimble seemed to have emerged triumphant by a whisker yet again, but what was different this time was the apparent willingness of both rivals to burn their bridges. Donaldson and two other anti-agreement UUP MPs, David Burnside and Martin Smyth, resigned the party's whip and were in turn suspended by the party. It was no wonder that newspapers, both north and south of the border, drew little comfort from Trimble's latest narrow victory.[214]

A variety of developments over the summer suggested a more upbeat interpretation. The marching season proceeded relatively peacefully and a number of blows were struck against the dissident republicans, including, in the Republic, the sentencing of Michael McKevitt, apparently a leader of the Real IRA, to twenty years' imprisonment for directing terrorism; the decision of the British government to offer financial assistance to the civil case proposed by relatives of the Omagh victims; and the first arrest in the United Kingdom in the Omagh case. Loyalist paramilitaries were, however, still active. Another UUC vote on 6 September 2003 appeared to offer a narrow endorsement of Trimble's policy of demanding the loyalty of Donaldson, Smyth and Burnside, but crucially only a less cagily stated affirmation than had earlier been flagged was thus ratified, and only after the British and Irish governments had offered some strategically timed concessions to unionists over the proposed Independent Monitoring Commission on paramilitary activity, concessions that in turn met with the disapproval of PSF.

Five years after the GFA the relationship between unionists and republicans had resorted to a zero-sum pattern reminiscent of earlier times, while the possibility of at least *effective* co-operation between the still recalcitrant Donaldson and the anti-agreement DUP remained an ominous one for the beleaguered forces of pro-agreement unionism. The time for a breakthrough that might save the latter was surely at the very least running short.

CONCLUSION

The current suspension has only recently become the longest
disruption to the life of the Assembly and of the Executive:
following its election in June 1998, the Assembly at first operated on
a shadow basis and commenced full operations only in December
1999. Past experience could still make optimism tempting late into
2003. On the other hand, a sequence of hurdles remained and the
clearance of all of them in succession seemed unlikely. In the event
of the PIRA's satisfying the British and Irish governments with a
new offer, Trimble would still have had to persuade his party to
accept it. Delays and increasing distrust had made this significantly
harder. It was also highly unlikely that the PIRA would as yet
propose its own disbandment, as Trimble had suggested, and the
Joint Declaration, which was clearly not popular among unionists,
would probably also have to be sold to the UUP with the package.
Even disbanding the PIRA might, in any case, serve only to disguise
what might well become a considerable secession towards dissident
republicanism (see Chapter 1). Further, painstaking attempts to
obtain the requisite adherence of the UUP could have been derailed
at any moment by further revelations about the 'extra-curricular'
activities of Provisionals, in Colombia or elsewhere. This possibility
was live, not because the Provisionals are bound to have been up to
anything particularly pernicious compared to the loyalists, but
because Provisional activity is certain to get more attention. Even if
all these obstacles had been navigated and the current suspension
ended, there would have remained the major project for *both*
moderate nationalists *and* unionists of trying to minimise their losses
in the Assembly elections due in November. Even if the pro-
agreement unionists had been successful in this, which seemed
difficult, it would have been hard to see how even moderate
unionists could acquiesce in a situation where PSF became the
largest nationalist party in the Assembly and advanced Gerry
Adams as its candidate for Deputy First Minister. Moderate parties
would thus still have struggled to sustain working majorities within
their communities for a period that would bring stability. The British
government's decision to deny the large and growing body of anti-
agreement unionists – two thirds of all unionists, at least if some

opinion polls are to be trusted – the means of expressing themselves in Assembly elections for as long as possible was utterly predictable, in view of both the unfavourable context and all the evidence of the government's preferred strategy, which is to control as many political developments as possible through choreography and spin, and leave as little as possible to be determined at the grassroots (on this see also Chapter 3). This would prove to have been a short-sighted measure, since denying opponents of the government's policy a voice until the very last moment consistent with the rules was always likely only to exacerbate frustration with, and disengagement from, politics, and thus from the peace process (see postscript). The continued suspension of the institutions also appears to confirm the predictions of the anti-agreement parties, unionist and republican.

It thus remains hard to see where a substantial breakthrough will come from without a material shift of attitudes affecting more parties more dramatically than any of those that have appeared to rescue the process in its many previous hiatuses. Indeed, the kind of material shift required is likeliest to come from a shift to a different path of progress in Northern Ireland, or a dramatic delivery from outside forces, particularly a major error or series of errors on the part of anti-agreement forces, whether republican or unionist. This does not mean that the GFA, or the peace process, should be erased from history, or that there is no alternative to a resumption of conflict on a similar basis to that seen in the 1970s or the 1980s. It does mean, however, that it is surely not premature, in the specific sense intended, to contemplate failure, to interpret the causes and to examine what the alternatives were and are. Indeed, to deny the extent of the difficulties, a leading strategy in the recent past, could prove still more disastrous.

Reasons for Failure

To explore why the Northern Ireland peace process has failed – especially in relation to developments since the Good Friday Agreement (GFA) was signed – is to undertake a different task from explaining the sources of the conflict or advancing possible 'solutions' to it. Nevertheless, the former objective necessarily involves making assumptions about the underlying causes of the conflict and carries implications for possible lines of advance in Northern Ireland. There are several important scholarly discussions of proposed 'futures' for Northern Ireland on which this chapter draws.[1] However, the recent failure in the Northern Ireland peace process justifies and necessitates a further consideration of these proposals in the context of the latest evidence. New developments also call for evaluation of other reasons that have been, or can be, advanced for the failure of the process.

This chapter considers eight aspects of recent British and Irish political developments as possible causes of the failure of the peace process. Some of these are cognate to proposed 'solutions' for Northern Ireland that have been advanced for some time; others have been hinted at in recent scholarly or political analysis of the peace process. In some cases pairs of the eight can be considered as polar opposites of each other, derived from starkly differentiated academic or political perspectives. Elements of each of these eight possible causes are sorted into misdiagnoses of the cause of failure in the peace process; aspects of political responses to the Northern Ireland conflict that are, in the main, unavoidable or secondary consequences of the peace process, or of any negotiation process; proximate causes of failure or difficulty that are sources of problems in the process, but are themselves consequences of other locally apparent factors; and causes of the failure of the process, or of the Northern Ireland conflict, which appear to be or arise from exogenous factors. Clearly, it is most important to consider how to neutralise those influences that fall in the last of these categories if there is to be future political advance in Northern Ireland (a task that is pursued as part of a broader discussion in Chapter 4).

These eight possible explanations all carry implications for analysis of past actions of parties to the conflict, and prescriptions for future actions, including those of the two governments. Each also comprises a different form of negation of the simplest glib and popular explanation (or non-explanation) of the conflict, and reaction to the failure of the peace process: that there is a deep-seated binary opposition between two communities in Northern Ireland, which leads them inexorably into conflict.[2] This simple explanation can often carry the implication that nothing or little can be done about the conflict, especially by external actors, although there are also more intelligent bases on which the argument that there is no solution to the conflict can be advanced. This particular explanation, however, can be refuted on both empirical and theoretical bases.

There are two empirical arguments that refute it. First, contrary to appearances, Northern Ireland is not stuck in a timeless binary ethnic conflict but is a dynamic society changing over time. Second, and again contrary to appearances, the conflict itself has never directly involved more than a minority of the members of each of the communities who appear to be represented in it. In John Whyte's words, 'small numbers of extremists on each side can force a situation where, by reprisal and counter-reprisal, the peacefully inclined majority are obliged to seek protection from, and then give support to, the paramilitaries of their own community'.[3]

The theoretical explanation for rejecting this simplest explanation of the conflict concerns an understanding of the nature and function of identification, and its connections to the dynamism of Northern Irish and other societies. There is a temptation to assume that identity in Northern Ireland has fundamentally different characteristics from its appearance elsewhere, or at least in more stable societies. Frank Wright has written of the 'deterrence relationship' between the two communities in Northern Ireland: 'when polarisation forces us to look pessimistically at the worst thing coming from "their" side, that which is redeeming often disappears from our attention. And indeed history is put together as a string of incidents which explain and rationalise the endless circles of hostility.' Wright does not suggest

FIGURE 3
Cartoon by Garland, *Daily Telegraph*, 25 October 2001

"PEACE IN OUR TIME..."

that this process is unique to Northern Ireland, even if it may have
been unusually pervasive there. Other examples of this 'deterrence
relationship' can be found in neighbouring societies in this
nineteenth-century period and later.[4]

The theoretical implications of this argument go beyond mere
rejection of superficial views of the conflict and failure of the peace
process to suggesting how these developments should be evaluated,
and how appropriate policies should be formulated. As many
theorists have realised, it is more useful to think in terms of *processes
of identification* rather than identity. The former implies the
contingent, specific and limited nature of identification, while the
latter leads too easily to assumptions that the community or entity
identified with is pre-existing or ahistorical.[5] All identification, in
other words, involves an act of imaginative construction that creates
or alters a conception of a community.[6] On these assumptions, even
in Northern Ireland, and even if expressed in extreme modes, the
identifications of Whyte's 'peacefully inclined majority' retain
elements of contingency and specificity, and even, under ideal

conditions, reversibility. Identification, however, even if contingent, is not infinitely indeterminate and flexible. Importantly, it is possible to posit theoretically coherent post-positivist notions of identity, between the extremes of essentialism and the postmodernist assumption that all identity is a matter of individual choice. Indeed, any coherent view of identity probably must avoid these extremes. In theoretical or political analysis the most potent error to avoid is not the absolute application of essentialist or postmodern notions of identity, but their differential application to different communities. Thus, in the present context, while an essential basis to unionist identity might be assumed, nationalist identity is deconstructed; or vice versa. A post-positivist view would hold that it is possible to evaluate processes of identification according to their grounding in real or material conditions of existence shared between individuals.[7]

Logically, therefore, Anthony Smith's understanding in relation to national identification may be adapted and extended to other forms of identification: while it may be possible for political and cultural policies to pay only a limited deference to presented identities that have a minimal grounding in such shared conditions, it would be inadvisable to ignore or ride roughshod over those that have a considerable grounding, not least because such policies may in fact intensify or exacerbate such processes of identification.[8] Both policies that recognise a given political movement (such as unionism, nationalism, loyalism or republicanism) and its demands, and policies that ignore any of them, may be valid, depending on an empirical assessment on the above grounds of the set of identifications concerned. As is argued at several points throughout this chapter, anti-agreement unionism, more mainstream levels of dissatisfaction with the peace process and even dissident republicanism cannot simply be explained as the product of construction, manipulation, monolithic control exerted by political leaders or mass delusion, as each partly relate to individuals' and groups' lived experience in Northern Ireland before and after the GFA. This awareness might seem to make seeing a way through the current impasse in Northern Ireland still harder. However, the relationship between lived experience and such political formations, like other forms of identification, is fluid and variable, and understanding sources of the relationship in particular cases may help one to understand, and ultimately to navigate, the impasse.

CHOREOGRAPHING OF THE PEACE PROCESS

This has been an explanation for weakness in the peace process intimated by several commentators, notably Paul Dixon. In a complex and impressive argument Dixon suggests that the peace process can be perceived less in terms of a juxtaposition between two communities of 'nationalists', or 'republicans', and 'unionists', as represented by their leaders, and more as a juxtaposition between both sets of pro-agreement leaders and the two governments, on the one hand, and the wider population on the other. The leaders have a shared interest in selling the GFA to the population across the political divide, and collude in various forms of manipulation and presentation in order to bring this about. Specific strategies include ambiguity, most evident in the GFA itself; misdirection; moderation or retractions being presented as hard-line policies or aggression; and other unconfessed shifts of position. Thus ideologically committed supporters may be persuaded that their interests are not being neglected by the leaders, when in fact considerable ground may be being conceded in order to facilitate agreement with ostensibly bitter ideological foes. The ensuing complexities are well-explored in a discussion of the dynamic relationship between Gerry Adams, David Trimble and their respective support bases just before the first gesture of decommissioning by the Provisional IRA (PIRA) in October 2001:

> 'Concessions' or restraint by republicans could help unionist leaders deliver their supporters and vice versa, unionists could come to the aid of republicans. If the IRA were to begin the process of decommissioning they could ease Trimble's problems within unionism. Concessions by unionists on policing or public restraint in celebrating unionist 'victories' could help Adams [to] manage the republican movement. An outraged reaction by Adams to a proposal can help Trimble to convince unionists that their side is winning, but it may have an adverse effect on the Sinn Fein leader's support base. Sinn Fein's restrained and disciplined reaction to its own concessions has created problems for Trimble in trying to sell the process to unionists.[9]

Dixon concedes that some manipulation may have been beneficial in containing the conflict, but advances a 'democratic realist' position according to which recent attempts among political elites in Britain and Ireland to 'spin' or choreograph the peace process over the heads of the people whom the process primarily affects may have become excessive or counterproductive.[10] There are limits, Dixon suggests, to the degree to which manipulation and appearance can cover over real grievances and misgivings.[11]

If the peace process revolves around a few elite actors, with little engagement in politics for the masses, this would appear to undermine its rationale of drawing individuals into politics rather than into support of paramilitary activity. Further, some leaks of information about the extent of manipulation and choreography have unavoidably been disseminated, and have added to popular disillusionment.[12] Some earlier observations by other commentators implicitly endorse Dixon's analysis. Joseph Ruane and Jennifer Todd for instance had intimated that elites are moving more rapidly towards transcending the sectarian divide than is most of the population of Northern Ireland, so that the 'moderates' risk losing vital electoral support.[13] Even enthusiasts further admit that 'consociationalism', which features strongly in the Good Friday Agreement (and is discussed further below), is elitist and is thus detached from the control of the people of Northern Ireland.[14]

Dixon does not suggest that choreography was fatal, or was necessarily going to be fatal, to the peace process. He articulated these arguments just before the impasse in the Northern Ireland Assembly of October to November 2001, which forms an interesting test case for these arguments and one against which they broadly stand up well. To recapitulate: in the autumn of 2001, an extraordinary contrivance was adopted to avoid new elections to the Northern Ireland Assembly. The PIRA having just decommissioned a quantity of weaponry, the election of David Trimble as First Minister, with Mark Durkan as Deputy First Minister, was needed to reactivate the Northern Ireland Executive. On account of defections from pro- to anti-agreement unionism, this re-election was achieved within the constitutional deadline imposed by the GFA (or, more accurately, in technical breach of it) only by means of several MLAs redesignating themselves from 'other' to 'unionist'. Results of the eventual 2003 elections add to the impression that the anxiety to avoid new Assembly elections in 2001 was a confession of the truth that such elections at such a time would have prompted a significant statement of unionist dissatisfaction with the peace process: in other words, a possible admission that the peace process no longer has a workable mandate within the operation of the terms of the GFA.

Other aspects of choreography in the peace process can be discerned. As has been suggested, from an anti-agreement unionist perspective one might suggest that every time that the Provisionals have furnished any progress on the issue of decommissioning, not least in the autumn of 2001, there is evidence that what Peter Robinson of the DUP has described as 'secondary deals' have been offered the Provisionals by someone, frequently, apparently, the British government, involving corresponding concessions on other points. If such a suspicious trail indeed can be taken as indicating a sequence of secret arrangements, these would have entailed repeatedly going over the heads of the population of Northern Ireland, in the process disenfranchising particular groups, especially anti-agreement unionists, but also, it might be suggested, moderate nationalists. It can be suggested that it defeats the object of devolved democratic government in Northern Ireland, which is supposed to have been a major gain of the peace process, if core issues are to be resolved on such a basis. Arguably a braver and wiser course of action in October 2001 would have been to allow Assembly elections in order to re-engage relevant sections of the population with the political process, even at the price of a temporary or permanent majority within the unionist camp hostile to mainstream interpretations of the peace process. On the other hand, avoiding elections in the manner described and thus exacerbating frustrations in the electorate may have made a still larger anti-agreement vote possible at a later stage.

However, a couple of criticisms of Dixon's interpretation may be advanced. First, he is dependent for evidence of 'choreography' on media sources, when the media too are components of the industry of political manipulation. Further, the media, especially in Great Britain, have, with the best will in the world, a pretty poor record of representing 'what is really going on' accurately in the Northern Ireland conflict.[15] At the same time a contradictory tendency in Dixon's analysis takes a disconcerting turn in the direction of Jean Baudrillard, in a suggestion that no single reality necessarily exists in the conflict.[16] This links to a second serious criticism of Dixon: that he is in danger of denying or trivialising the salience and centrality of an underlying ideological conflict in Northern Ireland. Choreography may have particularly misguided manifestations, especially from a government such as 'New' Labour's, which is predisposed to 'spin', but the fact that it is felt necessary to attempt it is a symptom and not a cause of the problem. The procedure adopted in the autumn of 2001 by and with the encouragement of the Secretary of State, John Reid, was, after all, not utterly gratuitous, even if it may have been misguided. If anti-agreement unionists probably would have done well in an election, efforts to avoid an election had a rationale. Although, as Dixon implies, it is simplistic to suggest that the alternatives are a choreographed peace process and no peace process, the sources of the strength of anti-agreement unionism are surely at least in part substantive and are exacerbated by, but not created by, choreography. In other words, fundamental problems in the peace process either originated in another source besides choreography, or, perhaps, have always been there.

THE MISLEADING OF PUBLIC OPINION ABOUT THE PEACE PROCESS

One dimension of Dixon's argument is worth looking at a little more closely, since it is often articulated, although necessarily more crudely, by political actors within or close to the peace process itself. The idea that the peace process has been derailed because expectations have been raised by inaccurate or dishonest statements about its course by politicians can, clearly, be cognate to the view that the peace process has been fatally over-choreographed: both involve political elites manipulating and deceiving electorates and followers. However, the diagnosis that the peace process has failed because of, to put it crudely, lies and betrayals, however, rather than involving multiple relationships between different leaders and their different groups of followers, has a specific and important dimension that pertains to what leaders of a particular faction or group tell their followers or kindred spirits. Party leaders, it is suggested, have failed to prepare followers for taking the steps necessary to the continuance of the process that might be difficult for the ideologically committed to stomach by falsely or incorrectly intimating that such steps are not requisite according to the letter or spirit of the GFA or the process. Mainstream republicans, for instance, have been criticised for failing to prepare 'volunteers' for what they have publicly insisted was the psychological and emotional trauma of giving up weapons. Moderate unionists, meanwhile, have proved unable to stick strictly to the formula of 'no guns, no government', or have found themselves sitting down in negotiation or government with Martin McGuinness, the very man whom they had previously labelled the 'godfather of godfathers' of terrorism.[17] The upshot has been that steps necessary to the peace process have not been taken, have been taken in a grudging way that undermines trust, or have been taken at the price of frustrating followers' expectations, leading to supporters' cries of betrayal and quests for more reliable political alternatives, usually in anti-agreement parties.

The allegation that political opponents are not keeping, or have not kept, to the letter or spirit of the GFA is on the lips of almost every party to the GFA itself. Most obviously, the Provisionals have been attacked for their reluctance to decommission, and over the continuation of paramilitary violence and preparation for violence, such as intelligence-gathering, by republican actors. Yet these are by no means the only alleged breaches. Republicans point to the undoubted continuation of loyalist violence, and complain that David Trimble has continually held them to ransom, notably by threatening to resign from, or refusing to join, the power-sharing Executive and by his barring of Provisional Sinn Féin (PSF) representatives from meetings of the North–South Ministerial Council in the autumn of 2000. British ministers, especially Tony Blair and Peter Mandelson, were criticised by republicans for the suspension of the Assembly and the Executive in February 2000, and over the limits of demilitarisation; by nationalists and republicans for alleged obstruction of policing reforms; and by unionists and other opponents for releasing prisoners on licence in advance of the decommissioning of paramilitaries' weapons.

The danger of this situation, which, it can be argued, has proved terminal to the peace process, is that all these sharp practices (if such they are) interlock in a way to imprison the parties concerned and stifle progress. The lack of loyalist decommissioning is treated as an obstacle to the PIRA's decommissioning. The lack of decommissioning by the PIRA, or of sufficiently rapid and thorough decommissioning, leads to unionist pressure for limits to policing reform, among other developments. The limits to policing reform have been used by PSF as an excuse for it to give only half-hearted support to the pursuit of dissident republicans. The strength of such dissidents leads to understandable reluctance on the part of the British government to advance measures of demilitarisation, which in turn proves another obstacle to republican hardliners' acceptance of decommissioning, leading to further unionist suspicion of republicans, and so on until the fragile trust is lost.

While some allegations of breaches of the GFA may be spurious, part of the problem is that key sections of the GFA itself are, first, very vague and, second, have been read, possibly with good intentions, but eccentrically. The main example, and the source of many difficulties over the past few years, is the passage in the GFA pertaining to the decommissioning of paramilitaries' weapons. It is worth citing the relevant section in full:

> All participants accordingly reaffirm their commitment to the total disarmament of all paramilitary organisations. They also confirm their intention to continue to work constructively and in good faith with the Independent [International] Commission [on Decommissioning], and to use any influence they may have, to achieve the decommissioning of all paramilitary arms within two years following endorsement in referendums North and South of the agreement[,] and in the context of the implementation of the overall settlement.[18]

Many parties to the GFA seem unable to agree upon, or even to understand, this passage. A key source of difficulty seems to be Tony Blair's speech in Belfast on 14 May 1998. In a relevant passage Blair stated:

> People want to know that, if these parties are going to benefit from proposals in the agreement, such as accelerated prisoner releases and ministerial posts, their commitment to democratic non-violent means must be established, in an objective,

meaningful and verifiable way. Those who have used the twin tactics of the ballot box and the gun must make a clear choice. There can be no fudge between democracy and terror.

The agreement is what has to be implemented, in all its parts. In clarifying whether the terms and spirit of the agreement are being met, and whether violence has genuinely been given up for good, there are a range of factors to take into account:

first and foremost, a clear and unequivocal commitment that there is an end to violence for good, on the part of republicans and loyalists alike, and that the so-called war is finished, done with, gone; that, as the agreement says, non-violence and exclusively peaceful and democratic means are the only means to be used;

that, again as the agreement expressly states, the ceasefires are indeed complete and unequivocal: an end to bombings, killings and beatings, claimed or unclaimed; an end to targeting and procurement of weapons; progressive abandonment and dismantling of paramilitary structures actively directing and promoting violence; full co-operation with the Independent Commission on decommissioning, to implement the provisions of the agreement; and no other organisations being deliberately used as proxies for violence.

These factors provide evidence upon which to base an overall judgment – a judgment which will necessarily become more rigorous over time. What is more, I have decided that they must be given legislative expression directly and plainly in the legislation to come before Parliament in the coming weeks and months.

We are not setting new preconditions or barriers.

This speech can be associated with the letter that Blair gave to Trimble on 10 April to ease the latter's last minute doubts as the GFA was being signed. Blair suggested in the letter that he supported changes to the provisions of the GFA pertaining to prisoner releases if these were 'shown to be ineffective'; and that he understood that decommissioning should begin straight away.[19]

In conjunction with the speech just quoted and some pledges that Blair made on 20 May 1998, he seemed to many to be saying that he would not allow access to ministerial posts in the Northern Ireland Executive for members of groups attached to paramilitary organisations – i.e., for immediate purposes, PSF – or continue to release paramilitary prisoners on licence ahead of the fulfilment of prison terms, unless the paramilitary organisations concerned implemented strict principles of non-violence and made an immediate commencement on the decommissioning of weapons. If this was the intention, Blair made promises beyond the terms of the GFA itself. Part of the subsequent difficulty was that at this time Blair was co-operating with members of the Conservative opposition, such as William Hague, its then leader, Sir Patrick Mayhew, a former Secretary of State for Northern Ireland, and Andrew MacKay, the then 'shadow' Secretary of State, in urging inhabitants of Northern Ireland, especially unionists, to vote 'yes' in the referendum on the GFA in May 1998. Blair's subsequent inability or unwillingness to enforce the Conservative and unionist readings of his pledges led to considerable bitterness, and allegations of betrayal from Conservatives and unionists.[20] Interpretations of the peace process put forward, at the same time by political leaders in the Irish Republic, including the Taoiseach, Bertie Ahern, have been similarly criticised.[21]

Interpreted literally, it is not clear that Blair in fact was making the promises later imputed to him, at least in his speech. Even apart from the studied 'get out clause' – 'We are not setting new preconditions or barriers' – and the curious tension between seemingly listing an array of activities in terms of absolute prohibition and weakly describing them as 'factors to take into account', it is noticeable that Blair declared that he was looking for a commitment to non-violence 'on the part of republicans and loyalists alike'. The subsequent and interminable claims by PSF that its commitment to non-violence was rendered harder by continued loyalist violence, while they have been dismissed by many political, journalistic and academic[22] commentators, were therefore, in this sense, consistent with Blair's speech. Trimble's reliance on Blair's letter of 10 April has also been depicted by one hostile critic, Brendan O'Leary, as at least politically inept: 'Communications from UK premiers do not, of course, have the force of law – outside of the ranks of New Labour!'[23] The point is that PSF did not sign up to Blair's letter to Trimble in the way that it did to the GFA, so from

10 April 1998 onwards Trimble and PSF's leaders have had different conceptions of the parties' obligations under the GFA. Nevertheless, even if Blair's letter was a lesser guarantee than Trimble hoped, it can be argued that, even if Blair did not make the pledges understood at the time, he came painfully close to doing so and made little effort to correct 'misunderstanding' of his declarations, at least until after the support of the majority of unionists for the GFA was secured a few days later. Given the marginal nature of this majority support, this does seem like sharp practice by the Prime Minister.

In this sense unionists' resentment of a perceived betrayal by Blair and their subsequent insistence that the Prime Minister stick to what was understood to be his word were, arguably, legitimate. The legacy of Blair's mixed messages at this time can be seen, for instance, in an interview given by David Trimble to the BBC in June 2002, when he suggested that the PIRA should have given up its weapons within a certain time frame.[24] It was also evident in a suggestion in an interview given by Andrew MacKay in January 2001, when he was still shadow Secretary of State, that the Provisionals were under a 'straightforward' obligation to respond to the licensed release of their prisoners by decommissioning weapons.[25] Where both MacKay and Trimble erred, and contributed with Blair to the confusion and falsely raised expectations of their supporters, was in the suggestion in both cases that the Provisionals were subject to these obligations under the terms of the GFA. Both Trimble and MacKay's statements were legitimate interpretations of Blair's speech and other declarations, but, irrespective of the question of the integrity of the Prime Minister, both MacKay and Trimble should have been capable of consulting the GFA themselves, and thus discerning that it does not literally place the Provisionals under the obligation suggested. MacKay may also have been confused by the fact that two-year time scales are mentioned in the clauses in the GFA relating both to prisoner releases and to decommissioning, but the two sections of the GFA are nonetheless phrased differently, and without close and explicit links.

If Trimble and MacKay's readings of the GFA are eccentric, however, they are positively close to the mark compared to a suggestion made by Martin McGuinness to a British radio audience, around the time of the referendum of 1998, that the agreement meant that a united Ireland would arrive in five years.[26] In terms of raising political supporters' expectations of the agreement, MacKay and Trimble were, compared to McGuinness, and other republicans stone-cold sober. Subsequent public declarations by McGuinness have shifted this time frame somewhat, suggesting that Ireland should be united by the 100th anniversary of the Easter Rising, in 2016, but this too seems like rather wishful thinking.

In fairness to the politicians, however, it must be conceded that these crucial clauses of the GFA are so vague that even intelligent academic observers have great difficulty in understanding them, as two examples will demonstrate. First, Brendan O'Leary rejects Trimble's famous formulation of the unionist position as 'no guns, no government'. O'Leary claims that this was unwarranted 'on any reasonable interpretation of the text of the agreement' and that, from late 1999, 'each move on Sinn Féin's part merely led the UUP [Ulster Unionist Party] to request more'. Where O'Leary errs is in claiming that the GFA is 'clear' on decommissioning. In fact, as has been shown, it suggests that relevant parties will 'use any influence they may have, to achieve the decommissioning of all paramilitary arms within two years following endorsement in referendums North and South of the agreement[,] and in the context of the implementation of the overall settlement'. The phrase 'in the context of the implementation of the overall settlement' is in fact sufficiently unclear to warrant Trimble's suggestion that the PIRA's weapons should have been decommissioned before members of PSF took up ministerial posts, if only as much as it justifies PSF's evident desire that the PIRA's decommissioning should occur only after as many other parties had effected as many obligations anticipated in the GFA as possible.[27] On the other hand, Henry Patterson suggests that 'under the Agreement the decommissioning of paramilitary weapons was supposed to be completed by May 2000'.[28] In fact the proviso regarding 'the context of the implementation of the overall settlement' makes it a good deal less simple than this and, in any case, Patterson discusses decommissioning throughout the relevant section of his book as if it relates only to the PIRA's decommissioning, which surely is unwarranted.[29]

The fact that relevant actors have not fulfilled the agreement, or have misunderstood the agreement, or have raised followers' expectations about the agreement and thus exacerbated subsequent disillusionment, cannot therefore just be related to deliberate deception by political leaders, although there do seem to have been some clear cases of dramatically wishful thinking in just about every pro-agreement political location. Instead, the foregoing discussion highlights the fact that the GFA is extremely vague in key particulars, thus rendering possible numerous later readings and inspiring sources of disagreement between its signatories as much as it has signified agreement. Indeed, there seems to have been misaligned perceptions from the first as to which documents comprised the 'settlement', specifically over the status of Blair's letter to Trimble. In other words, the agreement was always less of a breakthrough than it appeared, or than the international media made it appear. Those involved in drafting the GFA and other aspects of the settlement are perhaps not to be blamed for this. It is at least arguable that, without a level of imprecision, even a symbolic accord between the configuration of parties involved would not have been possible. Without Blair's letter Trimble and the other members of the UUP delegation would have had great difficulty accepting the agreement: after all, certain members of the party anyway rejected it, including, most crucially, Peter Weir and Jeffrey Donaldson.[30] Yet, if the terms of Blair's letter had been fully incorporated in the agreement, the approval of PSF, which was in the event not even achieved until after a number of PIRA prisoners were released by the British government as a goodwill gesture, could not have been achieved. Without Blair's apparent pledges of May 1998, majority unionist ratification of the agreement, which has barely ever clearly been replicated, would probably not have been achieved. Although it can therefore be suggested that the peace process has now failed, and that this failure was implicit in the limits of the GFA, it could be argued that those limits were imposed by the nature of the conflict anyway and that, in its very vagueness, the GFA has achieved several years' diminution of certain categories of violence, a result that, from a humanitarian standpoint, cannot be dismissed. On the other hand, it is arguable that misreadings of the situation by politicians, however profitable in the short term, have proved counterproductive in the medium term by more rapidly creating a more widespread sense of disillusionment with the peace process, especially among unionists.

Like the choreographing and manipulation of the peace process by the same actors, the errors – and perhaps also the deliberate deceptions – effected by politicians from Great Britain, Northern Ireland and the Irish Republic in relation to the peace process have been a proximate cause of its failure, but not an ultimate cause. It is equally arguable that such creative interpretations and misinterpretations were a condition of even the limited level of accord achieved in the peace process, or, perhaps, in any alternative negotiation process. In other words, perhaps the peace process succeeded in the first place to an extent more limited than commonly appreciated, so its failure should not be surprising and should require proportionately little explanation.

THE ENTRENCHING OF COMMUNALISM THROUGH THE INSTITUTIONS OF THE GFA

The GFA, as is well-known, contains important 'consociational' features, even if not all features of the agreement cohere to this model. Consociationalism is a system in use in the government of a number of societies. Typically, under the system, features of the government and organisation of a society recognise a sharp communal division or divisions in that society, and thus treat individuals primarily or additionally as members of those communities, in order to ensure a proportional measure of political and social representation for each community. Each community may also possess rights of veto over aspects of political and cultural life that particularly affect it. Key elements of consociation or similar arrangements in the institutions of the GFA, and subsequent arrangements, include the operation of the d'Hondt formula in appointments to posts in the Executive and to the Assembly's committee chairs and deputy chairs;[31] the requirement of parallel or weighted voting within the Assembly; the facilities for communities to make representation to the Parades Commission on marches and parades; and the attempt to enforce ratios by community on recruiting to the new police force. While the leading theoretical advocate of consociationalism is Arend Lijphart,[32] the scholars who have most energetically pressed for the application of the model to Northern Ireland are Brendan O'Leary and John McGarry.[33]

The rationale for consociation in Northern Ireland is that without some form of veto for the smaller nationalist community it would be overwhelmed by the numbers of the majority, as was the case before 1969, which is what gave rise to the conflict in the first place.[34] In several respects, however, the observable dynamics of Northern Ireland since the GFA was signed suggest that consociationalism may have had negative effects, and theoretical criticisms of consociationalism have been importantly advanced as a possible explanation of these facts. Empirically, it can be argued that encouraging political action by individuals as members of communities in relation, for instance, to parades has sharpened the conflict between communities on such issues. The Orange Order, for instance, complains that, if it is to be prevented from entering areas of predominantly nationalist or Catholic residence during its marches, a system of extreme communal segregation or even apartheid will be fostered. It is relevant to note that in some parts of Northern Ireland the degree of residential segregation between the communities has recently increased. On the other hand, some nationalists argue that the number of Orange marches in Northern Ireland has actually increased in recent years. Regular rioting in North Belfast and the stand-off around Holy Cross Girls' Primary School in the autumn of 2001 (discussed in Chapter 2) can be presented as further examples of communal conflict arising since the agreement was signed, and incidents aroused by the rivalries between supporters of the two Glasgow football clubs Rangers and Celtic (an aspect of ethnic conflict owing to the historic religious affiliations of each club) do not seem to have diminished. An empirical critic of consociationalism could also point to the fact that the workings of the d'Hondt formula sometimes appear to have been a sticking point in the Assembly, notably in the autumn of 2001. In spite of O'Leary's optimism,[35] it can be argued that at least from 2001 voting patterns in Northern Ireland have become more determined by religious affiliation rather than less, the decline in the numbers of votes cast for the Alliance Party of Northern Ireland (APNI) being particularly a symptom. McGarry and O'Leary also seem to be wrong in anticipating the decline of the DUP's electoral impact, at least if the results of recent elections in 2001 and 2003 are anything to go by.[36] David Trimble's comments in March 2002 about the 'pathetic sectarian, mono-ethnic, mono-cultural' nature of the Irish Republic and the ensuing republican outrage also seem symptomatic of an inflamed state of ethnic rivalry in politics. (That republican outrage itself is not without its amusing aspects: after all, it is barely a decade and a half ago that mainstream republicans were entirely denying the legitimacy of the Irish Republic, to the defence of which they now leap, a legacy of which is the fact that one still finds republican intellectuals making comments little different from Trimble's.) [37]

As well as these manifestations of ethnic conflict, a recent facet of ethnic display in Northern Ireland politics have also been linked to the cultural balkanisation allegedly effected, or intensified, by the peace process. This is the recent attempt by some unionists and loyalists to depict themselves as expressions of, and to sponsor, an 'Ulster Scots' culture. Just as the peace process has been associated with nationalists winning space to express their culture, under the rubric of 'parity of esteem' for the two traditions in Northern Ireland, so these unionists' and loyalists' efforts to associate themselves with a distinct Ulster-Scots tradition can be read as an attempt to reclaim cultural space and recognition, although it can also or instead be treated as a fracturing and diversification within unionism. It is suggestive that attempts are made to read and thus justify unionist agendas in the peace process, both pro- and anti-agreement, as expressions of this Ulster-Scots tradition:

> Some of the attitudes and attributes, both good and bad, of the present-day more inclusive Protestant and broadly unionist community in Northern Ireland probably derive from old Dissenter traits and tendencies, and may be better understood in the light of the history of the major Ulster-Scot and largely Presbyterian component within it.[38]

Ulster-Scots identity also appears in certain loyalist murals. The extent to which its articulation is a response to successful Irish nationalist claims for cultural recognition is indicated by the recent political prominence of what is described as either the Ulster-Scots language or dialect, given that the Irish language and the pursuit of its equality of status are closely linked in Northern Ireland to the republican agenda.[39] The often politicised nature of Ulster-Scots identity is indicated in the fact that it is hardly particularly clear as to its own historical roots. Whereas the 'Scots Irish epic' focuses heavily on the role of Presbyterians from Ireland in eighteenth-century America, especially at the time of the American revolution, the people concerned would rarely have described themselves as 'Scotch Irish' and still less as 'Ulster Scots', since the construction of such a separate 'race' took place in the nineteenth century, when they had even fewer separate characteristics.[40] That the 'Ulster-Scots tradition'appears little less factual than Irish nationalist or republican narratives of history further suggests its derivative nature, as does the increased figuring of the role of the 36th Ulster Division at the Battle of the Somme in 1916 in loyalist versions of history, especially those deployed by the Ulster Volunteer Force (UVF), as a form of 'blood sacrifice' analogous to the republican iconography that surrounds the Easter Rising of the same year.[41]

`There is an argument that it is wrong to protect the rights of one or other community in Northern Ireland, since that community's culture is not worth preserving or, alternatively, since it does not have one. In dismissing this nearly always partisan assertion Stephen Howe articulates very helpfully the second and more important theoretical basis for linking the recent features of Northern Ireland's society and politics just discussed to the consociational aspects of the GFA:

> The central ... objection to an approach based on 'cultural traditions' and 'parity of esteem', however, is that it freezes – potentially in perpetuity – the perception of their being two fixed, opposed blocs in Northern Ireland. Each of these is treated as an ensemble of culture, tradition, and political allegiance, with far more internal homogeneity and less permeable borders than is in fact the case. At best, such an approach restricts choice (often apparently assuming that everyone is a member from birth of one or other 'tradition' and will remain so), and may militate against the further development of an open, fully plural civil society. At worst, it may perpetuate or even deepen the sectarianism it is intended to overcome. It is probably incompatible with moves in such directions as towards a more integrated system of education in

Northern Ireland, which many commentators have viewed as crucial to long-term social peace.[42]

Further, it has been argued that these 'cultural traditions' are thus encouraged to 'unproductive competition' for cultural resources, a process that 'ends up being damaging to all'.[43] Howe suggests instead that 'frameworks urging critical interrogation of one's group identity' may be a more promising line of advance.[44] It can also be suggested that it is desirable to emancipate individuals from tradition, or at least from monolithic control by tradition's self-appointed guardians, to deconstruct an imposed binary opposition within Northern Ireland that has an endemic tendency to produce conflict, and to facilitate greater cross-community dialogue and interaction. Such proposals are to be associated in particular with the 'emancipatory' approach to the conflict of Joseph Ruane and Jennifer Todd,[45] with Alan Finlayson,[46] with Mairéad Nic Craith,[47] and, as Howe implies, with advocates of integrated education.[48]

Implicitly, therefore, it is suggested, consociational features of the peace process can be held responsible for its failure by exacerbating tensions between two stereotyped communities and thus giving rise to more conflicts. There is, as we have seen, evidence for this view. This communalist or communitarian approach (and therefore its advocates, such as McGarry and O'Leary) seems particularly to be associated with the Social Democratic and Labour Party (SDLP), although the measure is attacked on both the left and right.[49] That the complaint that 'the provisions of the Belfast Agreement entrench communalism, rather than transcend it' should have attractions to broadly unionist sources such as the *Daily Telegraph* and assorted writers in the magazine *Fortnight* should not surprise us,[50] and suggests one of the objections to the view that the consociationalism of the peace process has caused its failures. More broadly, one could perhaps turn Howe's argument on its head: at a political level the argument that it is desirable to deconstruct the hegemony of the unionist and nationalist identities can be too much motivated by a partisan desire particularly to deconstruct one or other of those identities.

This certainly seems to be a motivation among some unionists and their sympathisers, for whom a first-part-the-post electoral system, as is used in the United Kingdom, including Northern

Ireland, for parliamentary elections, has an obvious attraction, since unionists are in a narrow majority in the province.[51] One of the most bizarre interventions in the debate held in the British House of Commons in December 2001 on extending Westminster facilities to PSF MPs came from the maverick Conservative Eric Forth. Forth argued that, since the first-past-the-post system was obviously the best, if it left non-PSF voters in West Belfast unrepresented at Westminster, owing to the refusal of that constituency's MP, Gerry Adams, to accept the parliamentary oath, that was just tough.[52] Similarly, when addressing the Conservative Party's conference in 2001, David Trimble took the opportunity to link the allegedly ponderous response of certain continental European states that had coalition governments to the foreign policy imperatives of the 'war against terrorism' with his own misgivings about the fact that Northern Ireland was governed through a power-sharing coalition.[53] Doubtless the temptation to present such concerns before an audience of Conservatives, who have been persistent opponents of proportional representation and coalition governments for ideological and more interested reasons, was great, but such declarations at such a time do beg the question whether Trimble's inner wish is to effect a system of majority rule by unionists in Northern Ireland analogous to the discriminatory and disastrous regime before 1972, which, arguably, evoked the need for consociationalism. Conversely, an over-critical reading of some of Alan Finlayson's work could perhaps discern particular attention being paid to the deconstruction of loyalist identity.[54] More reasonably, it can be suggested that there is a popular argument that unionism should not be protected because it is less legitimate than Irish nationalism, and is inextricably linked to supremacism, racism and sexism, an argument that has a destructive and divisive potential of its own (see below).

A defence of the entrenched communalism of the GFA (if such it is) is thus that the very nature of the criticisms increasingly levelled at it show that such an uneasy compromise is needed: rather as in the familiar game of prisoner's dilemma, neither tradition is showing any willingness first to undergo deconstruction, lest the other community remain intact. Assertions that any given manifestation of Ulster-Scots, nationalist or any other identity is fictitious merely help liberals to underestimate the difficulty of transcending the communal divide.[55]

As Colin Harvey has put it, 'Irish nationalists and British unionists really do exist', and their voting preferences have not just been 'dictated by "ethno-political" entrepreneurs' since the GFA.[56] Loyalist and republican parades, for instance, were increasing in number even before the first PIRA ceasefire[57] and, although they did become more contested with the peace process, controversies were known before. McGarry and O'Leary further argue that 'when ethnic communities feel secure the pressure to sustain ethnic solidarity is reduced, and the greater the likelihood that a more pluralist politics can emerge within them. This pattern may occur within Northern Ireland, within both communities, rather than across them.' If this seems a little too optimistic as things stand, their less audacious rejection of the view that consociationalism 'necessarily institutionalizes ethnic hierarchies . . . [, which] rests on the erroneous premise that the sole alternative to liberal individualism is some form of racist apartheid', seems nearer the truth.[58]

A different method of approach might suggest that the GFA does not, in some senses, entrench communalism enough. This possibility is suggested by a perhaps uncharacteristic comment made by Gerry Adams in New York on 3 February 2002: 'I don't think [that] we can force upon unionism an all-Ireland state which doesn't have their assent or consent and which actually reflects their sense of being uncomfortable.' A reading of this comment, which was applauded by, among others, David Ervine, the leader of the Progressive Unionist Party (PUP), suggests a willingness to make the achievements of a united Ireland conditional on the approval of a majority of 'unionists'.[59] (Incidentally, Adams's comment seems confused on this point, since surely, if 'unionists' were to approve a united Ireland, they would cease to be unionists: perhaps he meant 'Protestants' when he said 'unionism'.) Fear of being forced into a united Ireland in the near future, on the back of its marginal approval in a ballot of all of the inhabitants of Northern Ireland (shortly, in the relevant disproportionate fear, after the population had become majority Catholic), is surely one reason for the high levels of resistance to political change among unionists and, to an extent, for loyalist violence. If Adams were to mean such a proposal seriously (and, contrary to Bew, Gibbon and Patterson's uncharacteristic faith in Adams at this point,[60] it seems highly likely that on the specific occasion in question he was merely attempting to impress an international media audience with his supposed moderation), and if he could carry a large number of republicans with him on it, this would surely therefore be a force for the diminution of tensions and violence in Northern Ireland. An equivalent unionist guarantee to nationalists about political change, although it would need to be framed differently, would also have a positive influence. The significant point, however, is that, while the GFA suggests the possibility, or indeed the likelihood, of a border poll, or several such polls, in Northern Ireland, it contains no provision for the results to be subjected in this way to assessment according to a d'Hondt formula, i.e., for change to be confirmed only if a majority in both communities approves. In this specific sense, one could argue that the GFA is not communalist enough. Yet it was surely all that could be expected in this regard, since Adams did not speak for all republicans or nationalists in his fleeting moment of moderation in February 2002.

It is arguable that the consociational features of the peace process have exacerbated certain tensions in Northern Ireland, but, contrary to increasingly current arguments, it is surely a more convincing argument to suggest that the implementation of these features was a reflection of the underlying conflict, rather than the cause of the failure of the peace process. In any case, there is an opposite argument: that the appealing liberal desire to transcend, and free individuals from, the shackles of communal or ethnic bonds is disturbing Northern Ireland's society as much as the bonds themselves.

NAIVE LIBERAL OPTIMISM ABOUT THE TRANSCENDING OF SECTARIANISM

It is a liberal article of faith, in relation not just to Northern Ireland, but to all modern multi-ethnic societies, that cross-community contact promotes tolerance and understanding. However, as Paul Mitchell notes, contact, particularly in its most forceful manifestations, is as necessary for sectarianism and prejudice as it is for tolerance and understanding.[61] Indeed, researchers such as Peter Shirlow have suggested that encouraged cross-communal activities in Northern Ireland may not always have much impact in eradicating sectarianism.[62] In some cases, bringing people together from different communities into contact actually appears, not to open minds, but to lead closed minds to seek and find confirmation for stereotypes and resentment.[63] This suggestion does, after all, conform to some readily observable historical experiences. When the first non-white inhabitants moved into any given previously all-white neighbourhood in western Europe in the late twentieth century, for instance, reactions were not always solely in the form of philosophical reflections along the lines of 'I never realized they were so like us . . .'[64]

This implies an interpretation of the failure of the peace process that would suggest that attempts to press communities into dialogue or close coexistence have been grounded in a liberal optimism that is ignorant of the actual nature of life in Northern Ireland. According to such an interpretation, liberal optimism could be criticised on three grounds. First, such attempts to create dialogue may have been well-intended but premature. Second, and more worryingly, such efforts may have exacerbated tensions by forcing individuals into contacts that they would never freely have made. Third, and cognately, a dialogic or liberal approach can be criticised for forcing parties into negotiations as equals when they are in fact unequal. This may have a number of detrimental consequences, including under-representing certain political tendencies, over-representing others without a real mandate and exposing moderates to disagreeable political risks by forcing them to compromise with extremists.

Examples of all these fears have been voiced in respect of the peace process. Notably, for instance, in late 1997 many observers were critical of the policies of the British and Irish governments in pressing unionists to negotiate with republican representatives. One can suggest, however, that examples of critical perspectives on naïve liberal optimism, especially in its British manifestations, in the relevant literature are by no means marked by one cast of unionism: Steve Bruce[65] and Patrick O'Farrell,[66] for instance, seem to advance similar views in this respect from very different perspectives.

There are two international dimensions of liberal optimism that, one can suggest, may be unhelpful in Northern Ireland, or even a positive hindrance. One is the broader globalisation framework: the argument, stated simply, that since national or ethnic identity has an increasingly reduced meaning in a world undergoing communication and transport revolutions, the ethnic divide in Northern Ireland will also cease to have a meaning. Alan Finlayson makes this argument in an interesting passage:

> Set against a background of an increasingly globalised culture, where a citizen of Northern Ireland is as likely to be watching satellite television as waving flags in an Orange march, it seems that the possibility of maintaining rigid definitions of political identity is waning. As people got used to a situation of non-violence they were apt to go about expressing themselves in a number of ways, and through a variety of cultural and political practices, that cannot be reduced to a binary opposition of Catholic/Protestant, Nationalist/Unionist.[67]

This assumption that nationalism in particular, and ethnic and national identity more generally, must inevitably decay in the modern (or postmodern) era is highly questionable, and runs counter to some of the most interesting theoretical work on the question,[68] as well as to readily identifiable manifestations, such as the political support in assorted locations for Jörg Haider, Jean-Marie Le Pen, the British National Party and Islamic fundamentalism. What makes Finlayson's passage such a good example of liberal optimism, however, is the casual flagging of satellite television as a symbol of growing liberation from the dead tradition represented by such institutions as the Orange Order. As is common in academic work influenced by postmodern methodologies, this loses sight of the question of agency: globalisation becomes a discourse (benign, in this analysis) operating beyond or exclusive of any individual's interests, so that the question of who controls forces of globalisation, such as satellite television, becomes irrelevant. This is erroneous, because nationalists, nationalists' allies and commercial parasites upon nationalism are as capable as internationalists of controlling and manipulating such institutions. The most powerful satellite television company in the British context is BSkyB, headed by Rupert Murdoch, who is also the controller of print media, in Britain and elsewhere, that have a well-deserved reputation for xenophobia and for inflaming, not deconstructing, monolithic and crudely constructed ethnic or national identities. Technological development also does not inhibit politically antagonistic forms of intolerant nationalism: PSF, for example, has proved quite capable of keeping its website accessible and updated.

A second international dimension of optimistic liberal views of Northern Ireland is specifically European. A number of scholars have recently articulated the view that the existence and influence of the European Union have recently been positive factors for Anglo-Irish settlement. There is also a view that, in the context of an emerging closer and larger European union, national boundaries between member-states will gradually cease to have the same importance; in particular, the boundary between Northern Ireland and the Irish Republic will cease to be a cause of perturbation to nationalists, and greater unity within the island of Ireland will not appear so threatening in a political sense to unionists.[69] This argument assumes that an ever closer European union will not only continue to evolve, which is itself debatable,[70] but also include the United Kingdom and the Irish Republic on an equivalent basis. As the United Kingdom (including Northern Ireland) is now not using the euro as its principal medium of exchange, while the Republic is, this is currently not the case. In the intervening period, more importantly, the question of closer European union is divisive, not primarily because of objections from Irish republicans, although there certainly are some, but because of a lack of attraction to unionists. Even if there is a sense in which logically there should be greater enthusiasm for the project among those committed to the union between Great Britain and Northern Ireland,[71] unionists' actual objections to closer European union range from a concern that diminution of the United Kingdom's sovereign control over its fiscal and monetary policy will jeopardise the British Treasury's subvention to Northern Ireland, to the eschatological notion that the European Union, underpinned as it is by the Treaty of Rome, must embody the Antichrist.[72] It is suggestive that the leading political advocate of such a 'European' solution to the Northern Ireland problem has been the SDLP's former leader, John Hume,[73] and that its intellectual sage, Richard Kearney, seems to inhere nationalist assumptions in at least a more diluted form, including the view that unionists need to be as self-critical about their positions as Hume is in relation to nationalism.[74]

However, a limitation of critiques of liberal optimism relevant to the present discussion is that these critiques demonstrate far more clearly that liberal assumptions are unlikely to 'solve' the Northern Ireland conflict than that such assumptions have caused the failure of the peace process. Moreover, proposals for the alleviation of the conflict put forward on intellectual assumptions similar to the critique are usually not particularly persuasive. It is relevant, for instance, to consider the idea of repartition in Ireland, the most cogent advocate of which is Liam Kennedy,[75] although it is notably also conceded by Arend Lijphart, as well as by McGarry and O'Leary, to have possible value as a 'default' solution.[76] The objections to repartition are familiar. It seems highly unlikely to remove all disaffected minorities either side of the new border and it is likely to leave still smaller minorities feeling more frustrated and isolated, at least without a large-scale transfer of populations, which would itself be extremely difficult to execute peacefully. The transformation of Northern Ireland into an independent state is favoured by some writers, such as Tom Nairn, who reject naïve liberal optimism as represented by 'New' Labour,[77] but notably not by Steve Bruce.

Bruce, an important and prolific scholar on the subject, is sometimes read as an advocate of the view that the conflict's causal grounding in religion, especially in Protestantism, is such not to admit of a solution.[78] This seems to be invalidated by Bruce's recent suggestions that aspects of religious belief, especially of Protestant fundamentalism, can actually limit the conflict,[79] a suggestion that seems validated by the noble piety of, for example, Gordon Wilson, whose daughter was killed by the PIRA at Enniskillen, and Michael McGoldrick senior, whose son was the victim of a sectarian loyalist killing in 1996, and who have both forgiven their children's killers.[80] However, Bruce suggests that it is in the nature of the conflict that there is no solution whatsoever[81] and it must be conceded that, on assumptions hostile to liberal optimism, this conclusion is at once depressing and persuasive.

There is at least something to be said in favour of the liberals, just as there is for 'talking up' the Northern Ireland peace process, a procedure that most liberals find very appealing, at least in the short term. It is true that, contrary to some suggestions, internationalisation and Europeanisation have not delivered, and seem singularly unlikely to deliver, any solution to the Northern Ireland conflict in the foreseeable future.[82] Yet, if liberal optimism has been naïve in relation to Northern Ireland, there is not a great deal of evidence that it has particularly exacerbated the difficulties, so that it cannot be said to be more naïve than any other philosophy underlying any proposed solution. It is also not a very compelling suspect for the crime of killing the peace process.

UNWISE AND UNILATERAL CONCESSIONS TO REPUBLICANISM

This is perhaps the explanation for difficulties in the peace process that has attained the highest profile in both Great Britain and Northern Ireland. Ordinarily it emanates from British Conservatives and unionists, although analogous concerns are also sometimes expressed by voices emanating (originally) from the Irish Republic and the British left, such as Kate Hoey, a minister during Blair's first term of office who is originally from Northern Ireland.[83] The argument is that the British Labour government and its counterpart in the Irish Republic have destroyed confidence in the peace process by appeasing republicans, or refusing to put pressure on republicans to meet reasonable requirements in areas such as decommissioning and non-violence, while going to gratuitous lengths to meet republican demands in areas such as policing, the licensed release of prisoners, demilitarisation and the activation of a Northern Ireland Executive including representatives of PSF. Since the neutralisation of the PIRA was the main, if not the only, attraction of the peace process to large numbers of unionists, the apparently terminal collapse of unionist support in the peace process is directly connected to such flaws in British policy. As early as 1998 the Conservative Andrew Hunter suggested that: 'what was intended to be a peace process long ago turned into a shameful process of appeasement'.[84] As David Trimble's resignation as First Minister came into effect in July 2001, Andrew MacKay told the British House of Commons: 'this is a very bad day for the people of Northern Ireland, but it is an almost inevitable day, because the Government have appeased the men of violence and are now paying the price'.[85] In December 2001 David Wilshire, another Conservative, complained that the government's decision to allow PSF MPs access to Westminster facilities amounted 'to appeasement. It will not work. It never has done and it never will.'[86]

There is some mileage in these criticisms. The governments have clearly permitted PSF/PIRA some latitude on issues such as decommissioning and the definition of a PIRA ceasefire, although the British government's critics commonly fail to point out that limitations to the sanctions that it can enforce on such issues are by no means all rooted in wanton 'New' Labour weakness, since the British government needs, for instance, to ensure the full co-operation of the Irish Republic's government and international backing. It is also true that the expectations and hopes of pro-agreement unionists regarding the peace process have continually been thwarted. Unionism is the source of most opposition to the peace process, so that, unless one subscribes to the view that unionism is an inherently supremacist and intransigent political ideology (which is not the view held here – see below), it must be the case that at least some unionist objections to the peace process are reasonable and that republican demands that are anathema to unionists have correspondingly been mollified too hastily. As has been suggested, however, there is a problem about the common framing of these criticisms of government policy as failing to ensure that PSF/PIRA meet their obligations under the GFA, since such critics in most cases do not understand the agreement. The more material weakness of these criticisms is that they are dependent upon impoverished understandings of 'appeasement', Northern Ireland and republican politics. To describe gratuitous appeasement of the republicans as the causal source of problems in the peace process is far too simplistic.

As long ago as 1961 W.N. Medlicott suggested that 'appeasement should now be added to imperialism on the list of words no scholar uses'.[87] This has not stopped politicians and commentators from using it. The general point must be made that the implicit invocation of analogies with the 1930s in order to explain or, more commonly, mystify present political crises almost always evinces abject historical ignorance on the part of the speaker. It is to be hoped that this ignorance can attain no greater depths than in the writings of certain apologists for the recent military intervention in Iraq.[88]

Professional historiography of the Second World War by and large long ago ceased to accept the crude assumption still evident in politicians' discourse that 'appeasers' in that conjuncture were all immoral and cowardly, and 'anti-appeasers' were all brave and wise.[89] In the wider context of British imperial history it is appreciated that policies that can and were labelled appeasement, with due respect to Wilshire, did occasionally, and possibly even in the 1930s, achieve a measure of success, at least in relation to limited objectives,[90] a fact of which Winston Churchill, who was a complex personality, was incidentally far more aware than more recent individuals who imagine themselves his admirers.[91] Indeed, one of the more obnoxious implications of politicised denunciations of 'appeasement', such as by the current US administration and its supporters, is an unbearably conceited attempt to identify oneself with Churchill, or the person whom Churchill is misunderstood to have been, while blackening one's opponents as cowards.[92] In fact, no matter what Andrew Hunter, Andrew MacKay or David Wilshire (or even George W. Bush) think of themselves, humanity would be ill-advised to believe any implications that these individuals possess the capacity to save civilisation.

A second more specific point is that, on the careless definition used by such critics of the British government, almost any measure taken within Northern Ireland could be presented as appeasement. For instance, the Anglo-Irish Agreement (AIA) of 1985, negotiated by Margaret Thatcher, a Conservative Prime Minister herself fond of being compared to Winston Churchill, was, and sometimes still is, overtly treated by right-wing critics as an act of appeasement: according to Andrew Alexander, for instance, 'Hillsborough is as pregnant with danger for Britain as Munich once was, an act of folly which also received spectacular bipartisan support in Parliament'.[93] In fact the AIA was intended to deprive the Provisionals' policy of 'long war' of support and was not altogether unsuccessful. Even entirely opposite policies could be presented as appeasement. Secretaries of State for Northern Ireland who reject republican demands, as Peter Mandelson did, may be applauded by some, but those sympathetic to PSF, such as the *Guardian* columnist Jonathan Freedland, can just as legitimately suggest that such policies are designed 'to appease unionists'.[94] War to the knife with the PIRA, which seems to be the objective in view for right-wing critics of the peace process, is rarely avowed in polite company, although the aspiration was given one airing, to polite if startled applause, by the maverick Conservative politician Alan Clark at the Conservative Party's conference in 1997.[95] Yet such a war could surely be presented, on the prevalent vague definition of 'appeasement', as a measure to appease loyalists. A linked justification of British government policy is that, irrespective of questions of 'appeasement', morality or principle, and on the basis solely of Realpolitik, it has worked. Concessions have persuaded the PIRA to keep to its ceasefire, on at least a minimalist definition; accept an essentially partitionist document, the GFA; and recognise the southern state. Further, notwithstanding the extent of recent Conservative fulminations against 'New' Labour's 'appeasement' of the PIRA, it is a fact that the PIRA has committed three acts of weapons decommissioning while the Labour government has been in office, which is three more than any Conservative government has ever come even close to securing. Indeed, there is a view that the only difference between Labour and Conservative policy in Northern Ireland is not that Labour appeases the PIRA, but that, while both parties appease the PIRA, Labour's appeasement actually works. However, as Henry Patterson shows, this is an unfair view, not only because of the similarities between Major's and Blair's policies on Northern Ireland,[96] but also because any inroads made on the republican position have usually been accompanied with a reluctant set of concessions from unionism, which have exerted too much strain on the movement.

The major problem with the argument that the weakness of the British and Irish governments has caused the failure of the peace process lies in the implicit assumptions made about the nature of Irish republicanism. These critics suggest that republican demands are rooted only in the movement's utterly insatiable and rapacious nature. Thus, while republican demands could be frustrated without any repercussions, and possibly with the beneficial consequence of forcing republicans to become a good deal more politically mature, concessions to the movement have been fatal to the peace process, not only by alienating unionists, but also by encouraging republicans to advance ever more outrageous and unrealistic demands. In the unionist Roy Bradford's words, 'The Sinn Féin appetite for concessions grows with what it feeds on.'[97] This is close, it may be recalled, to O'Leary's description of the UUP's 'appetite for concessions' a few years later (see above). A closer attention to the internal dynamics within both parties would surely have dispelled these comforting illusions in both cases, although the lack of such attention is surely less surprising in Bradford than it is in an acclaimed academic political scientist such as O'Leary.

In any event, the implication that republicans do not have any real grievances leads their critics to resort to extraordinarily crude pieces of essentialism to try to explain the movement's appeal in terms of an atavistic Irish love of violence. As Ruth Dudley Edwards argues: 'The Irish love the whiff of cordite and – most important of all – republican leaders discovered long ago that if you get the rhetoric right, you can literally get away with murder.'[98] How one would read Ruth Dudley Edwards' own work, and especially its occasionally confrontational implications, on the basis of such an assumption – given her own Irishness – is a question that she does not answer.

A still more critical assumption evident in the argument that appeasement has caused the failure of the peace process is that Irish republicanism is monolithic, with Gerry Adams 'in absolute control of the republican movement – its terrorist and political wings'.[99] More normally this has been implicit in the careless political and journalistic formulation, constantly reiterated for thirty years, 'the IRA', commonly assumed to be coterminous with republicanism or, at times, variously 'terrorism', 'Irish nationalism' or even 'the Irish', a movement of historical continuity and monolithic depravity. As an aside one might suggest that this gives the Provisionals a good deal more credit than they deserve, attributing to them, for instance, a direct line of apostolic succession from the forces that fought against the United Kingdom in the War of Independence. Even Richard English's *Armed Struggle*, one of the best, most highly acclaimed and most important academic histories of 'the IRA', can be criticised on this basis for exaggerating the level of continuity between the IRA of Michael Collins and the modern PSF/PIRA. Not surprisingly, this is a claim that the Provisionals are also very happy to make for themselves.

However, the assumption that Adams is 'in absolute control of the republican movement – its terrorist and political wings' can literally be maintained only if it is assumed that the well-publicised rift between the Provisional IRA and the Real IRA, as well as other potent divisions in republicanism, is fictional, the result of a conspiracy from top to bottom. This theory is crucial to the idea that there is a readily available path of progress in Northern Ireland, inside or outside the peace process, if only republicanism could be brought to recognise its obligations, probably through greater determination being shown about this by the two governments. This is the view sometimes advanced in the *Daily Telegraph*,[100] by Conor Cruise O'Brien, implicitly in some scholarly accounts[101] and, in a far less cerebral and more casual form, in assumptions underlying reports in the *Sun* and other tabloid newspapers that the Provisionals must be responsible for the Omagh atrocity because they are republicans.[102]

Admittedly republicans themselves should take a major share of the responsibility for the misreading of republicanism as monolithic, through their long stifling of public debate within their organisations; several cases where followers have been apparently overruled by the dictate of leaders, such as in the calling of the PIRA's first ceasefire in 1994;[103] and the long and ludicrous attempts of PSF's leaders to deny substantive connections with the PIRA. There is some evidence of fluidity between the membership of the PIRA and that of the Real IRA, and, of course, there are similarities of philosophy, but the argument that they are one and the same movement does not persuade for a number of reasons. First, the most feasible work on republicanism, as well as readily recognisable facts, both about republicanism and about the vast majority of political movements, demonstrates that it is simply not a monolith, but has historically been fissiparous, diverse and marked by internal debate.[104] Second, there is the intensity of the rhetorical and actual hostility between mainstream and dissident republicanism. The fact that at least one member of the Real IRA appears to have been murdered by the Provisionals does not indicate a unified sense of direction between the two, since republicanism, even taken in sum, surely has too few 'volunteers' to sacrifice any so freely.[105] Third, there is the fact that one can surely explain the existence of dissident republicanism in more plausible ways than conspiracy. Mainstream republicans have conceded ground in the peace process, for instance by signing a partitionist agreement and by decommissioning weapons, so that the genuine dissatisfaction of some republicans with the peace process is not utterly incomprehensible, especially given the continued violent activity, and lack of decommissioning, of most loyalist groups. Republicans may be misguided, but their existence is not just the product of a contrived culture of grievance; crucially, therefore, republicanism could not be obliterated by hunting down a few godfathers, or in a Tiananmen-Square-style blitz.[106] Fourth, there is the inaccuracy of the past predictions made by those, such as Conor Cruise O'Brien and Kevin Myers, who have been most willing to criticise the alleged 'appeasement' of republicanism.[107] In a sense these mistakes arose precisely because these commentators held the specific ideas about the republican movement here being reviewed. Myers, for instance, believed that the peace process was over in June 1996, in part because he was convinced that there would and could be no division in the republican movement.[108] The nature of the current predictions advanced by republicanism's most ostentatious critics suggests that their prescience has not improved. The guileless faith with which conspiracy theories have recently been embraced by right-wing critics of the British government[109] is matched by a readiness to believe the unbelievable in only one other political location, the republican movement itself.

In a limited sense the latitude shown to the Provisionals by the British and Irish governments has undermined the peace process by exacerbating unionist disaffection with the process. Yet the proposition that this weakness is gratuitous is unproven and is usually dependent on naïve views of the internal dynamics of republicanism. Moreover, unwarranted concessions to republicanism can perhaps, as we shall see, be linked to a broader excessive level of attention paid to the Provisionals within the context of Northern Ireland politics, so that this appears to be, at best, only part of one cause of the failure of the process.

HOSTILE ATTENTION TO REPUBLICANISM

This interpretation can be regarded as the polar opposite of the last: it is the view that the problem with British and, to an extent, also Irish policy is that, rather than showing too much latitude to republicanism, there is 'an uncomfortably close association between

British governments (Conservative and Labour) and unionism',[110] and the governments are thus too inflexible to republicans. This view is easily inferred from suggestions emanating from the republican movement itself, especially in its conceiving itself to be the victim of a conspiracy, incorporating elements of the British establishment and the Special Branch, to frame the Provisionals for breaches of their ceasefire.[111]

In recent manifestations, by definition, this has been a criticism targeting British policy since the GFA was signed and thus can be associated politically with mainstream (pro-agreement) republicanism. However, this is not to suggest that academic and media commentators who articulate this view, or who had articulated cognate ideas before the GFA was signed, are all by any means to be associated with PSF or the PIRA. Broadly, this republican criticism of the basis of peace process can be broken into criticism of the reactions to, and commentaries on, events in Northern Ireland from three quarters: the British government, academia and the British media.

Such analysts, first, point to the disproportionate interest that is paid in Britain, and especially by the British government and counter-terrorism experts such as Paul Wilkinson, to the threat of disorder posed by republican rather than loyalist paramilitaries.[112] This, it is suggested, is ultimately indicative of a commitment by British politicians to maintaining the union. Writing about the collapse of the PIRA's first ceasefire in 1996, James Anderson suggests that: 'the British authorities have been able to hide behind the unionists' intransigence, letting them take the blame for failure[,] but more attention should be given to British nationalism in Britain and to the ideological importance of the union for many mainstream British politicians'. There are '"hard-line militarists"' in the British establishment, he continues, '"irrational" nationalist elements' analogous to such elements in the PIRA, who believed that, softened up by the ceasefire, the PIRA could be 'decisively beaten'.[113] A strong case, as has been previously suggested (in Chapter 1), can be made for the view that the responses of the British government and others to loyalism under-estimate its importance, in so far as loyalist groups are not, as is commonly assumed, simply a reaction to the activities of the PIRA. The extent to which the issue of the PIRA's decommissioning is made salient in the peace process, to the point of almost occluding the importance of loyalists' decommissioning, can similarly be criticised: as far as disrupting the peace process is concerned, this was effective, for instance, in the suspension of the Assembly and the Executive in February 2000. The excuse for these prevalent British (but not just British) assumptions could be offered that loyalists, unlike the Provisionals, are not seeking posts on the Northern Ireland Executive, but this is not convincing, since in any serious attempt to erect a democratic polity in Northern Ireland it surely has to be conceded that, irrespective of the question of size and possession of arsenals, republicans are more entitled to ministerial representation than are loyalists, because republicans have more electoral support.

However, the claim that this expresses an intense desire of 'hard-line militarists' and '"irrational" nationalist elements' in the British establishment to terminate the peace process, so that the PIRA can be 'decisively beaten', is less strong. At several points in the peace process events have occurred or have been portrayed in a way that, even without prejudging the thesis that such events are concocted by elements in the British secret service or elsewhere, could have led a fiercely anti-republican British government to call time on the PIRA's ceasefire, declare the peace process over and pursue the decisive defeat of the PIRA. This was most obviously the case in the summers of 1999 and 2001, respectively following the murder of Charles Bennett and the arrest of three members of the PIRA in Colombia. One may contrast the decision of John Reid, also in 2001, to declare the UDA's ceasefire over. PSF was 'quarantined' from talks early in 1998, before the GFA, on account of action by the PIRA, but only briefly, and the loyalist UDP suffered a similar fate. Broadly, as Michael Cunningham suggests, there is simply not much reliable evidence that many British politicians are ideologically committed to the union in this way, and attempts to locate such evidence are usually weak in the extreme.[114]

Crucially, while one can expect the British establishment to defend the British state against an insurgent movement, the complication in the current case is that it is not immediately obvious what constitutes 'the state' in Northern Ireland, and how far that state is 'British'. Under the GFA, not only is Northern Ireland's status in the United Kingdom confirmed as conditional, but there is already a consultative 'Irish dimension' to the government of

Northern Ireland. Further, in relation to Northern Ireland the 'British national interest' (as opposed to the 'United Kingdom's national interest', a phrase which is suggestively used more rarely) may actually be ambiguous on the question of the union. When one considers the financial cost to the British Treasury of Britain's presence in Northern Ireland, and the recurrent cost in terms of Britain's global reputation whenever one of the many public relations fiascos associated with the British security operation in the North has taken place, a strong argument could be made, as Dixon suggests, that the 'British' national interest in Northern Ireland would comprise working for a united Ireland; indeed, several British administrators in the 1960s and 1970s seem to have come to that conclusion (as mentioned in Chapter 2).[115] Thus, even where any half-serious scholarly attempt is made to uncover a 'steadfast' commitment to the union from British politicians that is 'very popular . . . in Britain', such as in relation to the early 1980s, even an analyst such as Newsinger has to recognise that such a commitment had a very different upshot than was suggested by its rhetorical veneer of opposition to Irish nationalism.[116]

A related argument advanced by David Miller and David Lloyd posits anti-republican bias in academic representations of the conflict in Britain (and, in Lloyd's case, Ireland). In Miller's words, 'the vast bulk of research on Northern Ireland is either supportive of the military actions of the British state or sees it as some form of neutral umpire'.[117] Miller and Lloyd argue that this is partly linked to the fact that the British and Irish states, which are justified in academic accounts against their insurgent republican foes, themselves fund the British and Irish universities, and so pay the salaries of the academics in question.[118] Lloyd further suggests that particular disciplines, including academic history, are compromised in Britain and the Irish Republic by their dependence on state-funded and -controlled archives, and so articulate pro-state perspectives.[119] It is possible that there is some force in these views, but they are somewhat crudely expressed and ahistorical, and they overlook conflicting influences. From the 1980s in Britain, for instance, the universities, along with public services and the teaching profession, became centres of anti-Thatcherite dissent (or even conspiracy, according to some interpreters), and so absorbed pro-state perspectives to only a limited extent. Miller's view is also unable to accommodate the fact of work produced by academics employed by British universities that in some sense coheres, whatever the politics of the academics themselves, to an Irish republican agenda, although examples of such individuals, such as Mary Hickman,[120] can certainly be cited. It is also arguable that if career academics in the Irish Republic are influenced by the fact that the state pays their salaries, surely they may absorb a pro-state perspective on that state's aspiration to a united Ireland, which would hardly be likely to turn them into rabid anti-republicans.[121]

A third dimension of this view relates particularly to media coverage of republicanism, especially in Britain. Liz Curtis, David Miller, David Lloyd, Bill Rolston and a number of other writers complain that the British media have represented republicanism in a negative fashion; concentrated only on republican rather than other forms of violence in connection with Northern Ireland; and often represented that violence as 'Irish' in the senses that it arose from an atavistic disposition to irrational violence in the psyche of the Irish people, and that the entire (Catholic) Irish population, not just in Northern Ireland, but also in the South, in Great Britain and in the United States, was ultimately responsible for it.[122] Some of these observations are well-grounded: much evidence can be marshalled in their favour and it is certainly true that British media coverage of Northern Ireland deserves, and has found, few defenders. It is true, for instance, that many people in Great Britain would have gleaned from British media coverage of Northern Ireland in the 1970s and 1980s the entirely fallacious impression that all deaths from political violence in Northern Ireland were solely or ultimately the responsibility of the PIRA. Nevertheless, while criticism of the British media's coverage of Northern Ireland is well-deserved, these particular criticisms somewhat miss the mark.

First, there is a tendency among such writers to ignore counter-instances to their arguments and conflicting discourses, such as British media coverage of the Stalker affair in the late 1980s surrounding the inquiry into the security forces' alleged 'shoot to kill' policy.[123] Further, Curtis, supported by the pro-agreement PIRA member Patrick Magee, and apparently without irony, cites in her catalogue of anti-republican censorship in the British media the BBC's television programme *Real Lives*, which in 1985 included an interview with Martin McGuinness, the broadcast of which was delayed and amended on the prompting of the British government.[124] In fact this fleeting prohibition produced a storm of journalistic protest in Britain, including one-day industrial action by the National Union of Journalists, and thus is hardly evidence of anti-republican bias among large sections of British media workers.

Second, there are serious analyses of the role of the British media in the conflict that furnish very different conclusions. According to Alan Parkinson, the depiction of loyalism in the British media has hardly been much more sympathetic, even in right-leaning publications such as the *Daily Telegraph*.[125] It has been argued that the very demonisation of republicans has given them such a high profile in the British media that it has shifted the political agenda against loyalists and unionists, giving more attention to republican political demands as well as transgressions.[126] The 'counter-insurgency' or criminalisation analysis is perhaps also due closer attention than writers such as Rolston and Miller suggest.[127] As interestingly articulated by Shane Kingston in 1995, for instance, this suggests that media coverage in Britain is actually too favourable to 'terrorists', at least in the sense of offering them unmerited publicity.[128] There are weaknesses and inaccuracies in Kingston's argument, such as the suggestions that loyalists have no 'political wing' and are 'safe in the knowledge' that a majority in the North favours Northern Ireland remaining in the United Kingdom,[129] as well as the unexplained assertion that British authorities 'deserve' media assistance, which surely needs to be proved rather than assumed.[130] Yet, while Kingston's view is largely antagonistic to that of Curtis and Miller,[131] there is a suggestive level of concurrence between the two, and with Parkinson's interpretation, that the higher profile given to republican violence in the British media, whether a product of an outraged indignation or a treacherous pro-republican hidden agenda in the media, might actually advance republican objectives at specific points.[132] While it is trite to assume that where opposites agree there must lie truth, there are substantive grounds for thinking that the rival analyses may at this point share a germ of truth.

Republican terror matters to British politicians and to British media agencies more than loyalist terror because republicans, especially the PIRA, have been more likely to kill people in or from Great Britain, and therefore have been more likely to touch the British media's core audiences. It can be argued that, in the long term, this additional publicity has actually advanced republican political objectives by giving republicans a higher profile. While British media coverage of Northern Ireland can and should be criticised, the criticisms of Miller, Curtis and other scholars are not necessarily apposite (see below). While some of the arguments advanced by scholars (and pro-agreement republicans) who believe that British governments' commitment to the union with Northern Ireland has been a source of difficulty in the peace process are accurate, the hypothesis paradoxically points to the same ultimate source of the failure in the process as the polar opposite political argument that too much latitude has been shown to republicanism. In other words, both arguments point to the existence of a disproportionate level of political, media and popular attention to republicanism, especially the PIRA, as opposed to the many other aspects of Northern Ireland politics, which does seem to have been a source of distortion in the peace process and in the policies effected as part of it. Loyalism, after all, is in a close binary relation to republicanism: loyalist violence helped, and does help, to generate republican violence, much as the reverse is true, and loyalist and republican participations in the peace process are thus both important. The British and international media's accordance of vastly disproportionate levels of obloquy *and* of more positive manifestations of attention upon republicanism, while it may be comprehensible, does not reflect some of the realities of Northern Ireland, and is thus a distorting influence.

LACK OF INTEGRATION OF NORTHERN IRELAND WITHIN THE UNITED KINGDOM

It is possible to suggest that the peace process has 'exoticised' Northern Ireland, or treated it too much as a separate entity, rather than integrating it within wider political and cultural concerns, consolidating the obsession with parochial issues that is the source of difficulty. This is cognate to a set of proposed 'solutions' to the Northern Ireland problem that can be broadly described as 'integrationist'. Integrationist solutions have both unionist and nationalist dimensions, positing, respectively, that closer links should be established between Northern Ireland and Great Britain on the one hand, or between Northern Ireland and the 26-county Republic on the other. This section and the following consider the broad case for these two arguments. This section considers suggestions advanced by supporters of Northern Ireland's electoral and broader political integration within the state that is still formally called the United Kingdom of Great Britain and Northern Ireland.

Electoral integration is the idea that British political parties should campaign and run candidates more energetically in Northern Ireland.[133] This has been done little to date. Since Northern Ireland was established, the tendency of Conservative governments to leave the province as much alone as possible has led to a bifurcation between the Conservative Party and Northern Ireland unionism. Stronger criticisms still are particularly raised against the British Labour Party on this point, since it takes advantage of inhabitants of Northern Ireland who are members of trade unions affiliated to the Labour Party: the union dues of these members may help to fund the Labour Party, but they have no chance of voting for Labour candidates and have only latterly been able to join the party.[134] Proponents of integration, who are found on both the right and the left of British politics, believe that voting for British parties could transcend the sectarian divide that the parties unique to Northern Ireland effectively enforce. There is also an argument that incorporation within the British political system would have a beneficent influence, since that system has largely been successful. This case is summarised by Charles Moore, the former editor of the passionately pro-unionist *Daily Telegraph*. According to Moore, full integration of Northern Ireland within the United Kingdom is the one policy that has not been tried there and, since that it is the policy that keeps the peace elsewhere in the United Kingdom, this omission in itself has contributed largely to the North's troubled history.[135] Conversely, political structures such as those of the GFA that accentuate institutional differences between Northern Ireland and Great Britain exacerbate the conflict. Implicit in such a view also is the idea that the institution of devolution when Northern Ireland was created in 1920–21 was a mistake: if Northern Ireland had then been fully integrated with the rest of the United Kingdom, its membership of that state would not have been questioned and the conflict would never have emerged.[136]

These proposals ceased to have a great presence on the political agenda long before the signing of the GFA, and thus were not and are not a viable alternative to it. The Conservative Party flirted with the idea in its manifesto for the general election of 1979, but never actively pursued it. Richard Needham's description of the integrationist position as 'ridiculous' may be a little unfair,[137] but the position does lack realism. Efforts by both major British political parties to organise in Northern Ireland have yielded few results. While debates on this question within the Labour Party in the 1990s evoked divisions of a bitterness sometimes reminiscent of the politics of the six counties themselves,[138] the announcement in October 2003 that residents of Northern Ireland would be allowed to join the party was regarded as uncontroversial within the party itself and was little noticed by the media.[139] It seems unlikely to make much impact in the province. In so far as any party based in Great Britain would be able to avoid being drawn towards sectarian or partisan positions, the fate of this decision may repeat that of the Conservative Party's decision in the late 1980s to organise in the province, where its results have been miniscule. Alternatively, any party based in Great Britain may attain power and influence at the price of a detachment from populist political concerns: in other words, by populating undemocratic focus-group or 'quango' institutions, through a process cognate to that choreographing and manipulation from above that is already a source of weakness in post-GFA politics. After all, ostensibly non-sectarian parties already exist or have existed in Northern Ireland, yet even the most durable of them, the APNI, has attained relatively little support, while another, the Northern Ireland Labour Party, imploded as the conflict began and was powerless to arrest it. The mere existence of such parties is no guarantee of their success or of an end to the conflict.

As Graham Walker, a broad proponent of these ideas, concedes, there is a fear of importing further parameters of the Northern Ireland conflict into Great Britain.[140] Even if one dismisses such considerations as self-interested British fears, there remains a major question whether integrationist parties involving themselves in Northern Ireland in any case could transcend the national or sectarian questions that are the source of controversy. Irrespective of the decline of Protestantism in Great Britain,[141] recent leading

Conservative politicians and theorists have evinced a tendency to valorise what is miscalled 'the national Church'[142] and a suspicion of Catholicism, both of which could have disastrous consequences if the party were to become more closely involved in Northern Ireland's politics. In any case, electoral integration has its limits even in comparatively peaceful polities. Even before devolution in the 1990s there were notable differences between the Scottish and English manifestations of both the Conservative and Labour parties,[143] and if it is true that in Northern Ireland even Thatcher was a Keynesian,[144] much the same was sometimes suggested of contemporary Conservative policies in Wales under the superintendence of Peter Walker, the Secretary of State for Wales in the 1980s. There is nothing necessarily sinister about the fact that people in Northern Ireland vote for different parties, and the conflict surely has more substantive roots than this alone.

Integrationists are confused about relevant aspects of history. As has been explained, from a unionist perspective it was fortuitous that the full integration of Northern Ireland within the United Kingdom was not effective in the 1930s and the 1940s, as the British rulers of Northern Ireland might then have tried to effect the 'full integration' of the North within the Irish Republic (see Chapter 2). It is surely patronising in the extreme to inhabitants of Northern Ireland to suggest that they would have forgotten their political grievances if only the province had been regarded by British governments as being as British as Finchley. Implicitly, such proposals depend on what the Conservative politician John Redwood describes as 'the success of Britain as a governing entity over many centuries'.[145] This 'success' is greatly exaggerated and those who advance integration on this basis are (as will be explored below) as confused about British history as they are about Northern Ireland. This weakness of these erstwhile allies is a serious problem faced by unionists, and a serious barrier to progress in the peace process and unionist weakness within it. It is also, unfortunately (as will be explained in Chapter 4), in combination with other influences, a possible source of weakness to any negotiation process in Northern Ireland. Because the historical successes of the British political system are limited, it is not irrational to have misgivings about the prospect of being incorporated into it, and perhaps especially not if one is an Irish Catholic. While there persists an almost Victorian tendency among some unionists to conceive of Irish Catholics as the spoilt children of the British political system,[146] that system's historical record of politically managing Irish Catholic populations is undoubtedly poor. While this does not prove that it will continue to be poor, it does mean that the North's further integration within the United Kingdom would be highly politically problematic.

Integrationist criticism of the peace process also fails to accommodate the fact that the GFA and the peace process do have a significant British dimension (part of 'strand three'). The future evolution of the British–Irish Council is not clear, but it does suggest a form of integration in a predominantly British context.[147] This is especially the case in an era when devolved governments are elected on the basis of proportional representation, not just in Northern Ireland, but also in Wales and Scotland, while England has long been a problematic aberration.[148] Indeed, in 1999 it was the intention that the three new devolved bodies (the Scottish Parliament, the Welsh Assembly and the Northern Ireland Assembly) would begin active work around the same date. Also, as Arthur Aughey notes, notwithstanding some insistent Conservative propaganda avowing the view that 'New' Labour is plotting the destruction of Britain, and some premature separatist triumphalism, all four parts of the United Kingdom still contain unionist majorities.[149] It is also noticeable that a British–Irish Council was a proposal favoured by the integrationist James Molyneaux, the former leader of the UUP.[150] Of course, in other respects the treatment of Northern Ireland under the GFA and in the wider peace process is obviously different from the treatment of the rest of the United Kingdom: power-sharing and applications of the d'Hondt formula, for instance, are specific to Northern Ireland. However, it must be reiterated that it is not clear that such aspects of the differential treatment of Northern Ireland are all as unproductive as an integrationist might want to suggest. It could be held instead that they reflect a conflict that already served to differentiate Northern Ireland from Great Britain.

As Paul Mitchell suggests, electoral integration is not a solution: the fact that it is suggested is rather a symptom of the problem.[151] The Northern Ireland peace process did not fail because it did not incorporate Northern Ireland within the British political system and such an incorporation would not solve the Northern Ireland conflict.

Or at least it can be argued that incorporation would not solve it without major prior changes to British politics and culture.

LACK OF INTEGRATION OF NORTHERN IRELAND WITHIN THE IRISH REPUBLIC

There is a converse criticism of the peace process that it has failed and, indeed, deserved to fail because it militates against a united Ireland, which is the most legitimate political aspiration in relation to the island of Ireland. The rephrasing of the opening articles of the Irish Republic's Constitution is an obvious example of such aspects of the peace process. Unlike the mainstream republican criticism of aspects of the peace process since the signing of the GFA that were noted above, this criticism also targets the GFA itself and the principles that underlie it, and is thus to be associated in political manifestations with dissident republicans, although once again, those scholars who articulate or have articulated aspects of this case are not necessarily to be associated with the Real IRA or the 32-County Sovereignty Movement.[152]

As was suggested above, the view that British politicians are greatly ideologically attached to the union with Northern Ireland is not convincing. Nevertheless (as has also been argued in Chapter 2), the suggestion of dissident republicans that the GFA and the underlying policies are partitionist has some credibility. The GFA created all-Ireland institutions such as the North–South Ministerial Council (NSMC), but the dissident republican critique of these was most memorably summarised in Bernadette Sands-McKevitt's assertion that her brother, the hunger-striker Bobby Sands, did not die for cross-border tourism.[153] However, the partitionism of the GFA and the British government's approach to it can be exaggerated. Supporters of a united Ireland were infuriated at the following statement made by Tony Blair in his speech on Northern Ireland in May 1997: 'none of us in this hall today, even the youngest, is likely to see Northern Ireland as anything but a part of the United Kingdom'.[154] There are complaints that this is indicative that Blair is not neutral on Northern Ireland, but is committed to partition.[155] Leaving aside the view that there is not much reason why Blair should be neutral on such an issue, this fails to notice that Blair's actual policies rapidly reversed key clauses of this speech, in a direction that was effectively pro-republican, although the right-wing interpretation of this speech that suggests that Blair therein expressed his personal active wish for a united Ireland is surely still more perverse.

The GFA itself should also be read more carefully. While the imminence of a united Ireland can certainly be exaggerated, the GFA does at least detail a procedure whereby this would become 'binding' on the British government.[156] Complaints about the partitionism of the GFA may be moved by the idea that British governments will try to weasel out of this obligation. Nationalist and republican consciousness of British bad faith has certainly proved an obstacle to agreement in Ireland in the recent and distant past,[157] but in 2004, as in 1940 and 1996, the obstacles to a united Ireland are not all of the British government's making. Indeed, segments of British administrations have long viewed a united Ireland as, in the abstract, a desirable objective (as mentioned in Chapter 2). This is not to endorse the assumption of some unionists that there is a conspiracy involving the Foreign Office, among other elements of the British administration, to propel unionists into a united Ireland, nor to adopt the theory that the partition of Ireland is of Irish nationalists' own making,[158] but to suggest that the unionist presence in the North makes it hard for even a favourably disposed British government to press the question of unity. To posit the notion that the limited partitionism of the GFA renders it and the peace process illegitimate is thus to suggest that the core unionist conviction that Northern Ireland should stay part of the United Kingdom is itself not a legitimate aspiration, or, in other words, that unionism is not a legitimate political creed. This argument is worthy of some consideration, especially its dimensions that relate to aspects of Irish history, more recent allegedly unreconstructed features of unionism and interpretations of unionism's perceived defenders, especially in southern Ireland.

According to historical arguments, unionism and the province of Northern Ireland are inherently rooted in the British/English colonisation of Ireland.[159] In contrast, republicans claim a democratic mandate for Irish unity dating from the general election of 1918, which supposedly marked the people's affirmation of the actions of the Easter rebels of 1916.[160] Terry Eagleton, a British-born writer of Irish descent, advances a related 'non-nationalist case for a united Ireland', on the grounds of democratic self-determination: a majority in Ireland favours a united Ireland and 'one vital function of that democratic majority is to nurture the conditions in which minorities may flourish all round'.[161] This is reminiscent of Gerry Adams' suggestion at PSF's Ard Fheis (conference) in 1995 that 'unionists are an Irish national minority with minority rights'[162] and also of Declan Kiberd's suggestion, in a book published around the same time, that the case for minority rights for speakers of the Irish language within Ireland 'might have implications for the treatment of a unionist minority in some future "agreed" Ireland'.[163] Against this democratic case for a united Ireland, unionism is said to rest ultimately on force: it was unionists who were responsible for bringing the gun into Irish politics during their resistance to the third Home Rule Bill, especially the gun-running at Larne in April 1914, thus triggering the Easter Rising and the subsequent militarisation of Irish nationalism.[164] To enforce partition unionism also relied upon the violent ethnic cleansing of nationalists from parts of the North in subsequent years, most notably in Belfast in late July 1920; and for its continued existence it depended, before the imposition of direct rule from Westminster in 1972, on the discriminatory structures of an 'apartheid' Orange state.[165]

Contemporary facets of unionism are also criticised. It has been noted (see Chapter 2) that in some respects the work of loyalist paramilitaries can be regarded as more sectarian than that of republicans, and loyalist murals are also regarded as persistently more militaristic and sectarian than republicans' murals.[166] The strength of sectarian tendencies within wider unionist culture is evidenced by the prominence of the Orange Order in that culture. Recent manifestations of unionist 'identity politics' in Northern Ireland have also been linked to what one might describe as irrational postmodernism[167] and it has also been suggested that unionism suffers from an inability to express itself in cultural forms,[168] both of which features are clearly seen as expressive of some form of inherent corruption in the ideology. There is also an argument that unionism has no basis in geography, the six counties clearly being part of Ireland. A more sophisticated related attempt to tackle the fact that unionists claim a British identity is advanced by David Miller:

> No one now suggests that Northern Ireland is really part of 'Great Britain' and the mouthful which is the name of the state reflects this – the 'United Kingdom of Great Britain and Northern Ireland'. When people in Northern Ireland claim to be British they justify this in imperial and ideological terms since they don't actually live in Britain. Ulster [*sic*] is British in the sense that it is a colonial possession which the British state has tried to present as an integral part of the state.[169]

Finally, unionism's supremacism is said to be evinced in sexist features of unionist political thought and action.[170]

A cognate target of unionism's critics is the school in debates about Irish history and culture that is labelled 'revisionist', particularly its supposed chief representatives, Roy Foster and Conor Cruise O'Brien.[171] Such debates are rarely solely academic in nature and form an aspect of the political context that is worth some consideration. Revisionists are seen to be linked to the long-anticipated project of amending the opening articles of the Irish Constitution,[172] a project that was anathema to republicans and that came to fruition with the peace process in 1999. It is held that the 'revisionists' display characteristics closely correlated with the objectionable character of unionism, thus demonstrating both their own status as unionist/British apologists, and the fundamental flaws of the unionist case. To Seamus Deane, Foster's work is objectionable because of its contradictory combination of a veneer of naïve objectivism and its postmodern denial of metanarratives,[173] and demonstrates its incoherencies in its attempt to deconstruct Irish nationalism while espousing itself, variously, British nationalism, 'Ulster' (Northern Ireland) nationalism and imperialism:

> To legitimise partition Northern Ireland must be allowed its separate 'identity', 'tradition', 'essence', while nationalist Ireland must have those qualities denied it. Alas, you cannot have one without the other. If Ulster [*sic*] is 'different', its difference can be described only in contrast with the 'sameness' of the rest of the island. Abandon the sameness and you abandon the difference. The only grounds on which partition can be legitimised are the same on which it can be refused.[174]

It has also recently been argued that the identification of O'Brien with unionism is genealogically related, not to any sense of the reasonableness or rightness of its arguments, but to fear of a violent unionist backlash if any attempt is made to advance towards a united Ireland. Ultimately even O'Brien admits that Irish nationalism is more moderate, more flexible and more susceptible of being reasoned with than unionism is.[175] Revisionism is thus linked in such accounts to a tendency to self-criticism in Irish culture that is seen as excessive and damaging. In an extremely popular book of cultural commentary Kiberd emphasises the need for cultural self-criticism: 'There have been sustained, at times self-lacerating, attempts at just such an autocritique in the [Irish] Republic: but these have been matched by no similar revisions in other places.' The deficient 'other places' are among unionists and the British: the British have failed 'to explain how for fifty years one of the most civilized peoples of Europe' supported a one-party state in the North.[176] The fact that Kiberd had voiced this same charge in 1985 incidentally demonstrates his view that no progress had been made in British or unionist 'autocritique' in the intervening period.[177]

The idea that Irish culture is too self-critical is developed in a particularly interesting direction by Luke Gibbons. While 'xenophobic expressions of identity, with their ideas of racial purity and domination, come easily to habits of authority and a secure, organic basis in tradition', these make little sense, Gibbons suggests, in cultures whose national narratives 'are already porous and open-ended, and in which even natives were considered strangers in their own land'. Nationalisms 'in an anti-colonial frame', as in Ireland, 'have tended to mimic their masters' voices, and reproduce in their own idioms the closed, univocal expressions of identity articulated in the imperial centre' in order 'to win recognition and gain respectability', but 'threaded through these totalising images is ... contestation of identity and openness towards the other which that entails'. Thus the danger of intersection with manifestations of certain other cultures, such as 'supremacist Anglo-Saxon ideals of whiteness in the United States', is of 'accommodation with the values of powerful expansionist cultures already built on racism'.[178] To paraphrase, Irish nationalism has within itself the potential for inclusiveness 'and openness towards the other', manifestations of intolerance deriving instead from a misguided accommodation with, and attempt to win recognition from, 'powerful expansionist cultures already built on racism'. Understanding revisionism to be an attempt to suggest that the depredations of the Irish national past, mostly at the hands of the British, can be normalised, Gibbons rejects the idea that 'cultural diversity in a modern social polity' requires such 'cultural amnesia with regard to one's own past'. 'The capacity of a society to retrieve the memory of its own unacknowledged others', those 'who paid the price in different ways for its own rise to prosperity', instead provides 'deeply rooted and vital' forms of solidarity with other peoples oppressed or suffering in the present. On the other hand 'there is little likelihood' that revisionist amnesia, 'the surface optimism of a culture in self-denial', will enhance in Ireland the 'ability to look outward, and particularly to identify with the plight of refugees and asylum-seekers'.[179] Peter Berresford Ellis, another supporter of a united Ireland, states the argument in a different form: 'Racism is not, and never has been, part of Celtic national philosophy.'[180]

Most of these efforts to demonstrate that unionism merits no consideration whatsoever, and those that, implicitly or explicitly, criticise (aspects of)the peace process for failing sufficiently to advance the goal of a united Ireland, are confused, and all are one-sided. Northern Ireland and, indeed, Ireland as a whole can be helpfully understood as a colonial society to only a limited extent.[181] Links between Great Britain, especially Scotland, and the nine counties of Ulster, one of the bases of the North's differences from the South of Ireland, are not just reducible to the seventeenth-century Plantation.[182] In any case, settler-colonial origins would not entirely invalidate the unionist case. As has been suggested by John Hewitt (who is well known as an 'Ulster poet' rather than as a 'Northern Ireland poet'), surely after a certain period of settlement people deserve to be regarded as native to an area rather than as 'rootless colonists'.[183] Protestants' position, whether in historic Ulster (nine counties) or contemporary Northern Ireland (six counties), should certainly be regarded as more established than, say, the position of Israeli settlers in areas acquired during the war of 1967: if there were acts of dispossession in the nine counties or the six, they were not substantially within living memory. The result of the general election of 1918 may have been a mandate for the independence of nationalist Ireland, although republicans tend to forget that previous similar mandates predated the Easter Rising, but, even if it is allowed that an election result more than eighty years ago should determine the future of Ireland, it is by no means clear that it was also a mandate against partition.[184]

The problem with the argument for a united Ireland as an expression of 'democratic self-determination' is not just that the case of those claiming to be British in Ireland is surely different from that of Irish-language speakers, but that there is no reason why the island of Ireland has to be treated as the unit of democratic self-determination. Apart from the view, persistently urged by British governments, that the six counties should be considered as such a unit, from a historical perspective, at points before 1914, it could, perhaps legitimately, have been claimed that there was a democratic majority in the United Kingdom that furnished conditions in which, in Eagleton's terms, 'minorities may have flourished'. In other words, if one were rigorously true to this doctrine, there might be no question of a twenty-six-county, let alone a thirty-two-county, Irish state. If the assertion of the island of Ireland as the prime unit of self-determination has a basis, it seems to be geographical determinism, but it is rather odd geographical determinism at that, given that Belfast is after all geographically nearer to southwestern Scotland than it is to Cork.

The specific events that gave rise to the creation of Northern Ireland are also open to other interpretations. Unionist gun-running at Larne in 1914 occurred at a time when the Liberals and the Irish Nationalist Party had been trying to drive through home rule using a distinctly questionable procedure,[185] and in any case it is not clear that the unionist mobilisation caused the Easter Rising, nor that Irish nationalist politics was previously purged of militant or violent tendencies. Further, the years 1912–14 surely show that unionism was not dependent on being propped up by the British government. The sectarian violence in the North around July 1920 has been neglected by some historians,[186] but it needs to be seen in a context that included sectarian aggression against Protestants in the South during the War of Independence.[187] Unionist denials of discrimination under the Stormont regime are disingenuous, but (as has been explained in Chapter 2) judgement should be qualified in view of the nationalists' withdrawal from the institutions of Northern Ireland and the attitudes of southern leaders. There are also allegations that discrimination by nationalists took place in local government in locations such as Limavady and Newry, even under the majoritarian unionist regime.

There are occasional suggestions that the unionist argument is essentially a denial of history, a suggestion that the conquests of the seventeenth century, for instance, all occurred a long time ago and should be forgotten about.[188] Yet surely this is a misunderstanding, since the annual activities of the Orange Order hardly suggest a community renowned for forgetting about this phase of Irish history. In fact, as the foregoing suggests, unionism is textured by a particular narrative of history, much as Irish republicanism and Irish nationalism are.

The case for the allegedly unreconstructed character of unionism in the present is no more persuasive. Recent republican activities themselves have a sectarian dynamic, although Steve Bruce and Ruth Dudley Edwards, among others, exaggerate this,[189] in the process, ironically, coming close to articulating the solipsistic rationale of loyalist sectarian assassination, in which all Catholics are ultimately responsible for the PIRA's actions.[190] This logic is ultimately deplorable, although it seems an exaggeration to present it as genocidal,[191] yet other dimensions of republican provocation need to be cited. First, there is simply the fact that the PIRA has killed more people during the conflict than any other group has.[192] Second, arguments about the non-sectarian nature of the PIRA's attacks entitle the Provisionals to no credit whatsoever. If Patrick Magee is correct that the PIRA could have sought 'soft' Protestant targets in East Belfast, for instance, the PIRA's strategy of instead leaving bombs in city centres, such as in Donegall Street in Belfast in 1972, where they would kill indiscriminately, was hardly a moral alternative.[193] Republican murals are hardly much less provocative than loyalist murals, especially where they portray those active in the PIRA as martyrs. The influence given to the Orange Order in the politics of Northern Ireland after 1921 demarks a not particularly creditable phase for unionism, but portrayals of the Order as analogous to the Ku Klux Klan are inappropriate and it is in any case legitimate to ask whether the function of the Ancient Order of Hibernians within nationalist communities has, in specific times and places, been much different.

Seamus Deane is correct to indicate that deconstructionist postmodern analysis can serve to appear to legitimise reactionary political 'narratives',[194] although it would also foolishly saw off the branch on which it is sitting.[195] Since postmodern methodologies thus undermine as well as nurture identity politics,[196] if such were the basis of unionist identity, republicans would appear to have little to worry about. However, those who associate postmodernism with unionism and with 'revisionism' are surely wide of the mark. After all, a considerable body of work in the field of Irish studies operates from assumptions entirely opposed to the idea that the Irish nationalist subject is the product of full closure at the end of a long process of historical determinism, while unionism, or loyalism, or the 'Ulster [*sic*] British tradition', is an effete and indeterminate choice. In other words, such work would be a better object for strictures such as Deane's, even though such work is, as it happens, broadly favourable to Irish nationalism.[197] Arguments about unionism having no culture, which seem incidentally to involve an elitist definition of culture, omit many exceptions, not least John Hewitt himself.[198] Miller's effort to delegitimise British identities in Ireland as 'imperial' is unconvincing for reasons already discussed, while Irish nationalism is surely as 'ideological' as unionism is. Miller's core point appears thus to be semantic. The full name of the United Kingdom is, it is true, a mouthful, indeed too much so for most of its inhabitants to use on a regular basis,[199] although (as we have seen in Chapter 2) the rulers of Northern Ireland in its early years took a good deal of care in making sure that the semantics were got right. Nevertheless, the mere fact of living on the island of Ireland surely does not invalidate a British identity, just as (unless perhaps one is the former Chairman of the Conservative Party, Lord Tebbit) living in Britain makes it illogical for anyone to regard themselves as Irish. Miller presumably would not suggest that those in Great Britain who identified their ethnic group as Irish in the census of 2001 (the first time, amid right-wing protest,[200] that a checkbox was provided for the option) are thereby Irish imperialists. Miller's point merely renews the dependence of the case for a united Ireland on the half-baked geographical determinism and limited colonial analogy both criticised above. Finally, the argument that Irish nationalism/republicanism does not also have sexist tendencies is ultimately reducible to special pleading.[201]

The somewhat more intellectual attack on 'revisionism' also often misses the mark. The work of Roy Foster, for instance, is critical of aspects of British policy,[202] and hardly welcomed by a unionist such as Trimble.[203] As is also the case with a 'revisionist' such as Paul Bew, who has been linked to Trimble and to the political group the Friends of the Union, 'revisionism' can constitute an attempt to rethink 'Irishness' beyond certain previous monolithic frames, in a more plural and more open way that is better able to encompass previously excluded minorities. As such, 'revisionism', whatever the political inclinations of the writers concerned, does not appear to be inimical to a united Ireland.[204]

Talk of 'bloodbaths' or of the imminent violence of an alleged 'Protestant backlash' in the event of an attempt to effect a united Ireland may be excessive, and may imply that one should always give way to force in politics, but this is not the only basis on which one may feel that the consequences of a united Ireland may be detrimental. If the history of Northern Ireland after 1920 is indicative, the sullen, non-co-operative attitude of an unintegrated minority may be as much of a danger to the stability of a state or a province in the long term.[205] The idea advanced by Gibbons and Kiberd,[206] that 'revisionism' is symptomatic of uniquely and overly self-critical tendencies in Irish culture, reads strikingly like the now common complaints on the British right that an unprecedented attack on British culture by domestic 'politically correct' intellectuals has taken place (see Chapter 4). It is doubtful that that comparison would be appreciated by either party, but it at least demonstrates the reactionary nature of such complaints, even as articulated by advanced intellectuals. That such conflicting claims could be launched in neighbouring societies, evincing almost no awareness of the existence of other claims, and with little to choose between the relative accuracy of each, is also striking testimony to the autistic nature of nationalism in both societies.

There is also a strong similarity between Gibbons' argument that revisionism will detract from the 'ability to look outward, and particularly to identify with the plight of refugees and asylum-seekers', and arguments advanced by the British right that racism in Britain is the product of excessively self-critical tendencies in British culture (see Chapter 4). There is a severe problem of agency in both: racist attacks on asylum-seekers are not perpetrated by, and are not the responsibility of, liberal intellectuals, but broadly are committed by individuals with nationalist assumptions. In both the British and the Irish cases these contorted apportionments of responsibility seem to be the consequence of a colossally theoretically naïve assumption that an 'authentic' national culture provides the causal root of tolerance. In fairness to Gibbons, he recognises that connections with peoples historically or currently subjugated by western imperialism do not comprise the totality of the history of Irish nationalism. Nevertheless, his notion of 'Irish people's' 'own history' is at times crude and uncritical,[207] particularly his assumption that an imagined 'national' must be the frame of reference through which one interprets one's own past. Surely if the assumption is that empathy with victims is likely to be attained by connection with a history of oppression, it is best to widen the search for such connections, not limit them to a national frame. For example, Irish people deprived of land or the means of survival, while other Irish people thereby rose 'to prosperity' in the Famine years and after,[208] assuredly experienced oppression, but by definition not as a nation.

In other words, Gibbons' metaphor of therapy distorts historical perspective by providing the impression of intimacy with a select group of 'national ancestors', in much the same way and to much the same end as Gerry Adams' startling complaint in 1993 that 'revisionist' intellectuals in Dublin 'tell people they can't be satisfied with what they came from': 'That's putting things you thought of as constants under attack: the effect's like a family trauma, like discovering you've been adopted.'[209] In short, one can view the argument that Irish nationalism/republicanism does not also have racist tendencies as unconvincing[210] without endorsing the equally bogus unionist counter-argument that tolerance and diversity are more integral to the British than to the Irish political system (and see also the next chapter).[211]

Any solely electoral integration of the North with the Republic, it may be noted, holds out no greater prospect of gain than that with Great Britain. That the only significant party currently operating north and south of the border in Ireland is PSF is hardly promising. The idea of an association between the SDLP and Fianna Fáil has been aired, although such an association would be problematic, since most major parties in the Republic could equally claim to be supportive of the SDLP's style of constitutional nationalism. Audacious predictions as to all-Ireland labour or radical politics may be made,[212] but they have been heard before and proved forlorn to date.[213] It seems that, for the foreseeable future at any rate, even modest advances of an Irish dimension to Northern Ireland, such as a federal Ireland, a confederal Ireland or even joint British–Irish sovereignty, while there are some proponents, are inherently unlikely to be greeted by many unionists with even resigned acceptance.[214]

The republican notion that unionism is an inherently supremacist ideology, unworthy of major political consideration, ultimately has highly confrontational implications, suggesting either that unionists should surrender key tenets of unionist belief, or that they should be brushed aside, either by republicans themselves, or, as one assumes republicans would prefer, by the British. Justification of such drastic steps requires much stronger evidence of unionism's alleged fundamental depravity. Indeed, whatever suggestions emanate from the Real IRA that it did not intend its Omagh bomb to be quite so destructive, the logic of violence is implicit in the distance of dissident republican discourses from reality: this surely makes dissident republicanism a good deal more depraved than unionism. In this sense, it is arguable that the absence of a more marked Irish dimension to the peace process has actually been an influence for success, not failure. The attendant analysis that suggests the contrary is possibly the weakest of those reviewed in this chapter.

CONCLUSION

The difficulties in which the peace process finds itself demonstrate the elusiveness of inclusive political dialogue and agreement in Northern Ireland, and it is not surprising to find that there is no single reason for the failure of the peace process, or that there is no simple prescription for resolving the problems. Choreography and deception in the conduct of the process by political leaders have been factors in increasing disillusionment with the process, but these seem to have exacerbated pre-existing difficulties rather than created new ones, and it is more significant perhaps that, in academic as much as in political and journalistic commentary, these have worked to distract attention from the limits of the peace process even at its height. Consociationalism and liberal optimism may have had some undesirable consequences in Northern Ireland, but in other respects they have been beneficial and are unlikely in themselves to have been the source of failure. Those who decry either the appeasement of republicanism or supposedly excessively hostile attention to republicans in the peace process both offer no really strong analysis of the failure of the peace process, but there is a level of agreement in these two antagonistic analyses, from which it may be discerned that there has been an imbalance in the level of positive and negative attention given to loyalism and republicanism through the process. Since republican and loyalist activities and political formations are clearly linked in a number of ways, this imbalance has not been helpful. Diagnoses of the failure in the peace process that take as their main premise the idea that Northern Ireland should be more integrated within either the United Kingdom or the Irish Republic, and take the contrary direction of the peace process as the source of its failure, seem to be the least helpful.

There is one specific sense, however, in which the view that attitudes consonant to the peace process exaggerate the differences between Northern Ireland and surrounding societies connects with the more pertinent analysis focusing on the disproportionate level of attention given to republicanism in the peace process, and may thus be more helpful. This connects the high profile of republicanism in commentary on Northern Ireland to the high profile of political violence and, within that, republican violence. As Elisabeth Porter's criticism of the industry of media, journalistic and academic study that has been built up around the Troubles suggests, this industry normalises the Troubles 'as if they accurately reflect the lives of most people. They do not . . . most people have lives that are not defined entirely by the conflict.'[215] It is worth noting however that there is also of course a contrary and equally inaccurate journalistic cliché according to which people just carry on with their ordinary lives during the conflict.[216]

Paul Dixon takes as the methodological starting point for his commendable study the proposition that, in order to tackle the limited reliability of public language in relation to Northern Ireland, 'particular attention' should be paid to 'sources which indicate the attitudes of politicians when they are not in the public eye, for example to newspaper off-the-record briefings, other leaks of information, politicians' gaffes, private papers, committee minutes and private communication between elites'.[217] The evidence of such sources clearly influences Dixon at key points in arriving at his conclusion that there has been a failure to understand unionism in British policy (and elsewhere), leading British governments to try to push unionists to make too many concessions too rapidly.[218] The problem with this approach is that it assumes that the sources through which these reports of 'real intentions' reach the researcher are accurate and honest. A better methodology would also apply Dixon's critical method to the sources themselves, such as the media. One such off-the-record comment that had as its object not politicians but the media themselves, reported by a European academic to an academic conference, suggested that one British journalist professed to her a complete lack of interest in reporting life in Northern Ireland outside violence, as only the conflict itself was deemed 'sexy' enough to interest a British audience.

The media, especially newspapers and especially in Britain, are not simply anti-republican, but do have political and material interests in reporting the Northern Ireland conflict in ways that do not necessarily cohere to factual reporting of politicians' gaffes, or anything else, about Northern Ireland. In the mode of populist journalism, for instance, few subjects are likelier to catch popular attention and increase circulation, or to require less journalistic talent to write up, than a politician's gaffe that seems to suggest an elite conspiracy to betray the imagined national community to a sworn enemy. In this sense, sections of the media have an interest in engineering situations likely to promote or exaggerate gaffes indicative of, in a crude form, 'surrender to the IRA', so that it is not surprising that Dixon's methodology uncovers much evidence that suggests, if not a conspiracy, a significant interest in the British political establishment in working towards a united Ireland. This is not to suggest that there is no evidence that such an interest has existed (indeed, evidence for such an interest has been provided in Chapter 2), but that Dixon's methodology may have exaggerated it.

More importantly, however, newspaper and other media editors largely assume that their lucrative British market is most likely to be interested in some dimensions of life in Northern Ireland rather than others. For much of the Troubles these dimensions have particularly comprised conflict and violence, as these are assumed to have an intrinsic or voyeuristic interest, especially where they jeopardise the lives and freedom of people in or from Great Britain, as opposed to people in or from Northern Ireland or the Irish Republic. The strength of the media and popular assumption in Great Britain that anything that happens in Northern Ireland must be linked to the conflict is most evident in the frequency with which media agencies assume that it is necessary to supplement the rare media reports in Great Britain of events pertaining to Northern Ireland that are not connected to the Troubles with a bland statement such as 'police suspect no terrorist involvement' or 'police suspect no sectarian motivation'. One example was the reporting of the crash of a Royal Air Force Chinook helicopter on the Mull of Kintyre in June 1994, in which twenty-nine members of the Northern Ireland security forces, including a number of counter-terrorism experts, were killed.

A way of understanding resulting distortions in perceptions of Northern Ireland, in Great Britain and elsewhere, is suggested by Norbert Elias and John Scotson's notions of blame-gossip and praise-gossip. These explain, not only how individuals process data and events to form unwarranted conclusions about the actors, but also how this phenomenon coheres to the formation and consolidation of stereotypical assumptions about large groups of people in the face of reasonable inference.[219] Through blame- and praise-gossip negative images of the Other are endlessly replicated, while positive images are not reported: these, after all, are not 'sexy' enough. A prime example is the representation in the British media of the murderous lynching of two British soldiers at a republican funeral in March 1988. Decontextualised and gory images of these murders were subsequently deployed completely unnecessarily in certain British newspapers, in some cases years afterwards, with predictably detrimental consequences.[220]

Meanwhile, negative images of one's own imagined group are suppressed and positive images are frequently deployed. In relation to representations of Northern Ireland from British perspectives, blame and praise groups may be seen respectively as 'the Irish', or the people of Northern Ireland, and 'the British'. The former are seen as the source of the conflict, the latter as trying creditably to preserve order or as innocent victims. The distinction is subtly evident for instance in Blair's assumption that 'few would disagree' that 'the qualities that go towards . . . British identity' include 'tolerance, openness and adaptability, work and self-improvement, strong communities and families and fair play, rights and responsibilities and an outwardlooking approach to the world that all flow from our unique island geography and history'.[221] In common with other valorisations of Britishness, it is hard to imagine that Northern Ireland is as much in the view of the speaker at such moments as other parts of the United Kingdom. It is because the characteristic structure of gossip is so powerful in this way, in creating what is misrecognised as politically 'useful' notions of 'us' and 'them', that it is so often evident in nationalism, and especially in the way that British nationalism operates in relation to Northern Ireland. Far from having much now invested in the union, British nationalism thus often coheres to the aim of a united Ireland in emphasising differences between an imagined 'Britain' (or 'Great Britain') and an imagined 'Ireland', in order to flatter the vanities of the former. Press reportage of Northern Ireland plays a crucial role in this wider operation of praise- and blame-gossip. Northern Ireland is different from Great Britain and is a sharply divided society, but it appears to be peopled by bigots, imbeciles and barbarians who do nothing but commit acts of violence only because press reporting emphasises events that confirm this preformed impression, or presents events in ways that confirm this impression, or because sources of information about Northern Ireland are often interpreted in ways that cohere to this conventional wisdom.

The emphasis that is being placed here on the role of the media in forming British perceptions of Northern Ireland may be held to possess the weakness of models of hegemony commmonly invoked in studies of the media in the context of the Northern Ireland conflict: that these ignore the possibility that the message could be resisted. Undoubtedly, personal experience, alternative forms of information and popular cynicism about the press can furnish sources of resistance, but this would be to misunderstand the argument being advanced here. Counter-hegemonic discourses about the conflict do exist, but they can reinforce or collude with some of the same impressions as the hegemonic, in a pattern of response to terrorism that is by no means limited to Great Britain or Northern Ireland. Evidence suggests that it has become hard to shift the discursive frame of the core message that Northern Ireland is populated by strange and violent people, because it is replicated by diverse media agencies, whatever their political complexion. Even right-wing and left-wing newspapers in Britain can and do turn on their erstwhile respective unionist and nationalist allies.[222] Even intelligent people get their languages and assumptions from television and newspapers, including newspaper headlines, to a degree that they may not appreciate. As Elias and Scotson found, if one is exposed to the same message via blame- and praise-gossip for many years, especially if it is linked to one's own self-image, the prejudice may become almost insurmountable.[223] Further, it may be that sections of the British population participate in the perpetuation of fictions about Northern Ireland because of their close relationship to flattering self-images of the British.

Latterly, spectacular developments of a different sort have also been assumed to appeal to a British audience. Spectacular breakthroughs in political negotiations seem to cohere to a 'mainland' experience of the conflict marked by a diminution of violence. Both of these distortions are performative. Recent media coverage of Northern Ireland, with such notable exceptions as events at Drumcree, Omagh and Holy Cross School, has in several cases promoted over-optimistic views of the peace process, and cohered to dismissal of objections to the peace process as obscurantist, which they often are not. This has set up obstacles to policies designed to re-engage elements disaffected with the process. Before the peace process began, media reporting of the province exaggerated the level of violence, exacerbating Britain's and, to an extent, the Irish Republic's psychological withdrawal from the province,[224] discouraging British people from travelling there and, in some cases, even to the Irish Republic, and reducing many cultural interactions between Britain and Northern Ireland. Both these influences in turn distort British and Irish public opinion about Northern Ireland, thus imposing unwarranted limitations on the policies that can be attempted there.

These tendencies have a lasting political legacy in distorting attitudes to Northern Ireland. Attempts to accentuate the positive in Ireland since the GFA was signed are a source of misguided optimism, while efforts now to report the continued level of republican or loyalist violence in Northern Ireland, after the euphoria of Easter 1998, could have the effect of inducing despair in

Britain and the Irish Republic, and produce a further psychological withdrawal.[225] Yet there is undoubtedly still a great need of accurate coverage of Northern Ireland, particularly of the extent to which ordinary people's lives in the province are little affected by violence, conflict or even the peace process. Mere media representation, or popular extrapolation from it, by no means created the Northern Ireland conflict, nor the failure of the peace process, but erroneous perceptions to date pertain in part to an exogenous or ultimate cause of difficulty in Northern Ireland and have brought about dynamics that have built upon local weaknesses in the peace process.

If analysis of why the peace process has failed seems to locate only contributory causes, this coheres to the fact, first, that the causes are complex and interrelated, and, second, that failure really required the exertion of few new influences from the outset. The GFA comprised only a limited level of agreement from the first, always qualified by the significantly different meanings attached to it by its signatories, and always rendered fragile by the exclusion from it, even if it was self-inflicted, of a significant proportion of the population of Northern Ireland, especially of its unionist element. Unionist approval for the GFA was only marginally achieved. Participants in the peace process, and outsiders, were relatively unconcerned by this because of an unrealistic sense of the importance of what had been achieved in April 1998; a distorted sense of the importance of having PSF/PIRA on board; and exaggerations of the benefits that the peace process had brought to the people of Northern Ireland. A lack of straight-talking and some manipulation from above further seemed to gloss over the fragility of the peace process, while in fact exacerbating the level of popular disengagement. This created greater pressure on the parties to the process in Northern Ireland in particular to live up to the unrealistic initial expectations within their own constituencies of what the peace process offered them. Deprived of room for manoeuvre on all sides, the pro-agreement parties were unable to come to a new *modus operandi* and stalemate ensued.

The next chapter considers the chief alternative that has been proposed in Northern Ireland to the peace process. There follows a consideration of wider influences that stand in the way of this and other possibilities of political change in Northern Ireland.

Alternatives to the peace process and the obstacles to them

The preceding chapter has discussed a number of different factors that have been or can be suggested to have a causal connection with the 'failure' of the Northern Ireland peace process. It can be suggested that all of these factors have helped to destabilise Northern Ireland at some point or other in the past five years. Many of the same factors, however, such as concessions to republicanism, the entrenchment of communalism in the institutions of the Good Friday Agreement (GFA) and the choreographing of the peace process, were equally *preconditions* for progress in the peace process in the first place, or seem to have been necessary features of the environment of the conflict. These and other factors seem also only to have exacerbated, rather than originated, sources of instability.

Only two of the causal factors discussed in Chapter 3 seem to have acted as more ultimate causes of the problems in the peace process. These are the relatively high profile of republicanism, especially the Provisional IRA (PIRA), in representations of Northern Ireland; and the extent to which Northern Ireland is treated as *different*, and especially as being characterised by violence and conflict, and equally spectacular breakthroughs, within and beyond the peace process. With these findings in view, this chapter tries to isolate any alternative foundations that may have existed before 1998, or may exist for progress in Northern Ireland politics, or the possibility of alternatives to the peace process. Particular attention is paid to the most clearly articulated alternative, the proposals of anti-agreement unionists for either a renegotiation of the Good Friday Agreement or the making of a new agreement altogether. This chapter suggests that this proposal ultimately does not convince and demonstrates that the crystallisation of foundations for alternatives to the peace process is rendered more difficult by the wider political context. As some scholars of the issue have perceived, attention to this wider context is a necessity,[1] but it also brings both potential pitfalls and opportunities, which often daunt those who would rather turn Northern Ireland studies into a comfortable academic ghetto. Can such specialists manage the intellectually challenging task of engaging with a far more wide-ranging terrain? Is it practicable to offer recommendations to those whose actions have many other wider possible repercussions? Is it, in short, either feasible, or desirable from the perspective of the many interests affected, to envisage wider political changes as a means to advance in a conflict that can easily be regarded as local?

To answer these questions is not merely to propagate a methodological model for 'conflict studies', of relevance only to an esoteric academic elite, but to endorse a set of assumptions about the causes of the Northern Ireland conflict and its 'solution'. The assumption that would underlie negative responses to these three questions would entail, in Joseph Ruane and Jennifer Todd's terms noted earlier, the idea that 'the people of Northern Ireland are out of step with contemporary cultural trends'; with this assumption, the authors continue, go implications for the 'solution' of the Northern Ireland conflict, which is to be sought in 'education, exhortation and the reconciliation of traditions'.[2] Although there is in fact, given the context, surprisingly little evidence of gross moral turpitude in Northern Ireland,[3] moral exhortation certainly can play a positive role in Northern Ireland. It is surely wrong, and hardly possible, even to observe actions that are clearly inhuman without passing judgement; and in passing judgement one hopes, whether it is acknowledged or not, to have influence.

However, the above assumptions and implications are not endorsed in this chapter, for two other material reasons. First (as was indicated in Chapter 1), it is desirable to avoid the discourse of solutions in connection with the Northern Ireland problem, since this is suggestive of only one section of a spectrum of imaginable desirable political and social developments. Second, the external contexts of the Northern Ireland conflict are more than 'fig-leaves disguising the underlying local quarrel'.[4] While the structures through which extremists are able to exert influence in Northern Ireland may be largely beyond the control of external actors, only certain local causes of the Northern Ireland conflict are anything other than proximate. Political reconfigurations germane to Northern Ireland can therefore cohere to social and political change in wider frameworks. The implication of this chapter is that changes in the wider context that might at least facilitate the recovery of policy possibilities in Northern Ireland are less likely to be effected by dramatic interventions from powerful individuals than in many small acts of courage effected by many individuals with or without significant levels of political power, and both within and outside Northern Ireland. The obstacles to such beneficial external changes should certainly not be underrated, but they may at least be defined. This chapter therefore also addresses some issues of wider academic and political interest, beyond the 'local' context of Northern Ireland itself, including some of both wide-ranging and fundamental importance. These include political responses to global terrorism; the treatment of nationalism, and national and ethnic difference, in a world often misrecognised as postmodern and 'post-national'; and the cognate question of the post-Marxist treatment of social and economic inequality and disadvantage.

THE PEACE PROCESS AND NEGOTIATION PROCESSES

This first section expands on a distinction (mapped out in Chapter 1) between the current peace process in Northern Ireland and the broader category of possible negotiation processes. To recapitulate, the current *peace process,* if understood as minimising loss of life to political violence in Northern Ireland, seems laudable and, indeed, above criticism: there appears to be no alternative. This definition is, however, too problematic to accept. It would be better to define the current peace process as *the interaction of certain sets of political actors* to minimise loss of life or injury from political violence *(particularly in certain categories)* in Northern Ireland *within an immediate time frame.* This definition accords well with known facts relating to Northern Ireland such as the marginal participation of certain actors in the peace process and the continued presence of violence committed by agents whose motives appear to be political. Perhaps more crucially, it also accords better with relevant unknowable facts. Specifically, there is a view that, far from peace being cumulative, short-term paramilitary abstention from violence – even such a limited paramilitary abstention as currently exists – can only be maintained at the price of parallel political developments that actually render a greater level of future violence more likely (see Chapter 1). If the peace process is thus regarded as actually encompassing delimited objectives, then anti-agreement, rejectionist or dissident perspectives, from whatever source, become worthy of more serious consideration than they are currently usually given, because it becomes possible to conceive of alternative hypothetical *negotiation processes* targeting other desirable objectives, and therefore admissible to regard the *actual* peace process as having failed without despairing. Such other hypothetical negotiation processes in Northern Ireland would have been orientated, or could still be orientated, around a configuration of parties different from that commonly currently described as pro-agreement. Such an alternative configuration may entail, or would have entailed, more political violence in Northern Ireland in the short term, but could still be defended on the grounds that in the long term it might have produced, or might produce, greater stability.

The most pertinent evidence of the potential of alternative negotiation processes comes from tracing tracks that were not taken in the actual peace process. The best candidate for such a decisive shift relates to events between the Northern Ireland Forum elections of May 1996 and the resumption of the 'Stormont' talks in the autumn of 1997. Until the PIRA's second ceasefire was declared, in July 1997, the main parties that *seemed* to be set for participation in the autumn session of talks were David Trimble's Ulster Unionist Party (UUP), Ian Paisley's Democratic Unionist Party (DUP), the Alliance Party of Northern Ireland (APNI), and the nationalist Social Democratic and Labour Party (SDLP), with the smaller United Kingdom Unionist Party (UKUP), the loyalist Ulster Democratic Party (UDP) and Progressive Unionist Party (PUP), and the Northern Ireland Women's Coalition also being involved. The PIRA's second ceasefire changed this by persuading the British and Irish governments to admit Provisional Sinn Féin (PSF) to participation in the talks, notwithstanding the obvious unlikelihood of immediate decommissioning by the PIRA.[5] The DUP and the smaller UKUP decided not to stay in the talks in these conditions, but Trimble's UUP decided, with some difficulty, to participate in the talks alongside PSF's representatives.[6]

Closer consideration of this sequence of events begs the question as to how much progress would be, or would have been, possible with a group of parties such as the initial 'Stormont' talks parties, and specifically if the British and Irish governments had adopted policies other than to facilitate the *immediate* presence of PSF in a negotiation process. This coheres closely to the more recent proposal advanced by both the DUP and anti-agreement members of the UUP such as (until recently) Jeffrey Donaldson for the negotiation of a new agreement among Northern Ireland parties. It is clear that such an agreement would have been most likely to differ from the GFA in excluding PSF. *Democratic* grounds for rejecting this alternative appear at best marginal. The DUP and the UKUP combined persistently record as high a vote in parliamentary and other elections as PSF, more recently indeed a higher one, and if the subsequently emerging anti-agreement segments of the UUP are considered, the advantage is still clearer. (It is true that in the general election of May 1997 PSF, with 16 per cent of the vote in Northern Ireland, did slightly better than the DUP, which won 13.5 per cent, and the UKUP, with 1.5 per cent, combined, and that local government elections results around the same time yielded similar results; these, however, are rarities in recent history.) It can thus only tenuously be suggested that such an alternative negotiation process would have *represented* fewer of the inhabitants of Northern Ireland than does the current peace process. A practical consideration that is more immediately apparent is that any exclusion of PSF from a negotiation process would probably precipitate either an end to the PIRA's current ceasefire, or the reorientation of Provisional supporters and 'volunteers' towards dissident republican groups such as the Real IRA. Neither of these is a particularly attractive prospect. Many 'rejectionist' unionists argue that the abstention of the PIRA from violence is limited as things stand. Others point out that abstention can certainly be purchased by concessions that are excessive, especially if there is no guarantee that the republicans in any significant numbers are committed to non-violent political processes in the long term. Further, crucially, what facilitated the PIRA's ceasefire and PSF's entry into talks, and triggered the exit of the DUP and the UKUP, was a suspension of consideration of the question of decommissioning, the very issue that has proved problematic all through the subsequent peace process. Any resolution of the decommissioning issue in the GFA and subsequently was confused (as discussed in Chapter 3), and republican decommissioning was implemented, in so far as it has been, only after critical levels of unionist disaffection from the process had been reached. On this ground it can be argued that July 1997 was a crucial conjuncture, arguably at least as important as the agreement itself, and the level of accord achieved after July 1997 was significantly less than appears. More tendentiously, anti-agreement unionists could thus argue that their protest at the developments of July 1997 has been vindicated.

How much progress towards a more stable conjuncture could have been, or could be, made with a configuration of parties similar to those in the talks before July 1997? In any immediately available context, the answer is surely very little, for a number of reasons. First, agreement or dialogue among unionist parties themselves for any extended period cannot be assumed. The course of the 'Stormont' talks before July 1997 had been marred by recriminations among all the unionist parties, especially if the APNI is included under that heading, with the parties questioning the legitimacy of each other's presence. The talks chair, George Mitchell, recalled his relief when Paisley's DUP and McCartney's UKUP walked out: 'reaching agreement without their presence was extremely difficult; it would have been impossible with them in the room'.[7] Since Paisleyite unionism was a significant force missing from the agreement that Mitchell brokered, this could be dismissed as retrospective self-justification, and Mitchell is surely guilty prematurely of writing off Paisley as a political force in the North,[8] but there is no need so to question the value of Mitchell's labours or his integrity. The tendency of unionism to shoot itself in the foot must be acknowledged as an obstacle to an alternative negotiation process. Nevertheless, the absence of a significant section of unionism from the actual peace process can only be regarded as no misfortune if some version is accepted of an established stereotype of unionism, especially of Paisley's and McCartney's variants, as the selfish and unreconstructed ideology of a class, or of Britain's garrison in Ireland, which demonstrated its inveterately supremacist and illegitimate character in the years after partition. Such a view and the linked relatively crude case for a united Ireland are surely inadequate (as argued in Chapter 3), and in any case do not help us address the fact that anti-agreement unionism is now on the *in*crease.

The other important reason why the negotiation process as it was before July 1997 could not work, or could not have worked, is that it would proportionately under-represent the minority. It would incorporate the two main parties whose constituency lies overwhelmingly among Northern Ireland Protestants, yet include only one of the two main parties whose constituency lies overwhelmingly among Northern Ireland Catholics, the SDLP. Evidence suggests that the SDLP would resist such a negotiation process. Under the leadership of John Hume the SDLP began to develop closer contacts with PSF in the late 1980s, in a movement described as the Hume–Adams initiative or the pan-nationalist alliance.[9] At key moments within the peace process both Hume and

FIGURE 4
'The Last night of the Prods', *Private Eye*, No.954 (10 July 1998), p.1

Mark Durkan, Hume's successor as leader of the SDLP, stuck with the policy of pressing the British and Irish governments not to expel PSF from negotiations or, later, from Northern Ireland's power-sharing Executive. Such attitudes on the part of the leadership of the SDLP have been criticised in certain quarters, including within the party itself, as an unprincipled or unwise parleying with terrorists,[10] but it is surely at least understandable, notwithstanding the nature of PSF, that moderate nationalists should not want the community with which they are associated to be so disadvantaged by under-representation in negotiations.

If the exclusion of PSF from a negotiation process appeared irreversible, and had attracted the DUP into talks, the SDLP *might in certain conjunctures* regard it as better to represent nationalism at such a negotiating table rather than protest at the under-representation of this community. If that were the case, under pressure of isolation some fragment of republicanism might plausibly also be prevailed upon to take such steps as would facilitate its return to the negotiation process. It cannot, however, be taken for granted that such a strategy would appeal to the SDLP's leadership, even in these circumstances, and, if the SDLP were to receive support from the Irish government, nationalist protest would almost certainly be successful, resulting in a negotiation process featuring at best a group of parties identical to those figuring in the peace process itself. Since Northern Ireland has a large minority with substantial ethnic and cultural links with the majority community in the island as a whole, and because under-representation of that minority within Northern Ireland was to a large extent the cause of the outbreak of conflict from the late 1960s,[11] it will always be difficult to conceive of a negotiation process that reverts to this under-representation.

Yet, conversely, what is significant about the peace process is that it has proportionately *over*-represented the minority and *under*-represented unionists. Indeed, negotiations orchestrated by the Irish and British governments between the parties described as pro-agreement have sometimes amounted in practice to select meetings among representatives of the pro-agreement section of the UUP, of the SDLP and of PSF, clearly under-representing unionists. An example of this would be the Weston Park discussions in July 2001. Clearly, nationalists and republicans both have reasons to acquiesce in, or indeed orchestrate, these operational consequences of an assumption that the peace process consists of the tripartite contribution of unionists, nationalists and republicans. It is hard to see how such negotiations could work otherwise, in the short term, since it is clearly the case that the majority of the active unionist electorate opposes the course that the peace process has taken and has done so ever since soon after the GFA was signed. However, to under-represent a *majority* is also certainly a fragile strategy in the long term and should surely be seen as a factor necessitating that choreographing of the peace process that some have seen as at least exacerbating its weaknesses.

This under-representation of unionism within the peace process has largely been deemed acceptable, and in some quarters still is. This should be related to the apparently asymmetrical influence exerted by British and Irish political leaders on Northern Ireland: the most powerful forces in British politics do not offer support to unionism to the extent that Irish political leaders do to nationalists.[12] This does not mean that there is, as some unionists suggest, a pan-nationalist alliance or conspiracy involving the whole-hearted backing of the Irish Republic for mainstream republicanism in the North,[13] but at least some unionists are naturally suspicious about a peace process framed in this context of asymmetrical external influences.[14] It is because of this context that consideration of alternatives to the current peace process seems only to confirm the impression that 'any ["settlement"] train without Sinn Fein [*sic*] and the IRA on board could never succeed in heading along anything more significant than a minor branch line'.[15] The existence of a PIRA ceasefire is thus to an extent regarded as defining the peace process, and a negotiation process without primary PSF/PIRA participation seems implausible as things stand. A pessimistic interpretation of this fact would suggest that the PIRA has successfully bombed and murdered its way to the negotiating table: the military elimination of mainstream republican terrorism was attempted, but proved more difficult than its advocates had hoped, or was even found to be impossible.[16] Even counter-terrorism experts agree, however, that terrorist conflicts are not solely military and have important political dimensions.[17]

Realistically, within the given context, there does indeed appear to have been no alternative to the peace process, a process that (it is argued here) has failed. This is suggestive of the powerful obstacles that the wider political context creates to political alternatives and therefore political advance in Northern Ireland. The fact that the peace process under-represented unionism, which has fatally destabilised the process, was regarded from the outset simply as necessary on account of some wider contextual political factors. Unless it is held that unionism simply *is* illegitimate, conditions that create a problem of political legitimacy or plausibility for unionism are fundamental causes of the unpromising outlook in Northern Ireland.

SOURCES OF UNIONISM'S LACK OF LEGITIMACY

A number of explanations for unionism's lack of perceived political legitimacy can be discerned from existing cultural and political commentary. The first suggests the instrumentality of US opinion and the attitudes of US administrators. Even those who suggest that the role that the United States has played in the recent peace process has been positive largely seem to accept that US opinion is usually broadly pro-nationalist.[18] However, this is surely a *symptom* rather than a cause of the problem of unionist legitimacy. To assert that US opinion is broadly pro-nationalist is to offer no explanation of why that should be the case, given the large number of Protestants in the United States who can trace their ancestry to immigrants from the ancient province of Ulster, which included, of course, what is now Northern Ireland.[19] Indeed, the evidence that suggests that many such individuals are more likely to accept nationalist than unionist readings of Northern Ireland[20] is surely indicative of deeper problems. It can also be suggested that Irish nationalism, along with several other actors in global conflicts, gains prestige from being an anti-colonial struggle, but this too does not really explain why global opinion should focus on those aspects of Irish historical experience and the Northern Ireland conflict that seem to fit a typology of colonialism, as opposed to the many that do not.[21] A third assumption is that the relatively sympathetic hearing that global opinion gives to Irish nationalism/republicanism is a symptom of the strength of irrational Anglophobia in several parts of the world.

This sort of assumption has been evident, for instance, in British media reporting of any adverse judgements about British policy in Northern Ireland made by the European Court of Human Rights, in other European institutions and by US commentators.

One problem with all of these three arguments is that it is quite hard to see how they can intersect. Given that ill-informed radical critiques of colonialism and neocolonialism, such as lend credence to the case of Irish republicanism, tend to depict the United States as the world's leading 'neocolonial' power, the reason why US administrations should also have adopted a policy towards Northern Ireland broadly compatible with the same Irish republican goals is not immediately apparent. The reconciliation of these different vectors of influence is made still harder by the fact that British governments have frequently recently been perceived as close geopolitical allies of US administrations. Serious attempts to explain how these influences might interlock evince their complexity and therefore their indeterminacy. For instance, there is an argument that the pressure on Margaret Thatcher to sign the Anglo-Irish Agreement (AIA) in 1985 from her close ally President Ronald Reagan arose from a specific conjuncture in US foreign and domestic policy, whereby Reagan exerted such influence in order to placate critics of his funding of the right-wing Contra guerrillas in Nicaragua. If this reading is correct, it would suggest that an influence favourable to nationalism arose from the United States, in spite of the Anglo-American 'special relationship', but in a process inimical to 'anti-colonialism'.[22]

In any case, however (as will be argued below), the bases for the British nationalist mode of self-pity that detects a ubiquitous irrational Anglophobia are really rather flimsy. Explicit support for Irish republican terrorism in the United States and elsewhere has always been a minority creed, although selective reporting in low-quality British newspapers has persistently obscured that fact by occluding differences between supporters of moderate nationalists and supporters of republicans in Ireland, the United States and elsewhere.[23] In any case, as has been mentioned, it is crucially significant that unionism has as little legitimacy within Britain as anywhere, being dismissed, in the words of the pro-unionist right-wing journalist Charles Moore, by the Englishman 'who assumes that he alone defines what is British'.[24] According to Alan Parkinson (as mentioned in Chapter 3), negative attitudes to unionism are evident in both the right-wing and the left-wing media in Britain;[25] and at least one other informed recent observer has judged that even the right-wing British Conservative Party has failed to articulate a politically viable alternative to the current peace process.[26]

A second explanation, which often appeals to the same constituency as the arguments just discussed, emphasises the significance of Irish pan-nationalism, or the intransigence of Irish nationalism.[27] According to this view, violent and revolutionary action by those who claim to act on behalf of the minority in Northern Ireland, and, indeed, the majority in the island as a whole, has acquired a significant level of historical support among Catholics all over the island and elsewhere.[28] Over the past three decades there have been numerous suggestions that governments of the Irish Republic have not done enough to snuff out republicanism on their side of the border, making the military defeat of the PIRA by the British very difficult.[29] A number of leading British Conservatives, for instance, expressed disappointment with the level of co-operation on security issues that the Conservative government of the time received from Dublin in the aftermath of the signing of the AIA in 1985.[30] Proponents of this view could also cite the opening clauses of the Irish Republic's Constitution of 1937, which, though now revised, were altered, in their view, too slowly too reluctantly and perhaps insubstantially. John Hume's role in pushing the SDLP in a nationalist direction and opening a dialogue with Gerry Adams, while widely seen as a fundamental building block of the current peace process, has also been criticised.

For a number of reasons this view does not take us very far. If it is implied that Irish nationalists have no concrete grievances at all, so that republicanism or nationalism is all the product of clever propaganda, such a view is often dependent (as was suggested in Chapter 3) on essentialist notions of the Irish as immoral and deceitful, eloquent talkers and persuaders without talent for more tangible achievement, who are quick to organise behind even unwarranted political demands owing to a well-developed grievance culture. It is also often dependent on cognate stereotypes of Northern Ireland Protestants as hard-working and sober-minded, but inarticulate and poor at public relations.[31] Such views, it should be noted, while comforting to loyalists,[32] are actually condescending to both nationalists and unionists, and overlook conjunctures in which dubious interpretations advantageous to unionists – for instance, regarding the Irish Republic's neutrality during the Second World War[33] – have been widely accepted.

Further, it should be noted that there are some non-sinister or understandable reasons for aspects of the Republic's policy since 1968. The government of Northern Ireland before 1968 provides some evidence for the suggestion that the British took the concerns of the minority seriously only when powerful paramilitary groups began acting in its name, so that, from a certain perspective in Dublin, the continued existence of the PIRA could have been regarded as a guarantor of the minority's status. In any case, to assert the existence of an incestuous relationship between the Irish Republic and northern republicans would be to ignore the long-term distaste that each has felt for the other.[34] The Republic's record of punitive measures against republicans should not be overlooked; and it has also had notable successes recently in apprehending members of the Real IRA. It is true that public opinion surveys suggest that the Republic's population itself is broadly in favour of Irish unity, but more as an aspiration than as a measure of immediate policy.[35] After all, Irish unity would create obvious difficulties for the Republic of assimilating a recalcitrant Protestant minority. Irish opinion might even be prepared for partition to remain in effect in the medium to long term if a system of protection for the northern minority could be effected, in consultation with Dublin or via some other Irish dimension to the government of the North, which opinion in the Republic regarded as 'adequate'. If such were possible (and there are many other difficulties in its way), under the right conditions a Dublin government could even conceivably act as a crucial agent in the defeat of a troublesome republican fragment.

In any case, it is again necessary to return to the point that, even if the Republic, or at least a minority within it, has provided a level of moral, material and financial support for Irish republicans, the fact that Britain has not offered *symmetrical* support for unionists appears to be more of an ultimate cause in constraining the possibility of alternative negotiation processes. Thus, attitudes in the Irish Republic alone also do not explain the problems of unionist legitimacy.

Three other explanations of this problem seem more careful,

albeit suggesting only minor influences. First, as Adrian Guelke suggests, few affirmative global points of reference can be found for the partitionist nature of unionist ideology: divided islands are rare.[36] This is only a partial explanation, however, since lack of analogy surely does not preclude the possibility of such a political settlement. Second, as Steve Bruce suggests, loyalist paramilitaries suffer from the dilemmas of pro-state terrorism: to an extent, the division of function between loyalist paramilitaries and the British security forces in Northern Ireland has been unclear, and loyalism often seems to be most clearly demarcated by the naked sectarianism of many of its activities.[37] Third, whatever their slender basis of accuracy, aspects of popular stereotypes of Irish Protestants and Catholics have recently worked significantly to the advantage of the latter. The association of Irishness with alcohol, conviviality and sociability has long been an object of complaint for nationalists. However, due to the valorisation within postmodern capitalism of leisure and consumption rather than work as activities and as originators of identity,[38] global evaluations of these attributes have become significantly less negative. The global marketability of Irish music, entertainers and alcoholic beverages, as well as of St Patrick's Day festivities, all features of the 'Celtic Tiger' phenomenon, is the clearest evidence of a cognate re-evaluation of Irishness. Aspects of the stereotyping of Northern Ireland Protestants as hard-working and business-like, if dour and obstinate, formerly cohered to a form of metropolitan British nationalism that celebrated the United Kingdom as the 'workshop of the world'. Within this postmodern context, however, and perhaps also within the context of Britain's relative economic decline, these attributes clearly become less attractive. This is an important example of the way in which postmodern capitalism specifically disadvantages the unionist community of Northern Ireland.

It is not particularly clear that any of these causal influences can be changed, at least in the short term. However, it can be maintained that the problem of unionist political legitimacy is further exacerbated by aspects of the factors that were seen (in Chapter 3) as exogenous causes of the failure of the peace process, and specifically by their interaction with wider influences. To recapitulate, the profile of republicanism, and the media representation of Northern Ireland as defined by conflict (latterly mitigated by the peace process), are disturbing influences on

Northern Ireland's society and on policies executed towards it. These influences intersect with wider cultural formations to have a particularly detrimental effect on unionism. The profile of republicanism in Northern Ireland intersects with wider attitudes to terrorism and other structures in a way that impedes presentation of the unionist case. Meanwhile, representation of Northern Ireland as a violent society has produced tensions with 'core' conservative *and* liberal versions of national identity. Latterly, even more positive representations of Northern Ireland, which have been given a currency by the peace process, have produced problems for unionists because objections to the process, and set-piece occasions of residual conflict, such as at Drumcree and Holy Cross School, are frequently portrayed as emanating from obscurantist forms of unionism. The problematic influences external to Northern Ireland thus help to curtail alternatives to the failed peace process, and thus comprise obstacles to beneficial change in Northern Ireland.

The next three sections each elaborate on aspects of these crucial wider cultural dimensions. They address, in turn, terrorism, the political nation as viewed by conservatives and the political nation as viewed by liberals. Analysis particularly focuses on the United Kingdom as a whole, and on the island of Great Britain in particular, since unionist ideology involves aspiration to membership of the British political community and the lack of British support for unionism equivalent to the Irish state's for nationalism is a central cause of the non-viability of alternatives to the peace process. However, the inadequacies of the relevant formations are evident across a wide range of societies, and these international manifestations are also noted.

TERRORISM

In an attempt to demonstrate that the attributes of ideology are both affective and cognitive, John Cash suggested, in a book on aspects of the Northern Ireland conflict published in 1996, that there were contexts in which it is difficult to speak, especially as an outsider, without offending certain ideologies felt to belong to certain groups. His examples of such contexts – the United States during the

Embassy hostage crisis in Iran and Britain during the Falklands crisis[39] – were taken from, respectively, 1979–81 and 1982, and did not seem especially resonant in the late 1990s, although they at least illustrated the close relationship between the phenomena he described and nationalism. However, the aftermath of the events of 11 September 2001 ('9/11'), in the United States as well as elsewhere, provided some contexts that strikingly confirm Cash's point. Most obviously, those who raised even small practical issues about US policy within the political mainstream in the weeks after the attacks on New York, Washington, DC, and Pennsylvania risked condemnation for being unpatriotic, while those who openly criticised US policy frequently received a degree of ostracism that bordered on the threatening. Many Muslims and many of Middle Eastern descent, in the United States and elsewhere, encountered another level of intimidation altogether. Within an oppositional subculture, meanwhile, to pose certain questions was to appear to lend approval to US policy and also to be ostracised.

The climates generated after 9/11 dovetail with Cash's analysis since there is an obvious resonance between US experiences since that date and the experiences of inhabitants of Northern Ireland over three decades. Analysis of the strengths and weaknesses of wider attitudes to terrorism can certainly therefore not ignore the former terrain. Exploration of the precise context of Northern Ireland affairs on 11 September 2001 demonstrates that those closely involved in or affected by Northern Ireland affairs were quickly involved in attempts to understand, process and indeed politicise the relevance of the events to the province.

In September 2001 the Northern Ireland Executive was in the middle of a second successive suspension, resulting from unionist dissatisfaction with the rate (or absence) of decommissioning of weapons by the Provisional IRA (as discussed in Chapter 2). PSF/PIRA responses to the pressure under which this placed them were, broadly, threefold. First, in August 2001 the PIRA put forward what it heralded as a plan according to which it would begin to put its weaponry beyond use through the Independent International Commission on Decommissioning (IICD) headed by General John de Chastelain. David Trimble, as leader of the UUP, considered the scheme unsatisfactory and it was subsequently withdrawn by the PIRA. Second, PSF's leaders endeavoured to deflect concern about the PIRA's decommissioning by asking why similar political pressure was not being applied to loyalist paramilitary groups to decommission, especially given the continued level of sporadic loyalist violence in parts of Northern Ireland, some of which was directed at Catholics. Indeed, it was around this time that John Reid, then the British Secretary of State for Northern Ireland, declared the ceasefire of the loyalist Ulster Defence Association to be over. The third point that Provisionals made at this time to try to stall or diminish the pressure upon them to decommission was to posit different interpretations of the relevant sections of the GFA. As has been discussed (in Chapter 3), this is arguably a case in which the Provisionals had at least a semantic point.[40]

In this context the principal political responses to 9/11 can be placed into two categories. First, unionists and their supporters sought to suggest that there was no moral difference between Al-Qaeda and the PIRA. The implication was that, since the British government was playing a principal role in a self-styled 'war against terrorism' in Central Asia, it was hypocritical of that government not to lay down the gauntlet (at the very least) to republican terrorists who continued to harbour and sporadically use arms caches in Northern Ireland. As David Trimble argued in October 2001, 'if the response to Bin Laden and the Taleban is clear-cut, unfortunately at home in Northern Ireland the position is not so clear. The problem is uncertainty and the Government's reluctance to grasp the nettle.'[41] The Conservative Party's shadow Secretary of State for Foreign Affairs, Michael Ancram, implied that British Conservatives had a special understanding of the plight of those bereaved by the 9/11 attacks on account of their past experiences as targets of the PIRA.[42] The *Daily Telegraph* was unimpressed with the distinction that the British Prime Minister Tony Blair reportedly drew between the situation in Northern Ireland and the 'war against terrorism', which was that:

> whereas in Ulster [*sic*] and the Middle East, 'there is a genuine sense of conflict, a political disagreement, that [it] is best to try to resolve by dialogue and negotiation', the campaign waged by Osama bin Laden is 'a situation where you have got terrorists who have no demands'. The dangerous implication of this is that if bin Laden and his henchmen came up with a

shopping list of demands the West might sit down with them.[43] Such parallels drawn between Al-Qaeda and the PIRA were possibly the most politically influential at that moment. Some commentators suggest that it was in an attempt to dissociate itself from the attacks on New York, Washington, DC, and Pennsylvania that the PIRA delivered its first act of decommissioning in October 2001, perhaps waiting only for a quiet period in the war in Afghanistan in order to ensure the maximum of publicity and credit for its move. (It is worth noting that, typically, equivalent parallels involving loyalists were hardly noted. By way of example one might notice Alistair Little, formerly an active member of the Ulster Volunteer Force. Although he has now fully recanted violence, Little still has loyalist connections. He has argued that 'men of violence' often represent the concerns of attached communities, linking this observation to 9/11 in an implied critique of US policy.)

There were, however, contrary discourses. For some commentators the recent experience of flawed British counter-insurgency policies in Northern Ireland suggested that the US administration's analogous 'war against terrorism' would prove counterproductive. Carl Bromley, a US-based radical, recalled the state of British public opinion in the 1980s, where because 'Britain's racist newspapers . . . would often describe the Irish in terms not unidentical to the way Arabs and Muslims have been demonised in the US media, feelings against the IRA (and the Irish) intensified':

> Mrs. Thatcher took advantage of this . . . The IRA was demonized as an absolute enemy and approached with an extreme moral righteousness. The mantra, 'You're either with us or against us,' something familiar to us now, was a common Thatcher refrain. . . . the wider political culture was poisoned: Protest the British government's role during the Hunger Strikes, or call for withdrawal of its troops from Northern Ireland, would guarantee a number of political reflexes: many ordinary people would spit at you and call you 'IRA scum,' [and] the British state would undoubtedly label you as an IRA apologist . . .
>
> If we judge Thatcher by her war aims her crusade was a complete failure. The IRA . . . became the most formidable paramilitary force on the European continent thanks in many

ways to the sheer intensity that the British used in trying to defeat them . . . [It is] very likely that Bin Laden and his many allies will very likely [*sic*] feed off and are nourished by the forms of retaliation [that] the US and its allies propose.[44]

Bromley was able to cite in his support Matthew Parris, a British journalist (and former Conservative politician), who suggested around the same time that 'playing the world's policeman' would 'give Osama bin Laden his own Bloody Sunday', meaning that 'when you kill one bin Laden you sow 20 more'.[45] The post-9/11 context also echoed that of Northern Ireland in producing intense debates about the nomenclature of the conflict. In both cases some adopted the relativistic view that 'one man's terrorist is another man's freedom fighter',[46] while for others, such as Conor Cruise O'Brien, so to fight shy of calling groups such as the PIRA 'terrorists' was to give them moral and political assistance.[47] However, even Richard English, who could hardly be described as an apologist for the PIRA, has deemed the term 'guerrillas' a more appropriate descriptor than 'terrorists'.[48] The approach adopted here is that it is legitimate to describe republican and loyalist groups as 'terrorist' in the literal sense where such groups aim to enforce their political demands through 'terrorising' civilian populations, so long as it is recognised that certain state actions may also be so described, for it would comprise a biased pro-state or counter-insurgent position not to accept the latter proviso. (This latter caveat is a particularly important point to make since forms of state terrorism are often more inventively disguised by euphemism: the Anglo-American 'shock and awe' bombardment of Baghdad in March 2003 could, for instance, legitimately be described as the terrorising of a civilian population, as, to an extent, could the British Army's 'internment swoop' on nationalist communities in Northern Ireland in August 1971. These instances also suggest the uncomfortable but necessary question as to whether in any circumstance these or other forms of 'terrorism' might not be justified.) Distinctions between a group such as the PIRA and Al-Qaeda, based on the way in which civilian populations are treated, can and should be made, but this does not obviate the possibility of describing certain activities of each, and of loyalists, as 'terrorism'.

In response to 9/11, unionists, among others, thus articulated the fear, suggestively voiced earlier by Trimble in his speech on accepting the Nobel Peace Prize in 1998, that 'there is an appeasing strand in western politics' in dealing with terrorism. Trimble's self-consciously 'hard-headed advice' on handling terrorists was: 'Don't act chummy with them; don't assume a continuity of aims with them which does not really exist; don't make fatuous gestures of good will.'[49] (One might wonder how 'chummy' was Trimble's interaction with loyalists in resisting the Sunningdale settlement in 1974, or how 'chummy' was his conversation with the loyalist leader Billy Wright at Drumcree in July 1996.) However, others, such as Bromley, rather feared that 'western politics' was too judgemental in viewing terrorism as an absolute evil. These positions were symptoms of the salient problem of responses in the British and US democracies to terrorist activities such as those of Al-Qaeda and in Northern Ireland: they were not explanations. Most individuals in fact probably responded to the events of 11 September with sheer horror and feelings of humanitarian sympathy. Disinterested humanitarianism and patriotism were certainly also *constructed* as the response of most public figures in the United States. In a ceremony of studied simplicity on the first anniversary of 9/11, accompanied by the strains of Aaron Copland's 'Fanfare for the Common Man', President George W. Bush declared that 9/11 was not merely an attack

> on our nation [but] was also [an] attack on the ideals that make us a nation. Our deepest national conviction is that every life is precious, because every life is the gift of a Creator who intended us to live in liberty and equality. More than anything else, this separates us from the enemy we fight. We value every life; our enemies value none – not even the innocent, not even their own. And we seek the freedom and opportunity that give meaning and value to life.[50]

However, horror and humanitarian sympathy were, after all, only two of the elements of British and US *media* and *political* responses to 9/11. There were also many strikingly rapid attempts to enlist the event to assist specific political agendas. These included gratuitous attempts on the political right to use 9/11 as a justification for restrictions on immigration or asylum laws. Thus, a few days after

9/11 the right-wing British tabloid newspaper the *Daily Mail* suggested that 'The asylum system is near collapse, with nobody having a clue how many potential enemies are simply walking in and disappearing.'[51] They also included attempts to depict commentary from the political left as unpatriotic, while the most outrageously unpatriotic comments on the political right escaped such vilification,[52] as well as the more notorious left-wing uses of 9/11 in anti-globalisation or anti-American diatribes.[53] These responses, and a number of other more considered and humane reactions, all demonstrate how quickly the 'spectacular' comes to dominate political discourse in such democracies, especially in a 'postmodern' age.[54] The political agenda was dominated by 9/11 for so long because it is hard to imagine anything more *spectacular* than a sudden aerial attack leaving 3,000 dead in the media capital of the world. In terms of human significance, the Tutsi genocide in Rwanda in 1994, for instance, was undoubtedly a more substantial event, but it was not spectacular in media terms and thus was given relatively little media attention, a decision doubtless seasoned by the unspoken racist assumption in certain quarters that human life is worth rather less in Africa than in New York. Whether the United States, Britain or any other nation is the subject of analysis, this is thus hardly evidence of a national conviction, that 'every life is precious' (whatever one's conception of the 'Creator') and worthy of an 'equality' of attention, but it is, surely, evidence of certain other national convictions.

In the present context the bare statistics of casualties in Washington, DC, Pennsylvania and especially New York put many individual events in Britain, the Irish Republic and Northern Ireland into a chilling perspective (although not, however, the aggregate number of deaths during the Troubles since 1968, which exceeds the number of casualties on 9/11). Yet responses to both sets of barbaric actions, from widely differing political perspectives, share the risk of giving a wholly undeserved profile to acts of spectacular violence and, ultimately, an undue level of legitimation to those responsible for them. As Bromley suggests, a key text is Bush's famous declaration in the days following 9/11 that 'every nation, in every region, now has a decision to make. Either you are with us, or you are with the terrorists.'[55] Despite criticisms of such rhetoric,[56] Bush has, fortunately, been far more circumspect in applying the logical implications of this doctrine than some less responsible elements of the US right. However, the declaration does indeed have a striking resonance with rhetoric featuring in the Northern Ireland conflict. William Whitelaw, the Conservative politician who was the first-ever Secretary of State for Northern Ireland, protested at one point about media coverage in Great Britain of the 'Troubles', warning against lowering the morale of the security forces and declaring that it was not possible to be neutral in the 'fight for freedom': 'Surely one is either for it or against it.' This bold assertion of moral absolutes was made notwithstanding Whitelaw's personal direct negotiating contact with the PIRA.[57] Margaret Thatcher also suggested at one point: 'Either one is on the side of justice in these matters or one is on the side of terrorism.'[58]

This focus on the evil of 'terrorism' appears to be a function of the anxiety of conservatives, in both the United Kingdom and the United States, about the volatility of their democracies, and thus a belief that some complex issues, such as foreign policy questions, must be reductively presented as simple battles of good and evil in order to secure appropriately pliant domestic public opinion.[59] However, Bromley does not really display an understanding of what is detrimental about this specific language, only positing a counterintuitive and inadequate sense that the more force that is applied against the terrorists, the stronger they become.

In fact, the problem with the reductive media focus attracted by spectacular terrorist violence, and with attempts, conscious or unconscious, to taint all of those who can in any way be associated with 'the terrorists' with the moral responsibility for such actions, is that, by reducing the discursive space available to certain groups who are not supporters of terrorism, it actually creates allies that terrorists otherwise would not have. Such a strategy creates a situation in which individuals of the same ethnic group as any selected terrorist faction are charged with complicity in terrorism and, in some cases, visited upon with reprisals, either sanctioned by the state or not. This occurs in part because a reductive portrayal of an ethnic or other group in association with acts of violence creates a process whereby that group comes to appear to be defined by violence. This error is, of course, evident in the targeting of Muslims and individuals of Middle Eastern descent in the United States and elsewhere by misguided individuals, and in journalistic and political depictions of Islam as an inherently violent or backward religion, as well as in more academic discourses about a 'clash of civilisations', which often overtly treat Muslim immigrants as a source of danger.[60] There is abundant evidence that during periods when the PIRA was conducting bombing campaigns the Irish in Britain underwent experiences that in some respects were similar,[61] and that pro-state discourses occluded intermediate positions at the time, as two examples will demonstrate.

First, Lloyd Turner of the tabloid newspaper the *Daily Star* reportedly stated:

> Those fighting to overthrow the State – and the democratically elected representatives of the State – are terrorists . . . The people living in Northern Ireland have freedom of choice. They have democratic elections. They are not prevented from leaving Northern Ireland to live elsewhere. Those who want to change Northern Ireland are given the opportunity to do so at the ballot box. In fact they resort to bullets instead. That is terrorism.[62]

There are many problematic aspects to this argument, such as the neglect of *un*democratic features of the government of Northern Ireland until 1972, when change was at least subsequent to the resort to 'terrorism', and the confrontational implications of the idea that those who do not like the way the North is governed should just 'get out'. The binary opposition drawn between 'terrorists' and pro-statists further occludes many other positions. Turner seems unaware of the fact that there might also be 'terrorists' who seek to uphold 'the State' (i.e., loyalists), and that these play a role in Northern Ireland politics of some significance. More importantly, Turner skates over the existence of those who 'want to change Northern Ireland' but who do *not* 'resort to bullets', such as at that time, among other groups, the APNI and constitutional nationalists. For the sake of indulging a sense of moral outrage about 'terrorism', this is thus to create a situation in which those with objections to the status quo are not recognised as having any mode of expression other than sympathy for 'terrorism' itself.

Second, there is Shane Kingston's analysis of Sinn Féin's electoral support: 'Sinn Fein's vote comes from members, supporters and sympathisers of the IRA, and those who support violence are as guilty as those who perpetrate it.'[63] This again is to occlude distinctions in an overstatement of unconditional support for 'terrorists' in a way which can actually have performative and counterproductive effects. Particularly at the time when Kingston was writing (1995) it was definitely not true that all who were likely to vote for PSF in Northern Ireland were supporters of terrorism, since some at that stage instead sought to show the mainstream republicans the potential rewards of political campaigning, in order to lure them more to political rather than military activities. More significantly, however, Kingston overlooks the extent to which the support of some Northern Ireland Catholics for republicans, whether through the ballot box or otherwise, has been a contingent response to situations in which Catholic communities and individuals have been the perceived or actual victims of aggression by loyalists or the security forces. Indeed, once again the observer barely acknowledges loyalism and certainly understates its significance. Kingston is also close to inhering Turner's tabloid stereotype according to which large communities of 'the Irish' are really responsible for 'terrorism' and thereby cause *the* problem, presumably through some atavistic racial disposition to violence. Another variant of this error is a tendency to overstate the continuity across time of Irish republican tradition, thus ascribing the conflict largely to allegedly long-established confrontational implications of a republican ideology implicitly endorsed by large numbers of Irish people. Paradoxically, in the Irish case this is to give republicans undeserved credit as inheritors of a republican tradition with some reputable historical manifestations (see Chapter 3). A more subtle but similar error may be discerned even in certain high-quality academic productions that focus on a minority of terrorists as salient objects of study in a particular political context, unconsciously giving that minority an inflated importance and thus obscuring other causal factors.[64]

'The terrorists' own perverted discourse is evident in their portrayals of infidels or Americans or 'Brits' as the enemy, being based on the assumption that a binary opposition exists between 'cultures' or ethnic groups. Sharing that language thus helps the terrorists, by shifting attention from the fundamental weakness of their ideology, the solipsistic assumption that they have 'their people' on their side.[65] In some cases, indeed, the connections between the applications of these erroneous assumptions to the two contexts of Northern Ireland and 9/11 are closer still. In October 2001 the right-wing British commentator Paul Johnson argued that the 9/11 attacks had occurred because 'Islam remains a religion of the Dark Ages'.[66] This followed and contradicted an earlier bizarre effort by Johnson to suggest that the Irish were ultimately responsible for 9/11, since the historical process by which 'nationalist agitators became ruthless mass murderers' 'began in Ireland'.[67] Both suggestions in turn are thus to be linked to Johnson's long record of wrong-headed interventions in debates about the Northern Ireland conflict, including the suggestion in 1975 that 'monsters' such as the Guildford Four be executed,[68] which have similarly been ultimately inspired by the assumption that terrorism is an evil that emanates from the atavistic disposition towards violence of certain ethnic groups.

A better antidote to terrorists' solipsistic discourse is not the rhetoric of 'war against terrorism', or other exaggerated dichotomies between ethnic and other groups, but a representation of aspects of the relevant terrain that refute the notion that violence is ethnically determined. These would include the non-violent elements of Islam, Irish culture and life in Northern Ireland, all of which are persistently under-represented. Non-essentialist explorations of the causes of violence in such contexts would also demonstrate that the terrorists do not represent those cultures and do not have popular sanction. As discussed previously (in Chapters 2 and 3), the continuing relative equanimity of significant sections of the British media and political class about loyalist terror was, and is, a source of distortion, but it is also a political disaster for any serious effort to govern Northern Ireland within the union, since it was, and is, yet another form of treating Northern Ireland Catholics, the victims of sectarian loyalist attacks, as second-class citizens. In this context Margaret Thatcher's retrospective suggestion that 'my well-known attitude towards Irish terrorism' should have reassured unionists is particularly interesting. It would be possible to infer from this statement that Thatcher was not notably hostile to loyalist terrorism, while the 'Irish' as a whole were responsible for the mode of terrorism that she *did* abhor.[69] Bromley compounds the failure to acknowledge loyalist terror, treating loyalism as little more than an arm of the British state. In a manner analogous to the effects of the victimisation of individuals from diasporic ethnic groups associated with terrorism by a crudely soldered public opinion, such media and political representation appears to reduce the options available to individuals from the relevant ethnic groups beyond lending support to those most clearly opposed to the union, i.e., Irish republicans or other extremists.

At another level the position of individuals with doubts about particular counter-insurgency policies, even where they do not share the ethnicity of the targeted terrorists, is also occluded by such discourses. One could, or can, criticise the Prevention of Terrorism Act, or the convictions of the Guildford Four or the Birmingham Six, or the US Patriot Act, or aspects of Bush's diplomacy before the onset of the war in Iraq, without assisting terrorists, and to suggest that one cannot is to give those with doubts about such measures little discursive space short of trying to find excuses for the inexcusable: where their military defeat is not possible, the 'terrorists' thus come to dictate the political agenda (see Chapter 3). As John McGarry and Brendan O'Leary argued in the 1990s, for those who most indulged rhetorical animosity to 'terrorism', 'Northern Ireland had to be either British or Irish; the choice was dichotomous. Analysts who suggested otherwise were considered idealistic fools, stooges or fellow-travellers of the paramilitaries. Thankfully, this consensus, to which not all subscribed, has passed away.'[70] McGarry and O'Leary appreciate, although they possibly understate, the important point that, notwithstanding the power of hegemonic discourses at such moments, such discursive space can be found. Some dissentient intellectuals, as well as some members of victimised minorities, within societies at 'war against terrorism' in such situations do seem to have erred politically and morally in adopting the strategy of linking themselves to a framework that shares a counter-hegemonic rationale with terrorism. An obvious example would be the intellectual who claims that 9/11 happened because of an ill-defined 'they' hate 'us' or 'America', and offers what presents itself as a master-narrative of why 'they' hate 'us', thus claiming for themselves and others a close relationship to the inner working of the terrorist mind.[71] These too are guilty of promoting the domination of discourse by, and thus of constructing a legitimation of, the terrorist spectacular, as well as inadvertently refunctioning discourses painfully close to the racist notion that terrorism has an essential relationship to specific ethnic communities. The processes at work here may be demonstrated by analyses of two academic texts concerned with republican activity in Northern Ireland, both of which were published before 9/11 but significantly refer to largely Muslim insurgent movements, especially in the Palestinian context. First, in an article published in 1991 Claire Wills echoes the late Edward Saïd in reflecting on the irony of how the stereotyping of all 'Palestinians' or all 'Catholic Irish' as terrorists reinscribes the 'terrorists' in a relationship to their community. However, Wills immediately goes on to assert 'the symbolically representative function of militant republicanism's actions': in a symbolic sense, certain anonymous rituals of the republicans do actually represent the 'Catholic Irish'.[72] A second such moment appears in David Lloyd's discussion of Neil Jordan's film *The Crying Game*. Lloyd first laments the film's 'coeval stereotypes of the terrorist and the Irishman . . . In this conflation, the Irishman is drawn to terrorism because of the violent and sentimental or fanatic nature of his racial psychology.' He then complains that the film recapitulates

> another set of racial stereotypes . . . that terrorists and the Irish are *by nature* fanatical, pathological, [and] atavistic[,] and, by virtue of these characteristics, lack full humanity. Requisite to such representations is their radical severance of insurgency from any historical ground which might give it a rationale . . . and, above all, from any relation to the subordinated communities without whose at least passive acquiescence and often active support a long-lasting guerrilla campaign is unthinkable.

Lloyd further suggests that this coheres to aspects of the British and Irish governments' criminalisation policies, which in his view are misapplied and have the aim of cutting 'off the insurgents from any base in the community'.[73]

What is fascinating in these arguments is how the racist conflation of violence and an essential Irishness is first disavowed and then, tantalisingly, almost reinvoked in an anxiety to demonstrate that republican 'insurgents' 'often' have 'active support' from, and therefore 'represent', 'their community'. This is linked to an attempt to 'understand' the republican position: Lloyd at least aspires (at a low intensity) to a united Ireland and is a critic of the Northern Ireland peace process, apparently on the grounds that it is not doing enough to challenge the legitimacy of the British and Irish states, although he is also a critic of dissident republican violence.[74] From this position the domination of discourse by the spectacular is likely to conflate terrorism and an ethnic 'community' as much as from the position that Lloyd terms the counter-insurgent. While there is a measure of justification for Lloyd's hint that the PIRA's campaign has been dependent on a 'tense but often mutually supportive relationship' with certain nationalist neighbourhoods,[75] it misses the crucial point about the context in Northern Ireland, that the actions of small numbers of extremists on either side have created that 'deterrence' relationship in the first place (as discussed in Chapter 3).[76] The unusual set of conditions described by Cash, in which communal consciousness takes on exclusivist, even dehumanising and totalitarian forms is created by communities being on the receiving end of terrorism in the first place.[77] To regard terrorists as even symbolically representative of the community in such a context is to miss the critical fact that terrorism *creates* such a community and is thus in, not an essential, but a *very contingent* relationship to it. The overplayed notion of 'symbolic' representativity further deprives non-republican Catholics or nationalists of agency. To foreground symbolic rather than electoral representation[78] is to overlook the facts, not only that the 'Catholic Irish' have consistently professed their dissension from acts of terrorism by voting for non-republican parties in very considerable numbers, but also that those numbers might now be larger were it not for republican intimidation.

Within the British, US and Irish democracies, both establishment and counter-hegemonic narratives inscribe 'terrorists' in an unnecessarily strong relationship to certain ethnic or cultural groups. This works to the advantage of groups that can perpetrate the terrorist violence likely to be treated within mainstream media as the most 'spectacular'. In the British Isles this was the PIRA and now in the United States it is Al-Qaeda, only partly on account of the sheer military force of such groups, but also because societies' media are likely to be more fascinated by events yielding victims of 'their own'. Depending on the intersecting vectors of political, military and demographic forces, the depiction of terror groups, and their attached (and acquired) supporters, as an unmitigated evil might actually persuade, and it may be possible to bring overwhelming influence (or force) to bear to counter any initial political gains to the terrorist. However, where there is a disjuncture between the centre of such influence or force and political causes mostly directly opposed to such 'terrorists', the attention paid to the latter's outrages may detract from the legitimacy of opposed causes, such as Northern Ireland unionism. While the dynamics in effect since 9/11 thus *may* have a different upshot, it is indeed depressing, if understandable, to anyone who has lived through Britain in the 1980s, to see US administrators and opinion-formers repeating the same mistakes.

Bromley is quite wrong, however, to suggest that US Republicans, or, indeed, Democrats, need to rethink their attitude to Al-Qaeda because of a cosy relationship with PSF. The only fact about this cosy relationship that Bromley laments is that, by pollution, US Republicans have turned PSF, which 'was once quite an impressive radical political party, into a pro-business one'. Presumably Bromley felt that the Provisionals were more 'right on' when they were killing British people on a regular basis.[79] In a sense the *Daily Telegraph* and, in a sense, Trimble and Ancram (all quoted above) are right: reactions to 9/11 in the United States show that Northern Ireland unionism and, indeed, Irish nationalism are not exceptional, and should at least make aspects of Northern Ireland unionist and nationalist ideologies more comprehensible to more parties than they formerly were. There is a certain level of evidence that this has in fact taken place, for instance through contact between Bush and the families of victims of the Omagh bomb.

This argument would not suggest that the media attention that has been secured by republican (especially PIRA) outrages has had a particularly negative influence on unionist legitimacy unless there could be said to be an insistent disjuncture between British and, in a different sense, Irish society, on the one hand, and unionism and Northern Ireland on the other. This is where features, observable in many national contexts, of the imaginings of the conservative and liberal political nations have been particularly important.

THE CONSERVATIVE POLITICAL NATION: SELF-PITY
AND SELF-CONGRATULATION

On 1 June 1997, a few weeks after becoming Prime Minister of the United Kingdom, Tony Blair issued an apology for the negligence of British administrators during the Irish Famine more than 150 years before. The conservative *Daily Telegraph* was concerned that this apology would 'reinforce the self-pitying nature of Irish nationalism. A growing tendency within nationalist Ireland holds that the famine was an act of genocide. Feeding its grievance culture allows it to place the blame for all the country's ills at the door of the Brits, ultimately justifying terrorism.'[80] This notion of 'the self-pitying nature of Irish nationalism' enjoys a level of academic credibility, especially since Liam Kennedy's articulation of what he called a 'MOPE complex' in Irish culture: 'an almost palpable sense of victimhood and exceptionalism in the presentation of the Irish national past, particularly as reconstructed and displayed for political purposes. It is a syndrome of attitudes that might be summed up by the acronym MOPE, that is, the most oppressed people ever.'[81]

Journalistic uses of this interpretation may however suggest that self-pity is not an identifiable feature of nationalism elsewhere. In fact, it is at least as significant a feature of British nationalism as of Irish nationalism and, as Arthur Aughey notes, the British nationalist formations evident in certain columns of the *Daily Telegraph* itself provide many an example.[82] Influential recent conservative imaginings of the British nation suggest that that nation is under such attack from an enemy within that one might talk of a Most Self-Deprecating People Ever complex, or, indeed, a Most Self-Oppressing People Ever complex, according to which the British are fundamentally just too self-effacing for their own and everybody else's good. Minette Marrin argues that:

> for many Britons there [is] a profound self-doubt . . . which has deprived the indigenous Judaeo-Christian culture of confidence in itself, and in its true and admirable values. . .[There is] a deep-seated reluctance among the educated to speak up against cultural assaults and for the host culture . . .Tolerance is

not only one of the greatest achievements of our civilisation
and the bedrock of freedom; it is also its Achilles' heel.[83]

The educated 'enemy within' is thus supposedly responsible for a
dual assault on tolerance and the 'national' culture. This supposed or
predicted death of Britain is depicted by the influential Eurosceptic
British Conservative politician John Redwood, in a moment typical
of the contradictory products of such uncritical national self-
congratulation, as a self-inflicted attack on 'our decent, understated,
self-deprecating way of doing of things'.[84] As Peter Hitchens argues:
'alone of all European countries, [Britain's] recent past is unsullied
by collaboration or even by dishonourable neutrality . . . Yet she acts
as if she has something to be ashamed of. National pride is suspect,
patriotism rarely expressed.'[85] As the *Daily Telegraph* declared in an
editorial that appeared close to St George's Day in 2001, 'many'
Britons were supposedly 'afraid to speak' their fears that 'their own
country is being taken away from them' by 'the public sector attack
on British history and traditions, orchestrated by the
[Blair]Government's cheerleaders in the public sector, the BBC and
the race relations industry'. The basis of tolerance was under attack
along with this history and these traditions: 'the Government is
tearing Britain's ethnic and cultural settlement apart'.[86] The political
strength of this assumption that the British people's 'own country is
being taken away from them' was further reflected in a speech made
by the then leader of the British Conservative Party, William Hague,
at Harrogate on 4 March 2001, widely known as the 'foreign land'
speech. The 'foreign land' in question was a Britain misgoverned,
with inefficient public services, poor living conditions and rampant
crime, particularly after the supine hand-over of control of the
United Kingdom, by an elite of 'self-appointed experts', to
European institutions: 'we have a government that scorns and
despises all the things that have made our country what it is. A
government that holds Britishness cheap.'[87] Hague's speech mirrors
closely, and may well have been inspired by, the closing passages of
Hitchens' book.[88]

Many British newspapers' coverage of Northern Ireland is
uncannily similar to their more recent coverage of the perceived
problem of Britain being 'swamped' by asylum-seekers, usually
stereotyped as Islamic or non-white, in displaying this tendency to

self-pity. In both cases those few facts are selectively presented that seem to demonstrate that 'Britain' is being a 'soft touch',[89] uniquely taken advantage of by rapacious foes, respectively under-punished PIRA killers (see Chapter 2) and asylum-seekers exploiting the British welfare system, supporting terrorism or bringing disease into the country.[90] Evidence that contextualises these experiences, or suggests that they are by no means unique, is neglected. The British media have persistently under-reported violence by loyalists or the security forces in Northern Ireland (as has been discussed in previous chapters), and neglected cross-national comparisons and opportunities to report numbers of asylum-seekers in Britain as proportions of population rather than in absolute terms, both of which would help to refute the idea that Britain has recently been a uniquely burdened asylum destination.[91] In the case of asylum-seekers as in the case of Northern Ireland, the self-pitying notion that members of the white English middle class are in some way the most put upon, under-appreciated, badly treated people in the world is indulged partly in order to sell newspapers. This British mode of self-pity is potentially as productive of violence as the Irish self-pity so worrying to the *Daily Telegraph*. British media self-pity has appeared to legitimise heavy-handed and ham-fisted anti-republican policies in Northern Ireland, while the repeated sentiment that governments are failing to protect the country from asylum-seekers, of which 'Britain has had enough', encourages racist attacks, among other problems, injustices and inequalities, by giving individuals the utterly misguided sense that thus to take the law into their own hands is to protect 'Britain'.[92]

These self-pitying discourses are incoherent and wrong-headed, as well as implicitly violent. However, whether a mechanism by which British media coverage of the asylum issue can have an effect as ultimately counterproductive to the political aims declared in such locations as coverage of the Northern Ireland conflict has had remains to be seen. The source of these counterproductive effects in the case of Northern Ireland is that 'national' narratives that activate the display of self-pity are usually heavily focused on evidence (selective evidence at that) derived from a national 'heartland', and are, at best, ambivalent and, at worst, antipathetic to narratives emanating from national peripheries. Thus a disjuncture is created between such forms of British nationalism, on the one hand, and unionism and Northern Ireland on the other. This feature of nationalism, which is surprisingly under-appreciated in the rich thematic literature on the subject,[93] and which is especially, though not exclusively,[94] evident in conservative or right-wing nationalist formations in western societies, helps to explain why obstacles to the incorporation of a peripheral society such as Northern Ireland within the imagined conservative political nation are currently so intractable.

These obstacles do indeed require some explanation, since the *British* Conservative political nation is one to which a large number of members and supporters of the UUP (at least) appear to feel akin. Many such unionists, Aughey notes, feel

> a traditional understanding of the history of a free people, a freedom not unrelated, of course to their Protestantism. Free, though, in a very peculiar and in a very British way. The British genius is believed to lie in the capacity to fashion institutions which reconcile order with personal liberty. This faith has tied traditional unionism into the 'conservative political nation', in both the ideological and party-political senses of the word 'conservative'.[95]

For some Unionists and Unionist sympathisers Protestantism is passionately believed in and perceived as a key feature of Britishness and defence of the purity of the Protestant faith is an objective in itself. In other formations British institutions, including Protestantism or the Protestant settlement, serve a more instrumental function, furthering the higher aims of tolerance and liberty. There is a possible tension between these versions of conservative teleology, the unravelling of which (as will be shown) can adversely affect conservatives' relations with unionists. However, currently it does not appear that conservative awareness (at least) of such a consequence of these tensions is very great. In spite of difficulties when the Conservatives were in government,[96] British Conservatives and the UUP have more recently again sought closer links.

Three distinct contradictions resulting from politicised self-pity in conservative imaginings of the British nation may be identified, the third of which especially coheres with the obstacles to legitimation facing Northern Ireland unionism. First, politicised self-pity is a fragile basis for British patriotism, since it entails implicit and increasingly explicit despair about 'Britain'. The nationalism advanced by proponents of this imagined British nation is definitively not the same as territorialised patriotism. Indeed, such nationalists may be so bewitched by their image of a nation as to find unbearable a large number of the occupants of the *actual* territorial nation they claim to cherish. This is the cause of the curious fact that such conservative nationalists are those most ready to write Britain off. Hague's 'foreign land' speech should be criticised not for racism, as was suggested at the time, but for logical renunciation of the British nation, pending the fulfilment of a contingency that practically everyone knew at the time was inevitable: the heavy defeat of the party that Hague was leading in the then forthcoming general election of June 2001. Such renunciations emanated strikingly from the leader and chief organ of a political party that has often claimed to be the secure repository of British/English patriotism.[97] Other conservatives are prepared to declare that their nation is already dead, no contingency requiring fulfilment.[98] There is surely nothing here that could be defined as patriotism in conventional terms. It is indicative of the contorted psyche induced by such a Most Self-Oppressing People Ever complex that the sufferer begins by chiding fellow-nationals for exaggerated national self-deprecation (even though, as, notably, in Redwood's case, self-deprecation *in some forms* is also seen as a national virtue) and ends by deprecating the same nation in the most dogmatic, emotional and outrageous terms of all.

The second problem with this conservative vision of the political nation comprises its misconceptions about British and English history. It is rather hard to find solid historical groundings for this imagining of the nation, since it is as incumbent in such accounts to suppress instances of bombastic nationalism as it is to deny cases of racial and ethnic violence, indecency, intolerance, and sectarianism in British and, more especially, English history. There are surely, in fact, no small number of any of these.[99] There are cognate problems with the clear implication that one's own culture is *uniquely* self-deprecating: this is such an easy assumption to make among those whose knowledge is too concentrated within a single national frame that it is no surprise to find it appearing elsewhere. Witness the

domination of the US media by equivalent discourses in the
aftermath of 9/11, especially lamenting the failure of liberal elites,
notably in the same media and public-service professions reviled by
British right-wingers, to understand that 'an American patriotism' is,
in John O'Sullivan's words, 'among other things a celebration of
tolerance':

> today there is . . . a tendency to self-blame . . . A person in its
> grip has imbibed the notion that the patriotism of ordinary
> people is something simplistic, vulgar, and shameful, and thus
> to be avoided . . . Many of America's troubles stem in part
> from the fact that it is the first nation with a dissident ruling
> class. Our elites in government, cultural institutions, the courts,
> the media, and even business have increasingly adopted the
> view that the American people are racist, sexist, and
> homophobic.[100]

Admirer though he is of the US right,[101] Peter Hitchens might struggle
to respond to the view that the United States is the 'first nation' to
suffer this syndrome. Perhaps, however, he could learn from the
strategy adopted by a writer in the *Daily Telegraph* who was in an
analogous quandary when confronted by a reported comment, from
the former French Prime Minister Lionel Jospin, that 'France should
not undervalue itself or be self-deprecating': the writer concluded that
this was clear evidence that the French *should* be self-deprecating.[102]

Other examples of this 'complex' can be found in other national
contexts, including Irish anti-'revisionism' (see Chapter 3). To elide
oneself with an imagined nation and then to claim that 'we' fellow-
nationals deprecate 'our' country too much is a ubiquitously
convenient method of silencing critics. As Jürgen Habermas
explains, a 'naturalistic conception of the nation as a pre-political
entity' is unlikely to be 'combined seamlessly with the universalistic
self-understanding of the democratic constitutional state' and can
inspire 'repressive' tendencies in relation to those who fail to live up
to such a 'national' 'ideal'.[103] A dynamic of intolerance can emerge
towards those members of one's own group who evince dissent from
the imagined archetype of the national by disparaging the
supposedly authentic national culture, even, ironically, where that
culture is held to be uniquely tolerant. Further, where evidence of

violence, intolerance and xenophobia within this supposedly authentic national culture cannot be denied, intellectual cartwheels must be turned to suggest that these are not what they seem at all, but the fault of a liberal elite frustrating outlets for patriotic sentiment.[104] Roger Scruton thus argues in his historically challenged[105] book *England: An Elegy*. 'It is the fact that England has been forbidden – and forbidden by the English.'[106] Racist responses in England to immigration are, he suggests, results of this sense that 'England . . . is no longer "ours"': 'Until this fatal disenchantment, immigrants were regarded by the English as newcomers to the home, entitled to hospitality while they found their feet.'[107] Yet racist violence in Britain has by and large not been perpetrated by liberal intellectuals, but by individuals a good deal closer in political inclinations to some of Scruton's own.[108] Scruton's view is not exceptional and equivalent special pleading can be found in other national contexts among analysts, such (again) as Irish anti-'revisionists', desperate to defend the indefensible hypothesis that their own particular national 'traditions' constitute roots of tolerance (see Chapter 3).[109]

The third and most important problem with conservative imaginings of the political nation is the way in which they tacitly exclude, while claiming to incorporate, a peripheral society such as Northern Ireland. For geopolitical reasons a 'national' tradition of tolerance, whether associated with an imagined British, American or other nation, in spite of its inadequacies in each case, is a myth that it is easier to present in association with a national 'heartland', such as, in the British case, the Southeast of England. It seems to be far easier to congratulate oneself about one's tolerance where the centre of national sovereignty has largely been close by and within one's influence. This constitutes a tension between conservative ideology and the real conditions of existence in Northern Ireland, which, being intimately related to explosive political controversies over closer European union, is likely to become only more intense in the near future.

In a thought-provoking essay on British policy in Northern Ireland, published in 1993, Lord Armstrong of Ilminster, who was centrally involved as a civil servant in the construction of the AIA and now sits in the House of Lords as a 'crossbencher' (independent), provided a telling example of the tendency among some British commentators articulating relevant discourses to assume that they do not actually constitute a 'nationalism', or at any rate comprise truths too profound to deserve to be so regarded. Armstrong suggests that the English do not have an ethnicity: 'I can recognise an English national identity and character, but I cannot recognise an English "ethnicity". If there is any, it is certainly less than that of the Scots, the Welsh or the Irish.'[110] This hyper-rationality of the English was apparently demonstrated by the mastery of Northern Ireland policy demonstrated by one of Lord Armstrong's former bosses, Margaret Thatcher: 'it was for her just history and not – as it sometimes seems to be for the Irish – a backward extension of the present . . . She was relatively free of historical baggage or hang-ups.'[111]

This doctrine of cool English detachment is in fact itself inseparable from historical 'baggage', involving a clear refunctioning of a stereotypical Irish obsession with history[112] that features in many an apologetic for British policy. The selected subject is also singularly unfortunate, given the well-established tendency of Mrs (now Baroness) Thatcher and some of her close associates, before and after 1993, to display spectacular 'hang-ups' about Europe (the European Union in particular) and sundry other matters, all derived from their imperfect assimilation of historical contexts.[113] Such hang-ups themselves are a product of a powerful historical metanarrative in conservative Euroscepticism, closely linked to the conservative political nation's confidence in its own tolerance and decency. As Thatcher suggested in October 1999: 'In my lifetime all our problems have come from mainland Europe and all the solutions have come from the English-speaking nations of the world that have kept law-abiding liberty alive for the future.'[114] Apart from arguing that participation in an ever-closer European union does not really match Britain's economic and commercial interests, conservatives argue that there are important historical, cultural and political differences between Britain and the countries of continental Europe. Redwood juxtaposes a 'continental way' of autocracy, bureaucracy and violent revolution with a historical pattern of 'English evolution', which is supposed to have 'reigned' in British history from at least the Glorious Revolution at the end of the seventeenth century, continuing to a large extent into the present day.[115] British institutions, it is suggested, have proved the most successful in Europe, so it is illogical to reject them for institutions of dubious provenance largely devised elsewhere.

As James Loughlin suggests, the articulation of such rarefied and exclusive 'core' versions of British national identity as Redwood's has historically added to Northern Ireland unionists' difficulties, since their ability to conform to such metropolitan norms is popularly in doubt. In particular, while such British commentators as those quoted have perceived Great Britain as being characterised by 'humour, tolerance and compromise', the public image of Northern Ireland that prevails in Great Britain includes 'associations of bigotry, sectarianism and political extremism'. Thus 'the dominant image of Ulster [*sic*] was at variance with the characteristics identified as British'.[116] Redwood's narrative of British history is particularly dependent on *English* history. His consideration of the history of the non-English parts of the United Kingdom is far less coherent:

> An Englishman rejoices in his liberties, Scotsmen used to tolerate the union, with many coming to London to seek their fortunes. The Celtic countries provided a little bitter-sweet anger and romance to leaven the more sedate, less easily aroused English breed. The British remain . . . confident that their islands will remain forever free.[117]

A 'little bitter-sweet anger and romance' either constitutes a highly inappropriate trivialisation of any phase of the Northern Ireland conflict, or indicates that Redwood does not wish to think seriously about that conflict at all. The latter interpretation is certainly consonant with Redwood's treatment of parliamentary discussion of Northern Ireland as an irritating distraction from the business of holding the present Labour government to account within a ruthlessly metropolitan frame of reference.[118] So far as this Conservative is concerned, the best response to European integration is to ignore Northern Ireland altogether.

Another striking example of this conservative '"mainland" amnesia'[119] occurred in a speech given by William Hague in January 1999. Here Hague again suggested that the Labour government's supposed enthusiasm for closer European integration ignored the existence of a 'British way', distinct from continental norms. The

Times, until recently a traditionally conservative newspaper, particularly purred over one reported comment:

> It is indeed the case that, as Mr Hague asserted, 'where we invest our national identity in our political institutions, many other European countries have been let down by their political institutions within living memory'. For that reason the constitutional implications of close integration within the European Union are more profound and more destabilising for Britain than for almost all of our neighbours.[120]

Hague and the *Times* clearly had continental Europe's collapse before Nazism in mind. This doctrine that British institutions are distinctive because they have not failed overlooks the fate of the Stormont institutions in Northern Ireland, which, even disregarding more recent difficulties, were superseded by direct rule from Westminster amid a wave of political violence in 1972. The faith of Hague and the *Times* stands any chance of justification only if the unionist claim that the institutions of, and the majority in, Northern Ireland are British is overruled.

Relevant incoherencies are also evident in the *Daily Telegraph*. In April 2002 the far-right leader Jean-Marie Le Pen achieved a surprising level of success in the first round of voting in the French presidential election (before being crushed in the second round). Initially the *Daily Telegraph* gleefully used this event to draw attention to the supposed organic differences between British and (continental) European history and culture previously mapped by Hague, Redwood and the *Times*, posing Le Pen as 'the heir to a nasty, authoritarian tradition on the French Right, one that has no real equivalent in British politics'.[121] Boris Johnson, a Conservative MP who is also editor of the *Spectator*, joined in sounding the triumphalist note by suggesting that British liberals 'apologise' for criticising Baroness Thatcher's suggestion that 'extremist politicians sometimes do alarmingly well on the Continent'.[122] However, as part of an argument that blamed Le Pen's success on closer European integration, the *Daily Telegraph* went on to describe Le Pen as 'like Ian Paisley . . . a kind of perennial "no" man'. Thus the most popular unionist politician in Northern Ireland, it was suggested, represents a definitively 'nasty', 'extremist', non-British 'tradition'.[123] In

October 2000 the *Daily Telegraph* had self-consciously placed itself at the epicentre of rebuttals of the high-profile multiculturalist report of the Commission on the Future of Multi-Ethnic Britain set up by the Runnymede Trust, also known as the Parekh Report after the commission's chairperson, Bhikhu Parekh,[124] accusing its authors of an 'attempt to destroy a thousand years of British history'.[125] Such a wholly imaginary thousand-year-old British nation-state puts in no small number of appearances within right-wing Anglocentric British nationalism. It fails to incorporate the experience of the non-English peripheries of the United Kingdom[126] and especially, even in its more informed articulations, fails to appreciate how *any* attempted incorporation of Northern Ireland must render 'Britishness' a fundamentally modern formation.[127] The editorial policy of the *Daily Telegraph* has thus, ironically, been that of the Englishman 'who assumes that he alone defines what is British',[128] epitomising the metropolitan superciliousness that excludes Northern Ireland from its conceptions of Britain and Britishness.

In the short term these subtle influences may have little effect on Conservative policy for Northern Ireland. In the long term conservative stereotypes of British history accentuate pre-existing tendencies in Great Britain to regard the unionist population of Northern Ireland as not truly British, thus exacerbating the British public's psychological withdrawal from the province. This is a fact of which even policy-makers sympathetic to Northern Ireland unionism have ultimately to take account. Armstrong thus may hint at a truth when he suggests that the lack of English 'ethnicity' becomes a problem in British–Irish relations, since the English cannot understand in the Irish what they lack in themselves.[129] Certainly it is hard to see how a supercilious metropolitan assumption that the Irish are all irrationally obsessed with history, and thus predisposed to violence and intolerance, could be extended only to the *nationalist* inhabitants of the island of Ireland. Even when these assumptions emanate from right-wing or apparently unionist perspectives, they nourish the sense that inhabitants of Ireland are so alike, so uncivilised and so fundamentally 'Irish' that it is best that British governments clear out of the island of Ireland altogether, paving the way for a united Ireland. It is in this sense that Paul Dixon's observations as to the Thatcher government's 'English nationalist "weakness" on the Union' are so apposite.[130] Conservative discourses in relation to Europe are particularly important, since they show that these assumptions are likely to find continued sources of vivacity on the British right through political controversies that also will not go away.

THE LIBERAL POLITICAL NATION: DISCRIMINATION AND OVERSIGHT

Some unionists argue that it is more logical to forge connections between Northern Ireland and a United Kingdom that is a 'multi-national, multi-faith, multi-ethnic' state than between the province and 'the romantic nostalgia of contemporary Irish nationalism'.[131] There are those prepared to articulate the mirror image of this argument on the nationalist side.[132] If the above analysis of the conservative imagined political nation is correct, however, such arguments may proceed in entirely the wrong direction. A concept of either nation that would incorporate Northern Ireland would need, not to celebrate proudly or demonstrate its own tolerance, but to confront most boldly the limitations of the imagined national culture.

Although British conservative nationalists are not disposed to see it, there are in fact considerable narratives of sectarianism and xenophobia in British history. 'English evolution' in Britain has not contrasted with a 'continental way' of autocracy, bureaucracy and violent revolution, even in historical epochs where such a dichotomy appears most apposite. To provide one example: during the 1790s the numbers of casualties even in the year of French revolutionary Terror itself was roughly equalled in 1798 in Ireland, a much smaller society within the British orbit, most of these being victims of repression by British-sponsored authorities.[133] Irish conservative nationalists – and many Irish nationalists are more conservative than they would like to admit – are similarly averse to recognising equivalent narratives in the history of nationalist Ireland.[134] There are, of course, reasons for the conventional wisdom that, in John Whyte's words, 'Northern Ireland *is* different'.[135] Nevertheless, if equivalences such as between sectarianism in Scotland and sectarianism in Northern Ireland are sometimes overemphasised,[136] an unnecessary aversion to parallel consideration particularly of discrimination in Northern Ireland with analogous problems elsewhere exists in all sorts of political and academic perspectives.

The fact that this deficiency is liberal as well as conservative, especially in the British context, creates further problems of political legitimacy for those in Northern Ireland who would like to relate most closely to that context, the unionists. At least three definitions of the word 'liberalism' are relevant to this analysis: the aim of emancipating the individual from state or legal restriction, and a belief in the potent autonomy of the individual from determination by ethnicity or class (classical liberalism); a right-wing term of abuse of any orientation antagonistic to the goals of the political right ('liberalism'); and the project of removing impediments to international trade, involving indifference if not enthusiasm about the implicit extension of the power of wealthy multinational corporations (neoliberalism). All three of these definitions are pertinent to certain key actors in this section, such as, importantly, the British 'New' Labour Party, but where any specific sense of liberalism is intended the terms in brackets will be used.

Unionist efforts to claim a moral high ground in discussions of civil (or human) rights were problematised by a conjunction of international events from the 1960s. Analogies of widely varying degrees of accuracy between the civil rights movements in the US South and in Northern Ireland have been drawn ever since, and were clearly, to some extent, deliberately and ostentatiously explored by nationalists and others involved in agitation in Northern Ireland.[137] Almost simultaneously, a British movement on behalf of immigrants from the countries of the New Commonwealth emerged, influenced by the same examples and political points of reference as the civil rights movement in Northern Ireland.[138] Comparison with apartheid South Africa, another reference point that leaps to minds predisposed towards a sympathetic reading of Irish republicanism, carries still more tendentious implications: republicans thus boast of their empathy for the victims of apartheid.[139] The civil rights movement that overtly emerged in Britain in the 1990s in response to the fall-out from the murder of the black teenager Stephen Lawrence, although it has no overt connection to events in Northern Ireland, represents a renewal of a political discourse in Britain that has to date furthered Irish nationalist political objectives. Some observers have fallen into the error of depicting political representation of PSF within the peace process as an adequate solution to problems of discrimination against Catholics in Northern Ireland, or as a necessary restitution for such discrimination.[140] The global replacement in problems of citizenship of a discourse of 'civil rights' with one of 'human rights' created further problems for unionists. While the difference in the underlying concepts is subtle and elusive, often, as in Northern Ireland, such a development has marked a shift in the focus of radical criticism of institutional structures from reformist to separatist, internationalist or revolutionary objectives. The very sovereign power of existing national or state authorities was thus brought into question.[141] For unionists, who have often (though not always) regarded the defence of such structures in Northern Ireland as a defining element of their creed, such a shift marks a real challenge to their political plausibility. Unionists' further defensive strategies of throwing in their lot with British conservatives, and/or further entrenching their institutional bastions of defence within Northern Ireland *vis-à-vis* Irish nationalism, have yielded limited success.

This serious unionist dilemma has arisen because the prevalent mode of applying concepts and commentaries on discrimination to Northern Ireland politics is one-eyed. Discrimination against Catholics in Northern Ireland can be, and popularly is, compared with discrimination against non-white ethnic minorities in the United Kingdom, while individuals living in Great Britain who have moved there from Ireland (North or South), or are descended from such migrants, are increasingly considered *themselves* to form an ethnic minority experiencing prejudice and negative stereotyping. Racism and racial discrimination, as distinct from sectarianism, are also matters of increasing concern within Northern Ireland itself. There is, however, a further potential parallel between unionists in Northern Ireland and ethnic minorities in Britain, as groups whose aspiration to be considered full and equal members of the British national community is imperfectly accepted by other members of that community. That this latter dimension goes unexplored is linked to the nature of 'liberalism'. One explanation of this hiatus might suggest that 'liberals' believe, to quote Hague's criticism of the Parekh Report, that 'there is no such thing as "nation"'.[142] Yet in fact 'liberalism' in such recent articulations, while adopting a (limited) multicultural and transnational frame, subscribes to the ideas of 'nation' and membership of a nation as much as conservatism does, seeking rather to reimagine the nation in order to delegitimise assumptions that particular groups do not 'belong' in it.[143] Difficulties instead arise on the axis between 'liberal' consideration of groups' rights to belong to the 'political nation', a question closely linked to the facts of immigration and discrimination, and recent forms of 'liberal' internationalism whose existence, even in versions ostensibly antagonistic to capitalism, is dependent upon postmodern capitalism. In consequence, in many recent formulations liberals are willing to consider only *select* cases of struggles for social, economic and political equality by those who are underprivileged in terms of mobility when these struggles are articulated within a narrative of ethnic or national community. The limitations of liberal imaginings of the nation, as much as those of such conservative imaginings, thus help to create a context that is detrimental to the political legitimacy of unionism.

Conservative consideration of discrimination against the minority in Northern Ireland, influenced by the idea that Northern Ireland is different, has involved acquiescence in, and in some cases initiation of, institutions specifically designed to protect the Catholic minority in the province from discrimination and the abuse of political power. It is hard to escape the implication behind the implementing of structures of fair employment legislation and power-sharing in Northern Ireland, earlier than in Great Britain or even in the province alone: that the province's majority community is particularly not to be trusted. Those unionists who are committed to the free market, and thus predisposed to see inequalities experienced by Catholics as caused by internal problems within the Catholic community, read this disjuncture as an insult and/or a threat. In December 1994 an interviewee linked to the Ulster Defence Association reportedly expressed the underlying anxieties in unusually frank terms:

> Fair employment is against the Protestant people. Such policies are an attack against Protestant livelihoods. It's simple. The Fenians and their IRA have bombed the Brits into submission. It is the start of the process in which they will secure a united Ireland.[144]

However, it is not only on the right that British political leaders committed to economic neoliberalism[145] endorse the idea that, in Tony Blair's words, 'the circumstances of Northern Ireland are very particular, and do not necessarily have implications for the rest of the United Kingdom'. Meaningfully, the doctrine of Northern Ireland's exceptionalism also helps such 'liberals' as Blair to silence suggestions, such as those from John Hume, that, in view of the fact that proportional representation is now used for a number of elections in the United Kingdom, including elections to the Northern Ireland Assembly, it should be applied to elections to the Westminster Parliament.[146] British 'liberals' also advocate power-sharing solutions in Northern Ireland, yet turn pale when they are expected to share the power that they currently hold personally across the water.

Even a 'new Britain' as reimagined by 'liberals', such as Yasmin Alibhai-Brown, who are more sensitive to the existence of discrimination throughout the British Isles is as reluctant to incorporate the Northern Ireland problem as the conservative nation is. The concept of 'white diversity' offers multiculturalists one avenue of approach to Northern Ireland. If white inhabitants of the United Kingdom are acknowledged to be heterogeneous, 'in the name of multiculturalism', recognition of differences between inhabitants of Northern Ireland and those of Great Britain is not inimical to acceptance of Northern Ireland's status within the United Kingdom.[147] Research around the theme of anti-Irish racism in Great Britain is a leading academic derivative of the idea of white diversity. In their investigation into anti-Irish racism in Great Britain, undertaken for the Commission for Racial Equality in 1997, as well as in other writings, Bronwen Walter and Mary Hickman have argued that analysis of the experience of individuals of Irish descent in Britain, as an exercise in 'deconstructing' the fiction of white homogeneity,[148] could fruitfully inform wider studies of racism and ethnicity, and meet some of the objections put forward against racial and ethnic monitoring, by minimising projections of a binary opposition between 'black' and 'white'.[149] However, Walter and Hickman's intention to 'deconstruct' 'whiteness' is not matched by a desire to pay similar sustained critical attention to the concept of 'Irishness'. Although their research details cases of anti-Irish prejudice encountered in Great Britain by individuals with backgrounds in Northern Ireland, including unionist backgrounds,[150] Hickman and Walter can be criticised for a tendency to assume that the Irish who are discriminated against in Great Britain are definitively Catholic and nationalist, and consequently some of their recommendations overlook those who do not fit this typology.[151]

The Parekh Report itself was derivative of Walter and Hickman's approach in so far as it foregrounds individuals of Irish descent in Britain, and their experience of 'racism', as an aspect of 'white diversity'.[152] Surveys of prejudice against Catholic and nationalist Irish men and women in Britain, for all their faults, consciously or unconsciously offer mechanisms for the integration of these groups into the United Kingdom. These should therefore modulate perceptions of the apparent uniqueness within the United Kingdom of the Catholic Irish *in Northern Ireland*, which contribute to the psychological distancing of Great Britain from the province. As astute commentators sympathetic to unionism identify, unless one proposes not just repartition in Ireland, but also a forcible transfer of populations, the view that more energy, in whatever form, should be put into reconciling individuals from nationalist Irish backgrounds to life outside a united or an independant Ireland is consistent with, and perhaps even necessary to, the unionist position.[153] Logically, there appears to be no reason why a project such as the Parekh Report on discrimination incorporating assessment of anti-'Irish' prejudice should not take a United Kingdom perspective.

The report further depicts a British society that features ingrained prejudices and antipathies, largely towards non-white minorities within Britain, which require restraint by a 'neutral' umpire. It calls for thorough examinations of legal, educational, political and employment practice for prejudice through surveys, targets, policy drives and/or declarations of intent about equality of opportunity. Sensitivity about language and national symbols in Britain, and changes to British national institutions, are necessary, according to the report, because of divisions within the community. This 'island story' is so reminiscent of the politics of the six counties as to suggest that Northern Ireland could surely have been included in the report without perceptible incongruity.

Instead, however, the Parekh Report's authors saw their terms of reference as 'England, Scotland and Wales',[154] thus strangely omitting to consider the overwhelming evidence of prejudice against non-white minorities in Northern Ireland itself. Indeed, the report comes dangerously close to replicating the assumptions about Northern Ireland's society that are most complacent about and, arguably, thus complicit in, racism in the province, especially the idea that racism is not 'the' 'real' problem in Northern Ireland, which rather concerns established national and sectarian questions.[155] Opportunities are also missed by the report's authors in other publications to make a point of incorporating Northern Ireland within analysis of the wider problem.[156] It is true that fleeting references to Northern Ireland in the Parekh Report are used to map out the type of complex measures and multiple identities that the authors see as crucial to 'the new Britain'. One particularly revealing passage commences with the belated observation that the 'nation-state' to which England, Scotland and Wales belong is the United Kingdom, not Great Britain (the island on which these three countries are located). To

> one community in Northern Ireland, as among large numbers of Irish people in [Great] Britain, being British is not an acceptable self-description. In Scotland and Wales the conflation of Britishness with Englishness has always made being 'British' problematic. Now, with substantially more devolved political power, the term is being used less and less. The Good Friday Agreement of 1999 [*sic*] implies that there should be a sense of affiliation to the supranational entity known as 'these islands'. Perhaps one day there will be an adjective to refer to this entity, similar in power perhaps to the unifying term 'Nordic' in Denmark, Finland, [Iceland,] Norway and Sweden.

Instead of further exploring the possibility of incorporating Northern Ireland within the frame of analysis of 'British' multiculturalism, the report proceeds along the following lines:

> But for the present, no such adjective is in sight. It is entirely plain, however, that the word 'British' will never do on its own . . . [For] Asians, African-Caribbeans and Africans . . . Britishness is not ideal, but at least it appears acceptable, particularly when suitably qualified – Black British, Indian British, British Muslim and so on.

However, there is one major and so far insuperable barrier. Britishness, as much as Englishness, has systematic, largely unspoken, racial connotations. Whiteness nowhere features as an explicit condition of being British, but it is widely understood that Englishness, and therefore by extension Britishness, is racially coded. 'There ain't no black in the Union Jack', it has been said. Race is deeply entwined with political culture and with the idea of nation . . . Unless these deep-rooted antagonisms to racial and cultural difference can be defeated in practice, as well as symbolically written out of the national story, the idea of a multicultural post-nation remains an empty promise.[157]

The authors then introduce the term 'community of communities', which they regard 'as a possible way of describing Britain as a whole. (The term could also, incidentally, describe the United Kingdom or "these islands" as a whole.)'[158] This very passage was the report's most controversial, evoking wholly disproportionate attention and volleys of criticism from points across the political spectrum, including a prevalent misreading as 'Britain is racist'.[159] If the authors of the report were fearful of courting controversy because of the 'unionist' implications of analytically treating Northern Ireland as part of the United Kingdom (or Britain), either here or elsewhere, their fear thus seems singularly misplaced. It is certainly clear that their assumptions about Northern Ireland have gained the authors little credit.

Why, then, if there are so many logical and political reasons for incorporating Northern Ireland within the liberal political nation, are British 'liberals' so reluctant to do so? There are special historical features of unionism, such as its perceived closer relationship to British Conservatism and its affinity with fundamentalist Protestantism,[160] which have tended to detract from liberal sympathy. These seem not to be particularly powerful factors, however, since the relationship with Conservatism, as previously discussed, surely *seems* closer than it actually is, while the relationship between religion and politics is not one that liberals have to deal with in relation to Northern Ireland unionism alone (see further below). Another explanation might posit the historical intersections between Irish nationalism, interest in Irish nationalism, and the left. Irish nationalism has certainly had a number of left-wing valorisers, some of them British,[161] and it was during a militant phase in 1981 that the British Labour Party offered its most enthusiastic endorsement of the aspiration for a united Ireland.[162] On the other hand, an 'Old' Labour government in 1969 told the government of the Irish Republic to mind its own business in respect of the North; the next Labour government, in office from 1974 to 1979, was not anti-partitionist; and even in the 1980s Labour Party conferences rejected motions that would have given the party's support for the aspiration to Irish unity greater urgency.[163] There are surely few substantive reasons for believing that Irish nationalism has an intrinsically left-wing agenda,[164] and it is certainly possible to exaggerate the extent to which economic liberalism has been a hegemonic creed among Protestants in Northern Ireland.[165] Socialism continues to retain an influence on sections, for instance, of the PUP[166] and elements of the British left continue to be favourable to unionism.[167] It is a little far-fetched to see the Ulster Workers Council strike of 1974 as a proletarian revolt against multinational capitalism,[168] but many unionists opposed the privatisation and free-market policies of the British Conservative government of the 1980s, in part because of the province's high dependence on public-sector employment (Northern Ireland has frequently experienced the worst regional levels of unemployment in the United Kingdom).[169] Indeed, at the time, far from believing that 'state benefits . . . allow the average terrorist to spend his days polishing Kalashnikovs',[170] unionists treated the relative generosity of United Kingdom levels of social security *vis-à-vis* those in the Irish Republic as one of the most practical influences amongst Catholic residents of the province against the struggle for a united Ireland, and were alarmed by the reduction of this differential by Thatcherite governments, notwithstanding Thatcherites' vaunted commitment to the union between Great Britain and Northern Ireland, and their perplexment at unionist criticism.[171] (Conversely, the growing connections between paramilitaries in Northern Ireland and mafia-style activities and drug- and fuel-smuggling have, arguably, suggested that, even when unemployment payments are reduced, the financial resources of terrorism are not exhausted.) It is by no means just hard-left anti-American Marxists who ridicule Northern Ireland unionism, but also soft-left 'liberals'.[172]

There are clearly, therefore, specific factors reducing the common ground between unionism and the left, including 'New' Labour, and it is arguable that the latter's dependence on a globalised capitalist culture is an important such factor. Consideration of the cover of an issue of the magazine *Private Eye* from July 1998 will illuminate this point.[173] There is an argument that the content of such a pseudo-witty satirical publication is not politically constitutive, but 'a bit of banter' or even a cherished cultural artefact.[174] This naïve argument is not one that either proponents of the idea of anti-Irish racism,[175] or right-wing British commentators who complain of victimisation at the hands of 'alternative' comedians,[176] can consistently maintain. The cover in question features a photograph of a Portadown Orange Lodge parade, adorned by slogans clearly designed to trivialise the Order and delegitimise associated political aspirations. One such slogan, 'The future's bright, the past is Orange', is a fascinating text. This was clearly inspired by the advertising slogan of the multinational mobile telephone company Orange, 'The future's bright, the future's Orange.' As reworked by *Private Eye*, 'The past is Orange' denotes an uncritical reading on the part of someone at the magazine of at least one politically charged essay on Northern Ireland, possibly Michael Farrell's seminal *Northern Ireland: The Orange State*. As of July 1998 'the future's bright' is symptomatic of naïvety about a politically contentious peace process in the aftermath of the GFA. These two assumptions feed off each other, since a few weeks previously the Orange Order had declared its opposition to the GFA. This is a striking demonstration of the tendency of many metropolitan liberals, not only to refuse to consider unionists' objections to the peace process, which are by no means all rooted in anachronism, bigotry or supremacism, but also to imagine that it simply does not matter that at least half of all unionists in Northern Ireland shared, and share, such objections. To such commentators the unionist position simply deserves neither to be seriously studied nor even to be acknowledged.[177]

The performativity of such a reaction to unionism, so close to the working assumptions of prominent republicans, is strong evidence of a public discourse, especially among London-based British liberals, that articulates prejudice specifically against those from Northern Ireland of a *unionist* background. This arises because such 'liberals' naturalise international economic neoliberalism, replicating 'liberal' failings in dealing with communities victimised by global capitalism, including indigenous and non-white rooted cultures. A reading of the work of Epifanio San Juan, Jr., Peter McLaren and other theorists will elucidate this point.

San Juan's critique of the 'postcolonial academy' offers a fruitful intersection with the current problem. San Juan argues that particular scholarly applications of postcolonial analysis and postmodern deconstruction, in their valorisation of the semiotic and their reduction of social conditions to indeterminacy, are ultimately complicit in colonialist power and *internationalised* capitalism.[178] A salient object of San Juan's criticism is Homi K. Bhabha, who is charged with misreading the famous Martiniquan anti-colonial writer Frantz Fanon in his desire to valorise indeterminacy.[179] Bhabha criticises Fanon for withdrawing from his most 'radical' denial of Hegelian closure and humanist aspiration, and from an appreciation of the creativity of 'the depersonalised, dislocated colonial subject' and of the 'limits of identity'.[180] For Bhabha, as for Edward Saïd, the motif of both the radical dislocated subject and the truly creative critic is the diasporic individual, an archetype that – conveniently, one might suggest – corresponds to the nomadic condition of many contemporary career academics.[181] From such a perspective, San Juan suggests, the political struggles of indigenous peoples and others for whom 'the nation-state remains an effective horizon of politics' are ultimately suspect on account of their 'authenticity' and 'foundationism'.[182] As McLaren intimates, liberation movements of indigenous peoples, constituting a claim that a particular form of subjectivity should take precedence owing to the overwhelming need to combat forms of violence, deprivation or disenfranchisement, thus fall foul of postmodernist suspicion of 'metanarratives' and ironic denial of commitment.[183] Or, in Arif Dirlik's words, while postcolonial theory tends to disavow the existence of class,

> ethnicities [and] cultures, . . . as they appear presently, . . . represent conflicting claims to empowerment within a transnational class. This class needs to be distinguished, nevertheless, by the common interests in a current structural situation that define them as a class and distance them from the social hinterlands for which they claim to speak.[184]

Such socialist or socialist-influenced analysis may appear to have little relevance to the struggle of a 'rooted' Protestant subject in Northern Ireland, or to the problem of recovering the agency of such a subject, least of all, perhaps, for San Juan and McLaren.[185] It would indeed be incongruous to pair Protestants in Northern Ireland with the victims of the Mayan genocide, for all the allegations of republican ethnic cleansing that occasionally emanate from unionist sources: the pattern of historical causation in the two cases is very different. Yet equally, as has been suggested, there is no intrinsic correlation between socialism and Irish nationalism. San Juan, McLaren and Dirlik's ideas are thus suggestive because of the interplay between cosmopolitan liberal trivialisation of 'rooted' Protestant subjects in Northern Ireland, postmodern irony and multinational capitalism, as typified by *Private Eye*'s cover.

As was suggested above, postmodern capitalism further particularly disadvantages the Protestant community of Northern Ireland, compared to the Catholic community in the province, because of the postmodern capitalism's intersection with long-established ethnic stereotypes. A crucial symbol of the supposed emergence of the 'postmodern condition' was the appropriation of modernist art by commerce, indicating the expiration of modernism's radical potential, so that consumption came to be conceived of as a substitute for social existence and political commitment.[186] The refunctioning of advertising slogans as expressions of cosmopolitan elite disdain for political commitment thus symbolises the twofold parasitism of intellectuals influenced by postmodernism. The manipulation of the advertising slogan of a multinational mobile telephone company in this context is especially suggestive. The mobile phone was popularised in the 1980s and 1990s as a symbol of the bombastic young executive class profiting from the Thatcher–Reagan boom, at the exact 'end of history' conjuncture of neoliberal capitalism's (supposed) geopolitical triumph over Marxism–Leninism, and in which postmodernism came to predominate in the academy at the expense of economic determinism. For those British liberals who, whether they admit it or not, are ultimately dependent on the fruits of such a boom, society and nation are of only contingent significance. From such a perspective, those Northern Ireland Protestants to whom the nation-state is not only 'an effective horizon of politics', but also a matter of struggle and endurance, must indeed seem worthy merely of mockery. Crucially, the Orange Order ridiculed by *Private Eye* as an anti-agreement force of 'bigots in bowler hats' serves for British liberals, and not just liberals, as a synecdoche for the Paisleyite DUP,[187] the very force whose absence from talks marks the most significant difference between the current peace process and the alternative negotiation process described above. The implausibility of the latter to liberals is thus closely linked to liberals' dependence on postmodern capitalism.

To suggest that cosmopolitan liberal ridicule of unionism is a symptom of such cultural parasitism is not to fall into the converse error of misrecognising certain established modes of expression of communal identity in Northern Ireland as 'stationary forms of life'.[188] Indeed, negative stereotyping itself demonstrates that it is instead desirable to develop non-homogenising ways of viewing communities such as the Protestants of Northern Ireland, taking account of differences of gender, class, etc., and of changes over time, not least the variegated processes of identification with, in the case of the community here in question, 'Britain', 'Ulster' (or Northern Ireland) and/or 'Ireland'. Violence and bigotry are already over-represented in Northern Ireland by those who assume that these have some 'authentic' relation to 'community'. Nevertheless, some forms of community, whether constructed around ethnicity, class, religion or region, may be sufficiently grounded that, notwithstanding irrational or traditional signifiers that seem to invite ridicule, attempts to deconstruct them, especially from particular perspectives, are liable, not to liberate individuals, but to solidify communal identity.

In addition, the forces of globalisation may be less powerful and more ambivalent than their academic valorisers suggest (as discussed in Chapter 3). As Edna Longley observes: 'it is not quite enough to confront unionism with the obsolescence of "Britishness" . . . football supporters often cling to a team however badly it is doing'.[189] Indeed, post-positivist views of identity suggest that experiential differences within such communities may further entrench forms of communal identity, fiercely held so that they come to be aspirations to liberation.[190] Working-class elements in both communities in Northern Ireland, still disproportionately as affected by violence during the very peace process through which middle-class politicians in London and Belfast have procured relative immunity, are a case in point. Unionism, especially in such working-class supporters, constitutes a 'rooted' popular struggle for recognition within a nation-state framework, a chief obstacle to which is a transnational 'liberal' political and cultural establishment – empowered by globalised capitalism, superficially multicultural and containing members who often claim, or are made to seem, to represent 'social hinterlands' to which they appear to have an ethnic attachment – that attempts to replace material conditions of existence as the basis of politics with choreography and self-perpetuating elites. The chief symptom of this is the tension between this community and a peace process choreographed by those closely influenced by the transnational liberal framework.[191]

The limitations of this liberal framework highlighted by a consideration of its inabilities to come to terms with unionism are, like the analogous difficulties within the imagined conservative nation, worth addressing in any case for their own sake. Bhikhu Parekh's own dissection of John Stuart Mill's condescending attitudes to Indians and Indian culture, and, by extension, of contemporary liberals' attitudes to British Muslims since the Salman Rushdie affair,[192] demonstrates an awareness of cognate difficulties within liberalism. Parekh suggests that Mill's individualist conception of man ruled out traditional, communal and 'ethnically grounded ways of life, as well as those limited to a "narrow mental orbit"'. Mill's 'colonial contempt for native cultures' led him to tolerate the use of violence by imperial officials to break up such cultures. Parekh concludes that liberals are, in some respects, illiberal and inegalitarian:

> Liberals do believe in equal respect for all human beings, but they find it difficult to accord equal respect to those who do not value autonomy, individuality, self-determination, choice, secularism, ambition, competition, and the pursuit of wealth. In the liberal view, such men and women are 'failing' to use their 'truly' human capacities, to live up to the 'norms' of their human 'dignity' or 'status', and are thus not 'earning' their right to liberal respect.[193]

Parekh can be accused here (and elsewhere) of sidelining necessary criticisms of patriarchal or elitist leadership structures in some ethnic communities, thus helping to enshrine inadequacies that some liberals perceive as atavistic tendencies in the communities themselves, such as undesirable, often gendered restrictions on personal and individual mobility.[194] Yet an extension of Parekh's exercise in intellectual archaeology would produce an equally critical analysis of Mill's admirer, John Morley, the limitations of whose sympathy for Indian nationalism were demonstrated in his early twentieth-century stint as Secretary of State for India.[195] At the same time Morley was a leading sympathiser with Irish nationalism among mainstream British politicians: it was the outlook of the Protestants in the nine counties of Ulster, 'ethnically grounded' and defined by a religion (like the 'Hindu way' that Parekh seems to have in mind), that jarred against the secularism cherished by Mill and Morley.[196] The centrality of religious observance to unionist political culture thus does not logically explain, let alone excuse, the analytical neglect of manifestations of prejudice against unionists. Suspicion inhered by British pseudo-liberals towards conservative and religious Hindu, Muslim and Sikh individuals and communities (whether in Great Britain or elsewhere) is subjected to searching analysis, while the similar suspicion of pseudo-liberals towards conservative and religious Protestant individuals and communities in Northern Ireland is deemed unremarkable.

CONCLUSION

Although Arthur Aughey bases his main defence of the union between Great Britain and Northern Ireland on the existence of a predominantly unionist population in the six counties, he suggests that the following line of reasoning might be developed 'in order to disorder the senses of those who have exploited the language of minority disadvantage in their culture of complaint against the union': that unionists

> are also a *minority* within the United Kingdom as a whole, a minority which has the same rights to protection as any other minority within the United Kingdom. The idea that one could 'expel' the Unionists from the United Kingdom (which is what

the nationalist notion of British 'persuasion' actually entails) is just as insupportable as the idea that one could expel from the United Kingdom the Pakistani, the Indian or West Indian communities. The outrage with which liberal opinion has greeted the arguments of the National Front has not been directed at the arguments of those in Great Britain who have supported the 'repatriation' of one million Ulster [*sic*] Unionists (against their will) to a united Ireland. So perhaps Unionists might prosper that little more if they came to think of themselves as a minority who do not have to pass any politically imposed test to establish their unequivocal statehood. They might even become politically correct.[197]

Aughey's suggestion that black and Asian communities are relatively privileged in the United Kingdom, and, either in their own view or that of white Britons, have not had 'to pass any politically imposed test to establish their unequivocal statehood', is surely patronising and inaccurate, while his notion of a 'culture of complaint' in Britain or Northern Ireland could also be criticised.[198] Few unionists are quite willing to consider themselves on the same footing as such black and Asian communities. Some loyalists hold assumptions perhaps not too distant from those evident in parts of this passage and find the company of the British far right more congenial.[199] Some mainstream unionists meanwhile, along with Aughey, display an affinity with the assumptions of the British *Daily Express* and *Daily Mail* on immigration and asylum.[200] It is also true that Aughey advances this argument overtly merely as a political device, 'in order to disorder the senses' of political opponents, perhaps with an even greater level of irony than Stephen Howe surmises.[201] Nevertheless, Aughey may inadvertently be raising problems with the imagined British nation, in both conservative and liberal formulations, parallel to those raised by Paul Gilroy's work on the Black Atlantic.

Gilroy suggests that to write the history of the Black British or the 'Black Atlantic' is to purge English cultural studies of ethnocentrist assumptions, which may assist in 'the more ambitious and more useful task of actively reshaping contemporary England [*sic*] by reinterpreting the cultural core of its supposedly authentic national life'.[202] As Gilroy wrote in 1987: 'It is impossible to theorise black culture in Britain without developing a new perspective on British culture *as a whole.*[203] British positive self-images and negative stereotypes of Northern Ireland, which are respectively explicit and implicit in Britons' images of their 'supposedly authentic national life', are based on a selective reading of each. Conceiving this nation along other lines, a *United Kingdom* with a land frontier, a state containing within Northern Ireland (to adapt Frank Wright's phrase) an 'ethnic frontier between the British and the Irish nations',[204] also requires 'a new perspective on British culture *as a whole*'. It is a matter of reimagining, not only a national territory, but also a national history, and of representing neglected aspects of metropolitan and peripheral experience that are less diachronic, less supportive of British stereotypes and/or less suggestive of unionists' lack of 'Britishness'. Gilroy, like Parekh, can be criticised for homogenising his Black British/English subjects,[205] an error that it is also desirable to avoid in analysis of unionists or Protestants, and Catholics, in Northern Ireland. With this proviso in view, according to Gilroy's schema, the United Kingdom could alternatively be conceived as a plurality of non-exclusive, non-homogenous narratives – including Northern Ireland unionist, Northern Ireland Catholic, Black British and other narratives – or a nation consisting of heterogeneous elements, in a process conducive to a greater critical appreciation of the variety of British historical experience.[206] However, external political obstacles would intrude on such an object, as on Gilroy's.

Gilroy indicates that a leading obstacle to 'reinterpreting the cultural core' of Britain/England is a 'new left' ethnocentric tradition in writing the history of England. The tradition constituted a particular Marxist inflection of Whig interpretations of history.[207] Whatever their apparent status within academia, Whiggish discourses retain an operative political force. Crude assumptions about the peculiarities of the English, British and/or Irish are still evident in the performative perspectives on issues of tolerance and discrimination in Northern Ireland common to both the liberal and the conservative political nations. These perspectives, and discourses about terrorism, are unable, for diverse reasons, to offer an adequate acknowledgement of the Britishness of inhabitants of Northern Ireland and, in other words, undermine the political legitimacy of unionism. These powerful aspects of the wider political context have influenced peace process policies that overemphasise the marginality of Northern Ireland to the historical experience of neighbouring societies, including British society. There are many reasons why the Northern Ireland peace process has failed, but among the preconditions leading this particular *negotiation process*, among all the possible such processes, to be pursued, and alternatives to it precluded, the limitations of prevalent reactions to terrorism, and in liberal and conservative imaginings of the political nation, were critical factors.

The fact that global or widespread forces underpin these processes and influences should make the dilemmas of the parties in Northern Ireland, especially the unionist parties, more understandable. Unfortunately, the existence of these forces also makes the difficulties more chronic. This chapter has focused on the limitations and contradictions of British attitudes to Northern Ireland, and other contextual issues, not because these limitations and contradictions are unique, but because they have a particular relationship to the problem of unionist political legitimacy – and the related lack of alternatives to the peace process – on account of unionists' aspiration to a closer political relationship with Great Britain. The intractability of the Northern Ireland conflict, the limits of the current peace process and the lack of viable alternative negotiation processes relate, not just to the historical nesting and entrenching of British and Irish identities – in locally antagonistic but recognisable forms – in the North, but also to ongoing problems in British, Irish and other societies.

Conclusion

Our capacity to predict the future of Northern Ireland is limited. Post-mortems on the failure of the peace process can be criticised as premature, even if they turn out to have been based on well-founded assumptions. An unexpected upturn in the fortunes of the peace process will still be sought and could confound the future that has been assumed in these pages to be the most likely. Conversely, however, to understate the extent of the problems of the process is to adopt a blasé attitude to unionist disaffection with it in particular, and thus to accentuate the probability of the very failure that is denied (see Chapter 1).

Further, even a resuscitation of the peace process would not render the argument put forward here useless. The implication of this argument is that such an upturn is most likely to occur because of mistakes on the part of extremist and anti-agreement parties. This is necessarily true, since, as the proposition of failure implies, extremists and anti-agreement parties currently have considerable opportunities to exploit difficulties in the peace process. The likelihood of such errors is hard to assess precisely. However, past experience suggests that such extremist and anti-agreement parties have on occasion had a helpfully considerable capacity for political incompetence. At this point all that may be said is that failure – in the sense of stalemate rather than disaster – seems to be the likeliest immediate future, both because that hypothesis has proved accurate so far in predicting developments in the course of preparing this book, such as the postponements and ultimate results of the Northern Ireland Assembly elections (which eventually took place in November 2003), and because the obstacles in the way of any alternative future seem considerable.[1]

The foregoing analysis has also revealed the difficulties of proposing alternatives to the peace process, but there is another reason for reserve in such matters. Analysts who do not live in Northern Ireland can have only a limited right to recommend courses of action to its people, beyond the obvious moral exhortation and condemnations of the clearly malign, and are not in a position to demand new initiatives so radical as might, for instance, be likely to precipitate a campaign of full-scale military operations in the province by a loyalist or republican force possessing considerable resources. It is easy to be a purist in academic or political speculations at a comfortable distance, but if one actually lives in affected areas the ability to go about one's daily business in an atmosphere of even only partially reduced perceived threat may be invaluable. Recommendations should thus be indirect, focusing instead on those external actors whose assumption of new approaches might in turn facilitate new attitudes among those in Northern Ireland itself. Truly a great deal of room for improvement can be detected even among the subjects falling within the remit of this indirect approach.

There remains a level of disagreement in Northern Ireland for which it is hard to suggest a strategy of resolution, and the peace process never offered such a strategy. For instance, it has not integrated the Democratic Unionist Party into direct, face-to-face talks with republicans, and this may to an extent be regarded as having always made the process fragile. Each of these two groups, it has been suggested here, has a significant constituency, genuinely appearing to its supporters to represent lived experiences and concerns, and neither of them can be assumed to be easily susceptible to manipulation from above. It would therefore be misleading to suggest that outsiders, or even the political leaders themselves, can easily produce a dialogue between them. Serious issues of sovereignty, allegiance, identity, faith, and communal and personal survival and security are at stake, and hence constituencies are found for what appear from the outside to be hopelessly intransigent policies. The Good Friday Agreement always achieved less than was claimed for it in well-meaning, overenthusiastic commentary. If this seems a depressing conclusion, it should not: it just indicates that the failure of the process should be no surprise. Stalemate is not disaster. The peace process did demonstrate that the political and social life of Northern Ireland is not unchanging or insulated from external concerns, and that outsiders do possess some ability to facilitate new approaches in the province, so there is room for new influences to be brought to bear, for new dynamics and thus for hope.

A broad approach to the Northern Ireland conflict such as has been attempted here is valid because Northern Ireland and its people are different, but not radically different and separate from the outside world, not stuck in the seventeenth century or in the grip of processes of identification greatly at variance from those operative elsewhere. It is valid also, and tangentially, because Northern Ireland helps to focus questions about mainstream aspects of both the surrounding societies, British and Irish.

Whatever the aspiration to Irish unity in the Republic, there is currently little to suggest preparedness on the part of the Irish state for the complex and delicate process that would be involved in any settlement of Northern Ireland giving the province a primary political orientation to the Republic. Irish nationalist attitudes to unionists are still too often hectoring and judgemental, although this may change.

The British nationalist assumption that 'the success of Britain as a governing entity over many centuries' justifies the closest possible integration of Northern Ireland within the United Kingdom[2] is also flawed. It is not just in relation to Ireland or Northern Ireland that the British ruling classes' historical record of success is somewhat sullied. Moments of intolerance and xenophobia are not lacking in British history; British democracy is not as successful as it may appear; and the absence of violent political revolution in Britain in the nineteenth century is at best a marginal advantage over the French or the German experience and is, in any case, contrary to 'Eurosceptic' assumptions, not a direct contrast to 'Europe': after all, several Nordic countries can claim at least as much political continuity as Britain. More recently the results of the referendums on devolution in Scotland and Wales in 1997 must suggest serious questions as to whether British institutions can any longer be regarded as having repeatedly 'succeeded' since 1688, at least so far as the populations in those areas are concerned.[3]

However, the nature of these problems also suggests opportunities for change. The core problem is that of the political legitimacy of Northern Ireland unionism. A sense in the Republic 'of owning even what they criticise', i.e., the unionists, has not gone without deconstruction, including in self-critical modes,[4] yet these modes are often misunderstood and reviled in nationalist circles (see Chapter 3).

The dimension of the obstacles to unionist legitimacy that relates to the United Kingdom (the state) and to Great Britain (the island) is not such half-baked irredentism, but an inarticulate sense that inhabitants of Northern Ireland cannot be British because they are not perceived as acting in accordance with supposedly 'British' norms of decency, tolerance and moderation. This sense is, arguably, one of the influences on the large segments of opinion in Great Britain that, judging by opinion poll results, accept at least the aspiration to a united Ireland.[5] In fact, the chequered historical record and present condition of the British nation suggest that regarding the province's people as being incapable of Britishness may not be logically viable. It implies that there is a pure British nation, which is identified with by most British people, unmediated by local and partial considerations, and characterised by tolerance and continuity. Such assumptions are as integral to British 'liberalism' as to conservatism and, indeed, the 'liberal' project of transition to a tolerant 'multi-ethnic Britain' is in some ways the more dependent on this assumed building block.[6] Yet there is in fact no core 'British nation' that never invokes, even unconsciously, an imagined national 'we' as a tool of defence of its local, sectional or material interests when threatened. Sport, for instance, especially football (soccer), is increasingly a focus of expressions of British/English national identity, but it is hard to see what relevance the consonant displays have to the self-deprecating restraint featuring in self-congratulatory stereotypes of the British/English, the ensuing disorder occasionally bearing a closer resemblance to the results of a contentious Orange march or a bad night in North Belfast. If there were such a British nation as is imagined by the right, characterised by a disinterested tolerance that supersedes continental norms, the same British right's media would surely have condemned in a little less feeble and half-hearted a fashion those loyalist actions over the past thirty-five years that have occasionally resembled the St Bartholomew's Day Massacre in their sectarian depravity. For most people in Great Britain, in the Irish Republic and, for that matter, elsewhere, patriotism and the national 'we' are thus reflected and experienced through the local, partial or fragmentary. In this there is much affinity with the experiences and processes of identification of the people of Northern Ireland.

The Northern Ireland peace process may have failed, but, as things stand, conventional conceptions of national identity, whether in Great Britain, Northern Ireland or the Republic, do not easily admit of an alternative. The 'internationalisation' or 'Europeanisation' models may have borne some fruit in limited applications to date (see Chapter 3), but there is surely not yet enough in these dimensions to constitute the core of an alternative process. In view of the limitations of these assorted options it is tempting to revert to the line that there is no alternative to the peace process. Yet it is the very capriciousness of national identity, and the very inadequacy of its existing definitions in Great Britain, the province and the Republic, that perhaps hold out the greatest hope for change and for emerging alternatives. In all three of these political spaces the political nation is not the distillation of stereotypes and clichés, or the necessary result of history, 'national character' or essence, but the product of a series of contingent and ongoing processes, and any or all of them may change in ways that admit of alternative policies towards Northern Ireland.

Logic suggests that to incorporate Northern Ireland on a more secure basis requires a more adaptable version of national identity in either the United Kingdom (and, within it, Great Britain), or the Irish Republic, or both. Obstacles to this clearly remain in both, however, notably that those positing such versions are stigmatised as unpatriotic. In Great Britain there is the more complex problem that those advancing such a 'new Britishness' are generally targeting the inclusion of groups other than Northern Ireland Protestants, and are often apathetic about the circumstances of, if not antagonistic to, Northern Ireland Protestants, while those in Great Britain who are more concerned about the retention of Northern Ireland within the union are also preoccupied with other issues and have not confronted the inadequacies of their own vision of the issue in hand. The failure of the peace process suggests the need for a renewed effort to confront these obstacles, but it also suggests the continuing limits of a dogmatic approach to the fundamental issues of sovereignty relating to Northern Ireland. There is nothing sacrosanct about the composition, complexion, image or territorial limits of the United Kingdom of Great Britain and Northern Ireland, or of the Irish Republic. If the Northern Ireland question is to be addressed within an international context in which the nation-state remains a significant structure – which seems likely for the immediate future – the question of which of these two states Northern Ireland is to be primarily aligned with, residual links with the other still being possible, cannot be fudged within the formulas of Euro-optimism or benign internationalism.

Logically, this should be determined by which of the two political nations – British or Irish – demonstrates the facility to evolve in a way best fitted to the most peaceful incorporation of all traditions within Northern Ireland. This may work in the same direction as, though it is not necessarily consonant with, the consent formula mapped out in the Good Friday Agreement, and in different forms in earlier British or British–Irish declarations and arrangements; but the latter measure is somewhat less politically contentious and a good deal more measurable, and there is thus much to be said in its favour. The consent formula is one of the aspects of the agreement that could helpfully be retained, despite the failure of the peace process, and not thrown away or renegotiated (as anti-agreement unionists and dissident republicans suggest), because it would be useful if possible to maintain the level of agreement achieved in 1998, even if it was as limited as has been described here. The will of the majority seems to remain the only viable way of assessing the success of future departures in the government of Northern Ireland, and the past few years have shown that this by no means always functions as a 'unionist veto'.

Any sensible analysis should not propose solutions to the 'Northern Ireland problem', because of the intrinsic difficulties, and the inadequate nature of the language of 'solution' itself. Within the above considerations of the question of sovereignty, of course it is true that, as Paul Bew and Henry Patterson put it some years ago, '*any* path of development which might hold out the hope for a modest reduction in sectarian division in Northern Irish society ought to be seriously considered'.[7] However, two more limited and specific criticisms of, and cognate recommendations for, outside parties are implicit in this book. Both of these are concerned with the popular, political and journalistic presentation or conceptualisation of Northern Ireland, which, it has been argued, has been problematic to date. Both should, if it is possible to effect them, at least help to expand the range of policy options for Northern Ireland, and thus contribute contextually if indirectly to the improvement of the quality of life of the province's people.

The first step is to present events and political progress in Northern Ireland more frequently in a more sophisticated way than just in relation to the Provisionals. Proportionately less attention needs to be paid to both the transgressions and the political demands of the Provisionals, and more to those of other groups, including the loyalists. Loyalists sometimes (if not always) find it useful to present themselves as a mere reaction to the Provisional IRA (PIRA), but (as Chapter 2 tried to demonstrate), although Provisional actions seemed to come to define the conflict, the PIRA alone did not cause it, other factors being more crucial at important stages, and as the collapse of Sunningdale especially shows loyalism is also a disturbing force. There is also no humanitarian or political reason why loyalist violence, whether concurrent to loyalist ceasefires or not, should be ignored or considered as an afterthought,[8] especially in Great Britain. Indeed, from the point of view of preserving the union, there are in fact imperative reasons why such violence should not be ignored or downplayed. Similarly, there is no justification for the proportionate lack of pressure for loyalists to decommission.

Conversely, however, the relatively low profile of loyalist political demands and perspectives is also a source of distortion. Republicanism is a smaller aspect of Northern Ireland politics than it has been made to appear, particularly in Great Britain, a presentation that, it has been argued, is linked to the fact that over the course of the conflict the PIRA has been the group most likely to be responsible for fatalities of people in or from Great Britain (see Chapter 4). Steve Bruce wrote in 1995, 'circumstances produce the activists, not vice versa. A removal of 100 leading loyalist paramilitaries, without a complete halt to IRA violence, would only create 100 job opportunities for would-be paramilitaries.'[9] Bruce was largely correct, but a similar point could also be made about the removal, under certain conditions, of the PIRA from Northern Ireland politics.[10] This observation suggests that it is not adequate simply to look to the removal of the PIRA – whether by military means or as part of a political process – as a solution to the Northern Ireland conflict, but desirable to pay attention also to other aspects of the Northern Ireland context.

This is not to suggest, that the Provisionals should be either quarantined or exonerated. It is not desirable to turn on or provoke mainstream republicans. After all, forcing the PIRA into a renewed conflict and crushing it would not solve the problem, and some elements of the republican movement at any rate have made efforts for peace, whatever their motives for getting involved in the first place. Few would like to see an end to the PIRA's ceasefire in itself, although there are complaints about the political purchase it has given them, and, if there are pressing reasons to avoid overestimating the level of peace in Northern Ireland when writing from a distance, there are also pressing reasons, when writing from such locations, to avoid trivialising the cost of renewed conflict between the security forces and the PIRA for civilians, who would probably bear the brunt of it. In any case, a shift of perspective that implies less tolerance for loyalist violence and arsenals should have attractions for republicans, or would at any rate reduce the pretexts for republican violence.

What such a shift would imply is a realisation that a ceasefire by the PIRA does not, or should not be allowed to, necessarily define 'peace in Northern Ireland', because such a ceasefire is compatible with continued violence by the PIRA itself, and by loyalists, as well as, it seems – judging by the half-hearted assistance given by Provisionals to the investigation of the Omagh crime – a certain level of moral, material or passive Provisional assistance to dissident republicans. As analysis of a historical moment in July 1997 has demonstrated, it is not currently possible, but may at some time in the future be possible, to have a negotiation process without the Provisionals. Such a process might for instance include another representation of republicanism. A long period of keeping faith during a stalemate in the current peace process might also be concurrent with a further trickle of secessions from mainstream to dissident republicanism, so that even if the leadership of Provisional Sinn Féin (PSF) were ultimately to make a truly magnanimous gesture, 'peace' would not necessarily be any nearer.

Further, to focus reductively on PSF/PIRA is not democratic.

PSF is certainly a significant political force in Northern Ireland, but is still supported by little over 20 per cent of active voters. Its support was only 16 per cent before Tony Blair's famous declaration that the settlement train was leaving whether PSF was on it or not, whereupon he and others, as before most recent legs of the journey, ascertained that the Provisionals had a seat reserved. As Henry Patterson suggests: 'The peace process had put [Gerry] Adams and Martin McGuinness at the centre of national and international attention. Received respectfully in Downing Street, Leinster House, and the White House, they were listened to deferentially when they continued to complain of being marginalised.'[11]

Paying less attention to the Provisionals also implies paying more attention to constitutional nationalism: mainstream republicans do not speak for nationalism, and what Provisionals do does not determine what the SDLP does, as is indicated by their disagreement on policing, and still less what the Irish government does.

Finally, a lower profile for the Provisionals implies proportionately more attention to unionism and its concerns. After all, the peace process often entailed close examination of the position and activities of PSF/PIRA and a sometimes cavalier attitude to the doubts among unionists about the course that the process was taking. It is partly as a consequence of that attitude being displayed and perceived that the peace process has failed.

The second step required is a broad improvement in the standard of media reporting of Northern Ireland and/or a more critical reception of this reporting among its popular audiences in the province itself, in Great Britain, in the Irish Republic and, indeed, internationally. The media can in no way be regarded as causing the Northern Ireland conflict, but they can be fairly accused of distorting impressions of Northern Ireland, thus helping to limit policy possibilities and block lines of progression that might possibly have improved the quality of life in the province, and compounding the error by denying a proper right of reply. In these ways the influence of the media's, especially newspapers', coverage of Northern Ireland has been misguided. In particular, there is an urgent need for life in Northern Ireland outside violence, the conflict and, most recently, the peace process to be better-represented within the mainstream media around the world. An intelligent attempt by the British media to encourage the retention of Northern Ireland in the United Kingdom, for instance, would not have focused on violence, republican or otherwise, but would have demonstrated how normal life in Northern Ireland largely is and thus how far its inhabitants are like 'us'. Irish nationalists' denunciation or misrepresentation of unionism has similarly been flawed.

These steps may seem limited enough, and are in themselves certainly no formula to break the impasse in Northern Ireland politics, which requires at least reciprocal action, self-criticism by both nationalists and unionists,[12] and tough choices within Northern Ireland itself. On the other hand, there are considerable obstacles even to these limited steps. An attempt to diminish media blame-gossip about Northern Ireland would be most powerful in tandem with a form of British and/or Irish nationalism or patriotism in the media that was less orientated around praise-gossip. Even if there may be benefits from this second wider step, as has been suggested, and even if conventional forms of nationalism in both societies are wrong-headed, the attachment of significant segments of the populations in both Great Britain and the Irish Republic to such forms may have perceived connections with lived experience, much as does the attachment in parts of Northern Ireland to anti-agreement unionism or republicanism, which could only be overruled with difficulty. Further, the changes in attitudes to Northern Ireland suggested here would also clash with global influences (as discussed in Chapter 4), so change in specific locations alone may be of limited potency. The treatment of terrorist groups who attack 'us' as an overdetermined symbol of a political context, in a way that distorts responses and may produce counter-productive policies, is an understandable flaw, and is not a solely British or Irish phenomenon. Self-congratulatory forms of national identity, conservative or liberal, which implicitly occlude the very peripheral groups or societies that they claim to incorporate, also manifest themselves across nations and cultures.

Nevertheless, the external distorting influences should be highlighted for three reasons: because doing so enhances understanding of Northern Ireland; because it may be possible to bring influences to bear locally that may partially counteract universal tendencies; and because this is to counteract the prevalent stereotyping of Northern Ireland as a society with no features beyond the violence, which is a disservice to the vast majority of its people. The precise future of Northern Ireland is still to be made in Northern Ireland, but a context of external assumptions and influences will help to determine whether that future consists in anything beyond stalemate and futile or non-existent political dialogue.

Notes

CHAPTER 1

NB: Where not otherwise indicated by page numbers etc., articles cited and quoted from newspapers may be located on the website of the publication concerned. The transitory nature of www locations makes it undesirable and misleading to provide a specific location at the moment of citation in most cases.

1. Thomas Hardy, 'I Looked Up from My Writing', in Samuel Hynes (ed.), *The Complete Poetical Works of Thomas Hardy* (Oxford: Clarendon Press, 1982, 5 vols), Vol. 2, pp. 305–6.
2. K. Theodore Hoppen, *Ireland since 1800: Conflict and Conformity*, second edition (London: Addison Wesley Longman, 1999; first published 1989), p. 233.
3. Quoted in Jeremy Smith, *Making the Peace in Ireland* (Harlow: Pearson Education, 2002), p. 1.
4. Philip James Currie, *Canada and the Irish Question: 1867 to Present* (Victoria, BC: P.J. Currie, 2001), p. v.
5. Joseph Ruane and Jennifer Todd, '"Why Can't You Just Get Along with Each Other?": Culture, Structure and the Northern Ireland Conflict', in Eamonn Hughes (ed.), *Culture and Politics in Northern Ireland, 1960–1990* (Buckingham: Open University Press, 1991), pp. 27–44, especially pp. 27–8.
6. Ibid., p. 39.
7. Graham Walker, 'Scotland and Ulster: Political Interactions since the Late Nineteenth Century and Possibilities of Contemporary Dialogue', in John Erskine and Gordon Lucy (eds), *Cultural Traditions in Northern Ireland: Varieties of Scottishness. Exploring the Ulster–Scottish Connection* (Belfast: Institute of Irish Studies, 1997), pp. 91–109, especially p. 107; I. MacBride, 'Ulster and the British Problem', in R. English and G. Walker (eds), *Unionism in Modern Ireland: New Perspectives on Politics and Culture* (Basingstoke: Macmillan, 1996), pp. 1–18, especially pp. 6, 14–15.
8. Mick Fealty, Trevor Ringland and David Steven, *A Long Peace?: The Future of Unionism in Northern Ireland* (Wimborne: Slugger O'Toole, 2003), p. 10.
9. Quoted in S. Hartley, *The Irish Question as a Problem in British Foreign Policy, 1914–18* (Basingstoke: Macmillan, 1987), p. 161.
10. Smith, *Making the Peace in Ireland*, pp. 11, 10–15.
11. Paul Arthur, *Special Relationships: Britain, Ireland and the Northern Ireland Problem* (Belfast: Blackstaff Press, 2000), p. x. Many other optimistic journalistic and academic accounts could be cited from recent years.
12. Smith, *Making the Peace in Ireland*, p. 10.
13. Jonathan Freedland, 'Ten Steps to Peace', *Guardian*, 8 Aug. 2001, p. 13; see also the comments by John Reid, *Hansard's Parliamentary Debates*, 6th series, Vol. 389, c. 227 (16 July 2002); and W. Harvey Cox, 'Keeping Going: Beyond the Good Friday Agreement', in Marianne Elliott (ed.), *The Long Road to Peace in Northern Ireland: Peace Lectures from the Institute of Irish Studies at Liverpool University* (Liverpool: Liverpool University Press, 2002), pp. 153–68.
14. Mike Morrissey and Marie Smyth, *Northern Ireland after the Good Friday Agreement: Victims, Grievance and Blame* (London: Pluto Press, 2002), p. 93.

15. 'No Regrets, no Surrender', *Guardian*, 12 July 2003; see also Fealty, Ringland and Steven, *A Long Peace?*, pp. 8–10.
16. Michael Keating, 'Northern Ireland and the Basque Country', in John McGarry (ed.), *Northern Ireland and the Divided World: the Northern Ireland Conflict and the Good Friday Agreement in Comparative Perspective* (Oxford: Oxford University Press, 2001), pp. 181–208.
17. Arthur, *Special Relationships*, p. x.
18. Ken Whelan and Eugene Masterson, *Bertie Ahern: Taoiseach and Peacemaker* (Edinburgh: Mainstream Publishing, 1998).
19. See, for example, Eamonn Mallie and David McKittrick, *The Fight for Peace: The Secret Story behind the Irish Peace Process*, revised and updated edition (London: Mandarin, 1997; first published 1996). To an extent this may also be said of Gerard Murray, *John Hume and the SDLP: Impact and Survival in Northern Ireland* (Dublin: Irish Academic Press, 1998).
20. George Mitchell, *Making Peace* (New York: Knopf, 1999), pp. 113, 178; Tim Pat Coogan, *Wherever Green is Worn: The Story of the Irish Diaspora* (New York: Palgrave, 2001), pp. 264–71, 331–4, 343.
21. Peter Taylor, *Provos: The IRA and Sinn Fein* [*sic*] (London: Bloomsbury, 1997); Smith, *Making the Peace in Ireland*, p. 13.
22. Brendan O'Leary, 'The Conservative Stewardship of Northern Ireland, 1979–97: Sound-bottomed Contradictions or Slow Learning?', *Political Studies*, 45 (1997), pp. 663–76. Compare the comment by Paul Dixon, *Political Studies*, 46 (1998), pp. 795–6; and Henry Patterson, 'From Insulation to Appeasement: The Major and Blair Governments Reconsidered', in Rick Wilford (ed.), *Aspects of the Belfast Agreement* (Oxford: Oxford University Press, 2001), pp. 166–83.
23. Peter Taylor, *Loyalists* (London: Bloomsbury, 1999), p. 270.
24. Compare *Times*, 10 Feb. 1996, p. 21.
25. Paul Arthur, '"Quiet Diplomacy and Personal Conversation": Track Two Diplomacy and the Search for a Settlement in Northern Ireland', in Joseph Ruane and Jennifer Todd (eds), *After the Good Friday Agreement: Analysing Political Change in Northern Ireland* (Dublin: University College Dublin Press, 1999), pp. 71–95.
26. Smith, *Making the Peace in Ireland*, pp. 197–210.
27. Jonathan Freedland, 'The Key to Peace is Stuck', *Guardian*, 16 Feb. 2000.
28. Paul Arthur, 'Conflict, Memory and Reconciliation', in M. Elliott (ed.), *The Long Road to Peace*, pp. 143–52; and Morrissey and Smyth, *Northern Ireland after the Good Friday Agreement*.
29. Henry McDonald, *Trimble* (London: Bloomsbury, 2001; first published 2000), pp. 272–80.
30. *Times*, 2 Sept. 1999, p. 1.
31. Tony Blair, 'Finding a Way through the Crisis', speech in Belfast, 17 Oct. 2002, available at http://www.labour.org.uk/tbnispeech/, last accessed 15 May 2004.
32. Arthur, *Special Relationships*, p. ix.
33. Edward W. Saïd, *The End of the Peace Process: Oslo and After*, second edition (London: Granta, 2002), especially pp. xix–xxix.
34. Smith, *Making the Peace in Ireland*, pp. 7–9, explores cognate ambiguities.
35. Richard Deutsch, 'The Good Friday Agreement: Assessing its Implementation, 1998–2001', *Nordic Irish Studies*, 1 (2002), pp. 95–109.
36. *Daily Telegraph*, 11 April 1998, p. 23; 'But is There an Agreement in Ireland?', *Daily Telegraph*, 17 April 1998, p. 29.
37. 'Parliament Humiliated', *Daily Telegraph*, 19 Dec. 2001, p. 21. See also Dean Godson, *Himself Alone: David Trimble and the Ordeal of Unionism* (London: Harper Collins, 2004); Kirsten E. Schulze and M. L. R. Smith, *Dilemmas of Decommissioning* (London: Politeia, 1999).
38. *Daily Mail*, 18 Jan. 2001, p. 12.
39. Ed Moloney, *A Secret History of the IRA* (London: Allen Lane, 2002), p. 492.
40. Arthur Aughey, 'A New Beginning?: The Prospects for a Politics of Civility in Northern Ireland', in Ruane and Todd (eds), *After the Good Friday Agreement*, pp. 122–44.
41. Richard English, *Armed Struggle: A History of the IRA* (Basingstoke: Macmillan, 2003), p. 296.
42. Ibid. pp. 117–19. See also Chapter 2 of this book.
43. Morrissey and Smyth, *Northern Ireland after the Good Friday Agreement*, p. 189.
44. Marianne Elliot, 'Introduction', in M. Elliott (ed.), *Long Road to Peace*, pp. 1–8.

45. Mallie and McKittrick, *The Fight for Peace*, p. 410.
46. Kevin Myers, 'An Irishman's Diary', *Irish Times*, 19 June 1996, p. 15; *Daily Mail*, 17 June 1996, p. 8.
47. Kevin Myers, *From the* Irish Times *Column 'An Irishman's Diary'* (Dublin: Four Courts Press, 2000), pp. 141–3.
48. Karl Popper, *Conjectures and Refutations: The Growth of Scientific Knowledge* (New York: Basic Books, 1962), pp. 33–59.
49. *Belfast Telegraph*, 19 Feb. 2003; 'Forum: Northern Ireland', *Global Review of Ethnopolitics*, 2:3/4, March/June 2003, pp. 71–91, especially Colin Irwin, 'Devolution and the State of the Northern Ireland Peace Process', pp. 71–82.
50. Henry Patterson, *Ireland since 1939* (Oxford: Oxford University Press, 2002), pp. 340–1.
51. A more academic example of such a cavalier attitude was provided in Brendan O'Leary,, 'The Character of the 1998 Agreement: Results and Prospects', in Wilford (ed.), *Aspects of the Belfast Agreement*, pp. 49–83, especially pp. 52–3. O'Leary argued that, even in the event of new elections to the Northern Ireland Assembly returning an anti-agreement majority among unionists (as has now occurred), the Assembly could still be got to function by the procedure of resorting to 'weighted' majorities in some of its activities: thus, instead of requiring separate majorities among both unionist and nationalist representatives in the Assembly, the support of only 40 per cent of unionists might suffice on certain issues so long as there was near overwhelming support from nationalist delegates, and thus the support of at least a 60 per cent majority in the Assembly as a whole. The danger of such a procedure is that it would appear to be another contrived effort to avoid confronting the problem of lack of support for the peace process among unionists, seeming further to disenfranchise the increasing level of opposition to the agreement among unionists, and possibly creating more bitterness and further problems down the line.
52. Brendan O'Neill, 'The Edge of the Abyss . . . Again', *Blanket* (Spring 2003), pp. 1–3, especially 3.
53. Ibid., pp. 54, 75–6; see also Tim Pat Coogan's foreword to Chris Anderson, *The Billy Boy: The Life and Death of LVF Leader Billy Wright* (Edinburgh: Mainstream, 2002), pp. 11–14.
54. McDonald, *Trimble*, pp. 331–2, 346.
55. Paul Bew, Peter Gibbon and Henry Patterson, *Northern Ireland, 1921–2001: Political Forces and Social Classes*, revised and updated edition (London: Serif, 2002), p. 244.
56. Patterson, *Ireland since 1939*, p. 339.
57. Noel McAdam, 'SF Man Says Poll Results Expected', *Belfast Telegraph*, 20 Feb. 2003.
58. Steve Bruce, 'Northern Ireland: Reappraising Loyalist Violence', in Alan O'Day (ed.), *Terrorism's Laboratory: The Case of Northern Ireland* (Aldershot: Dartmouth, 1995), pp. 115–35, especially p. 133.
59. Steve Bruce, 'Paramilitaries, Peace, and Politics: Ulster Loyalists and the 1994 Truce', *Studies in Conflict and Terrorism*, 18 (July/Sept. 1995), pp. 187–202, especially 198, 202.
60. The name 'Red Hand Defenders' has since been used as a cover name by both the LVF and the UDA in terrorist activities.
61. Patterson, 'From Insulation to Appeasement', p. 178; Patterson, *Ireland since 1939*, p. 337; Bruce Anderson, 'We All Know who Holds the Key to Peace in Ireland', *Independent*, 2 July 2001.
62. Paul Wilkinson, *Political Terrorism* (London: Macmillan, 1974), p. 118; see also Conor Cruise O'Brien, *Herod: Reflections on Political Violence* (London: Hutchinson, 1978).
63. PIRA statement, 6 May 2003.
64. 'But is There an Agreement in Ireland?', *Daily Telegraph*, 17 April 1998, p. 29.
65. Peter Mandelson, 'The Good Friday Agreement: A Vision for a New Order in Northern Ireland', in M. Elliott (ed.), *Long Road to Peace*, pp. 115–19.

CHAPTER 2

1. See, for instance, A.T.Q. Stewart, *The Narrow Ground: Aspects of Ulster, 1609–1969* (London: Faber & Faber, 1977).
2. Peter Gibbon, *The Origins of Ulster Unionism: The Formation of Popular Protestant Politics and Ideology in Nineteenth-Century Ireland* (Manchester: Manchester University Press, 1975).
3. Christine Kinealy and Gerard Macatasney, *The Hidden Famine: Poverty and Sectarianism in Belfast, 1840–50* (London: Pluto Press, 2000).
4. B.M. Walker, *Ulster Politics: The Formative Years, 1868–1886* (Belfast: Institute of Irish Studies, 1989); B.M. Walker, 'The 1885 and 1886 General Elections – A Milestone in Irish History', in Peter Collins (ed.), *Nationalism and Unionism: Conflict in Ireland* (Belfast: Institute of Irish Studies, Queen's University of Belfast, 1994), pp. 1–15.
5. Alvin Jackson, *Home Rule: An Irish History, 1800–2000* (London: Weidenfeld & Nicolson, 2003); Alan O'Day, *Irish Home Rule, 1867–1921* (Manchester: Manchester University Press, 1998).
6. A.T.Q. Stewart, *The Ulster Crisis* (London: Faber & Faber, 1967), pp. 58–68.
7. Jeremy Smith, *The Tories and Ireland, 1910–1914: Conservative Party Politics and the Home Rule Crisis* (Dublin: Irish Academic Press, 2000); Michael Laffan, *The Partition of Ireland, 1911–1925* (Dublin: Dublin Historical Association, 1983), p. 26.
8. See Patricia Jalland, *The Liberals and Ireland: the Ulster Question in British Politics to 1914* (Brighton: Harvester Press, 1980).
9. Public Record Office of Northern Ireland (PRONI): Craigavon papers, T/3775/10/5, Notes on a conference between King George V and Sir James Craig, 24 July 1914.
10. Thomas Hennessey, *Dividing Ireland: World War I and Partition* (London: Routledge, 1998).
11. G.K. Peatling, *British Opinion and Irish Self-Government, 1865–1925: From Unionism to Liberal Commonwealth* (Dublin: Irish Academic Press, 2001); D.G. Boyce, *Englishmen and Irish Troubles: British Public Opinion and the Making of Irish Policy, 1918–22* (London: Cape, 1972).
12. Michael Hopkinson, *Green Against Green: The Irish Civil War* (New York: St. Martin's Press, 1988).
13. PRONI: CAB/4/29/5, Northern Ireland cabinet meeting, 10 Jan. 1922.
14. Kevin Matthews, 'Stanley Baldwin's "Irish Question"', *Historical Journal*, 43 (2000), pp. 1027–49.
15. Dennis Kennedy, 'Politics of North–South Relations in Post-Partition Ireland', in Patrick J. Roche and Brian Barton (eds), *The Northern Ireland Question: Nationalism, Unionism and Partition* (Aldershot: Ashgate, 1999), pp. 71–96.
16. The National Archives (TNA (PRO)), London: PREM 3/131/1, 'Note of a Talk between Mr de Valera and Mr MacDonald in Dublin, June 26th, 1940'; PRONI: T/3775/20/6, Craigavon to Chamberlain, 27 June 1940, and T/3775/20/7, Chamberlain to Craigavon and Craigavon's note, 28 June 1940; Brian Girvin, 'Politics in Wartime: Governing, Neutrality and Elections', in Brian Girvin and Geoffrey Roberts (eds), *Ireland and the Second World War: Politics, Society and Remembrance* (Dublin: Four Courts Press, 2000), pp. 24–46, especially pp. 30–1.
17. James Loughlin, *Ulster Unionism and British National Identity since 1885* (London: Pinter, 1995), pp. 91–162; PRONI: CAB/4A/26, minutes of the Cabinet Publicity Committee.
18. PRONI: CAB/9J/8/1, documents on the Commonwealth Parliamentary Association, especially Basil Brooke to Howard d'Egville, 4 Dec. 1946.
19. National Archives of Ireland (Dublin), Department of the Taoiseach papers, S 1957 A and S 1957 B, on misuse of the term Ulster for Northern Ireland.
20. PRONI: CAB/9J/48/4, Eric Montgomery to J. Scott (of the NI Ministry of Education), 12 Feb. 1964.
21. PRONI: CAB/9J/48/4, Lord Rathcavan to Michael Adeane, 6 Jan. 1965.
22. Stormont, the Northern Ireland Parliament building, was not opened until 1932, but it has since become a powerful symbol of the entire period in the province from 1921 to 1972. In fact, following the creation of the Northern Ireland Assembly under the Good Friday Agreement, Stormont has continued to be used to house the legislature of Northern Ireland, even in a period of power-sharing government.
23. See, for example, Michael Farrell, *Northern Ireland: The Orange State* (London: Pluto Press,

1976).

24. Michael Hopkinson, *The Irish War of Independence* (Montreal: McGill–Queen's University Press, 2002), pp. 153–64.

25. Bryan A. Follis, *A State under Siege: The Establishment of Northern Ireland, 1920–1925* (Oxford: Clarendon Press, 1995).

26 See Andrew Magill papers, Bodleian Library, University of Oxford: MS.Eng.c.2803; Magill's autobiography; Peter Hart, *The IRA and its Enemies: Violence and Community in Cork, 1916–1923* (Oxford: Clarendon Press, 1998).

27. Laura K. Donohue, 'Regulating Northern Ireland: the Special Powers Acts, 1922–1972', *Historical Journal*, 41 (1998), pp. 1089–1120; Michael Farrell, *Arming the Protestants: The Formation of the Ulster Special Constabulary and the Royal Ulster Constabulary, 1920–27* (London: Pluto Press, 1983).

28. Christopher Hewitt, 'Catholic Grievances, Catholic Nationalism and Violence in Northern Ireland during the Civil Rights Period: A Reconsideration', *British Journal of Sociology*, 32 (1981), pp. 362–80, especially pp. 375–7; Denis O'Hearn, 'Catholic Grievances, Catholic Nationalism: A Comment', *British Journal of Sociology*, 34 (1983), pp. 438–45. For the ensuing debate see Christopher Hewitt, 'Discrimination in Northern Ireland: A Rejoinder', *British Journal of Sociology*, 34 (1983), pp. 446–51; Denis O'Hearn, 'Again on Discrimination in the North of Ireland: A Reply to the Rejoinder', *British Journal of Sociology*, 36 (1985), pp. 94–101; Christopher Hewitt, 'Catholic Grievances and Violence in Northern Ireland', *British Journal of Sociology*, 36 (1985), pp. 102–5: Kassian A. Kovalcheck, 'Catholic Grievances in Northern Ireland: Appraisal and Judgement', *British Journal of Sociology*, 38, (1987), pp. 77–87; Christopher Hewitt, 'Explaining Violence in Northern Ireland', *British Journal of Sociology*, 38 (1987), pp. 88–93; Denis O'Hearn, 'Catholic Grievances: Comments', *British Journal of Sociology*, 38 (1987), pp. 94–100. See also John Whyte, 'How Much Discrimination was There under the Unionist Regime, 1921–68?', in Tom Gallagher and James O'Connell (eds), *Contemporary Irish Studies* (Manchester: Manchester University Press, 1983), pp. 1–35; Bill Rolston, 'Reformism and Sectarianism: the State of the Union after Civil Rights', in John Darby (ed.), *Northern Ireland: The Background to the Conflict* (Belfast: Appletree Press, 1983), pp. 197–224; Paul A. Compton, 'Employment Differentials in Northern Ireland and Job Discrimination: A Critique', in Patrick J. Roche and Brian Barton (eds), *The Northern Ireland Question: Myth and Reality* (Aldershot: Avebury, 1991), pp. 40–76.

29. See Paul Bew, Peter Gibbon and Henry Patterson, *The State in Northern Ireland, 1921–72: Political Forces and Social Classes* (New York: St. Martin's Press, 1979), and, to a lesser extent, Paul Bew, Peter Gibbon and Henry Patterson, *Northern Ireland, 1921–1996: Political Forces and Social Classes* (London: Serif, 1996).

30. PRONI: CAB/9B/38/1, Joynson-Hicks to Craigavon, 14 Dec. 1928.

31. See PRONI: HA/32/1/900 on surveillance of the Anti-Partition League during the 1940s.

32. Niall Ó Dochartaigh, *From Civil Rights to Armalites: Derry and the Birth of the Irish Troubles* (Cork University Press, 1997): PRONI: CAB/9B/13/2 and CAB/9B/13/3, memos and correspondence on redistribution and local government in the 1930s. The name of the city called 'Londonderry/Derry' here is contested, nationalists generally preferring the name 'Derry', unionists generally preferring 'Londonderry'. Sometimes it is referred to as 'Stroke City', for obvious reasons.

33. PRONI: CAB/9B/70/1, W.E. Orr and W.H. Fyffe to Sir James Craig, 20 Sept. 1923.

34. PRONI: CAB/9B/13/2, H.L. Glasgow to Dawson Bates, 8 March 1929.

35. PRONI: HA/32/1/900, J.G. Montgomery to E. Warnock, 16 May 1949.

36. PRONI: CAB/9B/13/3, 'Londonderry wards' memo, n. d.

37. Follis, *State under Siege*, pp. 190–1; Marianne Elliott, *The Catholics of Ulster: A History* (New York: Basic Books, 2001), pp. 373–481, especially p. 383.

38. John M. Regan, *The Irish Counter-Revolution, 1921–1936: Treatyite Politics and Settlement in Independent Ireland* (Dublin: Gill & Macmillan, 1999).

39. TNA (PRO: HO 284/45, documents pertaining to a meeting of Home Secretary with Ulster Unionists about IRA activities, 24 Nov. 1959. It can be argued that from its earliest years the southern state has displayed a readiness to adopt legislation against republi-

can extremists periodically even more severe than that in effect in the North: see Colm Campbell, *Emergency Law in Ireland, 1918–1925* (Oxford: Clarendon Press, 1994).

40. Ronan Fanning, *Independent Ireland* (Walkinstown, County Dublin: Helicon, 1983), pp. 120–7; Girvin, 'Politics in Wartime'.

41. Dennis Kennedy, *The Widening Gulf: Northern Attitudes to the Independent Irish State, 1919–49* (Belfast: Blackstaff Press, 1988).

42. Michael Kennedy, *Division and Consensus: The Politics of Cross-Border Relations in Ireland, 1925–1969* (Dublin: Institute of Public Administration, 2000).

43. David Fitzpatrick, *The Two Irelands, 1912–1939* (Oxford: Oxford University Press, 1998).

44. M. Elliott, *The Catholics of Ulster*, pp. 407–9.

45. Farrell, *Northern Ireland*; C. Desmond Greaves, *The Irish Crisis* (New York, International Publishers, 1972).

46. Patrick Crozier, *Ulster for Beginners* (London: Friends of the Union, 1998); Conor Cruise O'Brien, *Ancestral Voices: Religion and Nationalism in Ireland* (Dublin: Poolbeg, 1994); Hewitt, 'Catholic Grievances, Catholic Nationalism and Violence in Northern Ireland'.

47. John Whyte, *Interpreting Northern Ireland* (Oxford: Clarendon Press, 1990).

48. See Sabine Wichert, 'The Role of Nationalism in the Northern Ireland Conflict', *History of European Ideas*, 16:1–3 (Jan. 1993), pp. 109–14; Ó Dochartaigh, *From Civil Rights to Armalites*; Richard English, *Armed Struggle: A History of the IRA* (Basingstoke: Macmillan, 2003). For English's position in this debate, see ibid., p. 93, and also Richard English, 'The State of Northern Ireland', in Richard English and Charles Townshend (eds), *The State: Historical and Political Dimensions* (London: Routledge, 1999), pp. 95–108.

49. For a relatively recent statement of this view see Alex Callinicos, *The Revenge of History: Marxism and the East European Revolutions* (University Park, PA: Pennsylvania State University Press, 1991), pp. 21–40.

50. Lewis Namier, *1848: The Revolution of the Intellectuals* (London: G. Cumberlege, 1944); J.L. Talmon, *Political Messianism: The Romantic Phase* (London: Secker & Warburg, 1960); J.L. Talmon, *The Origins of Totalitarian Democracy* (London: Mercury Books,, 1961).

51. PRONI: CAB/4/1347, papers relating to meeting of the Northern Ireland cabinet held on 10 Nov. 1966, especially the memorandum by the Attorney General, E.W. Jones; TNA (PRO): CAB 164/574, James Callaghan to Harold Wilson, 27 Feb. 1969; PRONI: CAB/4/1353, Northern Ireland cabinet meeting, 24 Jan. 1967.

52. Liam O'Dowd, Bill Rolston and Mike Tomlinson, *Northern Ireland, Between Civil Rights and Civil War* (London: CSE Books, 1980) pp. 110–1: Marc Mulholland, *Northern Ireland at the Crossroads* (Basingstoke: Macmillan, 2000).

53. PRONI: CAB/4/1365, Northern Ireland cabinet meeting, 8 June 1967; John Daniel Cash, *Identity, Ideology and Conflict: The Structuration of Politics in Northern Ireland* (Cambridge: Cambridge University Press, 1996), pp. 119–202.

54. Brian Dooley, *Black and Green: The Fight for Civil Rights in Northern Ireland and Black America* (London: Pluto Press, 1998); Bob Purdie, 'Oppressive Solidarity: The Northern Ireland Civil Rights Movement and Irish America', *Irish Studies Review*, 2 (Winter 1992), pp. 6–8.

55. Bob Purdie, *Politics in the Streets: The Origins of the Civil Rights Movement in Northern Ireland* (Belfast: Blackstaff Press, 1990), pp. 121–58.

56. Richard English, 'The Same People with Different Relatives?: Modern Scholarship, Unionists and the Irish Nation', in R. English and G. Walker (eds), *Unionism in Modern Ireland: New Perspectives on Politics and Culture* (Basingstoke: Macmillan, 1996), pp. 220–35, especially p. 229.

57. Sabine Wichert, *Northern Ireland since 1945*, second edition (London: Longman, 1999; first published 1991), pp. 128–9; Paul Arthur, *The People's Democracy, 1968–1973* (Belfast: Blackstaff Press, 1974).

58. PRONI: Sam Napier papers, D/3702/C/1/9, Northern Ireland Labour Party reactions to political and civil instability, 1968–69; PRONI: CAB/4/1347, papers relating to meeting of the Northern Ireland cabinet held on 10 Nov. 1966, especially the Northern Ireland Labour Party's 'Joint Memorandum on Citizens' Rights'.

59. Purdie, *Politics in the Streets*, pp. 148–52.

60. PRONI: CAB/4/1405, minutes of cabinet meeting held 8 Oct. 1968.

61. Jeremy Smith, *Making the Peace in Ireland* (Harlow: Pearson Education, 2002), p. 77: English, *Armed Struggle*, p. 97.
62. English, *Armed Struggle*, p. 352.
63. Richard Davis, *Mirror Hate: The Convergent Ideology of Northern Ireland Paramilitaries, 1966–1992* (Aldershot: Dartmouth, 1994), p. 13; Ó Dochartaigh, *From Civil Rights to Armalites*, p. 311.
64. Feargal Cochrane, '"Meddling at the Crossroads": The Decline and Fall of Terence O'Neill within the Unionist Community', in English and Walker (eds), *Unionism in Modern Ireland*, pp. 148–68.
65. TNA (PRO): CAB 164/574, note by Peter Gregson, 26 June 1969.
66. Paul Arthur and Keith Jeffery, *Northern Ireland since 1968* (Oxford: Basil Blackwell, 1988), p. 11.
67. TNA (PRO): CAB 164/574, Oliver Wright to Harold Wilson, 19 Oct. 1969; PRO: PREM 13/983, A.G.B. to Wilson, 23 July 1965.
68. TNA (PRO): CJ4/45, internal Foreign Office memo entitled 'Northern Ireland'.
69. Links have been suggested between the Official IRA and the Workers Party, which still survives as one of the smaller political parties in Northern Ireland.
70. 'Provisional' was initially adopted as a label as it was assumed that the split would be short-lived, but an alternative meaning was later preferred suggesting an association with the Provisional Government proclaimed by the leaders of the Easter Rising in 1916, a foundational moment in republican tradition: see Davis, *Mirror Hate*, pp. 14–15.
71. M.L.R. Smith, *Fighting for Ireland? The Military Strategy of the Irish Republican Movement* (London: Routledge, 1997), pp. 83, 87–90, 93; Marc Mulholland, *The Longest War: Northern Ireland's Troubled History* (Oxford: Oxford University Press, 2002), pp. 87–98; English, *Armed Struggle*, pp. 105–12, 120–3; R.B. Finnegan, 'The United Kingdom Security Policy and IRA Terrorism in Ulster', *Éire–Ireland*, 23:1 (1988), pp. 87–110.
72. Gerard Murray, *John Hume and the SDLP: Impact and Survival in Northern Ireland* (Dublin: Irish Academic Press, 1998), pp. 3–10.
73. English, *Armed Struggle*, pp. 117–19.
74. Loughlin, *Ulster Unionism and British National Identity*, pp. 198–201.
75. See Fig. 1. For further examples see Roy Douglas, Liam Harte and Jim O'Hara, *Drawing Conclusions: A Cartoon History of Anglo-Irish Relations, 1798–1998* (Belfast: Blackstaff Press, 1998), pp. 272–300.
76. For such a partisan account see Paul Johnson, *Ireland, Land of Troubles: A History from the Twelfth Century to the Present Day* (New York: Holmes & Meier, 1982), especially p. 193.
77. PRO: FCO 87/114, F.F. Steele to D. Trevelyan, 26 Jan. 1972.
78. See Bill Rolston and David Miller (eds), *War and Words: the Northern Ireland Media Reader* (Belfast: Beyond the Pale, 1996).
79. TNA (PRO): CJ4/39, papers on relations between the government and the BBC, 1971.
80. TNA (PRO): CAB 128/50, cabinet conclusions from meetings: cabinet meeting, 1 Aug. 1972.
81. TNA (PRO): CAB 129/159 (Cmd 4823), 'Report of the Enquiry into Allegations against the Security Forces of Physical Brutality in Northern Ireland Arising out of Events on the 9th August 1971' [Compton Report], Nov. 1971, p. vi.
82. TNA (PRO): CAB 128/48, cabinet conclusions from meetings: confidential annex: cabinet meeting, 3 Feb. 1972.
83. TNA (PRO): CAB 128/48 cabinet meeting, 13 July 1972.
84. TNA (PRO): PREM 15/1005, Northern Ireland cabinet to Heath, 23 March 1972.
85. TNA (PRO): FCO 87/108, memorandum by Cromer, 11 Jan. 1972; FCO 87/91, W.T. Hull to R.B. Bone, 8 Feb. 1972; FCO 87/101, memorandum by Cromer, 3 Feb. 1972; FCO 87/117, communications with the Papacy about Northern Ireland.
86. TNA (PRO): FCO 87/114, D.E.S. Blatherwick to Roger Bone, 24 Nov. [1971], CJ4/196; Smith, *Making the Peace in Ireland*, p. 91.
87 *The Future of Northern Ireland: A Paper for Discussion* (London: HMSO, 1972); PRO: CJ4/141, papers on the Darlington conference.
88. Brian Girvin, 'Northern Ireland and the Republic', in Paul Mitchell and Rick Wilford

(eds), *Politics in Northern Ireland* (Boulder, CO: Westview Press, 1999), pp. 220–41, especially p. 230.

89. Paul Dixon, *Northern Ireland: The Politics of War and Peace* (Basingstoke: Palgrave, 2001), pp. 138–9.

90. TNA (PRO): CJ4/45, 'Willie' [Capt. L.P.S. Orr, MP] to 'Reggie' [Reginald Maudling], 30 Nov. 1970.

91. Jonathan Moore, *Ulster Unionism and the British Conservative Party: A Study of a Failed Marriage* (London: University of North London Irish Studies Centre, 1997).

92. Belinda Probert, *Beyond Orange and Green: The Political Economy of the Northern Ireland Crisis* (London: Zed Press, 1978), pp. 136–41.

93. TNA (PRO): CAB 128/48, cabinet conclusions from meetings: confidential annex: cabinet meeting, 6 July 1972.

94. Loughlin, *Ulster Unionism and British National Identity*, pp. 202–5: David W. Miller, *Queen's Rebels: Ulster Loyalism in Historical Perspective* (Dublin: Gill & Macmillan, 1978), pp. 163–4.

95. Henry Patterson, 'British Government and the "Protestant Backlash", 1969–74', in Yonah Alexander and Alan O'Day (eds), *Ireland's Terrorist Dilemma* (Dordrecht: M. Nijhoff, 1986), pp. 231–47.

96. Probert, *Beyond Orange and Green*, pp. 141–4.

97. BBC television and radio broadcast by Harold Wilson, 25 May 1974, quoted in Mulholland, *The Longest War*, p. 120; see also Merlyn Rees, *Northern Ireland: A Personal Perspective* (London: Methuen, 1985).

98. Paul Foot, 'Colin Wallace and the Propaganda War', in Rolston and Miller (eds), *War and Words*, pp. 158–90, especially pp. 172–7; Anthony Coughlan, 'A Unitary Irish State', in John McGarry and Brendan O'Leary (eds), *The Future of Northern Ireland* (Oxford: Clarendon Press, 1990), pp. 48–68, especially p. 63. Academic evaluation of such claims is hampered by the unavailability of primary documents under the British government's thirty-year rule covering many such documents from this and all subsequent periods.

99. Arthur, *Special Relationships*, pp. 160–78.

100. Paddy Hillyard, *Suspect Community: People's Experience of the Prevention of Terrorism Acts in Britain* (London: Pluto Press in association with Liberty, 1993).

101. Graham Ellison and Jim Smyth, *The Crowned Harp: Policing Northern Ireland* (London: Pluto Press, 2000), pp. 134–49; Peter Taylor, *Brits: The War against the IRA* (London: Bloomsbury, 2001), pp. 286–96.

102. Betty Purcell, 'The Silence in Irish Broadcasting', in Bill Rolston (ed.), *The Media and Northern Ireland: Covering the Troubles* (Basingstoke: Macmillan, 1991), pp. 51–68.

103. Charles Drake, 'The Provisional IRA: Reorganisation and the Long War', in Alan O'Day (ed.), *Terrorism's Laboratory: The Case of Northern Ireland* (Aldershot: Dartmouth, 1995), pp. 87–114.

104. *Today*, 6 July 1990, p. 6; *Daily Star*, 30 Aug. 1979, p. 6.

105. Philip Elliott, 'Reporting Northern Ireland: A Study of News in Great Britain, Northern Ireland and the Republic of Ireland', in *Ethnicity and the Media: An Analysis of Media Reporting in the United Kingdom, Canada and Ireland* (Paris: UNESCO, 1977), pp. 263–376, especially pp. 292–3.

106. Mike Morrissey and Marie Smyth, *Northern Ireland after the Good Friday Agreement: Victims, Grievance and Blame* (London: Pluto Press, 2002), pp. 45–63. It is generally agreed that, while republicans have been responsible for the larger share of violent deaths during the Troubles (the PIRA accounting for around a half of all violent deaths), loyalists have explicitly targeted and killed more civilians, often on sectarian grounds: see Dixon, *Northern Ireland*, p. 24, for full statistics.

107. Patrick Magee, *Gangsters or Guerrillas?: Representations of Irish Republicans in Troubles Fiction* (Belfast: Beyond the Pale, 2001), pp. 147, 176, 177–9.

108. Ibid., p. 75.

109. Richard English, 'Did Stakeknife Cut the Mustard?', *Fortnight*, 416 (July/Aug. 2003), p. 5; Magee, *Gangsters or Guerrillas?*, p. 195.

110. Smith, *Making the Peace in Ireland*, pp. 115–18: Oliver Rafferty, *Catholicism in Ulster, 1603–1983: An Interpretative History* (London: Hurst, 1994), pp. 277–82.

111. Brendan O'Leary and John McGarry, *The Politics of Antagonism: Understanding Northern Ireland* (London: Athlone Press, 1993), pp. 214–16.
112. Arthur and Jeffery, *Northern Ireland since 1968*, pp. 41–3.
113. Neave was killed by a bomb planted within the Palace of Westminster, the home of the British Parliament, by a republican splinter group, the Irish National Liberation Army (INLA), although the distinction between the INLA and the PIRA tended to be overlooked as the media concentrated on the implications of such an event occurring in such a place.
114. Dixon, *Northern Ireland*, pp. 178–9; Richard Needham, *Battling for Peace* (Belfast: Blackstaff Press, 1998), pp. 19–20.
115. Adrian Guelke, 'The United States and the Northern Ireland Question', in Brian Barton and Patrick J. Roche (eds), *The Northern Ireland Question: Perspectives and Policies* (Aldershot: Avebury, 1994), pp. 189–212, especially pp. 206–7.
116. Arthur and Jeffery, *Northern Ireland*, pp. 101–8.
117. Margaret Thatcher, *The Downing Street Years* (London: HarperCollins, 1993), p. 385.
118. David Trimble, 'Initiatives for Consensus: A Unionist Perspective', in Charles Townshend (ed.), *Consensus in Ireland: Approaches and Recessions* (Oxford: Clarendon Press, 1988), pp. 73–94.
119. Feargal Cochrane, *Unionist Politics and the Politics of Unionism since the Anglo-Irish Agreement* (Cork: Cork University Press, 1997), especially pp. 379–83; Arthur and Jeffery, *Northern Ireland since 1968*, pp. 49–50.
120. *Hansard's Parliamentary Debates*, 6th series, Vol. 163, c. 1147–8 (14 Dec. 1989).
121. Arthur Aughey, 'Unionism, Conservatism and the Anglo-Irish Agreement', in D. George Boyce and Alan O'Day (eds), *Defenders of the Union: A Survey of British and Irish Unionism since 1801* (London: Routledge, 2000), pp. 294–315.
122. O'Leary and McGarry, *The Politics of Antagonism*, pp. 248–9.
123. Compare Adrian Guelke, 'International Dimensions of the Belfast Agreement', in Rick Wilford (ed.), *Aspects of the Belfast Agreement* (Oxford: Oxford University Press, 2001), pp. 245–63, especially p. 262, with Adrian Guelke, *Northern Ireland: The International Perspective* (Dublin: Gill & Macmillan, 1988).
124. Dixon, *Northern Ireland*, pp. 225–7, especially p. 225.
125 Gerry Adams, *The Politics of Irish Freedom* (Dingle, County Kerry: Brandon, 1986), pp. 97–8.
126. A symptom of this split was the emergence of a small group, Republican Sinn Féin, notably featuring the former Provisional mainstay Ruairi Ó Brádaigh. Some believe that Republican Sinn Féin later established links with the Continuity IRA, which became prominent after a later split in the Provisionals resulting from their ceasefire in 1994.
127. David Miller, *Don't Mention the War: Northern Ireland, Propaganda and the Media* (London: Pluto Press, 1994), pp. 278–9.
128. David Murphy, *The Stalker Affair and the British Press* (London: Unwin Hyman, 1991).
129. Peter Taylor, *Provos: The IRA and Sinn Fein* (London: Bloomsbury, 1997), pp. 298–301. On Stone see Martin Dillon, *Stone Cold: The True Story of Michael Stone and the Milltown Massacre* (London: Hutchinson, 1992).
130. Michael J. Cunningham, *British Government Policy in Northern Ireland, 1969–2000* (Manchester: Manchester University Press, 2001), pp. 60–1.
131. Smith, *Fighting for Ireland?*, p. 176.
132. Patterson, *Ireland since 1939*, pp. 312–3.
133. Wichert, *Northern Ireland since 1945*, pp. 206–10.
134. *Sun*, 28 Oct. 1993, p.1.
135 John Major, *The Autobiography* (London: HarperCollins, 1999), p. 450.
136. John McGarry and Brendan O'Leary, *Explaining Northern Ireland: Broken Images* (Oxford: Blackwell, 1995), pp. 408–13. McGarry and O'Leary argue that the British declaration that it had no 'selfish strategic or economic interest' was carefully phrased so as not to occlude other possible 'selfish' British interests in the province: ibid., p. 418.
137. Steve Bruce, *The Edge of the Union: The Ulster Loyalist Political Vision* (Oxford: Oxford University Press, 1994), pp. 88–95; O'Leary and McGarry, *The Politics of Antagonism*, p. 284.
138. Arthur Aughey and Duncan Morrow, 'Frameworks and the Future', in Arthur Aughey

and Duncan Morrow (eds), *Northern Ireland Politics* (Harlow: Longman, 1996), pp. 213–21, especially p. 216; Eamonn Mallie and David McKittrick, *The Fight for Peace: The Secret Story behind the Irish Peace Process*, revised and updated edition (London: Mandarin, 1997; first published 1996), p. 298.

139. O'Brien, *Ancestral Voices*, pp. 195–7.
140. McGarry and O'Leary, *Explaining Northern Ireland*, p.384.
141. CLMC statement, 13 Oct. 1994; James McAuley, '"Flying the One-Winged Bird": Ulster Unionism and the Peace Process', in Peter Shirlow and Mark McGovern (eds), *Who are 'the People'?: Unionism, Protestantism and Loyalism in Northern Ireland* (London: Pluto Press, 1997), pp. 158–75, especially pp. 163–4.
142. Mallie and McKittrick, *The Fight for Peace*, p. 407.
143. PIRA statement, 31 Aug. 1994.
144. *Sunday Times News Review*, 4 Dec. 1994, News Review pp. 1–2.
145. Paul Bew, Henry Patterson and Paul Teague, *Northern Ireland between War and Peace: The Political Future of Northern Ireland* (London: Lawrence and Wishart 1997), p. 221; Aughey and Morrow, 'Frameworks and the Future', pp. 217–21.
146. Major, *The Autobiography*, pp. 466–7.
147. *Hansard*, 6th series, Vol. 255, c. 361 (22 Feb. 1995).
148. 'So Long, Nice while it Lasted', *Sunday Times*, 12 March 1995, pp. 14–15.
149. Chris Ryder and Vincent Kearney, *Drumcree: The Orange Order's Last Stand* (London: Methuen, 2001). For a presentation of successive years' events at Drumcree that is favourable to the Orange Order see Ruth Dudley Edwards, *The Faithful Tribe: An Intimate Portrait of the Loyal Institutions* (London: HarperCollins, 1999), pp. 278–430. For the wry humour, see ibid., p. 384.
150. Bew, Gibbon and Patterson, *Northern Ireland, 1921–1996*, p. 233.
151. Major, *The Autobiography*, pp. 487–9.
152. Guelke, 'International Dimensions of the Belfast Agreement', p. 256.
153. Taylor, *Provos*, pp. 351–2; Gerry Adams, *Before the Dawn: An Autobiography* (New York: William Morrow & Co., 1996), pp. 322–3.
154. Sean O'Callaghan, *The Informer* (London: Corgi, 1999; first published 1998), pp. 396–7.
155. John Major, 'Glimpses of Lasting Peace must be Turned into Reality', *Irish Times*, 16 May 1996, p. 14.
156. *Irish Times*, 18 May 1996, p. 1.
157. George Mitchell, *Making Peace* (New York: Knopf and London: Heinemann, 1999), pp. 50–4.
158. *Times*, 29 May 1996. Robert McCartney, the UKUP's leader, had described Ian Paisley as a 'fascist' in 1981: Wichert, *Northern Ireland since 1945*, p. 236. Later McCartney was to join Paisley in opposition to the GFA.
159. *Times*, 1 June 1996, p. 21.
160. Paul Arthur, 'Time, Territory, Tradition and the Anglo-Irish 'Peace' Process', *Government and Opposition*, 31 (1996), pp. 426–40, especially pp. 435–8; Cochrane, *Unionist Politics and the Politics of Unionism*, p. 393.
161. Kevin Myers, 'IRA's Baghdad Mentality', *Daily Telegraph*, 7 April 1997, p. 20. Myers's prediction that PSF would not gain access to all-party talks was proved less accurate.
162. Quoted in Dixon, *Northern Ireland*, p. 267.
163. James Loughlin, *The Ulster Question since 1945* (Basingstoke: Macmillan, 1998), p. 130.
164. Jerry Fitzpatrick, 'The Role of the British Labour Party in Ireland', in James Anderson and James Goodman (eds), *Dis/agreeing Ireland: Contexts, Obstacles, Hopes* (London: Pluto Press, 1998), pp. 126–40, especially p. 132.
165. Loughlin, *The Ulster Question*, p. 132.
166. See Chris Anderson, *The Billy Boy: The Life and Death of LVF Leader Billy Wright* (Edinburgh: Mainstream, 2002).
167. Wichert, *Northern Ireland since 1945*, p. 216: Mitchell, *Making Peace*, pp. 129–33.
168. Henry Patterson, 'From Insulation to Appeasement: The Major and Blair Governments Reconsidered', in Wilford (ed.), *Aspects of the Belfast Agreement*, p. 176.
169. See Fig. 2. For other aspects of Martyn Turner's work see Martyn Turner, *Railings: Political*

Cartoons, 1998–2000 (Belfast: Blackstaff Press, 2000).

170. Richard Deutsch 'The Good Friday Agreement: Assessing its Implementation, 1998–2001', *Nordic Irish Studies*, 1 (2002), p. 106; Peter Hitchens, *The Abolition of Britain: The British Cultural Revolution from Lady Chatterley to Tony Blair*, revised and expanded edition (London: Quartet, 2000; first published 1999), pp. 361–2.

171. Ken Whelan and Eugene Masterson, *Bertie Ahern: Taoiseach and Peacemaker* (Edinburgh: Mainstream Publishing, 1998), p. 204.

172 Hitchens, *The Abolition of Britain*, pp. 332, 359.

173. Ibid., pp. 361–2.

174. *Sunday Times News Review*, 17 May 1998, p.5.

175. Thomas Hennessey, *The Northern Ireland Peace Process: Ending the Troubles?* (Dublin: Gill & Macmillan, 2000), pp. 216–20: Henry McDonald, *Trimble* (London: Bloomsbury, 2001; first published 2000), p. 345.

176. Antony Alcock, 'From Conflict to Agreement in Northern Ireland: Lessons from Europe', in John McGarry (ed.), *Northern Ireland and the Divided World: the Northern Ireland Conflict and the Good Friday Agreement in Comparative Perspective* (Oxford: Oxford University Press, 2001), pp. 159–80.

177. Anthony McIntyre, 'Modern Irish Republicanism and the Belfast Agreement: Chickens Coming Home to Roost, or Turkeys Celebrating Christmas?', in Wilford (ed.), *Aspects of the Belfast Agreement*, pp. 202–22. Also see Breandán O Muirthile, 'Managing the Strategy', *The Blanket* (Spring 2003), p. 14.

178. Patterson, *Ireland since 1939*, pp. 332–3.

179. O'Callaghan, *Informer*, pp. 447–8.

180. Kirsten E. Schulze, 'Taking the Gun out of Politics: Conflict Transformation in Northern Ireland and Lebanon', in McGarry (ed.), *Northern Ireland and the Divided World*, pp. 253–75, especially pp. 270–1; see also Chapter 3 pp. 98–103 of this book.

181. *Independent on Sunday*, 21 May 2000, p. 28; 'Prize Specimen', *Daily Telegraph*, 12 Oct. 2002.

182. This view was aired most notably in connection with Neil Jordan's film *Michael Collins*, although more recently there was an impassioned debate about the BBC's drama series *Rebel Heart*, screened early in 2001. Objections to the screening of this production, which dealt with Irish history, and especially northern republicanism, at the time of independence and partition, were raised by David Trimble and the *Daily Telegraph*, among others, in view of the fact that its writer, Ronan Bennett, is himself a republican with alleged links to the conflict.

183. Gerry Adams' *Before the Dawn*, for instance, has been crushingly criticised for its silence on this score: see R.F. Foster, 'Selling Irish Childhoods: Frank McCourt and Gerry Adams', in *The Irish Story: Telling Tales and Making It Up in Ireland* (London: Allen Lane, 2001), pp. 163–86, especially pp. 174–86; see also Ed Moloney, *A Secret History of the IRA* (London: Allen Lane, 2002).

184. Tom McGurk, 'Coming to Terms: Brighton Bomber's Story', *Sunday Business Post*, 27 Aug. 2000.

185. Sean O'Callaghan, 'Finucane Should Not Have Been Killed – But He Was in the IRA', *Daily Telegraph*, 18 April 2003. PSNI chief Hugh Orde has also rejected the idea that Finucane was a PIRA member.

186. Hillsborough Declaration, 1 April 1999.

187. McDonald, *Trimble*, pp. 297–301; McGarry and O'Leary, *Explaining Northern Ireland*, pp. 200–1.

188. Patterson, *Ireland since 1939*, p. 338.

189. William Hague, 'Soft on Terror, Soft on the Causes of Terror', *Daily Telegraph*, 1 Sept. 1999, p. 20.

190. Statement by Gerry Adams, 18 Oct. 1999.

191. Brendan O'Leary, 'The Character of the 1998 Agreement: Results and Prospects', in Wilford (ed.), *Aspects of the Belfast Agreement*, p. 77.

192. Rick Wilford, 'Aspects of the Belfast Agreement: Introduction', in Wilford (ed.), *Aspects of the Belfast Agreement*, p. 1–10, especially p. 8.

193. There has been a certain identity of philosophy, and some evidence of links,

between the ANC and the PIRA, and both groups have been alternatively dismissed as 'terrorist' and described as 'freedom fighters'. Very shortly after his release from prison in 1990 the ANC's leader Nelson Mandela paid a visit to Britain, during which he suggested that the British government negotiate with the PIRA. The suggestion was condemned by almost all major political actors at the time, including Neil Kinnock, then Leader of the Labour Party, which was committed to securing unity by consent in Ireland: see 'Mandela Suggests Talks with IRA', *Independent*, 3 July 1990, p. 1. Mr Ramaphosa's perspective may thus have facilitated progress in the Provisionals' slow and difficult navigation between armed group and demilitarised party.

194.   McDonald, *Trimble*, p. 340.

195.   'Demilitarisation', like 'decommissioning', is something of a euphemism, intended to disguise what otherwise might look like a military retreat or surrender. 'Demilitarisation' corresponds to the withdrawal by the British authorities of elements of its military presence in Northern Ireland, such as personnel, equipment or installations.

196.   Patterson, *Ireland since 1939*, p. 340.

197.   *Hansard*, 6th series, Vol. 363, c. 893 (28 Feb. 2001).

198.   See the comments by two unionist MPs, Lady Sylvia Hermon (UUP) and Peter Robinson (DUP), in *Hansard*, 6th series, Vol. 371, c. 711 and 719 (10 July 2001).

199.   *Irish Times*, 2 Aug. 2001, p. 7.

200.   Northern Ireland *Hansard*, available at <http://www.ni-assembly.gov.uk/record/reports/011105.htm#4>, pp. 471–7, last accessed 15 May 2004.

201.   Deutsch, 'The Good Friday Agreement', p. 96.

202.   *Hansard*, 6th series, Vol. 377, c. 151–262 (18 Dec. 2001).

203.   Trimble, *McDonald*, p. 341.

204.   Quentin Davies, MP, 'Amnesty for Terrorists Would Kill Off the Peace Process', *Daily Telegraph*, 8 March 2002; Kevin Myers, 'Please, Someone, Explain This Amnesty to Me', *Daily Telegraph*, 10 March 2002 (press release not yet archived).

205.   Provisional Sinn Féin, 'Sustained Efforts to Create Contrived Crisis in the Peace Process', 20 April 2002, available at <http://www.sinnfein.ie/releases/02/pr022004.html>, last accessed 27 May 2002.

206.   *Daily Telegraph*, 17 July 2002, p. 23.

207.   John Hume, *Personal Views: Politics, Peace and Reconciliation in Ireland* (Enfield: Roberts Rinehart, 1996), pp. 72, 92.

208.   *Hansard*, 6th series, Vol. 389, c. 983–6 (24 July 2002).

209.   Niall Stanage, 'Trimble Puts Power before Peace', *Guardian*, 25 Sept. 2002.

210.   Blair, 'Finding a Way through the Crisis', speech in Belfast, 17 Oct. 2002, available at http://www.labour.org.uk/tbnispeech/, last accessed 15 May 2004.

211.   *Irish News*, 16 Aug. 2002, p. 6. Police statistics released in 2004 confirm the impression since 1998 that loyalist violence has predominated.

212.   *Hansard*, 6th series, Vol. 401, c. 861–2 (18 March 2003).

213.   Joint Declaration by the British and Irish Governments, April 2003 (published May 2003).

214.   *Belfast Telegraph*, 17 June 2003, p. 12; *Irish Independent*, 17 June 2003, pp. 1, 10.

CHAPTER 3

1.   Especially Paul Mitchell, '"Futures"', in Paul Mitchell and Rick Wilford (eds), *Politics in Northern Ireland* (Boulder, CO: Westview Press, 1999), pp. 265–84; John McGarry and Brendan O'Leary (eds), *The Future of Northern Ireland* (Oxford: Clarendon Press, 1990); John Whyte, *Interpreting Northern Ireland* (Oxford: Clarendon Press, 1990), pp.209–43; Jonathan Tonge, *Northern Ireland: Conflict and Change* (Harlow: Longman, 2002), pp. 2–5.

2.   Joseph Ruane and Jennifer Todd, '"Why Can't You Just Get Along with Each Other?":

Culture, Structure and the Northern Ireland Conflict', in Eamonn Hughes (ed.), *Culture and Politics in Northern Ireland, 1960–1990* (Buckingham: Open University Press, 1991), especially pp. 27–8; see also Chapter 1 of this book.

3. Whyte, *Interpreting Northern Ireland*, p. 232.
4. Frank Wright, *Two Lands on One Soil: Ulster Politics before Home Rule* (Dublin: Gill & Macmillan, 1996), pp. 513, 522; see also Frank Wright, 'Asymmetry in Cross-Community Meetings', in Adrian Guelke (ed.), *New Perspectives on the Northern Ireland Conflict* (Aldershot: Avebury, 1994), pp. 142–60; Frank Wright, 'Communal Deterrence and the Threat of Violence in the North of Ireland in the Nineteenth Century', in John Darby, Nicholas Dodge and A.C. Hepburn (eds), *Political Violence: Ireland in a Comparative Perspective* (Belfast: Appletree Press, 1990), pp. 11–28; Frank Wright *Northern Ireland: A Comparative Analysis* (Dublin: Gill and Macmillan, 1987).
5. James Clifford, *Routes: Travel and Translation in the Late Twentieth Century* (Cambridge, MA: Harvard University Press, 1997), p. 268; Avtar Brah, *Cartographies of Diaspora: Contesting Identities* (London: Routledge, 1996), pp. 93–4.
6. The classic demonstration of this is Benedict Anderson, *Imagined Communities: Reflections on the Origin and Spread of Nationalism*, revised edition (London: Verso, 1991; first published 1983), especially p.6.
7. Paula M.L. Moya, 'Introduction', in Paula M.L. Moya and Michael R. Hames-García (eds), *Reclaiming Identity: Realist Theory and the Predicament of Postmodernism* (Berkeley, CA: University of California Press, 2000), pp. 1–26.
8. A.D.S. Smith, *Nationalism in the Twentieth Century* (Oxford: M. Robertson, 1979), pp. 12–13, 184–97.
9. Paul Dixon, 'Political Skills or Lying and Manipulation?: The Choreography of the Northern Ireland Peace Process', *Political Studies*, 50:4 (Sept. 2002), pp. 725–41, especially p. 730.
10. Ibid., 740.
11. Paul Dixon, *Northern Ireland: The Politics of War and Peace* (Basingstoke: Palgrave, 2001), p. 306.
12. Dixon, 'Political Skills . . .', p. 739.
13. Joseph Ruane and Jennifer Todd, 'The Belfast Agreement: Context, Content, Consequences', in Joseph Ruane and Jennifer Todd (eds), *After the Good Friday Agreement: Analysing Political Change in Northern Ireland* (Dublin: University College Dublin Press, 1999), pp. 1–29, especially pp. 28–9.
14. Paul Arthur, *Special Relationships: Britain, Ireland and the Northern Ireland Problem* (Belfast: Blackstaff Press, 2000), p. 180.
15. Dixon, 'Political Skills . . .', pp. 733, 736–7. See below, pp. 127–30, 146–50, for further discussion of this point.
16. Dixon, 'Political Skills . . .', p. 732; Jean Baudrillard, *The Gulf War Did Not Take Place*, translated and with an introduction by Paul Patton (Sydney, NSW: Power Publications, 1995).
17. This epithet was applied to McGuinness by the moderate unionist Ken Maginnis on the television programme *Newsnight* (BBC 2) in August 1997.
18. Text of the Good Friday Agreement, available at <http://www.nio.gov.uk/issues/agreement.htm>, last accessed 15 May 2004.
19. George Mitchell, *Making Peace* (New York: Knopf and London: Heinemann, 1999), pp. 179–80.
20. William Hague, 'Soft on Terror, Soft on the Causes of Terror', *Daily Telegraph*, 1 Sept. 1999.
21. Kirsten E. Schulze, 'Taking the Gun out of Politics: Conflict Transformation in Northern Ireland and Lebanon', in John McGarry (ed.), *Northern Ireland and the Divided World: the Northern Ireland Conflict and the Good Friday Agreement in Comparative Perspective* (Oxford: Oxford University Press, 2001), pp. 270–1.
22. Henry Patterson, *Ireland since 1939* (Oxford: Oxford University Press, 2002), p. 341.
23. Brendan O'Leary, 'The Character of the 1998 Agreement: Results and Prospects', in Rick Wilford (ed.), *Aspects of the Belfast Agreement* (Oxford: Oxford University Press, 2001), p. 54.
24. David Trimble, interview on *Hearts and Minds* (BBC [Television] Northern Ireland), 27 June 2002.

25. Andrew MacKay, interview on *The Westminster Hour* (BBC Radio Four), 21 Jan. 2001.
26. Martin McGuinness, interview on BBC Radio Five Live on the weekend of 23 and 24 May 1998.
27. O'Leary, 'The Character of the 1998 Agreement', p. 70.
28. Patterson, *Ireland since 1939*, p. 339.
29. Ibid., pp. 332–43.
30. Jeremy Smith, *Making the Peace in Ireland* (Harlow: Pearson Education Limited, 2002), p. 230.
31. The d'Hondt formula underlies one possible system of proportional representation. Its most significant role in Northern Ireland is in determining parties' representation on the Executive, with the exceptions of the posts of First Minister and Deputy First Minister, which were to be elected in the Assembly. The formula thus ensured that posts on the Executive were divided among the four largest parties in the Assembly, the UUP, the SDLP, the DUP and PSF: see Brendan O'Leary, 'The Nature of the British–Irish Agreement', *New Left Review*, 233 (Jan./Feb. 1999), pp. 66–96, especially pp. 95–6. However, McGarry and O'Leary had expressed a preference for Sainte-Laguë rules to distribute seats on such an executive, rather than the d'Hondt formula, as the former function mathematically to ensure a larger representation for smaller political parties: John McGarry and Brendan O'Leary, *Explaining Northern Ireland: Broken Images* (Oxford: Blackwell, 1995), p. 374
32. Arend Lijphart, 'Foreword: One Basic Problem, Many Theoretical Options – and a Practical Solution', in McGarry and O'Leary (eds), *The Future of Northern Ireland*, pp. vi–viii; Arend Lijphart, *Democracy in Plural Societies: A Comparative Exploration* (New Haven, CT: Yale University Press, 1977), especially pp. 134–41.
33. Brendan O'Leary, 'The Character of the 1998 Agreement'; John McGarry and Brendan O'Leary, 'Conclusion: Northern Ireland's Options: A Framework and Analysis', in McGarry and O'Leary (eds), *The Future of Northern Ireland*, pp. 268–303: B. O'Leary and J. McGarry, 'Regulating Nations and Ethnic Communities', in A. Breton *et. al.*, *Nationalism and Rationality* (Cambridge: Cambridge University Press, 1995), pp. 245–89; John McGarry and Brendan O'Leary, *Explaining Northern Ireland*, pp. 354–82: Brendan O'Leary and John McGarry, *The Politics of Antagonism: Understanding Northern Ireland* (London : Athlone Press, 1993).
34. J. McGarry, 'The Anglo-Irish Agreement and the Unlikely Prospects for Power-Sharing', *Éire–Ireland*, 23:1 (1988), pp. 111–28, especially p. 111.
35. O'Leary, 'The Character of the 1998 Agreement', pp. 58–9.
36. McGarry and O'Leary, *Explaining Northern Ireland*, pp. 405–6.
37. See Henry McDonald, 'Anger over Trimble's Irish Insult', *Observer*, 10 March 2002; David Lloyd, *Ireland After History* (Notre Dame, IN: University of Notre Dame Press, 1999), p. 4.
38. W.A. Hanna, *Intertwined Roots: An Ulster-Scots Perspective* (Blackrock: Columba Press, 2000), p. 8.
39. C. McCall, 'Political Transformation and the Reinvention of the Ulster-Scots Identity and Culture', *Identities: Global Studies in Power and Culture*, 9:2 (April–June 2002), pp. 197–218.
40. Rory Fitzpatrick, *God's Frontiersmen: The Scots-Irish Epic* (London: Weidenfeld & Nicolson in association with Channel 4 Television and Ulster Television, 1989); Patrick Griffin, *The People with No Name: Ireland's Ulster Scots, America's Scots Irish, and the Creation of a British Atlantic World, 1689–1764* (Princeton, NJ: Princeton University Press, 2001); Michael Montgomery, 'The Problem of Persistence: Ulster–American Missing Links', *Journal of Scotch–Irish Studies*, 1:1 (Spring 2000), pp. 105–19, especially pp. 105–7; Matthew McKee, '"A Peculiar and Royal Race": Creating a Scotch-Irish Identity, 1889–1901', in Patrick Fitzgerald and Steve Ickringill (eds), *Atlantic Crossroads: Historical Connections between Scotland, Ulster and North America* (Newtownards: Colourpoint, 2001), pp. 67–83.
41. Brian Graham and Peter Shirlow, 'The Battle of the Somme in Ulster Memory and Identity', *Political Geography*, 21:7 (Sept. 2002), pp. 881–904.
42. Stephen Howe, *Ireland and Empire: Colonial Legacies in Irish History and Culture* (Oxford: Oxford University Press, 2000), p. 238.

43. Mick Fealty, Trevor Ringland and David Steven, *A Long Peace?: The Future of Unionism in Northern Ireland* (Wimborne: Slugger O'Toole, 2003), p. 29.
44. Howe, *Ireland and Empire*, p. 239.
45. Joseph Ruane and Jennifer Todd, *The Dynamics of Conflict in Northern Ireland: Power, Conflict, and Emancipation* (Cambridge: Cambridge University Press, 1996); Joseph Ruane and Jennifer Todd, 'Irish Nationalism and the Conflict in Northern Ireland', in David Miller (ed.), *Rethinking Northern Ireland: Culture, Ideology and Colonialism* (London: Longman, 1998), pp. 55–69.
46. Alan Finlayson, 'Discourse and Contemporary Loyalist Identity', in Peter Shirlow and Mark McGovern (eds), *Who are 'the People'?: Unionism, Protestantism and Loyalism in Northern Ireland* (London: Pluto Press, 1997), pp. 72–94: Alan Finlayson, 'The Problem of "Culture" in Northern Ireland: A Critique of the Cultural Traditions Group', *Irish Review*, 20 (Winter/Spring 1997), pp. 76–88.
47. Mairéad Nic Craith, *Plural Identities – Singular Narratives: The Case of Northern Ireland* (New York: Berghahn Books, 2002).
48. Seamus Dunn and Alan Smith, 'Education and the Conflict in Northern Ireland', in Alan O'Day (ed.), *Terrorism's Laboratory: The Case of Northern Ireland* (Aldershot: Dartmouth, 1995), pp. 75–86; Dominic Murray, 'Schools and Conflict', in John Darby (ed.), *Northern Ireland: The Background to the Conflict* (Belfast: Appletree Press, 1983), pp. 136–50; Dominic Murray, *Worlds Apart: Segregated Schools in Northern Ireland* (Belfast: Appletree Press, 1985).
49. Howe, *Ireland and Empire*, p. 238.
50. 'Blair and Ulster Riots', *Daily Telegraph*, 22 June 2001.
51. Arlene Foster, *'Parity of Esteem' and 'Consent': How Words Deceive* (London: Friends of the Union, 1996).
52. *Hansard*, 6th series, Vol. 377, c. 239 (18 Dec. 2001).
53. 'Speech by Rt. Hon. David Trimble MLA to the Conservative Party Conference', Blackpool, 10 Oct. 2001, available at <http://www.uup.org/current/displayfullpress.asp?pressid=274>, last accessed 10 Oct. 2001. Trimble's analysis fails when confronted with the foreign policy of Silvio Berlusconi's right-wing coalition government in Italy.
54. See Finlayson, 'Discourse and Contemporary Loyalist Identity'.
55. See Richard Kirkland, *Identity Parades: Northern Irish Culture and Dissident Subjects* (Liverpool: Liverpool University Press, 2002).
56. Colin Harvey, 'Stick to the Terms of the Agreement', *Fortnight*, 416 (July/Aug. 2003), p. 9.
57. Neil Jarman, *Material Conflicts: Parades and Visual Displays in Northern Ireland* (Oxford: Berg, 1997), pp. 118–19.
58. McGarry and O'Leary, *Explaining Northern Ireland*, pp. 135, 406.
59. Paul Bew, Peter Gibbon and Henry Patterson, *Northern Ireland, 1921–2001: Political Forces and Social Classes*, revised and updated edition (London: Serif, 2002), p. 246.
60. Ibid., p. 246.
61. P. Mitchell, '"Futures"', p. 272.
62. Peter Shirlow, 'Who fears to Speak': Fear, Mobility and etho-sectarianism in the two Ardoynes', *Global Review of Ethnopolitics*, 3:1. (Sept. 2003), pp. 76–91, and other recent articles by Shirlow..
63. Dominic Murray, 'Culture, Religion and Violence in Northern Ireland', in Seamus Dunn (ed.), *Facets of the Conflict in Northern Ireland* (Basingstoke: Macmillan Press, 1995), pp. 215–29, especially pp. 222–3.
64. Brah, *Cartographies of Diaspora*, pp. 9, 11, 23–47.
65. Steve Bruce, *The Edge of the Union: The Ulster Loyalist Political Vision* (Oxford: Oxford University Press, 1994), pp. 133–49.
66. See Patrick James O'Farrell, *Ireland's English Question: Anglo-Irish Relations, 1534–1970* (London: Batsford, 1971).
67. Alan Finlayson, 'Discourse and Contemporary Loyalist Identity', p. 94.
68. See Anthony D. Smith, *National Identity* (London: Penguin, 1991); Anthony D. Smith, *Nationalism and Modernism: A Critical Survey of Recent Theories of Nations and Nationalism* (London: Routledge, 1998).
69. See Rupert Taylor, 'Northern Ireland: Consocation or Social Transformation', in

McGarry (ed.), *Northern Ireland and the Divided World*, pp. 37–52; Bernard Crick, 'The Concept of Consent and the Agreement', in Charles Townshend (ed.), *Consensus in Ireland: Approaches and Recessions* (Oxford: Clarendon Press, 1988), pp. 110–27, especially p. 122; Michael Dartnell, 'The Belfast Agreement: Peace Process, Europeanization and Identity', *Canadian Journal of Irish Studies*, 26:1 (Spring 2000), pp. 72–85; Elizabeth Meehan, 'Europe and the Europeanisation of the Irish question', in Michael Cox, Adrian Guelke, and Fiona Stephen (eds), *A Farewell to Arms?: From War to Peace in Northern Ireland* (Manchester: Manchester University Press, 2000), pp. 199–213; Richard Kearney, 'Introduction: Thinking Otherwise', in *Across the Frontiers: Ireland in the 1990s: Cultural–Political–Economic* (Dublin: Wolfhound, 1988), pp. 7–28, especially p. 14.

70.   Anthony D. Smith, *Myths and Memories of the Nation* (Oxford: Oxford University Press, 1999), pp. 225–51.

71.   G.K. Peatling, '"Continental Crossings": European Influences on British Public Opinion and Irish Politics, 1848–2002', *History of European Ideas*, 27 (Aug. 2001), pp. 371–87, especially pp. 385–6.

72.   Dennis Kennedy, 'The European Union and the Northern Ireland Question', in Brian Barton and Patrick J. Roche (eds), *The Northern Ireland Question: Perspectives and Policies* (Aldershot: Avebury, 1994), pp. 166–88.

73.   Gerard Murray, *John Hume and the SDLP: Impact and Survival in Northern Ireland* (Dublin: Irish Academic Press, 1998), pp. 210–21; John Hume, 'A New Ireland in a New Europe', in Dermot Keogh and Michael H. Haltzel (eds), *Northern Ireland and the Politics of Reconciliation* (Washington, DC: Woodrow Wilson Center Press, 1993), pp. 226–33; John Hume, 'Europe of the Regions', in Kearney (ed.), *Across the Frontiers*, pp. 45–57.

74.   Kearney, 'Introduction: Thinking Otherwise', p. 18; see also Richard Kearney, *Postnationalist Ireland: Politics, Literature, Philosophy* (London: Routledge, 1997).

75.   Liam Kennedy, 'Repartition', in McGarry and O'Leary (eds), *The Future of Northern Ireland*, pp. 137–61.

76.   See Lijphart, 'Foreword: One Basic Problem . . .', and John McGarry and Brendan O'Leary, 'Conclusion: Northern Ireland's Options . . .'.

77.   See Tom Nairn, *The Break-Up of Britain: Crisis and Neo-Nationalism*, second, expanded edition (London: NLB, 1981); Tom Nairn, *After Britain: New Labour and the Return of Scotland* (London: Granta, 2000); John Baillie, *Solution for Northern Ireland: A King's Perspective* (Lewes: Book Guild, 1994).

78.   McGarry and O'Leary, *Explaining Northern Ireland*, pp. 180–5.

79.   Steve Bruce, 'Fundamentalism and Political Violence: The Case of Paisley and Ulster Evangelicals', *Religion*, 31:4 (October 2001), pp. 387–405.

80.   *Newsletter* [Belfast], 21 March 2003, p. 12; Adrian Guelke, 'Limits to Conflict and Accommodation', in Adrian Guelke (ed.), *New Perspectives on the Northern Ireland Conflict* (Aldershot: Avebury, 1994), pp. 190–206, especially p. 202.

81.   Steve Bruce, *God Save Ulster: The Religion and Politics of Paisleyism* (Oxford: Clarendon Press, 1986), p. 268; Steve Bruce, *The Red Hand: Protestant Paramilitaries in Northern Ireland* (Oxford: Oxford University Press, 1992), pp. 268–90, especially pp. 288, 290.

82.   G.K. Peatling, 'The Northern Ireland Peace Process and Europeanization: A Critical Response', *Canadian Journal of Irish Studies/Revue canadienne d'études irlandaises*, 27:2/28:1 (Autumn 2001/Spring 2002), pp. 102–9.

83.   Kate Hoey, 'To Keep his Pledge, Tony Blair Should Blame the IRA Terrorists', *Daily Telegraph*, 23 Aug. 2001.

84.   *Hansard*, 6th series, Vol. 322, c. 366 (9 Dec. 1998).

85.   *Hansard*, 6th series, Vol. 371, c. 21 (2 July 2001).

86.   *Hansard*, 6th series, Vol. 377, c. 232 (18 Dec. 2001).

87.   Quoted in D.C. Watt, 'Appeasement, the Rise of a Revisionist School', *Political Quarterly*, 36:2 (April–June 1965), pp. 191–213, especially p. 191.

88.   See, for example, Dick Morris, *Off with Their Heads: Traitors, Crooks and Obstructionists in American Politics, Media and Business* (New York: Regan Books, 2003), especially pp. 170–91.

89.   See F. McDonough, *Neville Chamberlain, Appeasement and the British Road to War*

(Manchester: Manchester University Press, 1998), pp. 2–7 for a review of recent historiography; and compare Fig. 3.

90. Paul Kennedy, *Strategy and Diplomacy, 1870–1945: Eight Studies* (London: Allen & Unwin, 1983), pp. 22–39; Ritchie Ovendale, *'Appeasement' and the English-Speaking World: Britain, the United States, the Dominions and the Policy of 'Appeasement', 1937–1939* (Cardiff: University of Wales Press, 1975), p. 320.

91. Graham Stewart, 'Churchill without the Rhetoric', *Historical Journal*, 43:1 (March 2000), pp. 303–07.

92. Richard Littlejohn, 'Blood, Sweat and Bogus Rhetoric', *Daily Mail*, 17 April 1997, p. 11, is a good example of the hypocrisy of the art.

93. Andrew Alexander, 'How Ulster Could Ruin Britain', *Spectator*, 29 March 1986, pp. 15–16, especially p. 16.

94. Jonathan Freedland, 'The Key to Peace is Stuck', *Guardian*, 16 Feb. 2000.

95. Philip Webster, 'Hague Slaps Down Tory "Dinosaurs"', *Times*, 8 Oct. 1997, p. 1.

96. Henry Patterson, 'From Insulation to Appeasement: The Major and Blair Governments Reconsidered', in Wilford (ed.), *Aspects of the Belfast Agreement*.

97. Roy Bradford, 'Unionists Fear Being Stranded on the Rock of Consent', *Irish Times*, 20 May 1996, p. 12.

98. See Ruth Dudley Edwards, 'SF Campaign Run on Fascist Lines', *Irish Times*, 11 June 2001, p. 16.

99. David Sharrock, 'Why Apology is Diversion Tactic for Gerry Adams', *Daily Telegraph*, 17 July 2002, p. 6.

100. 'No Justice, No Peace', *Daily Telegraph*, 6 Oct. 2000.

101. Patterson, 'From Insulation to Appeasement', p. 178.

102. *Sun*, 18 Aug. 1998, p. 11. That the *Sun* trailed this piece in its previous issue (*Sun*, 17 Aug. 1998, p. 16) suggests it was inordinately proud of it, which speaks volumes for the average quality of journalism in that execrable little publication.

103. See Eamonn Mallie and David McKittrick, *The Fight for Peace: The Secret Story behind the Irish Peace Process*, revised and updated edition (London: Mandarin, 1997; first published 1996), p. 298, for a different and not altogether persuasive reading of these events that foregrounds an alleged misrepresentation by the media.

104. See M.L.R. Smith, *Fighting for Ireland?: The Military Strategy of the Irish Republican Movement* (London: Routledge, 1997); Fearghal McGarry (ed) *Republicanism in Modern Ireland* (Dublin: UCD Press, 2003); Paul Arther, 'The transformation of Republicanism', in John Coakley (ed), *Changing Shades of Orange and Green* (Dublin: UCD Press, 2002), pp. 84–94. Kevin Bean, 'Shifting Discourses of New Nationalism and Post-Republicanism', in Marianne Elliott (ed.), *The Long Road to Peace in Northern Ireland: Peace Lectures from the Institute of Irish Studies at Liverpool University* (Liverpool: Liverpool University Press, 2002), pp. 129–42; Jennifer Todd, 'Nationalism, Republicanism and the Good Friday Agreement', in Ruane and Todd (eds), *After the Good Friday Agreement*, pp. 49–70. Evidence of these debates can be found, for instance, in the magazine *Fourthwrite*, available at http://www.fourthwrite.ie/.

105. Richard English, *Armed Struggle: A History of the IRA* (Basingstoke: Macmillan, 2003), pp. 320–1.

106. J. Bowyer Bell, 'The Irish Republican Army Enters an Endgame: An Overview', *Studies in Conflict and Terrorism*, 18 (July/Sept. 1995), pp. 153–74.

107. See Conor Cruise O'Brien, 'Appeasement is the Real Terror', *Independent*, 29 July 1994, p. 18, and also Conor Cruise O'Brien, *Independent*, 1 Sept. 1994 'This is not Peace' p. 17.

108. Kevin Myers, 'An Irishman's Diary', *Irish Times*, 19 June 1996, p. 15.

109. 'Helping Gerry Adams', *Daily Telegraph*, 24 April 2002.

110. Mike Tomlinson, 'Can Britain Leave Ireland?: The Political Economy of War and Peace', *Race & Class*, 37:1 (July–Sept. 1995), pp. 1–22, especially p. 2.

111. Sinn Féin, 'Sustained Efforts to Create Contrived Crisis in the Peace Process', 20 April 2002, available at <http://www.sinnfein.ie/releases/02/pr022004.html>, last accessed 27 May 2002 (a press release not yet archived on Sinn Féin's new website).

112. Mike Tomlinson, 'Walking Backwards into the Sunset: British Policy and the Insecurity

of Northern Ireland', in Miller (ed.), *Rethinking Northern Ireland*, pp. 94–122, especially p. 111.

113. James Anderson, 'Rethinking National Problems in a Transnational Context', in Miller (ed.), *Rethinking Northern Ireland*, pp. 125–45, especially p. 139.
114. Michael J. Cunningham, *British Government Policy in Northern Ireland, 1969–2000* (Manchester: Manchester University Press, 2001), pp. 153–9.
115. See also Dixon, *Northern Ireland*, p. 102.
116. John Newsinger, 'British Security Policy in Northern Ireland', *Race & Class*, 37:1 (July–Sept. 1995), pp. 83–94, especially p. 91; see also John Newsinger, *British Counterinsurgency: From Palestine to Northern Ireland* (Basingstoke: Palgrave, 2002).
117. David Miller, 'Colonial and Academic Representations of the Troubles', in Miller (ed) *Rethinking Northern Ireland*, pp. 3–39, especially p. 20.
118. Lloyd, *Ireland After History*, pp. 79–80; Miller, 'Colonial and Academic Representations of the Troubles', pp. 20–1.
119. Lloyd, *Ireland After History*, pp. 13, 37, 41, 47, 53–4.
120. See Mary Hickman, 'Alternative Historiographies of the Irish in Britain: A Critique of the Segregation/Assimilation Model', in Roger Swift and Sheridan Gilley (eds), *The Irish in Victorian Britain: The Local Dimension* (Dublin: Four Courts Press, 1999), pp. 236–53; Mary J. Hickman, *Religion, Class and Identity: The State, the Catholic Church and the Education of the Irish in Britain* (Aldershot: Ashgate, 1995); Mary J. Hickman and Bronwen Walter, *Discrimination and the Irish Community in Britain: A Report of Research Undertaken for the Commission for Racial Equality* (London: Commission for Racial Equality, 1997).
121. Edna Longley, 'What Do Protestants Want?', *Irish Review*, 20 (Winter/Spring 1997), pp. 104–20, especially p. 107.
122. See Lloyd, *Ireland After History*, p. 47; David Miller, *Don't Mention the War: Northern Ireland, Propaganda and the Media* (London: Pluto Press, 1994), p. 278; Liz Curtis, *Ireland, the Propaganda War: The Media and the 'Battle for Hearts and Minds'* (London: Pluto Press, 1984); Philip Elliott, 'Reporting Northern Ireland: A Study of News in Great Britain, Northern Ireland and the Republic of Ireland', in *Ethnicity and the Media: An Analysis of Media Reporting in the United Kingdom, Canada and Ireland* (Paris: UNESCO, 1977); Bill Rolston (ed.), *The Media and Northern Ireland: Covering the Troubles* (Basingstoke: Macmillan, 1991); Bill Rolston and David Miller (eds), *War and Words: the Northern Ireland Media Reader* (Belfast: Beyond the Pale, 1996).
123. Ibid.; see also David Murphy, *The Stalker Affair and the British Press* (London: Unwin Hyman, 1991).
124. Liz Curtis, 'A Catalogue of Censorship 1959–1993', in Rolston and Miller (eds), *War and Words*, pp. 265–304, especially pp. 278–9; Patrick Magee, *Gangsters or Guerrillas?: Representations of Irish Republicans in Troubles Fiction* (Belfast: Beyond the Pale, 2001), pp. 208–9.
125. See Alan F. Parkinson, *Ulster Loyalism and the British Media* (Dublin: Four Courts Press, 1998); see also James Loughlin, *Ulster Unionism and British National Identity since 1885* (London: Pinter, 1995), p. 200.
126. Parkinson, *Ulster Loyalism*, p. 165; P. Elliott, 'Reporting Northern Ireland', p. 355.
127. Rolston and Miller, 'Introduction: War, Words and Silence', in Rolston and Miller (eds), *War and Words*, pp. xv–xvii, especially p. xvi.
128. Shane Kingston, 'Terrorism, the Media and the Northern Ireland Conflict', *Studies in Conflict and Terrorism*, 18 (July/Sept. 1995), pp. 203–31.
129. Ibid., pp. 208–9. The assumption that loyalists are particularly assured by that piece of 'knowledge' surely indicates a low level of understanding of the loyalist paramilitaries' motivations.
130. Ibid., p. 228.
131. Ibid., p. 225.
132. Ibid., pp. 227–8: Miller, *Don't Mention the War*, pp. 245, 277–8.
133. Hugh Roberts, 'Sound Stupidity: The British Party System and the Northern Ireland Question', in McGarry and O'Leary (eds), *The Future of Northern Ireland*, pp. 100–36.
134. Paul Bew and Paul Dixon, 'Labour Party Policy and Northern Ireland', in Barton and

Roche (eds.), *The Northern Ireland Question: Perspectives and Policies*, pp. 151–65, especially pp. 162–3; Roberts, 'Sound Stupidity', pp. 103–9.

135. Charles Moore, *How to be British* (London: Centre for Policy Studies, 1995), p. 15; Charles Moore, *The Tale of a Round Table* (London: Friends of the Union, 1993).

136. Simon Heffer, *'Nor Shall My Sword': The Reinvention of England* (London: Weidenfeld & Nicolson, 1999), pp. 16–19; Peter Hitchens, *The Abolition of Britain: The British Cultural Revolution from Lady Chatterley to Tony Blair*, revised and expanded edition (London: Quartet, 2000; first published 1999), pp. 360–1.

137. Richard Needham, *Battling for Peace* (Belfast: Blackstaff Press, 1998), p. 19.

138. Campaign for Labour Representation, *Kate Hoey and Democracy Now: Labour's UlsterLoyalists* (Belfast: Campaign for Labour Representation Continuation Committee, 1996).

139. Henry McDonald, 'Now the Irish Can Join Three Labour Parties', *Observer*, 5 Oct. 2003.

140. Graham Walker, 'Scotland and Ulster: Political Interactions since the Late Nineteenth Century and Possibilities of Contemporary Dialogue', in John Erskine and Gordon Lucy (eds), *Cultural Traditions in Northern Ireland: Varieties of Scottishness: Exploring the Ulster–Scottish Connection* (Belfast: Institute of Irish Studies, 1997), pp. 103–6; Whyte, *Interpreting Northern Ireland*, pp. 216–21.

141. See Callum G. Brown, *The Death of Christian Britain: Understanding Secularisation, 1800–2000* (London: Routledge, 2001).

142. William Hague, 'Why I am Sick of the Anti-British Disease', *Daily Telegraph*, 13 Oct. 2000.

143. See Catriona M.M. Macdonald (ed.), *Unionist Scotland, 1800–1997* (Edinburgh: John Donald Publishers, 1998). The Conservative Party in Scotland even campaigned under a different name until the 1960s.

144. Patterson, *Ireland since 1939*, pp. 325–6.

145. John Redwood, *Stars and Strife: The Coming Conflicts Between the USA and the European Union* (Basingstoke: Palgrave, 2001), p. 8.

146. Patrick Crozier, *Ulster for Beginners* (London: Friends of the Union, 1998), pp. 21–9.

147. Graham Walker, 'The British–Irish Council', in Wilford (ed.), *Aspects of the Belfast Agreement*, pp. 129-41.

148. See G.K. Peatling, 'Home Rule for England, English Nationalism and Edwardian Debates about Constitutional Reform', *Albion*, 35:1 (Spring 2003), pp. 71–90.

149. Arthur Aughey, *Nationalism, Devolution and the Challenge to the United Kingdom State* (London: Pluto Press, 2001), p. 170.

150. Patterson, 'From Insulation to Appeasement', p. 176.

151. P. Mitchell, '"Futures"', pp. 268–70; McGarry and O'Leary, *Explaining Northern Ireland*, pp. 126–8, 133–6.

152. Most commentators suggest that the 32-County Sovereignty Movement has links to the real IRA, although the movement itself denies this. It is, however, overtly critical of the GFA and of the peace process from a republican perspective.

153. Patterson, *Ireland since 1939*, pp. 332–3; Francis Mackey, 'Southern Inaction Prolongs North Conflict', *Irish Times*, 13 June 2001, p. 14. Mackey is leader of the 32-County Sovereignty Movement.

154. Quoted in Dixon, *Northern Ireland*, p. 267.

155. Jerry Fitzpatrick, 'The Role of the British Labour Party in Ireland', in James Anderson and James Goodman (eds), *Dis/agreeing Ireland: Contexts, Obstacles, Hopes* (London: Pluto Press, 1998), p. 130; Jeremy Hardy, 'Betrayal', *Guardian*, 17 July 1999.

156. Text of the Good Friday Agreement.

157. See Mary Holland, 'Where even a touch of vision would not go amiss', *Irish Times*, 16 May 1996, p. 14; Kevin Toolis, 'Farewell to Arms', *Guardian*, 17 May 1996, p. 21; TNA (PRO): PREM 3/131/1; 'Note of a talk between Mr de Valera and Mr MacDonald in Dublin, June 26th, 1940'.

158. See Clare O'Halloran, *Partition and the Limits of Irish Nationalism: An Ideology under Stress* (Dublin: Gill & Macmillan, 1987).

159. McClintock, *Imperial Leather: Race, Gender and Sexuality in the Colonial Contest* (New York: Routledge, 1995), p. 12; Robbie McVeigh, 'The British/Irish "Peace Process" and the

Colonial Legacy', in Anderson and Goodman (eds), *Dis/agreeing Ireland*, pp. 27–53.

160. Mackey, 'Southern Inaction . . .'.

161. Terry Eagleton, 'Nationalism and the Case of Ireland', *New Left Review*, 234 (March–April 1999), pp. 44–61, especially pp. 55, 59.

162. Quoted in P. Mitchell, '"Futures"', p. 269.

163. Declan Kiberd, *Inventing Ireland: The Literature of the Modern Nation* (London: Cape, 1995), p. 652.

164. Joseph Johnston, *Civil War in Ulster: Its Objects and Probable Results*, Roy Johnston (ed.)(Dublin, University College Dublin Press, 1999), p. xix; Seamus Deane, 'Wherever Green is Read', in Máirín Ní Dhonnchadha and Theo Dorgan (eds), *Revising the Rising* (Derry: Field Day, 1991), pp. 91–105, especially p. 100.

165. See Michael Farrell, *Northern Ireland: The Orange State* (London: Pluto Press, 1976).

166. Bill Rolston, 'Changing the Political Landscape: Murals and Transition in Northern Ireland', *Irish Studies Review*, 11:1 (April 2003), pp. 3–16: Bill Rolston, *Drawing Support: Murals in the North of Ireland* (Belfast: Beyond the Pale, 2003).

167. Eagleton, 'Nationalism and the Case of Ireland', p. 55: Bill Rolston, 'What's Wrong with Multiculturalism?: Liberalism and the Irish Conflict', in Miller (ed.), *Rethinking Northern Ireland*, pp. 253–74; Ronan Bennett, 'Don't Mention the War: Culture in Northern Ireland', in ibid., pp. 199–210, especially p. 203.

168. Bennett, 'Don't Mention the War', and Ronan Bennett, 'Why the IRA Gets All the Good Lines', *Observer*, 12 Jan. 1997, p. 1.

169. Miller, 'Colonial and Academic Representations of the Troubles', p. 4.

170. See Carol Coulter, *The Hidden Tradition: Feminism, Women, and Nationalism in Ireland* (Cork: Cork University Press, 1993); Carol Coulter, 'Ireland's Metropolitan Feminists and Colonial Women', *Éire–Ireland*, 35:3–4 (Autumn/Winter 2000–01), pp. 48–78.

171. On revisionism particularly see D. George Boyce and Alan O'Day (eds), *The Making of Modern Irish History: Revisionism and the Revisionist Controversy* (London: Routledge, 1996); Ciaran Brady (ed.), *Interpreting Irish History: The Debate on Historical Revisionism, 1938–1994* (Blackrock: Irish Academic Press, 1994). Foster, incidentally, would entirely repudiate the usefulness of the label 'revisionist', although this need not concern us at present: see R.F. Foster, 'We Are All Revisionists Now', *Irish Review*, 1 (1986) pp. 1–5.

172. Desmond Fennell, 'Against Revisionism', in Brady (ed.), *Interpreting Irish History*, pp. 183–90.

173. Deane, 'Wherever Green is Read', p. 100; see also Terry Eagleton, 'A Postmodern Punch', *Irish Studies Review*, 6 (1994), pp. 2–3.

174. Seamus Deane, *Strange Country: Modernity and Nationhood in Irish Writing since 1790* (Oxford: Clarendon Press, 1997) pp. 191, 193; ibid; p. 102.

175. Barra Ó Séaghdha, 'The Celtic Tiger's Media Pundits', in Peadar Kirby, Luke Gibbons and Michael Cronin (eds), *Reinventing Ireland: Culture, Society and the Global Economy* (London: Pluto Press, 2002), pp. 143–59, especially p. 145.

176. Kiberd, *Inventing Ireland*, p. 647; see also Declan Kiberd, *Irish Classics* (Cambridge, MA: Harvard University Press, 2001), pp. 629–30.

177. Declan Kiberd, 'Anglo-Irish Attitudes', in Field Day Theatre Company, *Ireland's Field Day* (London: Hutchinson, 1985), pp. 83–105, especially p. 104.

178. Luke Gibbons, *Transformations in Irish Culture* (Cork: Cork University Press, 1996), pp. 176, 6–7.

179. Luke Gibbons 'The Global Cure?: History, Therapy and the Celtic Tiger', in Kirby, Gibbons and Cronin (eds), *Reinventing Ireland*, pp. 89–106, especially pp. 100, 102, 104, 105.

180. Peter Berresford Ellis, *The Celtic Revolution: A Study in Anti-Imperialism* (Talybont: Y Lolfa Cyf, 1985), pp. 203–4.

181. Howe, *Ireland and Empire*.

182. See Graham Walker, *Intimate Strangers: Political and Cultural Interaction between Scotland and Ulster in Modern Times* (Edinburgh: J. Donald Publishers, 1995); Ian S. Wood (ed.), *Scotland and Ulster* (Edinburgh: Mercat Press, 1994); Erskine and Lucy (eds.), *Cultural Traditions in Northern Ireland: Varieties of Scottishness*.

183. John Hewitt, 'No Rootless Colonist', in Patricia Craig (ed.), *The Rattle of the North: An Anthology of Ulster Prose* (Belfast: Blackstaff Press, 1992), pp. 121–31.
184. McGarry and O'Leary, *Explaining Northern Ireland*, pp. 35–44.
185. See Patricia Jalland, *The Liberals and Ireland: the Ulster Question in British Politics to 1914* (Brighton: Harvester Press, 1980); R. Fanning, 'The Irish Policy of Asquith's Government and the Cabinet Crisis of 1910', in Art Cosgrove and Donal McCartney (eds), *Studies in Irish History, presented to R. Dudley Edwards* (Dublin: University College, Dublin, 1979), pp. 279–303.
186. Michael Hopkinson, *The Irish War of Independence* (Montreal: McGill–Queen's University Press, 2002), p. 156.
187. See Peter Hart, *The IRA and its Enemies: Violence and Community in Cork, 1916–1923* (Oxford: Clarendon Press, 1998).
188. Terry Eagleton, *The Truth about the Irish* (Dublin: New Island, 1999), p. 131; R.A. Cosgrove, 'The Relevance of Irish History: The Gladstone–Dicey Debate about Home Rule, 1886–7', *Éire–Ireland*, 13:4 (1978), pp. 6–21.
189. Bruce, 'Fundamentalism and Political Violence', pp. 388–9; Ruth Dudley Edwards, *The Faithful Tribe: An Intimate Portrait of the Loyal Institutions* (London: HarperCollins, 1999), p. 35.
190. Bruce, *The Edge of the Union*, pp. 42–8, 108–12, 123–5, 146, 149.
191. Mike Morrissey and Marie Smyth, *Northern Ireland after the Good Friday Agreement: Victims, Grievance and Blame* (London: Pluto Press, 2002), pp. 61–2.
192. English, *Armed Struggle*, p. 378.
193. Magee, *Gangsters or Guerrillas?*, p. 204.
194. Ramón Flecha, 'Modern and Postmodern Racism in Europe: Dialogic Approach and Anti-Racist Pedagogies', *Harvard Educational Review*, 69:2 (Summer 1999), pp. 150–71, especially pp. 159–61; Henry A. Giroux, 'Living Dangerously: Identity Politics and the New Cultural Racism', in Henry A. Giroux and Peter McLaren (eds), *Between Borders: Pedagogy and the Politics of Cultural Studies* (New York: Routledge, 1994), pp. 29–55, especially pp. 34–9; Richard J. Evans, *In Defence of History*, new edition (London: Granta, 2000; first published 1997), pp. 232, 238.
195. R. Evans, *In Defence of History*, pp. 224–53.
196. Moya, 'Introduction', in Moya and Hames-García (eds), *Reclaiming Identity*.
197. Howe, *Ireland and Empire*, pp. 107–45.
198. Edna Longley, 'Ulster Protestants and the Question of "Culture"', in Fran Brearton and Eamonn Hughes (eds), *Last before America: Irish and American Writing: Essays in Honour of Michael Allen* (Belfast: Blackstaff Press, 2001), pp. 99–120.
199. Bernard Crick, 'An Englishman Considers his Passport', in Neil Evans (ed.), *National Identity in the British Isles* (Harlech: Coleg Harlech, 1989), pp. 23–34.
200. Stephen Glover, 'The Census that Obliterates the English Race', *Daily Mail*, 24 April 2001, p. 13.
201. G.K. Peatling, 'Emotion and Excess: Discourses and Practices of Women and Republicanism in Twentieth-Century Ireland', *Irish Studies Review*, 11:2 (2003).
202. Michael Laffan, 'Insular Attitudes: The Revisionists and their Critics', in Ní Dhonnchadha, and Dorgan (eds), *Revising the Rising*, pp. 106–21, especially p. 119.
203. Maurna Crozier (ed.), *Cultural Traditions in Northern Ireland: Inaugural Lecture by Roy F. Foster, 'Varieties of Irishness', and Proceedings of the Cultural Traditions Group Conference, 3–4 March 1989* (Belfast: Institute of Irish Studies, Queen's University of Belfast, 1989), p. 48.
204. See R.F. Foster, 'Storylines: Narratives and Nationality in Nineteenth-Century Ireland', in Geoffrey Cubitt (ed.), *Imagining Nations* (Manchester: Manchester University Press, 1998), pp. 38–56; Paul Bew, *Ideology and the Irish Question: Ulster Unionism and Irish Nationalism, 1912–1916* (Oxford: Clarendon Press, 1994).
205. There is at least superficial evidence that the nature of unionist political culture might conduce to such a sullen, non-co-operative attitude in such circumstances: see Colin Coulter, 'Direct Rule and the Unionist Middle Classes', in R. English and G. Walker (eds), *Unionism in Modern Ireland: New Perspectives on Politics and Culture* (Basingstoke: Macmillan, 1996), pp. 169–91, especially p. 187.

206. Declan Kiberd, 'The Elephant of Revolutionary Forgetfulness', in Ní Dhonnchadha and Dorgan (eds), *Revising the Rising*, pp. 1–20, especially pp. 3, 8, 17, 18.
207. Gibbons, 'The Global Cure?', p. 105.
208. Such events have been acknowledged by the vast majority of able writers on the Famine, including Christine Kinealy, whose representations of the Famine are sometimes criticised as cohering too closely to nationalist mythology: see Christine Kinealy, 'The Great Irish Famine – A Dangerous Memory?', in Arthur Gribben (ed.), *The Great Famine and the Irish Diaspora in America* (Amherst, MA: University of Massachusetts Press, 1999), pp. 239–53, especially p. 248; see also Cormac Ó'Gráda, *Black '47 and Beyond: The Great Irish Famine in History, Economy, and Memory* (Princeton, NJ: Princeton University Press, 1999), p. 4.
209. Quoted in Marianne Elliott, *The Catholics of Ulster: A History* (New York: Basic Books, 2001), p. 445.
210. G.K. Peatling, 'The Whiteness of Ireland Under and After the Union', *Journal of British Studies* (forthcoming, 2005).
211. Arthur Aughey, *Under Siege: Ulster Unionism and the Anglo-Irish Agreement* (Belfast: Blackstaff Press, 1989), pp. 28, 207–8: Richard English, 'The Same People with Different Relatives?: Modern Scholarship, Unionists and the Irish Nation,' in English and Walker (eds), *Unionism in Modern Ireland*, pp. 220–35, especially p. 230.
212. Denis O'Hearn, 'The Two Irish Economies: Dependencies Compared', in Anderson and Goodman (eds), *Dis/agreeing Ireland*, pp. 54–72.
213. See C. Fitzpatrick, 'Labour, Ideology and the States in Ireland, 1917–1932' (PhD thesis, University of Cambridge, 1993).
214. See, for instance, Claire Palley, 'Towards a Federal or a Confederal Irish State?', in McGarry and O'Leary (eds), *The Future of Northern Ireland*, pp. 69–99; Bruce, *The Edge of the Union*, pp. 69, 139.
215. Elisabeth Porter, 'Identity, Location, Plurality: Women, Nationalism and Northern Ireland', in Richard Wilford and Robert L. Miller (eds), *Women, Ethnicity and Nationalism: The Politics of Transition* (London: Routledge, 1998), pp. 36–61, especially p. 41.
216. Derick Wilson and Jerry Tyrrell, 'Institutions for Conciliation and Mediation', in Dunn (ed.), *Facets of the Conflict in Northern Ireland*, pp. 230–48, especially p. 244.
217. Dixon, *Northern Ireland*, p. 44.
218. Ibid., pp. 45, 62–3, 225–32, 306.
219. Norbert Elias and John L. Scotson, *The Established and the Outsiders: A Sociological Enquiry into Community Problems*, second edition (London and Thousand Oaks, CA: Sage Publications, 1994; first published 1965), pp. 89–105.
220. See, for instance, the *Sun*, 9 Sept. 1988, p. 1.
221. Michael White, 'Blair admits case for Regional Governments', *Guardian*, 29 March 2000.
222. See, for instance, the extraordinary article by Julie Burchill, 'Let's All Have a Flutter', *Guardian*, 29 June 2002.
223. Elias and Scotson, *The Established and the Outsiders*, p. 98.
224. Loughlin, *Ulster Unionism and British National Identity*, pp. 196–202.
225. Graham Spencer, *Disturbing the Peace?* (Aldershot: Ashgate, 1994), pp. 182–8; James Dingley, 'Peace in Our Time?, *Studies in Conflict and Terrorism*, 25:6 (Nov.–Dec. 2002) pp. 357–82; Thomas Taafe, 'Images of Peace', in Stefan Wolff and Jörg Neuheiser (eds.), *Peace at Last? The Impact of the Good Friday Agreement on Northern Ireland* (New York: Berghahn, 2002), pp. 111–31.

CHAPTER 4

1. See Adrian Guelke, *Northern Ireland: The International Perspective* (Dublin: Gill & Macmillan, 1988); John McGarry (ed.), *Northern Ireland and the Divided World: the Northern Ireland Conflict and the Good Friday Agreement in Comparative Perspective* (Oxford: Oxford University Press, 2001).
2. Joseph Ruane and Jennifer Todd, '"Why Can't You Just Get Along with Each Other?": Culture, Structure and the Northern Ireland Conflict', in Eamonn Hughes (ed.), *Culture and Politics in Northern Ireland, 1960–1990* (Buckingham: Open University Press, 1991), pp. 27–8.
3. Alan Bairner, 'Paramilitarism', in Arthur Aughey and Duncan Morrow (eds), *Northern Ireland Politics* (Harlow: Longman, 1996), pp. 159–72, especially p. 162.
4. Marianne Elliott, *The Catholics of Ulster: A History* (New York: Basic Books, 2001), p. 481.
5. James Loughlin, *The Ulster Question since 1945* (Basingstoke: Macmillan, 1998), pp. 129–30.
6. Paul Dixon, *Northern Ireland: The Politics of War and Peace* (Basingstoke: Palgrave, 2001), pp. 266–8.
7. George Mitchell, *Making Peace* (New York: Knopf and London: Heinemann, 1999), p. 110.
8. Ibid., p. 177.
9. John Hume, *Personal Views: Politics, Peace and Reconciliation in Ireland* (Enfield: Roberts Rinehart, 1996), pp. 91–7; Arthur Aughey and Duncan Morrow, 'Frameworks and the Future', in Aughey and Morrow (eds), *Northern Ireland Politics*, p. 214.
10. Conor Cruise O'Brien, *Ancestral Voices: Religion and Nationalism in Ireland* (Dublin: Poolbeg, 1994, pp. 176–7; Gerard Murray, *John Hume and the SDLP: Impact and Survival in Northern Ireland* (Dublin: Irish Academic Press, 1998), p. 175.
11. Marc Mulholland, *The Longest War: Northern Ireland's Troubled History* (Oxford: Oxford University Press, 2002), pp. 38–66.
12. James Loughlin, *Ulster Unionism and British National Identity since 1885* (London: Pinter, 1995), p. 194; Steve Bruce, *The Edge of the Union: The Ulster Loyalist Political Vision* (Oxford: Oxford University Press, 1994), pp. 65–6; Paul Dixon, 'Internationalization and Unionist Isolation: A Response to Feargal Cochrane', *Political Studies*, 43:3 (Sept. 1995), pp. 497–505.
13. Feargal Cochrane, 'Any Takers?: The Isolation of Northern Ireland', *Political Studies*, 42:3 (Sept. 1994), pp. 378–95.
14. Roy Bradford, 'Unionists Fear Being Stranded on the Rock of Consent', *Irish Times*, 20 May 1996, p. 12.
15. K. Theodore Hoppen, *Ireland since 1800: Conflict and Conformity*, second edition (London: Addison Wesley Longman, 1999; first published 1989), p. 230.
16. Yonah Alexander and Alan O'Day, 'Introduction – The Persistence of Irish Terrorism', in Yonah Alexander and Alan O'Day (eds), *Ireland's Terrorist Trauma: Interdisciplinary Perspectives* (New York: St. Martin's Press, 1989), pp. 1–11.
17. Paul Wilkinson, 'Support Mechanisms in International Terrorism', in Robert O. Slater and Michael Stohl (eds), *Current Perspectives on International Terrorism* (New York: St. Martin's Press, 1988), pp. 88–114, especially p. 100.
18. See, for example, Paul Arthur, '"Quiet Diplomacy and Personal Conversation": Track Two Diplomacy and the Search for a Settlement in Northern Ireland', in Joseph Ruane and Jennifer Todd (eds), *After the Good Friday Agreement: Analysing Political Change in Northern Ireland* (Dublin: University College Dublin Press, 1999), pp. 71–95; Conor O'Clery, *Daring Diplomacy: Clinton's Secret Search for Peace in Ireland* (Boulder, CO: Roberts Rinehart, 1997).
19. Donald Harman Akenson, *Irish Diaspora: A Primer* (Toronto, ON: P.D. Meany Co., 1996), pp. 219–20.
20. Míchéal D. Roe and Sybil Dunlap, 'Contemporary Scotch-Irish Social Identities and Attitudes toward the Troubles in Northern Ireland', *Journal of Scotch-Irish Studies*, 1:3 (Autumn 2002), pp. 12–36.
21. See Stephen Howe, *Ireland and Empire: Colonial Legacies in Irish History and Culture* (Oxford: Oxford University Press, 2000).

22. See Henry Patterson, *Ireland since 1939* (Oxford: Oxford University Press, 2002), p. 256.
23. See Andrew J. Wilson, *Irish-America and the Ulster Conflict, 1968–1995* (Washington, DC: Catholic University of America Press, 1995); Adrian Guelke, 'The United States and the Northern Ireland Question', in Brian Barton and Patrick J. Roche (eds), *The Northern Ireland Question: Perspectives and Policies* (Aldershot: Avebury, 1994), pp.189–212.
24. Charles Moore, 'Why Does Everyone Hate the Unionists So?', *Spectator*, 27 Nov. 1993, p. 7. Moore, a committed Conservative and unionist, was the editor of the *Daily Telegraph* until very recently.
25. See Alan F. Parkinson, *Ulster Loyalism and the British Media* (Dublin: Four Courts Press, 1998); Alan F. Parkinson, 'Bigots in Bowler Hats?: The Presentation and Reception of the Loyalist Case in Great Britain', in D. George Boyce and Alan O'Day (eds), *Defenders of the Union: A Survey of British and Irish Unionism since 1801* (London: Routledge, 2000), pp. 271–93.
26. Michael J. Cunningham, *British Government Policy in Northern Ireland, 1969–2000* (Manchester: Manchester University Press, 2001), pp. 117–52, 158–9.
27. Arthur Aughey, *Under Siege: Ulster Unionism and the Anglo-Irish Agreement* (Belfast: Blackstaff Press, 1989), pp. 207–8.
28. See O'Brien, *Ancestral Voices*.
29. Brendan O'Leary and John McGarry, *The Politics of Antagonism: Understanding Northern Ireland* (London: Athlone Press, 1993), pp. 248–9, 254.
30. Arthur Aughey, 'Unionism, Conservatism and the Anglo-Irish Agreement', in Boyce and O'Day (eds), *Defenders of the Union*, pp. 294–315.
31. This is largely the working assumption of, for instance, Ruth Dudley Edwards', Ruth Dudley Edwards, *The Faithful Tribe: An Intimate Portrait of the Loyal Institutions* (London: HarperCollins, 1999), especially p. 430.
32. Sarah Nelson, *Ulster's Uncertain Defenders: Protestant Political, Paramilitary and Community Groups and the Northern Ireland Conflict* (Belfast: Appletree Press, 1984), pp. 72, 75.
33. Ronan Fanning, *Independent Ireland* (Walkinstown, County Dublin: Helicon, 1983), pp. 120–7. For further disscusion, see Peatling, 'Unionist Identities, External Perceptions of Northern Ireland, and the Problem of Unionist Legitimacy', *Éire-Ireland*, (2004), forthcoming.
34. See Mark Ryan, 'From the Centre to the Margins: The Slow Death of Irish Republicanism', in Chris Gilligan and Jon Tonge (eds), *Peace or War?: Understanding the Peace Process in Northern Ireland* (Aldershot: Ashgate, 1997), pp. 72–84.
35. Brian Girvin, 'Northern Ireland and the Republic', in Paul Mitchell and Rick Wilford (eds), *Politics in Northern Ireland* (Boulder, CO: Westview Press, 1999), pp. 237, 239.
36. Guelke, *Northern Ireland*, pp. 11–12; Adrian Guelke, 'Northern Ireland and Island Status', in McGarry (ed.), *Northern Ireland and the Divided World*, pp. 228–52.
37. Steve Bruce, *The Red Hand: Protestant Paramilitaries in Northern Ireland* (Oxford: Oxford University Press, 1992), pp. 268–90; Steve Bruce, 'Northern Ireland: Reappraising Loyalist Violence', in Alan O'Day (ed.), *Terrorism's Laboratory: The Case of Northern Ireland* (Aldershot: Dartmouth, 1995), pp. 115–35.
38. David Ashley, *History without a Subject: The Postmodern Condition* (Boulder, CO: Westview Press, 1997), pp. 3, 11, 14.
39. John Daniel Cash, *Identity, Ideology and Conflict: The Structuration of Politics in Northern Ireland* (Cambridge: Cambridge University Press, 1996), p. 3.
40. Text of the Good Friday Agreement, available at <http://www.nio.gov.uk/issues/agreement.htm>, last accessed 15 May 2004; Kirsten E. Schulze, 'Taking the Gun Out of Politics: Conflict Transformation in Northern Ireland and Lebanon', in McGarry (ed.), *Northern Ireland and the Divided World*, pp. 253–75, especially pp. 270–1.
41. 'Speech by Rt. Hon. David Trimble MLA to the Conservative Party Conference'. Blackpool, 10 Oct. 2001, available at <http://www.uup.org/current/displayfullpress.asp?pressid=274>, last accessed 10 Oct. 2001; see also David Trimble, 'Even America Thinks [that] the IRA are Terrorists, So Why Doesn't Blair?', *Daily Telegraph*, 24 Sept. 2001; Iain Duncan Smith and David Trimble, 'There's No Such Thing as a "Good" Terrorist, Mr Blair', *Daily Telegraph*, 21 Nov. 2001; *Daily Mail*, 13 Sept. 2001, p. 16.
42. Michael Ancram, 'We Will Stay with This Fight until It is Won', speech to the

Conservative Party conference, 8 Oct. 2001, available at <http://www.conservatives. com/news/article.cfm?obj_id=17994>, last accessed 1 May 2004.

43.   'Troops Out, Troops In', *Daily Telegraph*, 28 Oct. 2001.

44.   Carl Bromley, 'There They Go Again: Bush's Proposed War on Terror Echoes Mrs Thatcher's in Northern Ireland', *Dispatch*, 26 Sept. 2001.

45.   Matthew Parris, 'The Bigger They Come[,] The Harder They Fall', *Times*, 15 Sept. 2001, p. 18. On the analogous effects of Bloody Sunday in boosting the membership of the PIRA, see Mulholland, *The Longest War*, pp. 97–8.

46.   Tim Pat Coogan, 'Michael Collins', in Peter Collins (ed.), *Nationalism and Unionism: Conflict in Ireland* (Belfast: Institute of Irish Studies, 1994), pp. 155–61, especially p. 161; see also Peter Taylor, 'The Semantics of Political Violence', in Bill Rolston and David Miller (eds), *War and Words: the Northern Ireland Media Reader* (Belfast: Beyond the Pale, 1996), pp. 329–39.

47.   Dixon, *Northern Ireland*, pp. 37–8.

48.   See Richard English, *Armed Struggle: A History of the IRA* (Basingstoke: Macmillan, 2003).

49.   Henry McDonald, *Trimble* (London: Bloomsbury, 2001; first published 2000), p. 279.

50.   George W. Bush, 'President's Remarks to the Nation, Ellis Island, New York, New York', available from the White House website at <http://www.whitehouse.gov/news/ releases/2002/09/20020911-3.html>, last accessed 15 May 2004.

51.   *Daily Mail*, 15 Sept. 2001, p. 18; see also *Daily Mail*, 13 Sept. 2001, p. 16; Simon Heffer, 'Our Way of Life is Worth Fighting For', *Daily Mail*, 15 Sept. 2001, p. 21; Minette Marrin, 'It is Decadent to Tolerate the Intolerable', *Daily Telegraph*, 22 Sept. 2001.

52.   See, for instance, John Derbyshire, 'Into the Realm of Chaos: Toward a Whole New World', *National Review*, 19 Sept. 2001; Janet Daley, 'A Strange Time to Decide [that] Political Debate is Pointless', *Daily Telegraph*, 10 Oct. 2001; Janet Daley, 'Self-Doubt Has No Place in the West's War on Terror', *Daily Telegraph*, 24 Oct. 2001. For examples of the US right's inaccurate post-9/11 claims that allegations that 'America had it coming' came solely or saliently from the 'left', see Kay S. Hymowitz and Harry Stein, 'Earth to Ivory Tower: Get Real!', *City Journal*, 11:4 (Fall 2001); Andrew Sullivan, 'The Agony of the Left', *Wall Street Journal*, 4 Oct. 2001; 'Blaming the US, Whitewashing Terror', *National Post*, 19 Sept. 2001.

53.   See, for instance, John Pilger, *The New Rulers of the World* (London: Verso, 2002), pp. 98–157.

54.   Zygmunt Bauman, *Intimations of Postmodernity* (London: Routledge 1992), pp. xix–xxi.

55.   George W. Bush, 'Address to a Joint Session of Congress and the American People', US Capitol, Washington, DC, 20 Sept. 2001. Available from the White House website, at <http://www.whitehouse.gov/news/releases/2001/09/20010920-8.html>, last accessed 15 May 2004. For other attempts to use the post 9/11 context to deflect criticism of US policy, see Dick Morris, *Off with Their Heads: Traitors, Crooks and Obstructionists in American Politics, Media and Business* (New York: Regan Books, 2003); Ann H. Coulter, *Slander: Liberal Lies about the American Right* (New York: Crown, 2002), especially pp. 4–6; Dinesh D'Souza, *What Makes America So Great* (New York: Penguin, 2003).

56.   By, for instance, Phyllis Bennis, *Before and After: US Foreign Policy and the War on Terrorism* (Moreton in Marsh: Arris Books, 2003).

57.   Dixon, *Northern Ireland*, p. 299; M.L.R. Smith, *Fighting for Ireland?: The Military Strategy of the Irish Republican Movement* (London: Routledge, 1997), pp. 105–9. Bromley, however, fails to intimate that the strategy of criminalisation attempted by successive British governments in Northern Ireland, including the Labour government that preceded Thatcher's Conservative one, coheres far more logically to the notion of the impossibility of neutrality than a 'war against terrorism' does. 'War', according to any meaningful definition in the context of international relations, entails combat between two belligerents, usually representing the recognised centres of sovereignty in different states. In such a conflict the neutrality of third parties is not only recognised by international law, but is also usually desirable in order to prevent an escalation of the conflict. To point out that 'war against terrorism' is a meaningless term is not merely a pedantic point, since it entails unnecessary moral disadvantage to the campaign 'against terrorism' in question. Noam Chomsky, while he is somewhat confused about the policy of 'England [*sic*]'

towards the PIRA, shows slightly more understanding on this point than Bromley does: Noam Chomsky, *9-11* (New York: Seven Stories Press, 2001), pp. 24, 26.

58.   Ed Moloney, 'Closing Down the Airwaves: The Story of the Broadcasting Ban', in Bill Rolston (ed.), *The Media and Northern Ireland: Covering the Troubles* (Basingstoke: Macmillan, 1991), pp. 8–50, especially p. 25.

59.   Arthur Aughey, Greta Jones and W.T.M. Riches, *The Conservative Tradition in Britain and the United States* (London: Pinter, 1992), p. 86.

60.   The leading example is Samuel P. Huntington, *The Clash of Civilizations and the Remaking of World Order* (New York: Simon & Schuster, 1996), pp. 198–206, 209–18.

61.   Mary J. Hickman and Bronwen Walter, *Discrimination and the Irish Community in Britain: A Report of Research Undertaken for the Commission for Racial Equality* (London: Commission for Racial Equality, 1997), pp. 184, 234; Paddy Hillyard, *Suspect Community: People's Experience of the Prevention of Terrorism Acts in Britain* (London: Pluto Press, 1993); Marella Buckley, 'Sitting on Your Politics: The Irish among the British and the Women among the Irish', in Jim Mac Laughlin (ed.), *Location and Dislocation in Contemporary Irish Society: Perspectives on Irish Emigration and Irish Identities* (Notre Dame, IN: University of Notre Dame Press, 1997), pp. 94–132, especially p. 115.

62.   Taylor, 'The Semantics of Political Violence', p. 332.

63.   Shane Kingston, 'Terrorism, the Media and the Northern Ireland Conflict', *Studies in Conflict and Terrorism*, 18 (July/Sept. 1995), p. 227.

64.   See, for instance, English, *Armed Struggle*; Rohan Gunaratna, *Inside Al Qaeda: Global Network of Terror* (New York: Columbia University Press, 2002). This is one of the reasons why the linked research methodology of interviewing figures linked to terrorist organisations has not been adopted here.

65.   Smith, *Fighting for Ireland?*, p. 138; Richard English, '"Pay No Heed to Public Clamour": Irish Republican Solipsism in the 1930s', *Irish Historical Studies*, 28:112 (Nov. 1993), pp. 426–39.

66.   Paul Johnson, 'Relentlessly and Thoroughly', *National Review*, 15 Oct. 2001, pp. 20–1. Such an assertion has been exposed as nonsense scores of times by more credible commentators than Johnson: see Bruce B. Lawrence, *Shattering the Myth: Islam Beyond Violence* (Princeton, NJ: Princeton University Press, 1998); Karen Armstrong, *Islam: A Short History* (London: Phoenix, 2001); Aziz Al-Azmeh, *Islams and Modernities* (London: Verso, 1993); Edward W. Saïd, *Covering Islam: How the Media and the Experts Determine How We See the Rest of the World* (New York: Pantheon Books, 1981); Tariq Ali, *The Clash of Fundamentalisms: Crusades, Jihads and Modernity* (London: Verso, 2002), pp. 73–8, 320–1; Bernard Lewis, *The Crisis of Islam: Holy War and Unholy Terror* (New York: Modern Library, 2003), p. xxxii.

67.   Paul Johnson, 'Dawn of a New Age', *Daily Mail*, 15 Sept. 2001, pp. 18–19.

68.   Paul Johnson, 'The Resources of Civilisation', *New Statesman*, 31 Oct. 1975, pp. 531–3. Johnson's resort to such misleading modes of moral absolutism, his justification of such punitive measures and his depiction (in 1975) of the PIRA as 'psychopathic murderers who delight in maiming and slaughtering the innocent, and whose sole object and satisfaction in life is the destruction of human flesh' is continued in his attitude to Al-Qaeda and, at a certain level, Islam, and his defence of the internment of terrorist suspects at Guantanamo Bay: Paul Johnson, 'Thought for the Day', *Daily Telegraph*, 23 July 2003; Paul Johnson, 'Why West is Best', *National Review*, 3 Dec. 2001, pp. 18–20.

69.   Margaret Thatcher, *The Downing Street Years* (London: HarperCollins, 1993), p. 402.

70.   John McGarry and Brendan O'Leary, *Explaining Northern Ireland: Broken Images* (Oxford: Blackwell, 1995), p. 392.

71.   See, for instance, Ziauddin Sardar and Merryl Wyn Davies, *Why Do People Hate America?* (Cambridge: Icon, 2002), especially pp. 193–211; Edward W. Saïd, *The End of the Peace Process: Oslo and After*, second edition (London: Granta, 2002), p. 382; Chomsky, *9-11*, pp. 3–5; Tariq Ali, *Clash of Fundamentalisms*, especially pp. 3–4; Andrew J. Bacevich, *American Empire: The Realities and Consequences of US Diplomacy* (Cambridge, MA: Harvard University Press, 2002); Noam Chomsky, *Power and Terror: Post 9/11 Talks and Interviews* (New York: Seven Stories Press, 2003) pp. 83–7; Chomsky, *Rogue States: The Rule of Force in World Affairs*

(Cambridge, MA: South End Press, 2000). Other attempts to 'understand' such 'hate' are still more lamentable. US administrations have indeed been responsible for or implicated in some wholly atrocious acts, far more atrocious than the US nationalists who have dominated the US media agenda since 9/11 would care to admit, but dissident Saudi millionaires can have no claim to speak, for instance, for the poor of Central America.

72. Claire Wills, 'Language, Politics, Narrative, Political Violence', *Oxford Literary Review*, 13: 1–2 (1991), pp. 21–60, especially pp. 53–4.

73. David Lloyd, *Ireland After History* (Notre Dame, IN: University of Notre Dame Press, 1999), pp. 66–7.

74. Ibid., pp. 3–4, 106–7.

75. Smith, *Fighting for Ireland?*, p. 93.

76. John Whyte, *Interpreting Northern Ireland* (Oxford: Clarendon Press, 1990), p. 232.

77. Cash, *Identity, Ideology and Conflict*, pp. 119–202, especially pp. 123, 154–5.

78. Wills, 'Language, Politics, Narrative, Political Violence', p. 54.

79. Bromley, 'There They Go Again'.

80. 'Bad History, Bad Politics', *Daily Telegraph*, 2 June 1997, p. 19.

81. Liam Kennedy, *Colonialism, Religion and Nationalism in Ireland* (Belfast: Institute of Irish Studies, 1996), p. 217; see also Donald Harman Akenson, *If the Irish Ran the World: Montserrat, 1630–1730* (Montreal: McGill–Queen's University Press, 1997), p. 175.

82. Arthur Aughey, *Nationalism, Devolution and the Challenge to the United Kingdom State* (London: Pluto Press, 2001), p. 15.

83. Marrin, 'It is Decadent to Tolerate the Intolerable'.

84. John Redwood, *The Death of Britain? The UK's Constitutional Crisis* (Basingstoke: Macmillan, 1999), p. 3; John Redwood, *Stars and Strife: the Coming Conflicts between the USA and the European Union* (Basingstoke: Palgrave, 2001), p. 39.

85. Peter Hitchens, *The Abolition of Britain: The British Cultural Revolution from Lady Chatterley to Tony Blair*, revised and expanded edition (London: Quartet, 2000; first published 1999), p. 315.

86. 'Racially Divided', *Daily Telegraph*, 24 Apr. 2001, p. 25.

87. 'The Last Chance Election for Britain – Hague', text of speech by William Hague to the Conservative Party Spring Forum in Harrogate, 4 March 2001, available at <http://www.conservatives.com/show_news_item.cfm?obj_id=2825&speeches=1>, last accessed 15 May 2004.

88. Hitchens, *The Abolition of Britain*, pp. 363–9.

89. *Sunday People*, 19 Aug. 2001, p. 8.

90. For claims that asylum-seekers exploit the welfare system or support terrorism, see *Daily Mail*, 24 July 2002, p. 1; *Daily Express*, 13 Aug. 2002, p. 1; *Daily Star*, 17 Dec. 2002, p. 1; 'Poison Gang are Asylum[-]Seekers', *Daily Express*, 9 Jan. 2003, pp. 1, 12; *Sun*, 9 Jan. 2003, p. 1; *Daily Express*, 7 July 2003, pp. 1, 5, 12. For examples of the periodic scares that asylum-seekers bring disease, involving the classic racist metaphor of immigration as contagion, see *Daily Mail*, 28 Dec. 2002, p. 21; *Sunday Telegraph*, 15 June 2003, p. 1; *Daily Telegraph*, 16 June 2003, p. 21.

91. *Daily Mail*, 23 May 2002, p. 1; *Daily Express*, 28 Dec. 2002, pp. 2, 16; *Daily Mail*, 28 Dec. 2002, pp. 12, 21; Anthony Browne, 'Some Truths about Immigration', *Spectator*, 2 Aug. 2003, pp. 18–19. Similarly, in September 2000, a contrived newspaper story in Britain suggested that if differential birth rates and rates of immigration to Britain between different ethnic groups continued on their present basis, by 2100 whites would be in a minority in Britain. This was presented as being 'the first time in history that a major indigenous population has voluntarily become a minority, rather than through war, famine or disease' (Anthony Browne, 'UK Whites will be Minority by 2100', *Observer*, 3 Sept. 2000), when in fact possibly no ethnic group in world history has benefited from emigration as much as the white British.

92. *Sun*, 13 March 2000, p. 1; Roger Andersson, Sako Musterd, and Vaughan Robinson, *Spreading the 'Burden'?: A Review of Policies to Disperse Asylum-Seekers and Refugees* (London: Policy, 2003). A common excuse made for such coverage of the asylum question is that, far from giving solace to racists, it expresses the 'legitimate concerns' of many people

within the pale of mainstream politics and thus eats away at the possible support base of neo-fascist political parties, which liberal negation of these concerns would enhance: see Browne, 'Some Truths about Immigration'; Kevin Myers, '"*From the* Irish Times *Column "An Irishman"' Diary'* (Dublin: Four Courts Press, 2000), pp. 199–202; *Daily Mail,* 28 Dec. 2002, p. 12. An interview with a member of the British National Party appears to blow this argument out of the water: 'Thrusting forward a folder of newspaper cuttings – the majority from the *Daily Mail* and the *Daily Express* – he says: "This is why I joined the BNP"'. The articles deal mostly with the asylum[-]seeker issue, illegal immigrants and racist attacks – but only those carried out on white people': Mary Fitzgerald, 'Right or Wrong?', *Belfast Telegraph,* 24 June 2003, p. 13. See also Benjamin Bowling, 'The Emergence of Violent Racism as a Public Issue in Britain, 1945–81', in Panikos Panayi (ed.), *Racial Violence in Britain in the Nineteenth and Twentieth centuries* (London: Leicester University Press, 1996), pp. 185–220, especially pp. 195–8.
93. See especially Craig Calhoun, *Nationalism* (Buckingham: Open University Press, 1997); E.J. Hobsbawm, *Nations and Nationalism since 1780: Programme, Myth, Reality* (Cambridge: Cambridge University Press, 1990): Benedict Anderson, *Imagined Communities: Reflections on the Origin and Spread of Nationalism,* revised edition (London: Verso, 1991; first published 1983); Ernst Gellner, *Nations and Nationalism* (Oxford: Basil Blackwell, 1983); Anthony D. Smith, *The Ethnic Origins of Nations* (Oxford: Basil Blackwell, 1986); Anthony D. Smith, *National Identity* (London: Penguin, 1991).
94. The *Daily Express,* for instance, was until recently a Labour-supporting newspaper.
95. Arthur Aughey, 'The Character of Ulster Unionism', in Peter Shirlow and Mark McGovern (eds), *Who are 'the People'?: Unionism, Protestantism and Loyalism in Northern Ireland* (London: Pluto Press, 1997), pp. 16–33, especially p. 21; Arthur Aughey, 'Conservative Party Policy and Northern Ireland', in Barton and Roche (eds), *The Northern Ireland Question: Perspectives and Policies,* pp. 121–50, especially pp. 125, 148; Paul Bew, 'The Union: A Concept in Terminal Decay?', in Boyce and O'Day (eds), *Defenders of the Union,* pp. 316–24, especially p. 322.
96. Brendan O'Leary, 'The Conservative Stewardship of Northern Ireland, 1979–97: Sound-bottomed Contradictions or Slow Learning?', *Political Studies,* 45 (1997), pp. 663–76.
97. A.J. Davies, *We, the Nation: The Conservative Party and the Pursuit of Power* (London: Little, Brown, 1995), pp. 198, 200; Robert Blake, *The Conservative Party from Peel to Major* (London: Arrow, 1998), p. 130; E. Green, *The Crisis of Conservatism: the Politics, Economics and Ideology of the British Conservative Party, 1880–1914* (London: Routledge, 1995), pp. 1, 59; see also Martin Francis and Ina Zweiniger-Bargielowska (eds), *The Conservatives and British Society 1880–1990,* Cardiff: University of Wales Press, 1996); B. Evans and A. Taylor, *From Salisbury to Major: Continuity and Change in Conservative Politics* (Manchester: Manchester University Press, 1996). Hague, Hitchens and others clearly imagine themselves to be the truest patriots at the same time as they issue such denunciations.
98. See, for instance, Roger Scruton, *England: An Elegy* (London: Chatto & Windus, 2000); and see especially '"The Abolition of Britain": Geoff Metcalf Interviews [the] Author Peter Hitchens on the End of England', *WorldNetDaily,* available at <http://www.worldnetdaily.com/news/article.asp?ARTICLE_ID=21407>, last accessed 15 May 2004.
99. See Tony Kushner and Kenneth Lunn (eds), *Traditions of Intolerance: Historical Perspectives on Fascism and Race Discourse in Britain* (Manchester: Manchester University Press, 1989); Panayi (ed.), *Racial Violence in Britain;* Panikos Panayi, 'The Historiography of Immigrants and Ethnic Minorities: Britain Compared with the USA', *Ethnic and Racial Studies,* 19:4 (Oct. 1996), pp. 823–40; Edwin Jones, *The English Nation: The Great Myth* (Stroud: Sutton, 1998).
100. John O'Sullivan, 'Their Amerika: the Song of the "Counter-Tribalists"', *National Review,* 15 Oct. 2001, pp. 28–30; see also Morris, *Off with Their Heads;* Coulter, *Slander,* especially p. 204.
101. See, for instance, '"The Abolition of Britain": Geoff Metcalf . . .'.
102. Philip Delves Broughton, '[The] French Lose their Passion for Power and Politics', *Daily Telegraph,* 19 April 2002.
103. Jürgen Habermas, *The Inclusion of the Other: Studies in Political Theory* (Cambridge: Polity Press, 1999; first published 1988), pp. 114, 115, 141.

104. Simon Heffer, *'Nor Shall My Sword': The Reinvention of England* (London: Weidenfeld & Nicolson, 1999), pp. 46–8; Hitchens, *The Abolition of Britain*, pp. 35–6; Andrew Roberts, *The Aachen Memorandum* (London: Weidenfeld & Nicolson, 1995), p. 142.
105. Scruton assumes that England, as the heartland of Britain, is only really safe in the hands of the Conservative Party. This leads him to make the assertion that the Labour Party 'would never have come to power, except for its support in Scotland and Wales, where it was seen as an anti-English force': Scruton, *England*, p. 252. On the contrary, in the general election of July 1945 the Labour Party won a large majority of English parliamentary constituencies, 331 to the Conservatives' 167. It substantially repeated this feat in 1997 and 2001, and also exceeded Conservative representation in England in the general elections of 1966 and October 1974. Meanwhile, at certain historical conjunctures the British Conservative (and Unionist) Party has drawn crucial electoral strength from the non-English parts of the United Kingdom, especially Scotland. In the general election of 1955, for instance, the Conservatives attained more than 50 per cent of the votes cast in Scotland. The Labour Party has never achieved such a predominance in Scotland, even in 1997 or 2001.
106. Scruton, *England*, p. 247.
107. Ibid., pp. 8, 8n, 7–8.
108. Roger Scruton, *The Meaning of Conservatism* (London: Macmillan, 1980), p. 68. Scruton has further suggested that 'political correctness' was ultimately responsible for the 9/11 attacks: Roger Scruton, *The West and the Rest: Globalization and the Terrorist Threat* (London: Continuum, 2002), pp. 68–83.
109. See, for instance, in relation to the BJP in India, Shri K.R. Malkani, 'BJP History: Its Birth, Growth and Onward March', available at <http://www.bjp.orghistory/history.htm>, last accessed 14 May 2004..
110. Lord Armstrong of Ilminster, 'Ethnicity, the English and Northern Ireland: Comments and Reflections', in Dermot Keogh and Michael H. Haltzel (eds), *Northern Ireland and the Politics of Reconciliation* (Washington, DC: Woodrow Wilson Center Press, 1993), pp. 203–7, especially p. 203.
111. Ibid., p. 204.
112. A.T.Q. Stewart, *The Narrow Ground: Aspects of Ulster, 1609–1969* (London: Faber & Faber, 1977), p. 16.
113. As exemplified in Nicholas Ridley's interview with the *Spectator*, in which he described the European Union as 'a German racket designed to take over the whole of Europe': *Spectator*, 14 July 1990, p. 8. This article cost Ridley his job as Secretary of State for Trade and Industry.
114. 'Thatcher Lauds [the] "English Peoples" above Europe', *Times*, 6 Oct. 1999, p. 16.
115. Redwood, *The Death of Britain?*, p. 4; Redwood, *Stars and Strife*, p. 2.
116. Loughlin, *Ulster Unionism and British National Identity*, pp. 99, 100, 210, 229.
117. Redwood, *The Death of Britain?*, p. 5.
118. Ibid., p. ix; *Daily Mail*, 18 Jan. 2001, pp. 1, 4, 12.
119. Liam O'Dowd, '"New Unionism", British Nationalism and the Prospects for a Negotiated Settlement in Northern Ireland', in David Miller (ed.), *Rethinking Northern Ireland: Culture, Ideology and Colonialism* (London: Longman, 1998), p. 84.
120. 'Hague's Identity: Strong Themes will Achieve Little without Policy Detail', *Times*, 20 Jan. 1999, p. 19.
121. 'French Malaise', *Daily Telegraph*, 22 April 2002.
122. Boris Johnson, 'Blunkett and Le Pen: What's the Difference?', *Daily Telegraph*, 25 April 2002.
123. 'Le Pen, Product of the E[uropean] U[nion]', *Daily Telegraph*, 23 April 2002.
124. The Runnymede Trust Commission on the Future of Multi-Ethnic Britain, *The Future of Multi-Ethnic Britain: Report of the Commission on the Future of Multi-Ethnic Britain* (London: Profile Books, 2000), [also known as the Parekh Report, as in further references below], p. 163.
125. 'Don't Diss Britannia', *Daily Telegraph*, 12 Oct. 2000.
126. See also *Daily Mail*, 12 Dec. 2001, p. 12; Jones, *The English Nation*, p. 246.

127. J.C.D. Clark, 'Protestantism, Nationalism, and National Identity, 1660–1832', *Historical Journal*, 43:1 (March 2000), pp. 249–76. Clark argues that the secession of the South of Ireland from the United Kingdom demonstrates no discontinuity in Britishness, since the South was 'scarcely a modern or a postmodern problem' (ibid., p. 276). A formation such as the South of Ireland and, therefore, any definition of Britishness that would incorporate Northern Ireland, is, on the contrary, extremely 'modern', since the 'hardcoding' of partition into Irish historical experience is not ancient, but dates from the late nineteenth century at the earliest (see Chapter 2 of this book, pp. 27–31).

128. Moore, 'Why Does Everyone Hate the Unionists So?'.

129. Armstrong of Ilminster, 'Ethnicity, the English and Northern Ireland', pp. 203–4.

130. Dixon, *Northern Ireland*, p. 206.

131. Aughey, *Under Siege*, p. 28; Richard English, 'The Same People with Different Relatives?: Modern Scholarship, Unionists and the Irish Nation', in R. English and G. Walker (eds), *Unionism in Modern Ireland: New Perspectives on Politics and Culture* (Basingstoke: Macmillan, 1996), p. 230. See also the Ulster Unionist Party's website <http://www.uup.org/>, last accessed 16 March 2002.

132. See Declan Kiberd, *Inventing Ireland: The Literature of the Modern Nation* (London: Cape, 1995), p. 645.

133. E. W. McFarland, *Ireland and Scotland in the Age of Revolution: Planting the Green Bough* (Edinburgh: Edinburgh University Press, 1994), p. 208.

134. See, for instance, Peter Hart, *The IRA and its Enemies: Violence and Community in Cork, 1916–1923* (Oxford: Clarendon Press, 1998).

135. Whyte, *Interpreting Northern Ireland*, p. 219.

136. See Graham Walker, 'Scotland and Ulster: Political Interactions since the Late Nineteenth Century and Possibilities of Contemporary Dialogue', in John Erskine and Gordon Lucy (eds), *Cultural Traditions in Northern Ireland: Varieties of Scottishness: Exploring the Ulster–Scottish Connection* (Belfast: Institute of Irish Studies, 1997), pp. 103–6.

137. Bob Purdie, *Politics in the Streets: The Origins of the Civil Rights Movement in Northern Ireland* (Belfast: Blackstaff Press, 1990), pp. 2–3, 156–7, 244–5; see also Brian Dooley, *Black and Green: The Fight for Civil Rights in Northern Ireland and Black America* (London: Pluto Press, 1998).

138. Benjamin W. Heineman, *The Politics of the Powerless: A Study of the Campaign Against Racial Discrimination* (London: Oxford University Press for the Institute of Race Relations, 1972), pp. x–xi, 16–18.

139. Gerry Adams, *Before the Dawn: An Autobiography* (New York: William Morrow & Co., 1996), pp. 278–9; Adrian Guelke, '"Comparatively Peaceful": South Africa, the Middle East and Northern Ireland', in Michael Cox, Adrian Guelke, and Fiona Stephen (eds), *A Farewell to Arms?: From War to Peace in Northern Ireland* (Manchester: Manchester University Press, 2000), pp. 223–33; John McGarry, 'Introduction: The Comparable Northern Ireland', in McGarry (ed.), *Northern Ireland and the Divided World*, pp. 1–33, especially pp. 3–14.

140. Dooley, *Black and Green*, p. 132.

141. Steven T. Walther, 'The Globalization of the Rule of Law and Human Rights', *Futures*, 31:9–10 (Nov. 1999), pp. 993–1003; T. Campbell, 'Human Rights: A Culture of Controversy', *Journal of Law and Society*, 26:1 (March 1999), pp. 6–26; Lawrence H. Fuchs, 'The Changing Meaning of Civil Rights, 1954–1994', in John Higham (ed.), *Civil Rights and Social Wrongs* (University Park, PA: Pennsylvania State University Press, 1999), pp. 59–85, especially p. 64.

142. Hague, 'Why I am Sick of the Anti-British Disease'.

143. To be fair to Roger Scruton, in one of his more forceful essays, which is, significantly, a critique of Bhikhu Parekh's work, he seems to show some appreciation of this fact: Roger Scruton, 'In Defence of the Nation', in J.C.D. Clark (ed.), *Ideas and Politics in Modern Britain* (Basingstoke: Macmillan, 1990), pp. 53–86, especially p. 76.

144. Quoted in Mark McGovern and Peter Shirlow, 'Counter-Insurgency, Deindustrialisation and the Political Economy of Ulster Loyalism', in Shirlow and McGovern (eds), *Who are 'the People'?*, p. 197; see also Bruce, *The Edge of the Union*, pp. 54–64; Paul A. Compton,

'Employment Differentials in Northern Ireland and Job Discrimination: A Critique', in Patrick J. Roche and Brian Barton (eds), *The Northern Ireland Question: Myth and Reality* (Aldershot: Avebury, 1991), pp. 40–76, especially p. 71; Patrick Crozier, *Plan B* (London: Friends of the Union, 2000).

145. On the extent of 'New' Labour's acceptance of Thatcherite neoliberalism, see, for instance, Richard Heffernan, *New Labour and Thatcherism: Political Change in Britain* (New York: St. Martin's Press, 2000).

146. *Hansard's Parliamentary Debates*, 6th series, Vol. 365, c. 954 (28 March 2001).

147. Yasmin Alibhai-Brown, *Who Do We Think We Are?: Imagining the New Britain* (London: Allen Lane, 2000), pp. ix, 275n, x; Yasmin Alibhai-Brown, *True Colours: Attitudes to Multiculturalism and the Role of the Government* (London: Institute for Public Policy Research, 1998), pp. 91–2, 131.

148. Hickman and Walter, *Discrimination and the Irish Community in Britain*, p. 11.

149. Ibid., pp. 88–9; Bronwen Walter, 'Challenging the Black/White Binary: The Need for an Irish Category in the 2001 Census', *Patterns of Prejudice*, 32:2 (1998), pp. 73–86; see also Bronwen Walter, *Outsiders Inside: Whiteness, Place and Irish Women* (London: Routledge, 2001); Mary J. Hickman and Bronwen Walter, 'Racializing the Irish in England: Gender, Class and Ethnicity', in Marilyn Cohen and Nancy J. Curtin (eds), *Reclaiming Gender: Transgressive Identities in Modern Ireland* (New York: St. Martin's Press, 1999), pp. 267–92.

150. Hickman and Walter, *Discrimination and the Irish Community in Britain*, p. 112; Walter, *Outsiders Inside*, pp. 165, 244–55, 270; Hickman and Walter, 'Racializing the Irish in England', pp. 284–5.

151. Hickman and Walter, *Discrimination and the Irish Community in Britain*, pp. 15–16, 50; Bronwen Walter, 'Contemporary Irish Settlement in London: Women's Worlds, Men's Worlds', in MacLaughlin (ed.), *Location and Dislocation in Contemporary Irish Society*, pp. 61–93, especially p. 82; see also G.K. Peatling, 'Recent Literature on the Irish Diaspora', *Studies in Travel Writing*, 6 (2002), pp. 108–26.

152. Parekh Report, pp. 61, 63. Evidence of the direct influence of this approach can be seen in the paper presented by Walter to the commission that produced the Parekh Report, 'The Irish Community – Diversity, Disadvantage and Discrimination' (18 June 1999), available at <http://www.runnymedetrust.org/projects/meb/bgIrishCommunity.htm>, last accessed 15 May 2004.

153. Paul Bew, 'The Ambiguous Dynamics of the Anglo-Irish Agreement', in Yonah Alexander and Alan O'Day (eds), *Ireland's Terrorist Trauma: Interdisciplinary Perspectives* (New York: St. Martin's Press, 1989), pp. 149–58, especially p. 156.

154. Parekh Report, pp. xiii, xxiii.

155. See Paul Hainsworth (ed.), *Divided Society: Ethnic Minorities and Racism in Northern Ireland* (London: Pluto Press, 1998); Robbie McVeigh, 'Is Sectarianism Racism?: Theorising the Racism/Sectarianism Interface', in Miller (ed.), *Rethinking Northern Ireland*, pp. 179–94.

156. Alibhai-Brown, *True Colours*.

157. Parekh Report, pp. 38–9; see also ibid., p. 18.

158. Ibid., p. 39.

159. Hague, 'Why I am Sick of the Anti-British Disease'. Although the Parekh Report may be said to be badly written at this point, this is certainly not its argument. See the letter from Bhikhu Parekh, *Times*, 17 Oct. 2000, p. 23; Robin Richardson, '"Children Will Be Told Lies"' Runnymede Bullitin (Dec. 2000), p. 126, available at <http://www.runnymedetrust.org/bullitin/pdf/324BullitinDec00.pdf>, last accessed 14 May 2004.

160. See Steve Bruce, *God Save Ulster: The Religion and Politics of Paisleyism* (Oxford: Clarendon Press, 1986); Duncan Morrow, 'Suffering for 'Righteousness' Sake?: Fundamentalist Protestantism and Ulster Politics', in Shirlow and McGovern (eds), *Who are 'the People'?*, pp. 55–71.

161. See, for instance, Geoffrey Bell, *The Protestants of Ulster* (London: Pluto Press, 1976); Geoffrey Bell, *The British in Ireland: A Suitable Case for Withdrawal* (London: Pluto Press, 1984); Paul Foot, *Ireland: Why Britain must Get Out* (London: Chatto & Windus, 1989), p. 28; [Sam Porter and Denis O'Hearn,] 'New Left Podsnappery: the British Left and Ireland', *New Left Review*, 212 (July–Aug. 1995), pp. 131–47; Chris Bambery, *Ireland's*

Permanent Revolution (London: Bookmarks, 1986); Ken Livingstone, *Livingstone's Labour: A Programme for the Nineties* (London: Unwin Hyman, 1989), pp. 125–49.

162. Paul Bew and Paul Dixon, 'Labour Party Policy and Northern Ireland', in Barton and Roche (eds.), *The Northern Ireland Question: Perspectives and Policies*, p. 153.

163. *Report of the . . . Annual Conference of the Labour Party* (London: Labour Party, 1983), pp. 249–58; *Report of the . . . Annual Conference of the Labour Party* (London: Labour Party, 1984), pp. 238–42; *Report of the . . . Annual Conference of the Labour Party* (London: Labour Party, 1985), pp. 73–9.

164. Austen Morgan, *Labour and Partition: The Belfast Working Class, 1905–23* (London: Pluto Press, 1991), especially pp. xvi–xix; Howe, *Ireland and Empire*, pp. 172–88.

165. See Graham S. Walker, *The Politics of Frustration: Harry Midgeley and the Failure of Labour in Northern Ireland* (Manchester: Manchester University Press, 1985); Bob Purdie, 'An Ulster Labourist in Liberal Scotland: William Walker and the Leith Burghs Election of 1910', in Ian S. Wood (ed.), *Scotland and Ulster* (Edinburgh: Mercat Press, 1994), pp. 116–33; Henry Patterson, 'British Government and the "Protestant Backlash", 1969–74', in Yonah Alexander and Alan O'Day (eds), *Ireland's Terrorist Dilemma* (Dordrecht: M. Nijhoff, 1986), pp. 231–47.

166. James McAuley, '"Flying the One-winged Bird": Ulster Unionism and the Peace Process', in Shirlow and McGovern (eds), *Who are 'the People'?*, pp. 165.

167. Notably Democracy Now and Kate Hoey, MP. Even within academic circles, while pro-nationalist or pro-republican scholars influenced by Marx and Gramsci, such as David Lloyd, David Miller or Terry Eagleton, are influential, there is a more subtle residual influence of Marxism evident in the work of leading historians who are broadly favourable to unionism, such as Peter Gibbon, Henry Patterson or Paul Bew: see McGarry and O'Leary, *Explaining Northern Ireland*, pp. 138–67.

168. See Belinda Probert, *Beyond Orange and Green: The Political Economy of the Northern Ireland Crisis* (London: Zed Press, 1978): Tom Nairn, *The Break-up of Britain: Crisis and Neo-Nationalism* (London: NLB, 1981), p. 247.

169. J. Esmond Birnie, 'The Economics of Unionism and Nationalism', in Patrick Roche and Brian Barton (eds), *The Northern Ireland Question: Nationalism, Unionism and Partition* (Aldershot: Ashgate, 1999), pp. 139–62, especially p. 149.

170. Crozier, *Plan B.*

171. Padraig O'Malley, *The Uncivil Wars: Ireland Today* (Belfast: Blackstaff, 1983), pp. 86–9; Arthur Aughey, 'Unionism' in Aughey and Morrow (eds), *Northern Ireland Politics*, p. 38.

172. See, for instance, Jonathan Freedland, *Bring Home the Revolution: How Britain Can Live the American Dream* (London: Fourth Estate, 1998); Jonathan Freedland, 'No Epitaph Yet for Ulster's Moderate Hardman', *Guardian*, 2 July 2001.

173. See Fig. 4.

174. Christie Davies, *Jokes and their Relation to Society* (Berlin: Mouton de Gruyter, 1998), pp. 20–4, 41. In fact this is not an argument Davies is able to sustain, since he is unable to resist the temptation to suggest that jokes 'are a mere barometer of political pressure'. He chooses, however, to apply this precept only to the study of a political system that he dubiously describes as 'socialist tyranny': Ibid., pp. 200n., 87.

175. Liz Curtis, *Nothing but the Same Old Story: The Roots of Anti-Irish Racism* (Belfast: Sasta, 1996; first published London: Information on Ireland, 1984), pp. 86–95.

176. Peter Hitchens, for instance, articulates the weak partisan argument that, while the significance of left-wing comedy 'in changing our national life' is 'beyond calculation', right-wing humour is by its very nature 'non-political': Hitchens, *The Abolition of Britain*, pp. 156, 170; see also James Delingpole, 'Why I Daren't Admit to Being Tory', *Spectator*, 4 Jan. 2003, pp. 12–13.

177. Cp. Brendan O'Leary, 'A Bright Future – and Less Orange', *Times Higher Educational Supplement*, 19 Nov. 1999. In fairness to O'Leary, who comments here on the Patten Report, it should be noted that writers for such publications have a limited degree of control over the headlines.

178. E. San Juan, Jr., *Beyond Postcolonial Theory* (New York: St. Martin's Press, 1998), pp. 6–7, 10, 13, 24–5, 74–5.

179. Ibid., pp. 28–9; see also Gautam Premnath, 'Remembering Fanon, Decolonizing Diaspora', in Laura Chrisman and Benita Parry (eds), *Postcolonial Theory and Criticism* (Cambridge: D.S. Brewer, 2000), pp. 57–73.

180. Homi Bhabha, 'Remembering Fanon: Self, Psyche and the Colonial Condition', in Frantz Fanon, *Black Skin, White Masks*, trans. Charles Lam Markmann (London: Pluto Press, 1986; originally published as *Peau noire, masques blanc*, 1952, without, it should be noted, this piece by Bhabha, which was written much later), pp. vii–xxv, especially pp. xxiii, xxii.

181. Edward W. Saïd, 'Reflections on Exile' in *Reflections on Exile, and Other Essays* (Cambridge, MA: Harvard University Press, 2000), pp. 173–86; Edward W. Saïd, *Culture and Imperialism* (New York: Knopf, 1993), pp. 332–3; Homi K. Bhabha, 'DissemiNation: Time, Narrative, and the Margins of the Modern Nation', in Homi K. Bhabha (ed.), *Nation and Narration* (London: Routledge, 1990), pp. 291–322, especially pp. 318–20.

182. San Juan, *Beyond Postcolonial Theory*, pp. 29–30, 43.

183. Peter McLaren, *Che Guevara, Paulo Freire, and the Pedagogy of Revolution* (Lanham, MD: Rowman & Littlefield, 2000), pp. xxiv–xxv, 190–1; Peter McLaren, *Critical Pedagogy and Predatory Culture: Oppositional Politics in a Postmodern Era* (London: Routledge, 1995), pp. 12–16; San Juan, *Beyond Postcolonial Theory*, pp. 85–6; see also Ziauddin Sardar, *Postmodernism and the Other: The New Imperialism of Western Culture* (London: Pluto Press, 1998).

184. Arif Dirlik, *The Postcolonial Aura: Third World Criticism in the Age of Global Capitalism* (Boulder, CO: Westview Press, 1997), p. xii.

185. Ibid., pp. 13, 21–52.

186. Ashley, *History without a Subject*, pp. 9–12; McLaren, *Critical Pedagogy . . .* pp. 13–14.

187. See Parkinson, 'Bigots in Bowler Hats?'; Parkinson, *Ulster Loyalism and the British Media*.

188. Habermas, *The Inclusion of the Other*, pp. 221–3, especially p. 223.

189. Edna Longley, 'What Do Protestants Want?', *Irish Review*, 20 (Winter/Spring 1997), p. 113.

190. See Paula M.L. Moya and Michael R. Hames-García (eds), *Reclaiming Identity: Realist Theory and the Predicament of Postmodernism* (Berkeley, CA: University of California Press, 2000).

191. A similar argument, adjusted for historical specificities, might also explain the disengagement of 'New' Labour from what was formerly the core constituency of the British Labour Party, the working class of the North of England, large numbers of whom, in many areas, did not vote in the general election of 2001, albeit without affecting the ultimate result (another Labour 'landslide' victory, following the one in 1997, but based on the votes of an even smaller proportion of the electorate). Those conservatives, such as Roger Scruton, who have belatedly realised that Thatcherite neoliberalism comprised an attack on certain communities have a point here: Scruton, *England*, p. 256.

192. Bhikhu Parekh, 'Liberalism and Colonialism: A Critique of Locke and Mill', in Jan Nederveen Pieterse and Bhikhu Parekh (eds), *The Decolonization of Imagination: Culture, Knowledge and Power* (London: Zed Books, 1995), pp. 81–98, especially p. 82.

193. Ibid., pp. 97, 95; see also Bhikhu Parekh, *Rethinking Multiculturalism: Cultural Diversity and Political Theory* (Basingstoke: Macmillan, 2000), pp. 36–47, 109–11.

194. Parekh Report, p. x.

195. See Stephen E. Koss, *John Morley at the India Office, 1905–1910* (New Haven, CT: Yale University Press, 1969).

196. John, Viscount Morley, *Recollections* (London: Macmillan, 1917, 2 vols), Vol. 1, p. 222.

197. Arthur Aughey, *The Union: Two Conflicting Interpretations* (London: Friends of the Union, 1995), pp. 14–15.

198. Ibid., p. 15; see also Asifa Maaria Hussain, *British Immigration Policy under the Conservative Government* (Aldershot: Ashgate, 2001).

199. Henry McDonald, 'Why the Streets of Bolton Echo to the Sounds of a Loyalist Vendetta', *Observer*, 13 July 2003.

200. Eric Waugh, 'What Cheriegate Means to Ulster', *Belfast Telegraph*, 18 Dec. 2002, p. 10. In a more positive unionist view of immigration, Patrick Crozier argues that the immigration into Northern Ireland of 'up to a million people' from outside the United Kingdom would change 'the demographics' of the province, with a positive effect on the conflict: Crozier

Plan B. In at least the short term, however, there must be a doubt whether Crozier's proposal would seriously affect the nature of Northern Ireland politics. Further, Crozier seems to overlook the evidence of racism in Northern Ireland, which, in view of the likelihood of further immigration into the province, requires, no less than racism in Great Britain, serious remedial or educative measures.

201. Howe, *Ireland and Empire*, p. 205; Aughey, *The Union*, p. 14.
202. Paul Gilroy, *The Black Atlantic: Modernity and Double Consciousness* (Cambridge, MA: Harvard University Press, 1993), p. 11.
203. Paul Gilroy, *'There ain't no Black in the Union Jack': The Cultural Politics of Race and Nation* (London: Hutchinson, 1987), p. 156.
204. Frank Wright, *Two Lands on One Soil: Ulster Politics before Home Rule* (Dublin: Gill & Macmillan, 1996), p. 510.
205. James Clifford, *Routes: Travel and Translation in the Late Twentieth Century* (Cambridge, MA: Harvard University Press, 1997), pp. 265–7.
206. W. Harvey Cox, 'On Being an Ulster Protestant', in Neil Evans (ed.), *National Identity in the British Isles* (Harlech: Coleg Harlech, 1989), pp. 35–45.
207. Gilroy, *The Black Atlantic*, p. 14.

CHAPTER 5

1. For early versions of this prediction, see Peatling, 'Rumbling Troubles outsde Ireland's Political Ghetto', *Times Higher Education Supplement*, 27 Sept. 2002, p. 36; Peatling, 'The Northern Ireland Peace Process and Europeanization: A Critical Response', *Canadian Journal of Irish Studies*, 27:2/28:1 (Fall 2001/Spring 20023), pp. 102–9
2. John Redwood, *Stars and Strife: the Coming Conflicts between the USA and the European Union* (Basingstoke: Palgrave, 2001), p. 8; see also Charles Moore, *How to be British* (London: Centre for Policy Studies, 1995), pp. 15, 17.
3. See Richard Weight, *Patriots* (London: Pan Macmillan, 2003).
4. Edna Longley, 'What Do Protestants Want?', *Irish Review*, 20 (Winter/Spring 1997), p. 147.
5. Jonathan Freedland, 'Surge in Support for Irish Unity', *Guardian*, 21 Aug. 2001.
6. See, for instance, 'Celebrating Britishness', speech by Robin Cook, [then] Secretary of State for Foreign and Commonwealth Affairs, Open Society, London, 19 April 2001, available at <http://www.labour.org.uk/>, last accessed 21 May 2001.
7. Paul Bew and Henry Patterson, 'Scenarios for Progress in Northern Ireland', in John McGarry and Brendan O'Leary (eds), *The Future of Northern Ireland* (Oxford: Clarendon Press, 1990), pp. 206–18, especially p. 218.
8. Among hundreds of other examples of this discursive practice, see *Hansard's Parliamentary Debates*, 6th series,: Vol. 255, c. 368 (22 Feb. 1995); Vol. 323, c. 900–3 (20 Jan. 1999); Vol. 324, c. 333–7 (27 Jan. 1999); Vol. 333, c. 1161–2 (23 June 1999); Vol. 334, c. 641–3 (5 July 1999).
9. Steve Bruce, 'Northern Ireland: Reappraising Loyalist Violence', in Alan O'Day (ed.), *Terrorism's Laboratory: The Case of Northern Ireland* (Aldershot: Dartmouth, 1995), p. 133.
10. J. Bowyer Bell, 'The Irish Republican Army Enters an Endgame: An Overview', *Studies in Conflict and Terrorism*, 18 (July/Sept. 1995), p. 173.
11. Henry Patterson, *Ireland since 1939* (Oxford: Oxford University Press, 2002), p. 337.
12. However, a number of commentators suggest that unionism has been particularly averse to self-criticism: Stephen Howe, *Ireland and Empire: Colonial Legacies in Irish History and Culture* (Oxford: Oxford University Press, 2000), p. 105; Colin Coulter, 'Direct Rule and the Unionist Middle Classes', in R. English and G. Walker (eds), *Unionism in Modern Ireland: New Perspectives on Politics and Culture* (Basingstoke: Macmillan, 1996), pp. 169–91, especially p. 187.

Postscript

The first draft of the preceding was completed in the summer of 2003. Within a few months, a notion of failure (however defined) in the peace process would have seemed to most casual observers chary and pedantic in the extreme. In October 2003, when John de Chastelain's IICD reported that it had witnessed the third and reportedly most substantial measure of PIRA decommissioning to date, an understanding appeared to have been reached which would have involved David Trimble leading his UUP back into a reconstituted Northern Ireland Executive alongside representatives of PSF. Trimble however regarded the nature of the step taken by the PIRA as insufficient to warrant his seeking his party's approval for this course of action. Trimble's reasons for taking this view are understandable: there are long-term misgivings within the unionist community about the lack of transparency in republican decommissioning, and a UUC approval for reentering the Executive on this basis would probably have been at best even closer than has become customary.[1] But as was suggested in the introduction, such was the lack of room for maneuver for *all* pro-Agreement parties in Northern Ireland, that reluctance to give further ground such as Trimble thus displayed invariably created difficulties for other parties. As has been argued here, PIRA decommissioning prior to any significant loyalist decommissioning *appeared* potentially to leave Catholic communities more vulnerable to loyalist (or other) assault by limiting the extent of protection mainstream republicans can offer. In turn, to those conscious of republicanism's fissiparous history, such a scenario can appear close to a repetition of the conjuncture in 1969 which precipitated the Official IRA's journey into political obscurity and eclipse by the more militarized PIRA.[2] Any eventuality where mainstream republicanism would now similarly fully lose its constituency within

beleagured Catholic communities to dissident republicans is actually
unlikely, and the level of community sanction for the 'policing' and
protection functions of republican paramilitary violence can be
exaggerated (though a variable level of support can be detected):[3]
but the emergence of problematic divisions within republicanism in
response to any dramatic new initiative from the leadership is a
somewhat more plausible possibility. The existence of fears of
divisions among mainstream republicans explains their frustration[4]
at Trimble's denying them anticipated political rewards in October
2003 in spite of their undertaking the perceived risks of
decommissioning. This sequence was thus likely to leave
republicans still more reluctant about further unreciprocated
decommissioning, and thus does not thus bode well for the future.
In the short term, however, the extremely optimistic expectations
which had featured in the international and local media in weeks
prior to these events, probably with the encouragement of both
sovereign governments, may have conduced to the ensuing sense of
disappointment when a deal proved impossible.[5]

It had been suggested here that 'denying opponents of
government policy a voice could only exacerbate frustration with
and disengagement from politics, and thus from the peace process'.[6]
The British government, after two postponements in the spring, had
little alternative, even in the absence of a deal to facilitate a
reconstitution of the Executive, other than to permit new Assembly
elections on 26 November 2003: even the earlier delays had not met
with the favour of nationalist forces (including republicans and the
Irish government). Several observers have suggested that the
original strong 'yes' vote in the Northern Ireland referendum on the
GFA of May 1998 was produced by usually politically inactive
groups (especially in the unionist community) being successfully
mobilised (a fact evident in the high turnout in the referendum).[7] In
contrast to the official efforts during that referendum, and at other
times in the process,[8] the two sovereign governments played a low-
key role in these November 2003 elections, although it may be that
analogous efforts would have made no difference to the results of
these elections.[9] These results furnished a continuation of the
established tendency of moderate parties in Northern Ireland
proportionately to lose support,[10] and the DUP emerged as the
largest party in the Assembly, and PSF the largest nationalist party.

(The PSF incidentally also garnered more first preference votes than the UUP.) The DUP's lead in terms of MLAs over the UUP would be enhanced over the start of the new year as Jeffrey Donaldson and two other MLAs first left the UUP,[11] and then joined the DUP,[12] a move which indicates the potential of at least some anti-Agreement unionist forces to organize more coherently than in the past.[13] With the more radical parties in both communities emerging the stronger, it was clear that current voting procedures in the Assembly offered no immediate prospect for the reconstitution of the Executive.

There has long been a tendency, perhaps most evident at the time of the 1998 referendum itself,[14] to perceive the DUP as a chief focus of political absolutism in Northern Ireland. Before the election, the DUP had called for a re-negotiated agreement (opposed by both governments), and opposed direct negotiation with, and participation in government for, 'terrorists' (meaning PSF).[15] Yet the DUP's election success has certainly not marked the termination of all political dialogue in Northern Ireland.[16] The governments may indeed have hoped that a shift in the balance of forces in representative politics in Northern Ireland might have provided a jolt to attitudes in certain quarters and thus an end to the deadlock, and certainly British government rhetoric had gradually become somewhat less dismissive of anti-Agreement unionism forces. Further, the DUP, like many political movements, has to reflect the considerations of potential and actual supporters. Many DUP supporters and leaders undoubtedly in principle dislike the ideas of sharing power with nationalists and of *any* all-Ireland dimension to the government of Northern Ireland: but anti-Agreement unionist sentiment, as has been argued above, has also been critically swelled by other issues such as policing reform, decommissioning and republican participation in government.[17] The responsibility incumbent in its expanding support base has entailed that the DUP reflect these concerns, and in February 2004, after the two governments had opened a review of the process (as provisioned under the GFA), the DUP advanced its *Devolution now* plan, proposing the fulfilling of most of the functions of devolved government through a so-called "Corporate Assembly".[18] The proposals would entrench a position of privilege for the DUP's MLAs within the Assembly, but they won grudging praise in even some surprising quarters,[19] and at least took the initiative away from alternative proposals, such as those which had suggested amending the operations of the d'Hondt formula in the Northern Ireland Assembly in order to sidestep any anti-Agreement majority within unionism.[20] Nonetheless, clear water remained between the DUP's and the nationalist positions: the DUP's position paper notably for instance reserved the party's views on strand 2 of the process, dealing with the all-Ireland dimension to the government of the North,[21] and it appeared unlikely to see eye-to-eye with nationalists on this. Whether any considerable bridging of such differences can be achieved remains to be seen, and even on the most optimistic interpretations evident at the time of writing (May 2004), the new review certainly represented a very different balance of political forces from those evident in cross-party talks in Northern Ireland ever since the formative moment of July 1997 discussed above.[22] Even if a new equilibrium could evolve in these circumstances, whether it could any longer best be regarded as part of the *same* peace process remained to be seen: the DUP would probably be unable to accept any settlement which did not exhibit at least the appearance of a different *negotiation process* altogether.

Other influences were more certainly not cheering at the time of writing (June 2004). Externally, the potentially highly unproductive mode of nationalist self-pity seemed to have become a still more dominant default in representation of issues relating to asylum in Britain and Ireland[23] (with political consequences in both), as well as in sundry political debates in the United States and elsewhere. Continued paramilitary activity in Northern Ireland itself, however, of course, more tangibly continued to disturb the review process. Late in 2003 and early in 2004, Michael McDowell, the Republic of Ireland's Justice Minister, suggested that mainstream republicans were involved in organised crime in the south. Meanwhile, in late January 2004, Jane Kennedy, the UK's then direct rule minister for Northern Ireland, suggested that the UDA's ceasefire could no longer be taken seriously. At the same time, there were implications that senior individual members of the south Belfast UVF might have been involved in racist attacks (a continuing feature of life in Northern Ireland), and the nationalist press was still concerned about loyalist attacks on Catholics.[24] It was noted above that 'further revelations about the "extra-curricular" activities of Provisionals' were particularly likely to have repercussions for the process, not 'because the Provisionals are bound to have been up to anything particularly pernicious compared to the loyalists, but because Provisional activity is certain to get more attention'.[25] So it was that the violent abduction and beating of republican dissident Bobby Tohill on 20 February 2004 has had the highest media profile because of PIRA involvement.[26] In the circumstances this may symptomize the disaffection of certain elements within the PIRA with the current political constellation in Northern Ireland, as may have occurred during previous periods of stalemate,[27] though that too would hardly be a good omen for the process. The response of the two governments was to encourage the Independent Monitoring Commission (IMC) proposed in the governments' *Joint Declaration* of the spring of 2003 to report earlier than had been planned,[28] but this was insufficient to satisfy David Trimble, who left the review in March 2004. The IMC's report, published on 20 April 2004 confirmed PIRA involvement in the Tohill case, and also publicized other continued paramilitary activities, republican and loyalist, including alleged involvement in murders, over the previous calendar year. The UK's Northern Ireland Secretary of State Paul Murphy immediately declared a punitive gesture, abating the financial assistance paid through the Northern Ireland Assembly to the PUP and the PSF. This was little more than a mild slap on the wrist,[29] but it led the PUP's David Ervine to express loyalist frustrations and declare he no longer wished to cooperate with the IMC,[30] and Gerry Adams to declare on 23 April 2004 that the peace process was 'in deep crisis'.[31]

Many secrets of the troubles remain opaque. In late April Irishmen with republican connections were cleared by a Colombian court of assisting left-wing guerillas in the country, but the nature of their presence in the country remains a subject of considerable suspicion for many. A civil case, brought by the relatives of the victims of Omagh against its alleged perpetrators, now with British government assistance, is ongoing. The investigations of retired Canadian Judge Peter Cory into a number of cases of alleged police collusion with paramilitaries on both sides of the Irish border has led to public inquiries being announced in both countries. The protracted Saville Inquiry into Bloody Sunday continues to sit, and Gerry Adams is under increasing pressure to admit to a leading past role in the PIRA. The future remains the most inscrutable secret of all, but, as the foregoing has suggested, some parameters can be drawn. In the aftermath of the 1998 referenda on the GFA, the elated *Irish Times* had declared: 'There is every reason to believe that most of the momentum [in Northern Ireland] of the coming weeks will be towards the centre and away from the extremes'.[32] Recent academic investigators are now notably less certain,[33] and such a momentum, if it ever existed, has long since dissipated. The effects of the peace process in enhancing mutual understanding and transcending sectarianism have been, to say the least, ambiguous.[34] At the analytical level, there is disagreement between those who suggest that the peace process was flawed from the outset and who thought Northern Ireland better off without the GFA,[35] and those who supported the GFA and believe that the more recent difficulties within the peace process could have been avoided if key parties to it and had not been either wantonly weak in discouraging violence or intransigent: the parties singled out for blame from the latter pro-Agreement perspectives, in all but a few academic cases,[36] are of course the analysts' political polar opposites.[37] It has been argued here that all of these views are wrong: while only the churlish or partisan can really deny that the peace process has brought benefits, the difficulties such as have been recently more and more evident were from the outset harder to avoid than most superficial commentators suggested, on account of the limitations of the process and of the GFA,[38] limitations partly, although only partly, the product of influences also evident in a wide range of societies beyond Northern Ireland.

Neither crisis nor stalemate comprises Armageddon however. On the other hand, it has been argued here that dealing with difficulties in the process has not been helped by public positions taken by the two governments, and by numerous other observers, which have often seemed to approximate to a state of denial as to the extent of these difficulties. Such denial seems an increasingly obviously forlorn option, and the soil should now, if belatedly, be receptive to the message that new postures are necessary. Indeed, new postures are perhaps already evident.[39] Although long deemed impossible, whether it has been admitted or not, from sheer necessity, a plan B will be invoked.

Notes

1. James W. McAuley, 'Unionism's last stand? Contemporary unionist politics and identity in Northern Ireland', *Global Review of Ethnopolitics*, 3:11 (September 2003), pp. 60–74, especially p. 63.
2. See for instance Brendan Anderson, *Joe Cahill: a life in the IRA* (Dublin: O'Brien Press, 2002), pp. 152–91 and Gerry Adams' recent *Hope and history: making peace in Ireland* (London: Brandon, 2003), especially pp.369, 371, 385–6. As a justification of Adams' leadership and strategy however, both this argument and the latter book are inadequate.
3. Kathleen A Cavanaugh, 'Interpretations of Political Violence in Ethnically Divided Societies', *Terrorism and Political Violence*, 9:3 (1997), pp. 33–54, especially pp. 44–9; Ian McAllister, '"The armalite and the ballot box": Sinn Fein's; electoral strategy in Northern Ireland', *Electoral Studies*, 23:1 (March 2004), pp. 123–142, especially pp. 137–9.
4. Evident for instance in the PIRA's statement of 29 October 2003.
5. Chris Gilligan. 'Constant crisis/permanent process: diminished agency and weak structures in the Northern Ireland peace process', *Global Review of Ethnopolitics*, 3:.1 (September 2003), pp. 22–38.
6. See Chapter 1.
7. Paul Bew, Peter Gibbon, Henry Patterson, *Northern Ireland, 1921-2001: political forces and social classes* (London: Serif, 2002, revised and updated edition.), p. 238.
8. Graham Spencer, 'Pushing for peace: the Irish government, television news and the Northern Ireland peace process', *European Journal of Communication*, 28:1 (March 2003), pp. 55–80; Roger MacGinty and John Darby, *Guns and government: the management of the Northern Ireland peace process* (Houndmills: Palgrave, 2002), pp. 163–6.
9. The lower turnout in the Assembly elections was also thus surely in part a symptom of the noted 'frustration with and disengagement … from the peace process'.
10. Jonathan Tonge, 'Victims of their own success? Post-Agreement dilemmas of political moderates in Northern Ireland', *Global Review of Ethnopolitics*, 2:1 (September 2003), pp. 39–59.
11. *Irish News*, (19 Dec. 2003), p.1.
12. Arlene Foster 'What's a nice girl like you doing in a party like this?', *Fortnight*, 422 (Feb. 2004), pp. 8–9.
13. Tonge, 'Victims of their own success?'.
14. John Darby and Roger Mac Ginty, 'Northern Ireland: long, cold peace', in John Darby and Roger MacGinty (ed), *The management of peace processes* (Houndmills: Macmillan Press, 2000), pp .61–106, especially p. 80.
15. 'Towards a new Agreement', DUP position paper 2003, available at <http://www dup2win.com/pdf/DupNewAgree.pd>, last accessed 16 Feb. 2004.
16. Mick Fealty, 'A deal is possible', *Fortnight*, 422 (Feb. 2004), p. 5.
17. McAuley, 'Unionism's last stand', pp. 60–74; Duncan Morrow, 'Nothing to fear but . . . ? Unionist and the Northern Ireland Peace Process', in Dominic Murray (ed.), *Protestant perceptions of the peace process in Northern Ireland* (Limerick: Centre for Peace and Development Studies, 2000), pp. 11–42, especially p. 39; MacGinty and Darby, *Guns and government*, pp. 42–3.
18. DUP, *Devolution now*, available at <http://www.dup.org.uk/pdf>DUPDevolution.pdf, from the DUP's website, <http://www.dup.org.uk/>, last accessed 14 Apr. 2004; Peter Robinson, 'The DUP plan for devolution', *Belfast Telegraph*, 6 Feb. 2004, p. 17.
19. *Belfast Telegraph*, (6 Feb. 2004), p. 16: *Irish Independent*, 26 Feb. 2004, p. 16.
20. See Brendan O'Leary, 'The character of the 1998 agreement: results and prospects', in Rick Wilford (ed.), *Aspects of the Belfast Agreement* (Oxford: Oxford University Press, 2001), pp. 49–83, especially pp. 52–3.
21. DUP, *Devolution now*, p. 3.
22. See above part 3, pp. 155–61.
23. Martin Conboy, 'Parochializing the global: language and the British tabloid press', in Jean Aitchison and Diana M. Lewis (eds.), *New media language* (London: Routledge, 2003), pp.45–54. See above part 3.

24. *Irish News*, (19 Dec. 2003), p. 3.
25. See above Chapter 1, p. 88.
26. Initially the PIRA denied all involvement, and then admitted that 'Volunteers' had been involved, but denied sanctioning the incident. This shifting pattern of denial and evasion has been evident in a number of Provisional statements in relation to recent incidents (including the arrest of republicans in Colombia in 2001), and creates much uncertainty among outsiders as to whether explanations advanced by mainstream republicans can ever be trusted.
27. Eamonn Mallie and David McKittrick, *The Fight for Peace: The Secret Story behind the Irish Peace Process* (London: Mandarin, 1997, revised and updated edition, first published 1996), pp. 398–9.
28. The IMC was ostensibly designed to give investigation of cases of alleged paramilitary involvement in crimes greater insulation against allegations of political motivation.
29. The UDA (which is without equivalent political representation) was also notably somewhat incongruously exempt from this sanction, notwithstanding its ongoing alleged paramilitary activities.
30. A number of loyalists have long felt that loyalist paramilitary organisations are judged more harshly than are the PIRA in matters such as the maintenance of ceasefires, and also feel that their contribution to the peace process is underecognised: on the latter see Roy Garland, *Gusty Spence* (Belfast: Blackstaff, 2001) pp. 277–311; Henry Sinnerton, *David Ervine: uncharted waters* (Dingle: Brandon, 2002); Gary McMichael, *An Ulster voice: in search of common ground in Northern Ireland* (Boulder, Colorado: Roberts Rinehart Publishers, 1999); Jim Cusack and Henry McDonald, *UVF* (Dublin: Poolbeg, 2000).
31. News release from Provisional Sinn Féin's web site, available at <http://www.sinnfein.ie/news/detail/4397>, last accessed 26 Apr 2004.
32. *Irish Times*, 25 May 1998, p. 13.
33. Richard Bourke, *Peace in Ireland: the war of ideas* (London: Pimlico, 2003), pp. 310–2: Gilligan. 'Constant Crisis/Permanent Process'.
34. Peter Shirlow, '"Who Fears to Speak": Fear, Mobility, and Ethno-sectarianism in the Two "Ardoynes"' *Global Review of Ethnopolitics*, 3:1 (September 2003), pp. 76–91; Peter Shirlow, 'Fear and ethnic division in Belfast', *Peace Review*, 13:1 (2001), pp. 67–74; Liam Kennedy, 'They shoot children don't they? An analysis of the age and gender of victims of paramilitary "punishments" in Northern Ireland', 2001, available via the University of Ulster's Conflict Archive on the INternet at <http://cain.ulst.ac.uk/issues/violence/docs/kennedy01.htm>, last accessed 26 Apr. 2004; Colin Knox, 'The "deserving" victims of political violence: "punishment" attacks in Northern Ireland', *Criminal Justice*, 1:2 (2001), pp. 181–199; Jeremy Harbison and Anna Manwah Lo, 'The impact of devolution on community relations', in *Social attitudes in Northern Ireland: the ninth report* (London: Pluto, 2004), pp. 107–120.
35. Patrick J. Roche, *The appeasement of terrorism & the Belfast Agreement* (Ballyclare: Northern Irish Unionist Party, 2000); J. Dingley, 'Peace in our time? The stresses and strains on the Northern Ireland peace process', *Studies in Conflict and Terrorism*, 25:6 (November/December 2002), pp. 357–82: Robert McCartney, 'Britain Feeds Political Monsters', *Irish Times*, 25 May 1998, p. 11.
36. Mac Ginty and Darby, *Guns and government*, p.182
37. *Belfast News Letter*, (20 Dec. 2003), p. 8; Tim Pat Coogan, 'Forged in the crucible of his hatred', *Sunday Independent*, (29 Feb. 2004), p.10;: Adams, *Hope and history*, pp. 377–88.
38. Adrian Guelke, 'Violence and electoral polarization in divided societies: three cases in comparative perspective', *Terrorism and Political Violence*, 13:3, 4 (2000), pp. 78–105, especially pp. 94–5; Kirsten E. Schulze and M.L.R. Smith, 'Decommissioning and paramilitary strategy in Northern Ireland: a problem compared', *Journal of Strategic Studies*, 23:4 (Dec. 2000), pp. 77–106.
39. Note for instance the Irish government's apparent decreasing fund of patience towards mainstream republican paramilitary activity after the Assembly elections of 2003.

Select Bibliography

As was explained in the introduction, this book 'is not, contrary to appearances, a book about the "Northern Ireland problem" or "conflict in Northern Ireland"', still less does it purport to be a comprehensive survey of Northern Ireland politics during the full period of the peace process. This has not been attempted partly because, in the vast literature on Northern Ireland, there is no shortage of such accounts, but in the main because it has been argued here that recent events in Northern Ireland are best considered in the light of a broad understanding of dynamics that also have effects on a large number of societies beyond Northern Ireland. This book comprises, amongst other things, an effort to grasp such an understanding from the broadest range of sources possible. In consequence it is more than usually difficult to itemize all the sources, dealing with matters both internal and external to Northern Ireland, which have been garnered in an effort to grasp such an understanding. What follows thus, necessarily, is merely a list of many of the principal sources which have contributed to this goal.

MANUSCRIPT SOURCES

National Archives of Ireland: Department of the Taoiseach and Department of Foreign Affairs papers.
Public Record Office of Northern Ireland: Northern Ireland Cabinet papers (CAB series) and Lord Craigavon Papers (T/3775).
The National Archives (PRO), London: Prime Minister's Office papers (PREM), Cabinet papers (CAB), Home Office papers (HO), and Foreign and Commonwealth Office papers (FCO).

NEWSPAPERS AND PERIODICAL PUBLICATIONS

Northern Ireland

The *Belfast Telegraph*
The Blanket
Fortnight
Fourthwrite magazine, available at http://www.fourthwrite.ie/
The *Irish News*
The *Newsletter* (Belfast)
An Phoblacht/Republican News

Republic of Ireland

The *Irish Independent*
The *Irish Times*
The *Sunday Business Post*

United Kingdom

The *Daily Express*
The *Daily Mail*
The *Daily Star*
The *Daily Telegraph*
The *Financial Times*
The *Independent*
The *Guardian*
The *New Statesman*
The *Observer*
The *Spectator*
The *Sun*
The *Times*
Today (1986-95)

United States of America

The *National Review*

BOOKS

Adams, Gerry. *Before the Dawn: An Autobiography* (New York: William Morrow & Co., 1996).

____. *Hope and History: Making Peace in Ireland* (London: Brandon, 2003).

Donald Harman Akenson, *God's Peoples: Covenant and Land in South Africa, Israel, and Ulster* (Montreal: McGill-Queen's University Press, 1992).

____. *Irish Diaspora: A Primer* (Toronto: P.D. Meany Co., 1996).

____. *If the Irish Ran the World: Montserrat, 1630–1730* (Montreal: McGill-Queen's University Press, 1997).

Alexander, Yonah, and Alan O'Day (eds.). *Ireland's Terrorist Dilemma* (Dordrecht, The Netherlands: M. Nijhoff, 1986).

____. *Ireland's Terrorist Trauma: Interdisciplinary Perspectives* (New York: St. Martin's Press, 1989).

Ali, Tariq. *The Clash of Fundamentalisms: Crusades, Jihads and Modernity* (London : Verso, 2002).

Alibhai–Brown, Yasmin. *Who Do We Think We Are? imagining the New Britain* (London: Allen Lane, 2000).

Anderson, James, and James Goodman (eds.). *Dis/agreeing Ireland: Contexts, Obstacles, Hopes* (London: Pluto, 1998).

Ansell, Amy Elizabeth. *New Right, New Racism: Race and Reaction in the United States and Britain* (Washington Square, N.Y.: New York University Press, 1997).

Arthur, Paul. *The People's Democracy, 1968–1973* (Belfast: Blackstaff, 1974).

____. *Special Relationships: Britain, Ireland and the Northern Ireland Problem* (Belfast: Blackstaff, 2000).

Arthur, Paul, and Keith Jeffery, *Northern Ireland since 1968* (Oxford: Basil Blackwell, 1988).

____. *Northern Ireland since 1968* (Oxford: Basil Blackwell, 1996, 2nd ed.).

Ashley, David. *History Without a Subject: the Postmodern Condition* (Boulder, Colorado: Westview Press, 1997).

Aughey, Arthur. *Under siege: Ulster Unionism and the Anglo-Irish Agreement* (Belfast: Blackstaff, 1989).

____. *The Union: Two Conflicting Interpretations* (London: Friends of the Union, 1995).

____. *Nationalism, Devolution and the Challenge to the United Kingdom state* (London: Pluto, 2001).

Aughey, Arthur, Paul Hainsworth, Martin J. Trimble. *Northern Ireland in the European Community : An Economic and Political Analysis* (Belfast: Policy Research Institute, Queen's University of Belfast and the University of Ulster, 1989).

Aughey, Arthur, Greta Jones and W.T.M. Riches. *The Conservative Tradition in Britain and the United States* (London: Pinter, 1992).

Aughey, Arthur, and Duncan Morrow (eds.), *Northern Ireland Politics* (Harlow: Longman Group Limited, 1996).

Bauman, Zygmunt. *Intimations of Postmodernity* (London: Routledge 1992).

Bell, Geoffrey. *The Protestants of Ulster* (London: Pluto, 1976).

____. *The British in Ireland: A Suitable Case for Withdrawal* (London: Pluto, 1984).

Bennis, Phyllis. *Before & After: US Foreign Policy and the War on Terrorism* (Moreton-in-Marsh: Arris Books, 2003).

Bew, Paul, Peter Gibbon and Henry Patterson. *The State in Northern Ireland, 1921-72: Political Forces and Social Classes* (New York: St. Martin's Press, 1979).

____. *Northern Ireland, 1921–1996: Political Forces and Social Classes* (London: Serif, 1996, revised and updated edition).

____. *Northern Ireland, 1921–2001: Political Forces and Social Classes* (London: Serif, 2002, revised and updated edition).

Bew, Paul, Henry Patterson, and Paul Teague, *Northern Ireland, Between War and Peace: the Political Future of Northern Ireland* (London: Lawrence and Wishart, 1997).

Bhabha, Homi K. (ed.). *Nation and Narration* (London: Routledge, 1990).

Bourke, Richard. *Peace in Ireland: The War of Ideas* (London: Pimlico, 2003).

Boyce, D. George. *Nationalism in Ireland* (London: Routledge, 1995, 3rd ed.).

Boyce, D. George, and Alan O'Day (eds.). *The Making of Modern Irish History: Revisionism and the Revisionist Controversy* (London: Routledge, 1996).

____. *Defenders of the Union: A Survey of British and Irish Unionism Since 1801* (London: Routledge, 2000).

Boyle, Kevin, and Tom Hadden. *Northern Ireland: The Choice* (Harmondsworth: Penguin, 1994).

Brady, Ciaran (ed.). *Interpreting Irish History: The Debate on Historical Revisionism, 1938–1994* (Blackrock, Ireland : Irish Academic Press, 1994).

Brah, Avtar. *Cartographies of Diaspora: Contesting Identities* (London: Routledge, 1996).

Brewster, Scott, *et alia*, (eds.). *Ireland in Proximity: History, Gender, Space* (London: Routledge, 1999).

Brown, Callum G. *The Death of Christian Britain: Understanding Secularisation, 1800–2000* (London: Routledge, 2001).

Bruce, Steve. *God Save Ulster: The Religion and Politics of Paisleyism* (Oxford: Clarendon Press, 1986).

____. *The Red Hand: Protestant Paramilitaries in Northern Ireland* (Oxford: Oxford University Press, 1992).

____. *The Edge of the Union: The Ulster Loyalist Political Vision* (Oxford: Oxford University Press, 1994).

Cairns, David, and Sean Richards. *Writing Ireland: Colonialism, Nationalism and Culture* (Manchester: Manchester University Press, 1988).

Calhoun, Craig. *Nationalism* (Buckingham: Open University Press, 1997).

Cash, John Daniel. *Identity, Ideology and Conflict: The Structuration of Politics in Northern Ireland* (Cambridge: Cambridge University Press, 1996).

Chomsky, Noam. *Rogue States: The Rule of Force in World Affairs* (Cambridge, MA: South End Press, 2000).

____. *9–11* (New York: Seven Stories Press, 2001).

Clark, J.C.D. (ed.). *Ideas and Politics in Modern Britain* (Basingstoke: Macmillan, 1990)

Cochrane, Feargal. *Unionist Politics and the Politics of Unionism Since the Anglo-Irish Agreement* (Cork: Cork University Press, 1997).

Collins, Peter (ed.). *Nationalism and Unionism: Conflict in Ireland* (Belfast: Institute of Irish Studies, Queen's University of Belfast, 1994).

Connolly, Claire (ed.). *Theorising Ireland* (Basingstoke: Palgrave, 2003).

Connolly, S.J. (ed.). *Kingdoms United? Great Britain and Ireland Since 1500: Integration and Diversity* (Dublin: Four Courts Press, 1999).

Coulter, Ann H. *Slander: Liberal Lies about the American Right* (New York: Crown, 2002).

Coulter, Carol. *The Hidden Tradition: Feminism, Women, and Nationalism in Ireland* (Cork: Cork University Press, 1993).

Cox, Michael, Adrian Guelke, and Fiona Stephen (eds.). *A Farewell to Arms? From War to Peace in Northern Ireland* (Manchester: Manchester University Press, 2000).

Cubitt, Geoffrey (ed.). *Imagining Nations* (Manchester: Manchester University Press, 1998).

Cunningham, Michael J. *British Government Policy in Northern Ireland, 1969–2000* (Manchester: Manchester University Press, 2001).

Curtis, Liz. *Ireland: The Propaganda War, the Media and the 'Battle for Hearts and Minds'* (London: Pluto, 1984).

_____. *Nothing but the Same Old Story: The Roots of Anti-Irish Racism* (Belfast: Sasta, 1996, first published, London: Information on Ireland, 1984).

Darby, John (ed.). *Northern Ireland: The Background to the Conflict* (Belfast: Appletree Press, 1983).

Darby, John, and Roger Mac Ginty (eds.). *The Management of Peace Processes* (Houndmills: Macmillan Press, 2000).

Darby, John, Nicholas Dodge and A.C. Hepburn (eds.). *Political Violence: Ireland in a Comparative Perspective* (Belfast: Appletree, 1990).

Davies, Christie. *Jokes and their Relation to Society* (Berlin: Mouton de Gruyter, 1998).

Davis, Richard. *Mirror Hate: The Convergent Ideology of Northern Ireland Paramilitaries, 1966–1992* (Aldershot: Dartmouth, 1994).

Deane, Seamus. *Strange Country: Modernity and Nationhood in Irish Writing Since 1790* (Oxford: Clarendon Press, 1997).

Dirlik, Arif. *The Postcolonial Aura: Third World Criticism in the Age of Global Capitalism* (Boulder, Colorado: Westview Press, 1997).

Dixon, Paul. *Northern Ireland: The Politics of War and Peace* (Basingstoke: Palgrave, 2001).

Dooley, Brian. *Black and Green: The Fight for Civil Rights in Northern Ireland and Black America* (London: Pluto, 1998).

Douglas, Roy, Liam Harte and Jim O'Hara. *Drawing Conclusions: A Cartoon History of Anglo-Irish Relations 1798–1998* (Belfast: Blackstaff Press, 1998).

Dunn, Seamus (ed.). *Facets of the Conflict in Northern Ireland* (Basingstoke: Macmillan Press, 1995).

Edwards, Ruth Dudley. *The Faithful Tribe: An Intimate Portrait of the Loyal Institutions* (London: HarperCollins, 1999).

Elcock, Howard, and Michael Keating (eds.). *Remaking the Union: Devolution and British Politics in the 1990s* (London: Frank Cass, 1998).

Elias, Norbert, and John L. Scotson. *The Established and the Outsiders: A Sociological Enquiry into Community Problems* (London; Thousand Oaks, Calif.: Sage Publications, 1994, 2nd ed., first published 1965).

Elliott, Marianne. *The Catholics of Ulster: A History* (New York: Basic Books, 2001).

Elliott, Marianne (ed.). *The Long Road to Peace in Northern Ireland: Peace Lectures from the Institute of Irish Studies at Liverpool University* (Liverpool: Liverpool University Press, 2002).

Ellison, Graham, and Jim Smyth, *The Crowned Harp: Policing Northern Ireland* (London: Pluto, 2000).

English, Richard. *Armed Struggle: A History of the IRA* (Basingstoke: Macmillan, 2003).

English, Richard, and Graham Walker (eds.). *Unionism in Modern Ireland: New Perspectives on Politics and Culture* (Basingstoke: Macmillan, 1996).

Erskine, John, and Gordon Lucy (eds.). *Cultural Traditions in Northern Ireland: Varieties of Scottishness. Exploring the Ulster-Scottish Connection* (Belfast: Institute of Irish Studies, the Queen's University of Belfast, 1997).

Evans, Neil (ed.). *National Identity in the British Isles* (Harlech: Coleg Harlech, 1989).

Evans, Richard J. *In Defence of History* (London: Granta, 2000, new ed., first published 1997).

Fanning, Ronan. *Independent Ireland* (Walkinstown, Dublin: Helicon, 1983).

Farrell, Michael. *Northern Ireland: The Orange State* (London: Pluto, 1976).

_____. *Arming the Protestants: The Formation of the Ulster Special Constabulary and the Royal Ulster Constabulary, 1920–7* (London: Pluto, 1983).

Fealty, Mick, Trevor Ringland, and David Steven. *A Long Peace? The Future of Unionism in Northern Ireland* (Wimborne: Slugger O'Toole, 2003).

Fitzgerald, Patrick, and Steve Ickringill (eds.). *Atlantic Crossroads: Historical Connections between Scotland, Ulster and North America* (Newtownards: Colourpoint, 2001).

Follis, Bryan A. *A State Under Siege: The Establishment of Northern Ireland, 1920–1925* (Oxford: Clarendon Press, 1995).

Foot, Paul. *Ireland: Why Britain Must Get Out* (London: Chatto & Windus, 1989).

Foster, R.F. *Modern Ireland, 1600–1972* (London: Penguin, 1989, first published 1988).

Francis, Martin, and Ina Zweiniger-Bargielowska (eds.). *The Conservatives and British Society, 1880–1990* (Cardiff: University of Wales Press, 1996).

Freedland, Jonathan. *Bring Home the Revolution: How Britain Can Live the American Dream* (London: Fourth Estate, 1998).

Freire, Paulo. *Pedagogy of the Oppressed*, trans. Myra Bergman Ramos (Harmondsworth: Pelican, 1985, first published 1972).

Galligan, Yvonne, Eilís Ward, and Rick Wilford (eds.), *Contesting Politics: Women in Ireland, North and South* (Boulder, Colo.: Westview Press, 1999).

Gibbon, Peter. *The Origins of Ulster Unionism: The Formation of Popular Protestant Politics and Ideology in Nineteenth-Century Ireland* (Manchester: Manchester University Press, 1975).

Gibbons, Luke. *Transformations in Irish Culture* (Cork: Cork University Press, 1996).

Gilligan, Chris, and Jon Tonge (eds.), *Peace or War?: Understanding the Peace Process in Northern Ireland* (Aldershot: Ashgate, 1997).

Gilroy, Paul. *'There Ain't No Black in The Union Jack': The Cultural Politics of Race and Nation* (London: Hutchinson, 1987).

_____. *The Black Atlantic: Modernity and Double Consciousness* (Cambridge, Mass.: Harvard University Press, 1993).

Graham, Colin. *Deconstructing Ireland: Identity, Theory, Culture* (Edinburgh: Edinburgh University Press, 2001).

Greaves, C. Desmond. *The Irish Crisis* (New York, International Publishers, 1972).

Griffin, Patrick. *The People with No Name: Ireland's Ulster Scots, America's Scots Irish, and the Creation of a British Atlantic World, 1689-1764* (Princeton, N.J.: Princeton University Press, 2001).

Guelke, Adrian. *Northern Ireland: The International Perspective* (Dublin:

Gill and Macmillan Ltd, 1988).

Guelke, Adrian (ed.). *New Perspectives on the Northern Ireland Conflict* (Aldershot: Avebury, 1994).

Habermas, Jürgen. *The Inclusion of the Other: Studies in Political Theory* (Cambridge: Polity Press, 1999, first published 1988).

Hainsworth, Paul (ed.). *Divided Society: Ethnic Minorities and Racism in Northern Ireland* (London: Pluto, 1998).

Haseler, Stephen. *The English Tribe: Identity, Nation and Europe* (Basingstoke: Macmillan, 1996).

Hepburn, A.C. (ed.). *The Conflict of Nationality in Modern Ireland* (New York: St. Martin's Press, 1980).

Heffer, Simon. *Nor Shall My Sword: The Reinvention of England* (London: Weidenfeld & Nicolson, 1999).

Heffernan, Richard. *New Labour and Thatcherism: Political Change in Britain* (New York: St. Martin's Press, 2000).

Hennessey, Thomas. *Dividing Ireland: World War I and Partition* (London: Routledge, 1998).

____. *The Northern Ireland Peace Process: Ending the Troubles?* (Dublin: Gill & Macmillan, 2000).

Hickman, Mary J. and Bronwen Walter, *Discrimination and the Irish Community in Britain: A Report of Research Undertaken for the Commission for Racial Equality* (London: Commission for Racial Equality, 1997).

Hillyard, Paddy. *Suspect Community: People's Experience of the Prevention of Terrorism Acts in Britain* (London: Pluto in association with Liberty, 1993).

Hitchens, Peter. *The Abolition of Britain: The British Cultural Revolution from Lady Chatterley to Tony Blair* (London: Quartet, 2000 Rev. & exp. ed., first published 1999).

Holmes, Martin (ed.). *The Eurosceptical Reader* (Basingstoke: Macmillan, 1996).

Hopkinson, Michael. *Green Against Green: The Irish Civil War* (New York: St. Martin's Press, 1988).

____. *The Irish War of Independence* (Montreal: McGill-Queen's University Press, 2002).

Howe, Stephen. *Ireland and Empire: Colonial Legacies in Irish history and Culture* (Oxford: Oxford University Press, 2000).

Hughes, Eamonn (ed.). *Culture and Politics in Northern Ireland, 1960-1990* (Buckingham: Open University Press, 1991).

Hume, John. *Personal Views: Politics, Peace and Reconciliation in Ireland* (Enfield: Roberts Rinehart, 1996).

Huntington, Samuel P. *The Clash of Civilizations and the Remaking of World Order* (New York: Simon & Schuster, 1996).

Hussain, Asifa Maaria. *British Immigration Policy Under the Conservative Government* (Aldershot: Ashgate, 2001).

Hutton, Sean, and Paul Stewart (eds.). *Ireland's Histories: Aspects of State, Society, and Ideology* (London: Routledge, 1991).

Insight team of the Sunday Times. *Ulster* (London: Deutsch, 1972).

Jackson, Alvin. *Home Rule: an Irish History, 1800–2000* (London: Weidenfeld & Nicholson, 2003).

Jarman, Neil. *Material Conflicts: Parades and Visual Displays in Northern Ireland* (Oxford: Berg, 1997).

Jones, Edwin. *The English Nation: The Great Myth* (Stroud: Sutton, 1998).

Kearney, Richard, *Postnationalist Ireland: Politics, Literature, Philosophy* (London: Routledge, 1997).

Kearney, Richard (ed.). *The Irish Mind: Exploring Intellectual Traditions* (Dublin: Wolfhound, 1985).

_____. *Across the Frontiers: Ireland in the 1990s: Cultural-Political-Economic* (Dublin: Wolfhound, 1988).

Kendle, John. *Federal Britain: A History* (London: Routledge, 1997).

Kennedy, Dennis. *The Widening Gulf: Northern Attitudes to the Independent Irish State, 1919–49* (Belfast: Blackstaff Press, 1988).

Kennedy, Liam. *Colonialism, Religion and Nationalism in Ireland* (Belfast: Institute of Irish Studies, 1996).

Kennedy, Michael. *Division and Consensus: The Politics of Cross-Border Relations in Ireland, 1925–1969* (Dublin: Institute of Public Administration, 2000).

Keogh, Dermot, and Michael H. Haltzel (eds.). *Northern Ireland and the Politics of Reconciliation* (Washington: Woodrow Wilson Center Press, 1993).

Kiberd, Declan. *Inventing Ireland: The Literature of the Modern Nation* (London: Jonathan Cape, 1995).

_____. *Irish Classics* (Cambridge, Mass.: Harvard University Press, 2001).

Kirby, Peadar, Luke Gibbons and Michael Cronin (eds.). *Reinventing Ireland: Culture, Society and the Global Economy* (London: Pluto, 2002).

Kushner, Tony, and Kenneth Lunn (eds.). *Traditions of Intolerance: Historical Perspectives on Fascism and Race Discourse in Britain* (Manchester: Manchester University Press, 1989).

Lawrence, Bruce B. *Shattering the Myth: Islam Beyond Violence* (Princeton, N.J.: Princeton University Press, 1998).

Lee, J.J. *Ireland, 1912–1985: Politics and Society* (Cambridge: Cambridge University Press, 1989).

Lijphart, Arend. *Democracy in Plural Societies: A Comparative Exploration* (New Haven: Yale University Press, 1977).

Lloyd, David. *Ireland after History* (Notre Dame, Ind.: University of Notre Dame Press, 1999).

Lloyd, Katrina, *et alia. Social Attitudes in Northern Ireland: The Ninth Report* (London: Pluto, 2004).

Loughlin, James. *Ulster Unionism and British National Identity Since 1885* (London: Pinter, 1995).

____. *The Ulster Question Since 1945* (Basingstoke: Macmillan, 1998).

MacDonagh, Oliver. *States of Mind: A Study of Anglo-Irish Conflict, 1780–1980* (London: Allen & Unwin, 1983).

Macdonald, Catriona M.M. (ed.). *Unionist Scotland, 1800–1997* (Edinburgh: John Donald Publishers, 1998).

Mac Ginty, Roger, and John Darby. *Guns and Government: The Management of the Northern Ireland Peace Process* (Houndmills: Palgrave, 2002).

Magee, Patrick. *Gangsters or Guerrillas? Representations of Irish Republicans in Troubles Fiction* (Belfast: Beyond the Pale, 2001).

Mallie, Eamonn, and David McKittrick. *The Fight for Peace: The Secret Story Behind the Irish Peace Process* (London: Mandarin, 1997, revised and updated edition, first published 1996).

Mawhinney, Brian, and Ronald Wells, *Conflict and Christianity in Northern Ireland* (Grand Rapids: Eerdmans, 1975).

McAliskey, Bernadette Devlin. *The Price of My Soul* (London: Deutsch, 1969).

McClintock, Anne. *Imperial Leather: Race, Gender and Sexuality in the Colonial Contest* (New York: Routledge, 1995).

McDonald, Henry. *Trimble* (London: Bloomsbury, 2001, first published 2000).

McDonough, Frank. *Neville Chamberlain, Appeasement and the British Road to War* (Manchester: Manchester University Press, 1998).

McFarland, E. W. *Ireland and Scotland in the Age of Revolution: Planting the Green Bough* (Edinburgh: Edinburgh University Press, 1994).

McGarry, John (ed.). *Northern Ireland and the Divided World: The Northern Ireland Conflict and the Good Friday Agreement in Comparative Perspective* (Oxford: Oxford University Press, 2001).

O'Leary, Brendan, and John McGarry. *The Politics of Antagonism: Understanding Northern Ireland* (London: Athlone Press, 1993).

____. *Explaining Northern Ireland: Broken Images* (Oxford: Blackwell, 1995).

____. *Policing Northern Ireland: Proposals for a New Start* (Belfast: Blackstaff Press, 1999).

McGarry, John, and Brendan O'Leary (eds.). *The Future of Northern Ireland* (Oxford: Clarendon Press, 1990).

____. *The Politics of Ethnic Conflict Regulation: Case Studies of Protracted Ethnic Conflicts* (London: Routledge, 1993).

McIntosh, Gillian. *The Force of Culture: Unionist Identities in Twentieth-Century Ireland* (Cork: Cork University Press, 1999).

McLaren, Peter. *Critical Pedagogy and Predatory Culture: Oppositional Politics in a Postmodern Era* (London: Routledge, 1995).

____. *Che Guevara, Paulo Freire, and the Pedagogy of Revolution* (Lanham (Md.): Rowman & Littlefield Publishers, 2000).

McMichael, Gary. *An Ulster Voice: In Search of Common Ground in Northern Ireland* (Boulder, Colorado: Roberts Rinehart Publishers, 1999).

McVeigh, Robbie. *The Racialization of Irishness: Racism and Anti-Racism in Ireland* (Belfast: Centre for Research and Documentation, 1996).

Miller, David. *Don't Mention the War: Northern Ireland, Propaganda and the Media* (London: Pluto, 1994).

Miller, David (ed.). *Rethinking Northern Ireland: Culture, Ideology and Colonialism* (London: Longman, 1998).

Miller, David W. *Queen's Rebels: Ulster Loyalism in Historical Perspective* (Dublin: Gill and Macmillan, 1978).

Mitchell, George. *Making Peace* (New York: Knopf, 1999).

Mitchell, Paul, and Rick Wilford (ed.). *Politics in Northern Ireland* (Boulder Co.: Westview Press 1999).

Moloney, Ed. *A Secret History of the IRA* (London: Allen Lane, 2002).

Moore, Charles. *How to be British* (London: Centre for Policy Studies, 1995).

Morgan, Austen. *Labour and Partition: The Belfast Working Class 1905-23* (London: Pluto, 1991).

Morris, Dick. *Off with their Heads: Traitors, Crooks & Obstructionists in American Politics, Media & Business* (New York: Regan Books, 2003).

Morrissey, Mike, and Marie Smyth, *Northern Ireland after the Good Friday Agreement: Victims, Grievance and Blame* (London: Pluto Press, 2002).

Moya, Paula M.L. and Michael R. Hames-García (eds.), *Reclaiming Identity: Realist Theory and the Predicament of Postmodernism* (Berkeley: University of California Press, 2000).

Murphy, David. *The Stalker Affair and the British Press* (London: Unwin Hyman, 1991).

Murray, Dominic. *Worlds Apart: Segregated Schools in Northern Ireland* (Belfast: Appletree, 1985).

Murray, Dominic (ed.). *Protestant Perceptions of the Peace Process in Northern Ireland* (Limerick: Centre for Peace and Development Studies, 2000).

Murray, Gerard. *John Hume and the SDLP: Impact and Survival in Northern Ireland* (Dublin: Irish Academic Press, 1998).

Murtagh, Brendan. *The Politics of Territory: Policy and Segregation in Northern Ireland* (Houndmills: Palgrave, 2002).

Nairn, Tom. *The Break-Up of Britain: Crisis and Neo-Nationalism* (London: NLB, 1977).

____. *After Britain: New Labour and the Return of Scotland* (London: Granta, 2000).

____. *Pariah: Misfortunes of the British Kingdom* (London: Verso, 2002).

Nelson, Sarah. *Ulster's Uncertain Defenders: Protestant Political, Paramilitary and Community Groups and the Northern Ireland Conflict* (Belfast: Appletree, 1984).

Ní Dhonnchadha, Máirín. and Theo Dorgan (eds.). *Revising the Rising* (Derry: Field Day, 1991).

Norton, Philip (ed.). *The Conservative Party* (London: Prentice Hall, 1996).

O'Brien, Conor Cruise. *States of Ireland* (New York: Pantheon, 1972).

____. *Herod: Reflections on Political Violence* (London: Hutchinson, 1978).

____. *Ancestral Voices: Religion and Nationalism in Ireland* (Dublin: Poolbeg, 1994).

O'Clery, Conor. *Daring Diplomacy: Clinton's Secret Search for Peace in Ireland* (Boulder, Colo.: Roberts Rinehart, 1997).

O'Day, Alan. (ed.). *Terrorism's Laboratory: The Case of Northern Ireland* (Aldershot: Dartmouth Pub. Co., 1995).

Ó Dochartaigh, Niall. *From Civil Rights to Armalites: Derry and the Birth of the Irish Troubles* (Cork: Cork University Press, 1997).

O'Dowd, Liam. *Whither the Irish Border? Sovereignty, Democracy and Economic Integration in Ireland* (Belfast: Centre for Research and Documentation, 1994)

O'Dowd, Liam, Bill Rolston, Mike Tomlinson. *Northern Ireland, Between Civil Rights and Civil War* (London: CSE Books, 1980).

O'Halloran, Clare. *Partition and the Limits of Irish Nationalism: An Ideology Under Stress* (Dublin: Gill and Macmillan, 1987).

O'Malley, Padriag. *The Uncivil Wars: Ireland Today* (Belfast: Blackstaff, 1983).

Ovendale, Ritchie. *"Appeasement" and the English Speaking World: Britain, the United States, the Dominion and the Policy of "Appeasement", 1937–1939* (Cardiff: University of Wales Press, 1975).

Panayi, Panikos (ed.). *Racial Violence in Britain in the Nineteenth and Twentieth Centuries* (London: Leicester University Press, 1996).

Parekh, Bhikhu. *Rethinking Multiculturalism: Cultural Diversity and Political Theory* (Basingstoke: Macmillan, 2000).

Parkinson, Alan F. *Ulster Loyalism and the British Media* (Dublin: Four Courts, 1998).

Patterson, Henry. *The Politics of Illusion: A Political History of the IRA* (London: Serif, 1997).

Patterson, Henry. *Ireland Since 1939* (Oxford: Oxford University Press, 2002).

Paul, Kathleen. *Whitewashing Britain: Race and Citizenship in the Postwar Era* (Ithaca, N.Y.: Cornell University Press, 1997).

Phoenix, Eamon. *Northern Nationalism: Nationalist Politics, Partition and the Catholic Minority in Northern Ireland, 1890–1940* (Belfast, 1994).

Pilger, John. *The New Rulers of the World* (London: Verso, 2002).

Popper, Karl Raimund. *Conjectures and Refutations: The Growth of Scientific Knowledge* (New York: Basic Books, 1962).

Porter, Norman. *Rethinking Unionism: An Alternative Vision for Northern Ireland* (Belfast: Blackstaff Press, 1996).

Probert, Belinda. *Beyond Orange and Green: The Political Economy of the Northern Ireland Crisis* (London: Zed Press, 1978).

Purdie, Bob. *Politics in the Streets: The Origins of the Civil Rights Movement in Northern Ireland* (Belfast: Blackstaff Press, 1990).

Rafferty, Oliver. *Catholicism in Ulster, 1603–1983: An Interpretative History* (London: Hurst, 1994).

Redwood, John. *Stars and Strife: The Coming Conflicts Between the USA and the European Union* (Basingstoke: Palgrave, 2001).

Rickard, John S. (ed.). *Irishness and (Post)Modernism* (Lewisburg (Pa.): Bucknell University Press, 1994).

Roche, Patrick J. *The Appeasement of Terrorism & the Belfast Agreement* (Ballyclare: Northern Irish Unionist Party, 2000).

Roche, Patrick J., and Brian Barton (eds.). *The Northern Ireland Question: Myth and Reality* (Aldershot: Avebury, 1991).

_____. *The Northern Ireland Question: Perspectives and Policies* (Aldershot: Avebury, 1994).

_____. *The Northern Ireland Question: Nationalism, Unionism and Partition* (Aldershot: Ashgate, 1999).

Rolston, Bill (ed.). *The Media and Northern Ireland: Covering the Troubles* (Basingstoke: Macmillan, 1991).

Rolston, Bill, and David Miller (eds.). *War and Words: The Northern Ireland Media Reader* (Belfast: Beyond the Pale, 1996).

Rose, Richard. *Governing Without Consensus: An Irish Perspective* (London: Faber and Faber, 1971).

Ruane, Joseph, and Jennifer Todd. *The Dynamics of Conflict in Northern Ireland: Power, Conflict, and Emancipation* (Cambridge: Cambridge University Press, 1996).

Ruane, Joseph, and Jennifer Todd (eds.). *After the Good Friday Agreement: Analysing Political Change in Northern Ireland* (Dublin: University College Dublin Press, 1999).

The Runnymede Trust Commission on the Future of Multi-Ethnic Britain. *The Future of Multi-Ethnic Britain: Report of the Commission on the Future of Multi-Ethnic Britain* (London: Profile Books, 2000).

Said, Edward W. *Culture and Imperialism* (New York: Knopf, 1993).

Said, Edward W. *The End of the Peace Process: Oslo and After* (London: Granta, 2002, second edition).

San Juan, Jr., Epifanio. *Beyond Postcolonial Theory* (New York: St. Martin's Press, 1998).

Sardar, Ziauddin. *Postmodernism and the Other: The New Imperialism of Western culture* (London: Pluto, 1998).

Sardar, Ziauddin, and Merryl Wyn Davies. *Why Do People Hate America?* (Cambridge: Icon, 2002).

Scruton, Roger. *The Meaning of Conservatism* (London: Macmillan, 1980).

____. *England: an Elegy* (London: Chatto & Windus, 2000).

Sharrock, David, and Mark Devenport. *Man of War, Man of Peace? The Unauthorized Biography of Gerry Adams* (London: Pan, 1998, first published 1997).

Shirlow, Peter, and Mark McGovern (eds.). *Who are 'The People'? Unionism, Protestantism and Loyalism in Northern Ireland* (London: Pluto, 1997).

Smith, Anthony D.S. *Nationalism in the Twentieth Century* (Oxford: M. Robertson, 1979).

____. *National Identity* (London: Penguin, 1991).

____. *Myths and Memories of the Nation* (Oxford, 1999).

Smith, Jeremy. *Making the Peace in Ireland* (Harlow: Pearson Education Limited, 2002).

Smith, M.L.R. *Fighting for Ireland? The Military Strategy of the Irish Republican Movement* (London: Routledge, 1997).

Spencer, Ian R.G. *British Immigration Policy Since 1939: The Making of Multi-Racial Britain* (New York: Routledge, 1997).

Stewart, A.T.Q. *The Ulster Crisis* (London: Faber and Faber, 1967).

____. *The Narrow Ground: Aspects of Ulster, 1609–1969* (London: Faber and Faber, 1977).

Talmon, Jacob Leib. *The Origins of Totalitarian Democracy* (London: Mercury Books, 1961).

Taylor, Bridget, and Katarina Thomson (eds.). *Scotland and Wales: Nations Again?* (Cardiff: University of Wales Press, 1999).

Taylor, Peter. *Provos: The IRA and Sinn Fein* (London: Bloomsbury, 1997).

Tonge, Jonathan. *Northern Ireland: Conflict and Change* (Harlow: Longman, 2002, 2nd ed., first published 1998).

Townshend, Charles. *Political Violence in Ireland: Government and Resistance Since 1848* (Oxford: Clarendon Press, 1983).

Townshend, Charles (ed.). *Consensus in Ireland: Approaches and Recessions* (Oxford: Clarendon Press, 1988).

Walker, Graham S. *The Politics of Frustration: Harry Midgeley and the*

Failure of Labour in Northern Ireland (Manchester: Manchester University Press, 1985).

Walker, Graham, and Tom Gallagher (eds.). *Sermons and Battle Hymns: Protestant Popular Culture in Modern Scotland* (Edinburgh: Edinburgh University Press, 1990).

Walker, Graham. *Intimate Strangers: Political and Cultural Interaction Between Scotland and Ulster in Modern Times* (Edinburgh: J. Donald Publishers, 1995).

Whyte, John. *Interpreting Northern Ireland* (Oxford: Clarendon Press, 1990).

Wichert, Sabine. *Northern Ireland Since 1945* (London: Longman, 2nd ed., 1999, first published 1991).

Wilford, Rick (ed.). *Aspects of the Belfast Agreement* (Oxford: Oxford University Press, 2001).

Wilkinson, Paul. *Political Terrorism* (London: Macmillan, 1974).

____. *Terrorism and the Liberal State* (Basingstoke: Macmillan, 1986, 2nd ed., revised, first published 1977).

Wilson, Andrew J. *Irish-America and the Ulster Conflict, 1968–1995* (Washington, D.C.: Catholic University of America Press, 1995).

Wood, Ian S. (ed.). *Scotland and Ulster* (Edinburgh: Mercat Press, 1994).

Wright, Frank. *Two Lands on One Soil: Ulster Politics Before Home Rule* (Dublin: Gill & Macmillan Ltd), 1996).

ARTICLES AND ESSAYS

Arthur, Paul. 'Time, Territory, tradition and the Anglo-Irish "peace" process', *Government and Opposition*, xxxi (1996), 426-40.

Aughey, Arthur. 'Northern Ireland: the modification of circumstances', *Parliamentary Affairs*, lv, no. 3 (July 2002), 600-4.

Bankoff, Greg. 'Regions of risk: western discourses on terrorism and the significance of Islam', *Studies in Conflict and Terrorism*, xxvi (2003), no.6, 413-28.

Bell, J. Bowyer. 'The Irish Republican Army enters an endgame: an overview', *Studies in Conflict and Terrorism*, xviii, no.3 (July/September 1995), 153-74.

Bhabha, Homi. 'Remembering Fanon: self, psyche and the colonial condition' in Frantz Fanon, *Black skin, white masks*, trans. Charles Lam Markmann (London: Pluto, 1986, originally published as *Peau noire, masques blanc*, 1952), pp. vii-xxv.

Bradshaw, Brendan. 'Nationalism and historical scholarship in modern Ireland', *Ir.Hist.Stud.*, xxvi (Nov. 1989) no.104, 329–351.

Bruce, Steve. 'Paramilitaries, peace, and politics: Ulster loyalists and the 1994 truce', *Studies in Conflict and Terrorism*, xviii, no.3 (July/September 1995), 187–202.

____. 'Victim selection in ethnic conflict: motives and attitudes in Irish republicanism', *Terrorism and Political Violence*, ix, no.1 (Spring 1997), 56–71.

____. 'Terrorism and politics: the case of Northern Ireland's loyalist paramilitaries', *Terrorism and Political Violence*, xiii (2001), no.2, 27-48.

Cavanaugh, Kathleen A. 'Interpretations of political violence in ethnically divided societies', *Terrorism and Political Violence*, ix (1997), no.3, 33–54.

Clark, J.C.D. 'Protestantism, nationalism, and national identity, 1660-1832', *Hist.Journ.*, xliii, no.1 (Mar. 2000), 249–76.

Cochrane, Feargal. 'Any takers? The isolation of Northern Ireland', *Political Studies* 42, no.3 (September 1994), 378–95.

Conboy, Martin. 'Parochializing the global: language and the British tabloid press', in Jean Aitchison and Diana M. Lewis (eds.), *New media language* (London: Routledge, 2003), pp. 45–54.

Deutsch, Richard. 'The Good Friday Agreement: assessing its implementation 1998–2001', *Nordic Irish Studies*, i (2002), 95-109.

Dingley, James. 'A reply to White's non sectarian thesis of PIRA targeting', *Terrorism and Political Violence*, x (1998), no.2, 106–17.

____. 'Marching down the Garvaghy Road: Republican tactics and state response to the Orangemen's claim to march their traditional route home after the Drumcree church service', *Terrorism and Political Violence*, xiv, no.3 (Fall 2002), 42–79.

____. 'Peace in Our Time? The Stresses and Strains on the Northern Ireland Peace Process', *Studies in Conflict and Terrorism*, xxv, no. 6 (November/December 2002), 357–82.

Dixon, Paul. 'Internationalization and Unionist isolation: a response to Feargal Cochrane', *Political Studies*, xliii, no.3 (September 1995), 497–505.

____. 'Political skills or lying and manipulation? The choreography of the Northern Ireland peace process', *Political Studies*, 1, no. 4 (September 2002), 725–41.

Donohue, Laura K. 'Regulating Northern Ireland: the Special Powers Acts, 1922–1972', *Historical Journal*, xli (1998), 1089–1120.

Eagleton, Terry. 'Nationalism and the case of Ireland', *New Left Review*, no.234 (Mar.Apr. 1999), 44–61.

Elliott, Philip. 'Reporting Northern Ireland: a study of news in Great Britain, Northern Ireland and the Republic of Ireland', in *Ethnicity and the media: an analysis of media reporting in the United Kingdom, Canada and Ireland* (Paris: UNESCO, 1977), pp. 263–376.

English, Richard. '"Pay no heed to public clamour": Irish republican solipsism in the 1930s', *Ir.Hist.Stud.*, xxviii, no.112 (Nov. 1993), 426-39.

____. 'The state of Northern Ireland', in Richard English and Charles Townshend (eds.), *The state: historical and political dimensions* (London: Routledge, 1999), pp.95–108.

Fanning, Ronan. 'The Irish policy of Asquith's government and the Cabinet crisis of 1910', in Art Cosgrove and Donal.McCartney (eds.), *Studies in Irish history, presented to R. Dudley Edwards* (Dublin: University College, Dublin, 1979), .279–303.

Farrington, Christopher, 'Ulster Unionism and the Irish historiography debate', *Irish Studies Review*, xi, no.3 (Dec 2003), 251–61.

Feldman, Allen. 'Retaliate and punish: political violence as form and memory in Northern Ireland', *Éire-Ireland*, xxxii, no.4 & xxxiii, nos.1 & 2 (Winter, Spring and Summer 1997/8), 195–235.

Finlayson, Alan. 'The problem of "culture" in Northern Ireland: a critique of the Cultural Traditions Group', *Irish Review*, xx (Winter/Spring 1997), 76–88.

Finnegan, R.B. 'The United Kingdom security policy and IRA terrorism in Ulster', *Éire-Ireland*, xxiii (1988), no.1, 87–110.

Flecha, Ramón. 'Modern and postmodern racism in Europe: dialogic approach and anti-racist pedagogies', *Harvard Educational Review*, lxix, no.2 (Summer 1999), 150–71.

'Forum: Northern Ireland', *The Global Review of Ethnopolitics*, ii, nos.3/4 (March/June 2003), 71–91.

Fuchs, Lawrence H. 'The changing meaning of civil rights, 1954–1994', in John Higham (ed.), *Civil rights and social wrongs*

(University Park, Pa.: Pennsylvania State University Press, 1999), pp.59–85.

Gilligan, Chris. 'Constant crisis/permanent process: diminished agency and weak structures in the Northern Ireland peace process', *Global Review of Ethnopolitics*, iii, no.1 (September 2003), 22–38.

Giroux, Henry A. 'Living dangerously: identity politics and the new cultural racism', in Henry A. Giroux and Peter McLaren (eds.), *Between borders: pedagogy and the politics of cultural studies* (New York: Routledge, 1994), pp.29–55.

Graham, Brian, and Peter Shirlow. 'The battle of the Somme in Ulster memory and identity', *Political Geography*, xxi, no.7 (Sept. 2002), 881–904.

Guelke, Adrian. 'Violence and electoral polarization in divided societies: three cases in comparative perspective', *Terrorism and Political Violence*, xii, nos.3 & 4 (2000), 78-105.

Harrison, Brian. 'The rise, fall and rise of political consensus in Britain since 1940', *History*, lxxxiv, no.274 (April 1999), 301–24.

Hewitt, Christopher. 'Catholic grievances, Catholic nationalism and violence in Northern Ireland during the Civil Rights period: a reconsideration', *British Journal of Sociology*, xxxii (1981), pp. 362–80.

Hewitt, John. 'No rootless colonist', in Patricia Craig (ed.), *The rattle of the North: an anthology of Ulster prose* (Belfast: Blackstaff Press, 1992), pp.121–31.

Hickman, Mary J. and Bronwen Walter. 'Racializing the Irish in England: gender, class and ethnicity', in Marilyn Cohen and Nancy J. Curtin (eds.), *Reclaiming gender: transgressive identities in modern Ireland* (New York: St. Martin's Press, 1999), pp.267–92.

Jackson, Alvin. 'Unionist myths, 1912-85', *Past & Present*, no.136 (1992), 164–85.

Knox, Colin. 'The "deserving" victims of political violence: "punishment" attacks in Northern Ireland', *Criminal Justice*, i (2001), no.2, 181–199.

Kingston, Shane. 'Terrorism, the media and the Northern Ireland conflict', *Studies in Conflict and Terrorism*, xviii, no.3 (July/September 1995), 203–31.

Longley, Edna. 'What do Protestants want?', *Irish Review*, xx (Winter/Spring 1997), 104–20.

_____. 'Ulster Protestants and the question of "culture"', in Fran Brearton and Eamonn Hughes (eds.), *Last before America: Irish and American writing: essays in honour of Michael Allen* (Belfast: Blackstaff, 2001), pp.99–120.

Lutz Brenda J., James M. Lutz, Georgia Wralstad Ulmschneider, 'British trials of Irish nationalist defendants: the quality of justice strained', *Studies in Conflict and Terrorism*, xxv (2002), no.4, 227–44.

McAllister, Ian. '"The armalite and the ballot box": Sinn Fein's electoral strategy in Northern Ireland', *Electoral Studies*, xxiii, no.1 (March 2004), 123–142.

McAuley, James W. 'Unionism's last stand? Contemporary unionist politics and identity in Northern Ireland,' *Global Review of Ethnopolitics*, iii, no.1 (September 2003), 60-74

McCall, Cathal. 'Political transformation and the reinvention of the Ulster-Scots identity and culture', *Identities: Global Studies in Power and Culture*, ix, no. 2 (Apr-June 2002), 197–218.

McGarry, John. 'The Anglo-Irish agreement and the unlikely prospects for power-sharing', *Éire-Ireland*, xxiii (1988), no.1, 111-28.

McVeigh, Robbie. 'The last conquest of Ireland? British academics in Irish universities', *Race & Class*, xxxvii, no.1 (July-September 1995), 109–22.

Monaghan, Rachel. 'The return of "Captain Moonlight": informal justice in Northern Ireland', *Studies in Conflict and Terrorism*, xxv (2002), no.1, 41–56.

Munck, Ronnie. 'Rethinking Irish nationalism', *Canadian Review of Studies in Nationalism*, xiv (1987), 31–48.

Neumann, Peter R. 'The myth of Ulsterization in British security policy in Northern Ireland', *Studies in Conflict and Terrorism*, xxvi (2003), no.5, 365–77.

Newsinger, John. 'British security policy in Northern Ireland', *Race & Class*, xxxvii, no.1 (July-Sept 1995), 83–94.

O'Leary, Brendan. 'The Conservative stewardship of Northern Ireland, 1979–97: sound-bottomed contradictions or slow learning?', *Political Studies*, xlv (1997), 663–76.

_____. 'The nature of the British-Irish Agreement', *New Left Review*, no.233 (Jan./Feb. 1999), 66–96.

_____. 'The protection of human rights under the Belfast Agreement',

The Political Quarterly, lxxii, no.3 (July-Sept 2001): 353–65.

O'Neill, Shane. 'Pluralist justice and its limits: the case of Northern Ireland', *Political Studies*, xlii, no.3 (Sept. 1994), 363–77.

Panayi, Panikos. 'The historiography of immigrants and ethnic minorities: Britain compared with the USA', *Ethnic and Racial Studies*, xix, no.4 (Oct. 1996), 823–40.

Parekh, Bhikhu. 'Liberalism and colonialism: a critique of Locke and Mill', in Jan Nederveen Pieterse and Bhikhu Parekh (eds.), *The decolonization of imagination: culture, knowledge and power* (London: Zed Books, 1995), pp.81-98.

Porter, Elisabeth. 'Identity, location, plurality: women, nationalism and Northern Ireland', in Richard Wilford and Robert L. Miller, *Women, ethnicity and nationalism: the politics of transition* (London: Routledge, 1998), pp.36–61.

[Porter, Sam. and Denis O'Hearn,] 'New Left Podsnappery: the British Left and Ireland', *New Left Review*, no.212 (July-Aug 1995), pp.131–47.

Roe, Mícheál D. and Sybil Dunlap, 'Contemporary Scotch-Irish social identities and attitudes toward *the troubles* in Northern Ireland', *Journal of Scotch-Irish Studies*, i, no.3 (Fall 2002), 12–36.

Rolston, Bill. 'Changing the political landscape: murals and transition in Northern Ireland', *Irish Studies Review*, xi, no.1 (April 2003), 3–16.

Said, Edward W. 'Reflections on exile' in *Reflections on exile and other essays* (Cambridge, Mass.: Harvard University Press, 2000), pp.173–86.

Schulze, Kirsten E. and M.L.R. Smith. 'Decommissioning and paramilitary strategy in Northern Ireland: a problem compared', *Journal of Strategic Studies*, xxiii, no.4 (Dec. 2000), 77–106.

Shirlow, Peter. 'Fear and ethnic division in Belfast', *Peace Review*, xiii (2001), no.1, 67–74.

————. 'Devolution in northern Ireland/Ulster/the North/six counties: Delete as appropriate', *Regional Studies*, xxxv, no.8 (Nov 2001), 743–752.

————. '"Who fears to speak": fear, mobility, and ethno-sectarianism in the Two "Ardoynes"' *Global Review of Ethnopolitics*, iii, no. 1 (September 2003), 76–91.

Silke, Andrew. 'Drink, drugs, and rock'n'roll: financing loyalist terrorism in Northern Ireland - part two', *Studies in Conflict and*

Terrorism, xxiii (2000), no.2, 107-27.

Smith M. L. R., 'The trouble with guns . . . and academics', *Studies in Conflict and Terrorism*, xxii (1999), no.4, 363–6.

Spencer, Graham. 'Pushing for peace: the Irish government, television news and the Northern Ireland peace process', *European Journal of Communication*, xviii, no.1 (March 2003), 55–80.

Tomlinson, Mike. 'Can Britain leave Ireland? The political economy of war and peace', *Race & Class*, xxxvii, no.1 (July-Sept 1995), 1–22.

Tonge, Jonathan. 'Victims of their own success? Post-Agreement dilemmas of political moderates in Northern Ireland', *Global Review of Ethnopolitics*, iii, no.1 (September 2003), 39–59.

Walter, Bronwen. 'Challenging the black/white binary: the need for an Irish category in the 2001 census', *Patterns of Prejudice*, xxxii (1998), no.2, 73–86.

Walther, Steven T. 'The globalization of the rule of law and human rights', *Futures*, xxxi, nos. 9–10 (November 1999), 993–1003.

White, Robert W. 'The Irish Republican Army: an assessment of sectarianism',
Terrorism and Political Violence, ix, no.1 (Spring 1997), 20–55.

____. 'Don't confuse me with the facts: more on the Irish Republican Army and sectarianism', *Terrorism and Political Violence* x (1998) no.4, 164–89.

Wichert, Sabine. 'The role of nationalism in the Northern Ireland conflict', *History of European Ideas*, xvi, nos.1-3 (Jan. 1993), 109–14.

Wilkinson, Paul. 'Support mechanisms in international terrorism', in Robert O. Slater and Michael Stohl (eds.), *Current perspectives on international terrorism* (New York: St. Martin's Press, 1988), pp.88–114.

Wills, Claire. 'Language, politics, narrative, political violence', *Oxford Literary Review*, xiii (1991), nos. 1–2, 21–60.

OTHERS

Hansard's Parliamentary Debates.

Dáil Éireann, Díosóireachtaí parliaminte, Tuairise oifigiúil (parliamentary debates official report).

ARK, Northern Ireland social and political archive, available at http://www.ark.ac.uk.

The CAIN Web Service, Conflict Archive on the Internet, available at http://cain.ulst.ac.uk/.

Northern Ireland Assembly debates, available at http://www.ni-assembly.gov.uk/record/hansard.htm.

'The agreement', available at http://www.nio.gov.uk/issues/agreement.htm.

Political party web sites in Britain, Ireland, and elsewhere.

Index